Rural Revolt in Mexico

A book in the series

AMERICAN ENCOUNTERS/GLOBAL INTERACTIONS

A series edited by Gilbert M. Joseph and Emily S. Rosenberg

. . . on Mexican Rural Revolts

[During the last week of April 1987] there were more than 1,000 peasants in place, for four days and nights, at the doors of the Legislative Palace in Mexico City. They failed to provoke the least bit of solidarity from the deputies attending the extraordinary session of Congress or even from progressive social and political organizations. . . . The yells and chanting characteristic of marches by workers or students are not heard during peasant demonstrations; the most one might hear is the occasional jubilant shout. The demonstrations of the peasants are silent; they appear to have little political content.

But that is the case only for those who fail to listen to the silence.

Heberto Castillo, *Proceso* 548, 4 May 1987, p. 34.

. . . on United States Interventions

Whatever President Wilson intended, however innocent of imperialism the American people were, the Americans who were at all interested in Mexico coveted the country, wanted to change its laws and the people, and to possess or anyhow to govern Mexico. Yes, they understand us, those backward Mexicans, and we don't understand them or ourselves. As I said to President Wilson once when he was asking me why the friendly landing of troops was resented as an invasion, we Americans don't seem to get it, that you can't commit rape a little.

Lincoln Steffens, *The Autobiography of Lincoln Steffens* (New York: Harcourt, Brace, and World, 1931), 2:716.

Contents

Foreword *William Roseberry*   xi

Preface   xvii

Introduction: Reasons to Be Cheerful   *Daniel Nugent*   1

I *Popular Nationalism and Anti-Imperialism in the Mexican Countryside*

The United States and the Mexican Peasantry, circa 1880–1940
Alan Knight   25

Measuring Influence: The United States and the Mexican Peasantry
John H. Coatsworth   64

Social Unrest, Nationalism, and American Capital in the Mexican
Countryside, 1876–1920   *John Mason Hart*   72

Villismo: Nationalism and Popular Mobilization in Northern Mexico
Rubén Osorio   89

II *Class, Ethnicity, and Space in Mexican Rural Revolts*

Rancheros and Rebellion: The Case of Northwestern Chihuahua, 1905–
1909   *Jane-Dale Lloyd*   107

Mixtec Political Consciousness: From Passive to Active Resistance
Michael Kearney   134

Space and Revolution in Northeastern Chihuahua
María Teresa Koreck   147

III *U.S. Intervention and Popular Ideology*

The United States, Feuding Elites, and Rural Revolt in Yucatán, 1836–
1915   *Gilbert M. Joseph*   173

U.S. Military Intervention, Revolutionary Mobilization, and Popular
Ideology in the Chihuahuan Sierra, 1916–1917   *Ana María Alonso*   207

From Alliance to Dependency: The Formation and Deformation of an
Alliance between Francisco Villa and the United States
Friedrich Katz   239

IV *Resistance and Persistence*

Chiapas and the Rebellion of the Enchanted World   *Adolfo Gilly*   261

Bibliography   335

Index   365

Contributors   381

Foreword

The first edition of this book marked the beginning of Daniel Nugent's intellectual career; the publication of the second edition marks its unexpected end. Daniel died, suddenly and much too soon, while the book was in press.

Reading again the essays in this book, along with the new introduction and Adolfo Gilly's conclusion, we can place this effort in relation to Daniel's other contributions. Setting aside some of his articles and the edited book with John Calagione and Doris Francis (*Workers' Expressions*, 1992), we have his historical ethnography of Namiquipa (*Spent Cartridges of Revolution*, 1993), a second edited book on popular culture and practice in relation to fields of power (*Everyday Forms of State Formation*, 1994, edited with Gilbert Joseph), and a substantial record of his editorial work with the *Journal of Historical Sociology* and, less actively, with *Critique of Anthropology*. With these introductory lines, I want to consider, first, the remarkably coherent and innovative intellectual and political project that connects this book with *Spent Cartridges* and *Everday Forms*, and, second, the creative and stimulating editorial practice he brought to this book along with *Everyday Forms* and the journals.

The intellectual and political project is given clear expression in Daniel's introduction:

Social groups such as the "peasantry" or the "rural working class" . . . do not exist in a social and historical vacuum. They are connected to global structures of power. At the same time, through the modalities of their own structure, they give expression to global structures of power. However this "giving expression to" does not operate only in one direction. Rural revolt for instance also affects or is "expressed in" global structures of power; there is a multidirectional character to this articulation. The "expression" of rural revolt and forms of popular mobilization in global structures of power is as important a determinant of historical process as the more routinely recognized manner in which global structures of power are expressed in rural revolt. If the former expression is more opaque than the latter, I suspect the reason for this has more to do with the conventions, the bias, and the political project of liberal social science than it does with the inefficacy of those popular movements.

   This passage, slightly revised from the introduction to the first edition, points to two poles of action: "global structures of power" on the one hand and "forms of popular mobilization" on the other. In this book, Nugent invited contributors to consider the relationship between a particular structure of power—U.S. intervention (though it became clear that a necessary path beyond some of the disagreements among authors was to see a more complex and pervasive structure of U.S. *imperialism*)—and a specific form of popular mobilization—rural revolt, especially but not exclusively in the Mexican Revolution. In *Everyday Forms,* Joseph and Nugent invited contributors to examine a different structure of power—the Mexican state in its complex process of formation and elaboration—and a broader range of popular forms, from comic books to schools to *ejidos* to structures of community governance. Connecting the two edited projects is the study of Namiquipa, in *Spent Cartridges* and elsewhere, which provided a singular vantage point from which to view both structures of power. From its formation as a *presidio* community to its early twentieth century attempt to reject the state's donation of an *ejido*, Namiquipa's constitution as a community was intimately connected to processes of state formation. Located in what was to become Mexico's far north (on a frontier that became a border, as Ana Alonso and Friedrich Katz have stressed), Namiquipa is physically distant from Mexico City and close to the United States. From such a locale, Daniel had ample opportunity to reflect, ethnographically and historically, upon the tension between structures of power and popular forms of mobilization.

   It is that tension that I want to stress here. In the quoted passage and throughout his work, Daniel was locating a field of relations through which both the structures of power (be they associated with U.S. imperialism, in this book, or with the state, in *Everyday Forms*) and the popular forms were constituted. In terms of Mexican studies, this intervention was critically important, coming in the wake of a revisionist historiography that had replaced a romantic celebration of peasant revolutionaries with a "top-down" depiction of elite machinations and state control. When Joseph and Nugent called for a "post-revisionist" historigraphy, they were signaling a return to a concern for the creative actions and capacities of common people as political actors, but these actions and capacities were to be placed in the context of power relations that both shaped and limited, and were in turn shaped and limited by, the actions and capacities themselves. As a conceptual framework, it identifies not a privileged site of agency but a field of relations and tensions through which critical actions unfold. The essays in both books, and subsequent studies that have been influenced by them, demonstrate the generative power of this framework.

But if I take from the quoted passage an identification of a field of tension and imagine a range of historical and ethnographic projects that explore particular dimensions of that field, Daniel's own claims were more sharply focused. The passage is also, fundamentally, a claim for the creative power of common people. "This book is about people," Daniel announces at the beginning of both editions, and references to "the people" abound in his writings. He was probably drawn to Namiquipa because of its revolutionary reputation in the first place, and while he carefully examined the pueblo's formation as a military garrison on the colonial frontier of Hispanic civilization, I suspect he was most attracted, personally and affectively, to the moment when a group of Namiquipenses said no to an *ejido* and, by interpretive extension, no to the state. And the quoted passage argues that analysts have overemphasized the shaping and limiting dimensions of the structures of power and remained blind to the transformative potential of . . . the people. Indeed, the most significant changes Daniel made to the quoted passage between the two editions was to replace more conditional with definitive statements about the power of the folk.

In this, Daniel was a romantic, at times too much so for this reader. I kept wishing he would tell us more about social differentiation and inequality within Namiquipa or explore the complex and difficult relationship between leaders and followers even at heroic moments of revolutionary refusal. And there is much more to be said about the nasty things people do to each other in households, communities, and organizations, in part because of the wider field of power relations and tensions in which they try to make their livelihoods and, occasionally, history. But I am willing to grant Daniel his romanticism, partly because it was never naive (he retained a clear vision, throughout his work, of the structures of power in which peoples are formed) and partly because some sort of romantic vision is necessary to avoid a cynical celebration of power itself.

In the present volume, we can see one tangible result of this vision in the remarkable new essay by Adolfo Gilly, which is a product of, first, Gilly's own long-term reflections on Mexican politics and history; second, a sustained examination of the *Zapatista* movement (including exchanges with Marcos and participation in the wider democratizing ferment of which the movement is part); and, third, an engagement with post-revisionist literature on Mexican politics and culture. Gilly's essay offers a clear-eyed assessment of the modalities of power, both Mexican and international, yet is suffused with a belief in, and demonstration of, the capacity of ordinary people to imagine social worlds outside, or beyond, the power relations that constrain their daily lives—and, on rare and explosive occasions, to act on and through those imaginings to create something new. Gilly's essay is an excellent example of a romanticism that remains essential to the revolutionary and humanistic spirit. Printed here, it is a fitting tribute to Daniel's memory.

I have mentioned that one source of Gilly's essay is an engagement with the post-revisionist literature on Mexican politics and culture (to which his essay is a substantial advance). This leads to a brief consideration of Daniel's considerable contribution as an editor, about which I would say three things. First, he encouraged disagreement and controversy and used it to generate fresh ideas. Consider the essays of Alan Knight and John Mason Hart in this book, and the way John Coatsworth's commentary serves to clarify the issues for the book as a whole. Or take the juxtaposition of the work of James Scott and of Philip Corrigan and Derek Sayer in *Everyday Forms,* and the editorial invitation to contributors to look beyond obvious disagreements and consider the ways in which their positions could speak to each other—again, the invitation itself, organized around contrasting views, generates new work.

Second, Daniel was no respecter of academic rank and hierarchy. This does not mean that he neglected the work of senior scholars: both *Rural Revolt* and *Everyday Forms* contain contributions by central figures. But this book in particular also includes contributions by junior or marginally employed scholars, including graduate students (and it should be remembered that Daniel began working on this volume while writing his dissertation). For some, writing for this book was a first publication; if we add to this Daniel's editorial work at the *Journal of Historical Sociology* we would find a noticeably larger proportion of authors publishing their first essays.

Providing a venue for authors was in itself a significant editorial achievement, but, perhaps more importantly, it included these young authors in a dialogue with senior scholars. Daniel's vision of a common intellectual community, marked more by differences in perspective than by differences in rank, is increasingly uncommon in academic culture.

Finally, I would stress Daniel's role in stimulating new work. One sees this first in the two edited books and the conferences that led to them. Many of us were cajoled into writing things we would not otherwise have produced, and we remain grateful to Daniel for his obsessive vision and heavy hand. But the real measure of this dimension of his work is in the new writings that emerge out of the frameworks elucidated here and in *Everyday Forms*. For this, Gilly's essay is exemplary. I am confident there will be others.

William Roseberry
New York, December 1997

Preface

In October of 1985 I loaded up my 1967 GMC pickup and left Namiquipa, Chihuahua, with my then wife. We were anthropology graduate students and, having just conducted two and a half years of fieldwork in rural Mexico, were looking forward to returning to the States, settling in, and writing up the results of our research. Matters were not helped when, at a party in Chicago a few weeks later, one of my thesis supervisors welcomed me back with the observation, "You know, Daniel, generally it takes about twice as long to write up as it does to do the research." I headed for the back porch and drank some tequila.

As it turned out, the major "life difficulty" in the years that followed had less to do with a thesis-like albatross hanging about my neck and more to do with the impermanence of my residences: eight months in Chicago, two more months in Namiquipa, nine months in San Diego, four months in Tucson, four months in Providence, six months in Riverside, then a move to Austin for two years (the '67 GMC died on the way there). I actually defended my thesis within *less* than two and a half years of leaving the field. But in the interval, I'd gotten involved in some other projects which directly flowed into the production of the volume you now hold in your hands. Teaching students at the University of Chicago for $75 a week did not cut it in the Reagan years; I needed some support.

I found it in southern California. In San Diego I was a visiting research fellow at the Center for U.S.-Mexican Studies, UCSD. That remarkable and wonderful institution (I hated my time there at the time) was founded in 1980 under the direction of Wayne Cornelius. The greatest feature of the Center, in my opinion, is its Resident Fellows program, which throws together scholars of radically different backgrounds and divergent experiences from Asia, Europe, Mexico, and the United States, provides them each a desk and a monthly check, and permits them to get on with their own work, whatever it might be. The results are as varied and provocative as the fellows that spend time at the Center. Admittedly, there is a Noah's Ark–like quality to the fellows each year: a communist economist for every apparatchik from the Mexican Ministry of Budget and Planning; a former *panista diputado* for every Brit lounging about on the beach reading Foucault; a Marxist anthropologist for every medical anthropologist. And even if one of its first visiting research fellows was named president of Mexico within a few years of his residence, while a more recent fellow was put behind bars in Mexico even more promptly, the Center has always been a supportive place of refuge for a diverse range of researchers, including political exiles alongside career academics.

Shortly before I left Chicago in 1986, John Coatsworth reminded me, "You know, Wayne likes to sponsor these little workshops in San Diego. If you can think up something the Center might do in, say, the middle of February, I hope you will invite me." That reminder provided a wonderful distraction from working on my thesis; by the conclusion of my residency at the Center all I'd done of that was come up with a title. I did, though, spend a fair bit of time with Ana María Alonso organizing a two-day workshop for a couple dozen participants which took place in February 1987. The workshop would not have been possible without the support, supervision, and enthusiasm for original ideas offered by Wayne Cornelius, then director of the Center, and Gabriel Székely, assistant director. With financial backing for the workshop from the Center for U.S.-Mexican Studies, the Ford Foundation, the Andrew Mellon Foundation, and the William and Flora Hewlett Foundation, what had begun as an opportunity to invite some friends from the frozen rustbelt to southern California in the middle of the winter turned into a stimulating and important gathering during which we discussed what turned out to be a theretofore neglected topic: the relation between U.S. intervention and rural revolt in Mexico.

The event had a cumbersome title: Rural Revolt in Mexico, Mexican Nationalism and the State, and Forms of U.S. Intervention. The staff at the Center, particularly Graciela Platero, Diane Platero, and Patti Rosas, coordinated the workshop despite my unhelpful efforts to understand what was going on. The participants were a diverse lot including graduate students and distinguished senior scholars; anthropologists, historians, political scientists, and sociologists; Europeans, Mexicans, and North Americans; visiting fellows and UCSD faculty. Working papers were read by Ana Alonso, John Hart, Evelyn Hu-DeHart, Gil Joseph, Friedrich Katz, Michael Kearney, Alan Knight, María Teresa Koreck, Jane-Dale Lloyd, Rubén Osorio, and Cynthia Radding. Responses were prepared by

John Coatsworth, Ann Craig, Paul Drake, David Mares, Enrique Semo, Eric Van Young, and Leon Zamosc. Sessions were chaired by Ana, Wayne, Joe Foweraker, Peter Smith, and Gabriel. When it was over, Wayne promptly secured support from the Tinker Foundation to underwrite publication of a volume, and then left me at complete liberty to make a book out of the papers as I saw fit. I didn't really know how to go about that, but Wayne let me do it anyway.

As it turned out, the commentaries along with the stimulating open discussions during the meeting were very useful to the authors in revising their papers and of inestimable value to me in editing the papers and writing an introduction. Not ever having authored a book, never mind having edited one, I had only a shaky understanding of what was involved, but Sandra del Castillo, managing editor at the Center, proved to be a realistic and constructive guide to the process. In bringing that effort to fruition I received help and a wealth of good suggestions through conversation and correspondence with Ana Alonso (with whom I was living when the work began), Romana Falcón (who refereed the manuscript), Paul Friedrich, Gil Joseph, Friedrich Katz, Michael Kearney (with whom I was living when the manuscript went to the printers), and Terri Koreck.

Rural Revolt in Mexico and U.S. Intervention was originally published by the Center for U.S.-Mexican Studies in 1988 as no. 27 of their Monograph Series. Some people with whom I discussed the work found that curious, assuming I had merely assembled what David Schneider would have called "a conference proceedings type" of volume. The book was in fact something very different. Prior study of social movements and popular mobilization in the Mexican countryside had revealed a wide range of organized efforts through which peasants and Indians had struggled to create political and cultural spaces for themselves, thereby shaping profoundly their own history and affecting the forces and classes ranged against them. What was missing from most studies, though, was a clear sense of how that activity engaged or connected with imperialism, with the extension and elaboration of a capitalist world system, and with the influence of the United States throughout Latin America during the twentieth century. (Much of that prior work in fact anticipated the "new social movements" literature of the 1980s and 1990s.)

This book argued, somewhat differently, for understanding rural revolt in terms of the specific historical contexts of particular regions and peoples, the national-historical context of Mexico, and the broader context of the unequal cultural, political, and economic relations between Mexico and the United States. In each of the studies presented, equal importance was attached to the sociocultural experiences of the protagonists of revolt and to the fact that revolts are not isolated events or objectifiable "cases," but material social processes profoundly influenced by the United States. By drawing together empirical materials from the rich historiography and ethnography of rural Mexico with political, economic, and sociological studies of the United States and capitalism on a world scale, these chapters illuminated the multifaceted reality of Mexican rural revolts and U.S. power in an original light. What in the past had been regarded as discrete types of events, structures, and relationships were now demonstrated as being unified. In short, the collection made sense as a monograph.

The themes and topics of the essays, and the directions for further research indicated by the contributions from anthropologists and historians, were almost unprecedented for an English-language study of rural Mexico. The reasons for that are several, including the then emerging shifts and fissures in the historiography of revolutionary Mexico south and north of the U.S.-Mexico border. Powerfully affecting me was the circumstance that shortly before the conference took place, Barney Cohn turned me on to *Subaltern Studies* and, just as I began editing the book, put me in contact with Philip Corrigan and Derek Sayer (in the Faculty Club of the California Institute of Technology). The effect those introductions had on my work, including this book, should be obvious.

After *Rural Revolt* went to press, I got on to other things: like finding a job (took a while), co-editing a book with John Calagione on the anthropology of work, writing a monograph about Namiquipa, working with Gil Joseph and a dozen other collaborators on what became *Everyday Forms of State Formation* (published by Duke Press in 1994), and enduring a midlife crisis that has still not abated. I was annoyed some years later when some Latin Americanist scholars, enthralled by the postmodern turn in literary studies, the social sciences, and the northern academy generally, began to address issues such as "postcoloniality" in Latin America; to my mind, for reasons having to do as much with securing greater market share in the academy as with explaining Latin American realities. The work of the *Subaltern Studies* group was "discovered" by more Latin Americanists (a good thing), but was recast in a manner that avoided coming to terms with the political consequences of certain types of anthropological and historical writing (a bad thing, particularly if one is writing about, say, Mexico in the 1990s). The last issue in particular was one that I felt had at least been broached, however obliquely, in *Rural Revolt,* which was in any event the very first effort by Latin Americanists to sympathetically embrace and enrich the work published in *Subaltern Studies* by projecting it onto a different region of historical experience.

In the present edition, the organization of the book has been improved and slight changes and corrections have been made to several of the essays. Most significant, it includes an entirely new section, "Resistance and Persistence," comprising a long essay written expressly for the new edition by Adolfo Gilly in late 1996. Commissioned with the modest task of writing a brief afterword that would at least mention recent instances of rural revolt in Mexico, Adolfo assumed the immodest task of amplifying the perspective and approach encouraged by this book through an investigation of *neozapatismo*—the popular movement of Indians and peasants that organized itself in the 1990s as the Ejercito Zapatista de Liberación Nacional in the southeastern state of Chiapas—that demonstrates it to be not so "neo." The result was his brilliant essay on "the rebellion of the enchanted world," a more detailed version of which was published as a book in Mexico by Ediciones Era in October 1997.

Some 150 additional entries are included in the bibliography, primarily material published since 1987. This new edition has an index. My introduction has been completely rewritten. I resisted the temptation to simply tag on another 12,000 words discussing recent developments in Mexican revolutionary historiography or theoretical advances over the past decade that have occurred as a result of the convergence of anthropological and historical practices. Gil Joseph and I outlined new historiographic tendencies in the study of revolutionary Mexico in our introduction to *Everyday Forms of State Formation;* not only would it be redundant to re-cover that ground here, but I feel strongly that the chapters in this book serve rather well as examples of what we pointed to in *Everyday Forms* as "postrevisionist" or "neopopulist" studies *avant la lettre.* The new introduction does include some terse remarks regarding more literary appropriations of the work of the *Subaltern Studies* group; terse because a protracted theoretical exegesis would run the danger of drawing the reader away from the more interesting feature of these studies. The point, again, is that it is possible to analyze rural revolt in Mexico and U.S. intervention as aspects of a single historical process without losing sight of the political character of their relationships as articulated both from below and from above. As for the theoretical results of the convergence of anthropological and historical practices, "The proof's in the pudding," as Friedrich Engels was fond of pointing out.

The chapters by Jane-Dale Lloyd and Rubén Osorio were translated from the Spanish original by Fay Henderson de Díaz and myself in 1987. I translated the new chapter by Adolfo Gilly with the assistance of Timothy B. Jafek.

This book would have languished in photocopy-reproduction limbo were it not for the efforts and encouragement of my friend Paul Gootenberg, who urged me to contact Valerie Millholland, an editor at Duke. I want to express my heartfelt thanks and appreciation to Valerie; not because that's the sort of thing authors—or, even more pathetically, the editors of out-of-print anthologies—are "supposed to do" but because she has proved to be the most intelligent, realistic, and supportive editor I have ever worked with. Thanks also to the seven anonymous experts whom Valerie consulted before agreeing to go ahead with the project; their comments, criticisms, and suggestions were extremely helpful. My hope is that this new edition lives up to their expectations, and that readers find it valuable as we hurtle toward the next *fin de siècle.*

Daniel Nugent
Tucson, Arizona

DANIEL NUGENT

Introduction: Reasons to Be Cheerful

This is not another book about the Mexican revolution. Nor is it a collection of essays on the modalities of state formation or nationalism in Mexico. Even less is it a series of analyses of forms of U.S. intervention in Mexican political life. This book is about people.

The essays that follow are concerned with understanding the people of the Mexican countryside, peasants and Indians who for centuries have participated in a succession of revolts and rebellions thereby forcing changes in the society as a whole and determining the character of the Mexican nation. By their actions they have, in compelling and occasionally heroic fashion, given the lie to an assumption often shared by liberal and Marxist analysts alike that the peasantry is essentially limited and backward or comparable to a "sack of potatoes." Despite this well-documented history of struggle, however, the custom in recent decades has been to aver the judgment that rural revolts in Mexico have resulted only in a series of defeats for the peasantry.

When first assembling these essays in 1987, I shared that judgment. What I did not share was the cynical basis routinely informing it, a basis generally linked to perspectives articulated from above by intellectuals or state functionaries. And neither is that cynicism (whether pragmatic, realistic, or shamelessly neoliberal in character) evident in the chapters that follow. Instead they make original contributions toward understanding the setbacks experienced by the Mexican peasantry—in ways that do not write peasants, and subaltern social groups and classes generally, out of the picture, out of history. Hence the evidence they provide, combined with the impact of the EZLN since 1994 in refashioning the languages of political discourse and political struggle throughout Mexico, convince me that that judgment is no longer valid in 1997.

The political defeats rural Mexicans have suffered, and yet persisted in the face of, are historical outcomes of their active engagement with other classes of Mexican society. As Adolfo Gilly persuasively argues below, the roots of and reasons for that active engagement may be uncovered by investigating the ongoing process of negotiation between rulers and ruled that has been a characteristic of Mexican society for several centuries. To attribute the supposed defeat of Mexican peasants to their inherent or essential "backwardness" in the face of "modernity," or to some iron law of history dictating that peasants must take a back seat to the proletariat or to any other hypostatized "perfect subject-object of history" (the post-Enlightenment "individual" comes to mind as another example), is a lame surrender to one or another variety of essentialism. No more tenable is the naive enthusiasm informing some northern intellectuals' embrace of *neo-zapatismo* as an example of a "postmodern political movement" (Burbach 1994; cf. Nugent 1995a, 1995b). Among the many things demonstrated by the EZLN uprising in Chiapas in 1994 and the subsequent negotiations between the EZLN and the Mexican state—however many times they have been interrupted—is that the peasantry in Mexico, even the residents of the most impoverished indigenous regions of the country, still have the capacity to resist. Popular insurgencies and mobilizations throughout Mexico during the 1980s and 1990s—in Chiapas and Chihuahua, in Guerrero and Michoacán and Tabasco—serve as potent reminders that however unfashionable peasant studies have become for the social science establishment, the peasantry remains, on the ground, rather like the figure Mark Twain invoked about himself: rumors of its death are highly exaggerated.

The Premise

The basic premise of the studies presented here is that rural revolt and popular protest in Mexico are best understood in simultaneous relation to the particularities of local or regional experience, the national-historical context of Mexico, and the broader dimension of U.S.-Mexican relations. A necessary starting point, then, is to determine how participants in rural revolts see themselves historically and to examine their actions in relation to global organizations of power without surrendering the analysis to those supralocal structures that erase or hide particular histor*ies* of struggle. This recasting of the context in which Mexican rural revolts are analyzed introduces issues that earlier studies of peasant insurgency did not have to confront.

Walter Goldfrank long ago pointed out that the possibilities and outcomes of popular insurrection are critically conditioned by international
relationships of power (Goldfrank 1979). The other side of the coin,
though—if one that is generally ignored when it does come up—is that
international relationships of power are critically conditioned by the form
and direction of popular insurrection. As John Coatsworth indicated in an
essay published the same year as the first edition of the present collection,
"Little has been written to acknowledge the effects of rural revolt on
the transition to modern capitalist societies in nineteenth-century Latin
America, nor has attention been focused on the relationship between rural
social movements and the development of modern political systems"
(Coatsworth 1988:59). The achievement of the essays collected here is to
provide empirically grounded demonstrations of that point by examining
relationships between rural revolt and state formation in Mexico and
showing how the two—either together or singly—present challenges to
forms of U.S. intervention.

This introduction sets out a general formulation of the historiographic
and theoretical issues considered in the chapters that follow. It indicates
how those issues are addressed by highlighting some important insights
that emerge from these studies. Particular attention is paid to the manner
in which the sociocultural and historical understanding of rural revolt in
Mexico is revised in light of a radical reconceptualization of the relationships between popular social movements, capitalist state formation, and
U.S. intervention. A compelling example of this sort of "postrevisionist"
analysis and explanation (Joseph and Nugent 1994a:9–12) is offered in the
new chapter written by Adolfo Gilly in late 1996. Beyond that, I make
some effort to discuss these arguments in relation to the theoretical and
substantive advances that have occurred in Mexican revolutionary historiography in the decade since these essays were originally written.

Rural Revolt, Mexico, and the United States: The State of Play

The nature of rural revolt and popular protest have long been central
concerns of historical research in Mexico. Not all of this work has focused
on the period of the Mexican revolution of 1910–20 (for which see, e.g.,

Gilly 1971, Womack 1969 [on *zapatismo*] or Katz forthcoming [on *vi-llismo*]). Colonial-period and nineteenth-century antecedents, as well as postrevolutionary popular movements, have received considerable scholarly attention (see, e.g., Bartra 1985; Cockcroft 1968; Guerra 1985; Joseph and Nugent 1994a; Reina 1980; Semo 1983; Tutino 1987); some scholars have even dealt with the entire period from conquest to the present focusing either on specific regions (García de León 1985) or on rural Mexico as a whole (Katz 1988a). Historical and political analyses of the Mexican state are plentiful (e.g., J. Alonso 1982; Cockcroft 1983; de la Garza et al. 1986; Garciadiego et al. 1986; Hamilton 1982; Leal 1985). And while the United States has had, to say the least, a peculiar historical relationship with Mexico, and while U.S. interventions—particularly but not exclusively economic and political—have been legion, for the past fifteen years at least it has been difficult to conceive of these except as "current events" (e.g., Castañeda 1996; Cornelius 1986; *NACLA* 1987; Oppenheimer 1996). More than that, with the 1980s—the decade of *La Crisis* and the "regime of zero growth"—now absorbed into the past, the present we are living through in the 1990s provides little in the way of vantage points (see García de León 1995) from which to coherently track the character of U.S. interventions in Mexico, where the now evident disaster that was *salinastroika* concluded with the highly visible assassinations of Cardinal Posadas, the PRI presidential candidate Luis Donaldo Colosio, and PRI Chairman José Francisco Ruiz Massieu (alongside the less visible assassinations of hundreds of political opponents of the regime in power), the peso devaluations, a "bailout" imposed by the IMF, the World Bank, and President Clinton, and the uprising of the EZLN in Chiapas coincident with the implementation of the NAFTA (see Gilly, below).

For a long time, scholarship concerning rural Mexico tended to fragment the multifaceted reality of social and political processes into discrete types of events, structures, or relationships; here a seemingly isolated "peasant revolt," there a particular form of the state ("colonial," "national," "revolutionary," "capitalist"), here again intervention from the "outside" by a colonial power or the United States. One of this book's innovations is to link together the themes of rural revolt, the Mexican state, and the United States to the end of challenging that fragmentation of perspectives by examining the social and historical processes implicated in rural revolts at the local level as they are actively related to the global context. This new focus for studies of Mexican rural revolt and U.S.-Mexican relations forms part of the recasting of the terms in which peasant rebellion and insurgency are now being understood, in relation to bourgeois state formation in the world as a whole (Wolf 1969, 1982; Worsley 1984) and with respect to particular regions such as Southeast Asia (Scott 1985, 1990), South Asia (Ahmad 1995; Alavi 1982; Guha 1983a), Africa (Comaroff and Comaroff 1991; Ranger 1985; Saul 1979) and, above all, Latin America (Katz 1981; Joseph and Nugent 1994a; Stern 1987; *Radical History Review* 1983; also see various issues of *Latin American Perspectives* and the *Journal of Peasant Studies*).

This expanded perspective has yielded nourishing fruit in studies of rural revolt in Mexico. Remarkable and influential examples of such work include Adolfo Gilly's studies of the Mexican revolution (1971, 1983, 1986) and of *cardenismo* (1994) and Friedrich Katz's *The Secret War in Mexico* (1981), which developed a rich sociohistorical perspective that articulated the struggles of social groups at the local level with global structures of power. Alan Knight's two-volume study of the Mexican revolution took as one of its premises the insight that "there can be no high politics without a good deal of low politics" (Knight 1986a, 1:x) and proceeded to a brilliant and challenging exploration of macro- and micro-level processes and structures interacting. Now it is possible to demonstrate with greater precision that the relationship between the United States and rural revolt in Mexico is not only maintained at the level of "international relations" but is also sustained through lower-level, and often very subtly effected, connections.

Such lower-level connections figured in the results of research by Mexicanist scholars published in the 1980s. Gilbert Joseph and Allen Wells' investigations of the International Harvester Company in Yucatán (Joseph 1980, 1982; Joseph and Wells 1986; Wells 1985), Jane-Dale Lloyd's study of the Galeana district of Chihuahua (Lloyd 1983, 1987), and Ann Craig's research on Los Altos de Jalisco (Craig 1983), for example, all presented abundant evidence of the relationship between peasant mobilization and U.S. economic crises, while detailing the impact of North American enterprises and immigration on local peasants, workers, and ranchers at the beginning of this century. Similar relationships and forms of engagement across cultures and national boundaries were indicated in a pathbreaking study by the anthropologist Paul Friedrich, published more than a decade earlier (Friedrich 1970; see also Gill 1993). My own monograph on Chihuahua—which drew as well on research by Ana Alonso and Terri Koreck in the 1980s—underlined the myriad connections linking the United States to Mexican rural revolt in the present and in the past (Nugent 1993).

Until the 1990s, work on this important subject in Mexico had been carried out largely through the individual contributions of historians, sociologists, anthropologists, and political scientists. This volume has been designed to advance those efforts collectively, publishing a group of original studies by anthropologists and historians engaged in research in Mexico that address debates on popular nationalism and anti-imperialism in the Mexican countryside, the pertinence of notions of class, ethnicity, and space in Mexican rural revolts, and the relationship between U.S. intervention and Mexican popular ideology. Already it has borne fruit, as demonstrated in the new chapter by Gilly which draws on the pioneering work of scholars such as Corrigan and Sayer, Guha and Scott, Bonfil and Rus, and the contributors to *Everyday Forms of State Formation* and the original edition of this book.

The simultaneous inclusion of subjects as diverse as rural revolt, Mexican state formation, and forms of U.S. intervention in a unified research agenda is extremely challenging and points to a new area of research that Latin Americanists are now beginning to explore systematically. As Norman Long put it: "All forms of external intervention enter the existing lifeways of the individuals and groups affected and thus, as it were, pass through certain social and cultural filters. In this way, external factors are both mediated and transformed by internal structures" (Long 1984:2). However, an examination of the reciprocal effects that external and internal or macro- and micro-level processes and structures have on one another (cf. DeWalt and Pelto 1985; Friedman 1974; C. Smith 1984; Wolf 1982)—or between what John Comaroff, in a lucid and concise synthesis of a host of arguments regarding the persistence of the peasantry (1982), termed "the dialectic of articulation" and the "internal dialectic" of community formation—cannot be conducted in a purely theoretical manner. The studies presented below are based on the empirically rich materials that the authors have uncovered in their investigations of Mexican society and on their knowledge about the ideology and action of the people of the Mexican countryside.

The analyses that follow consider both the diverse forms of U.S. political, economic, and ideological penetration conducted through a variety of agencies (i.e., not exclusively state power) and the forms of organization and response created at the local and regional level in specific sets of concrete circumstances within which rural Mexicans have advanced their own struggles. A variety of social agents, such as North American capitalist enterprises, North American colonists, and U.S. military forces, have penetrated Mexico for more than a century. But the Mexican bourgeoisie and petite bourgeoisie—or national, regional and micro-regional elites— are not the only social classes in Mexico to develop attitudes and take action in relation to the many forms of U.S. penetration. A vitally important issue that the following chapters address concerns the engagement of subordinated or subaltern classes and groups in rural Mexico with these diverse U.S. forces. In short, these essays demonstrate how it is possible to "listen to the silence" of peasant demonstrations, *and* understand that "you can't commit rape a little" (see the Castillo and Steffens epigraphs, p. vii above). While not eschewing theoretical discourse, the focus is on the examination of concrete instances in which the connections between rural revolt in Mexico and U.S. intervention are manifest.

Rural Revolt, Mexico, and the United States: Empirical Studies

All of the chapters that follow were written by anthropologists and historians and prepared especially for this volume. The arguments and data they provide are the direct result of original archival research, of ethnographic investigation, and of radical reinterpretation of the literature on U.S. intervention in Mexico. Most bring to light evidence from heretofore overlooked oral, archival, and secondary sources. Together they embody the fruitful results of innovative, multidisciplinary research methodologies.

Nevertheless, they are not all identical with respect to the manner in which they identify the units of analysis. Coatsworth, Hart, Katz, and Knight, for example, discuss the issue of U.S. intervention in Mexican rural revolts in terms of international relations, either over fairly long periods of time (Knight and Hart) or, in the case of Coatsworth, by leaping to a higher level of abstraction. Other authors examine the problem in terms of developments in particular regions, or among particular groups of people, generally focusing on periods of much shorter duration. It is significant that all of these other examples come from frontier regions of Mexico, whether political frontiers in the southeast or northwest or cultural and historical frontiers such as, for example, frontiers of capitalist development (see Katz 1988a). Finally, Gilly writes about the EZLN in Chiapas in the 1990s—the rebellion of the enchanted world—as a recent example of what he detects as a long-standing pattern of negotiation between the "Mexican state community" and "the agrarian community," a pattern that is in many respects impermeable to U.S. intervention and ineradicable by the penetration of capital.

Taking Mexico and the United States as units that provide a point of departure for their interpretations, Knight and Hart proceed to disaggregate those elements they identify as critical for analysis ("the United States," "the Mexican peasantry," "U.S. economic hegemony," "the rural working class") in very different ways. Alan Knight deconstructs the different types of U.S. intervention or influence that affected the Mexican peasantry before and during the revolution, noting differences between latent and manifest effects of U.S. influence, and suggests distinguishing between observable consequences of U.S. government policy on the one hand and of U.S. capital on the other. U.S. government policy toward Mexico, by this account, was inconsistent and frequently ineffectual (and also easily chronicled), while the manifest effects of U.S. capital in Mexico were much more profound (if more difficult to detect). Ironically, though, in the wake of an accelerated process of proletarianization during the *porfiriato*, it was peasants who played the crucially important role, both on battlefield during the revolution and to the extent that they succeeded (however indirectly) in shaping state policy since the revolution: "the revolution (1910–20) was fundamentally . . . popular, rural, and agrarian in character, and heavily dependent on peasant participation."

John Hart disaggregates the various actors involved in U.S. intervention and rural revolt in Mexico differently, drawing attention to specific programs and practices of U.S. enterprises throughout Mexico, rather than to the somewhat more abstract concept of "U.S. capital." In a tour de force of "naming names" and systematically identifying which U.S. actors and investors were involved in what kinds of economic activity in Mexico and where, Hart links those processes to the many different class actors in the Mexican countryside. He demonstrates the links between U.S. finance, industrial, and merchant capital, and provides a sense of the distinct social groups in the Mexican countryside who responded to the formation of those transnational relationships by participating in the armed period of revolutionary struggle in Mexico and who, in the final analysis, were defeated by the end of the revolution.

John Coatsworth indulges in an exercise in comparative counterfactualism, basically asking "How would the Mexican Revolution have been different *without* the influence or intervention of the United States?" Expressing a preference for "the implicitly structuralist Knight [over] the explicitly empiricist one," Coatsworth argues that the United States played a decisive role both in creating the conditions that produced the revolution and in powerfully affecting its outcome, particularly with regard to the delay in the institution of a massive agrarian reform. And while agreeing, by contrast to Hart and Osorio for example, with Knight's assertions regarding "the notable lack of xenophobic anti-Americanism among . . . the peasantry," Coatsworth points out that, "in rebelling against the Porfirian regime, Mexico's peasants . . . called into question all that imperialism had accomplished in their country, and did so in a way that U.S. business interests and the U.S. government correctly perceived as prejudicial."

That theme reappears in Friedrich Katz's examination of the unraveling of an alliance between Francisco Villa and different actors (government, military, and business leaders) in the United States during the revolution and of the factors and the personalities involved in the warming and cooling of relationships between the United States and Villa during the period leading up to the U.S. recognition of Venustiano Carranza in October 1915. Katz notes that by the end of 1914, "even before Villa's crushing defeat at Celaya, his relationship with the Wilson administration and with U.S. businessmen was already deteriorating rapidly." An explanation for this turn of events may be found in the fact that U.S. leaders such as President Wilson only belatedly recognized that they had been courting the leader of a peasant army and not "the only instrument of civilization in Mexico"; since those categories were regarded as contradictory and mutually exclusive, Villa's former supporters in the United States betrayed him.

They likely had reason to, if Rubén Osorio's account of the ideological continuities in popular revolts in the north from the 1880s through the final, *guerrillero* period of the Villa movement are considered. Pointing to the continuities of forms of organization and resistance to the state and to capitalism in Chihuahua from the 1880s through the revolution, Osorio illustrates the profoundly nationalist character assumed by some of the northern movements, citing from Villa's proclamations issued during the later period of armed struggle which invoked the slogan "Mexico for the Mexicans."

The different interpretations offered by Knight and Hart, by Coatsworth and Osorio, underline the diversity of perspectives regarding the relevance of economic nationalism and anti-imperialism as motivations for popular-class participation in revolutionary mobilization, whether viewed from "above" or from "below," from the standpoint of international relations or of particular communities. Where Knight persuasively argues that such factors were of little significance, Hart insists they were crucial; where Coatsworth endorses Knight's general point while observing that, regardless of popular motivations, imperialist fears of mobilization from below were genuine and well justified, Osorio provides examples of explicitly anti-imperialist currents within the northern revolutionary tradition.

Of more general significance is the fact that investigations of more circumscribed regions and peoples of Mexico can reveal how social-class differentiation, ethnic identity, and conceptualizations of space or territory figure in the articulation of rural revolt in Mexico with U.S.-Mexican relations. For example, Jane-Dale Lloyd documents the effects of Chihuahua's Municipal Land Law of 1905 on communities in the northwestern part of the state. While for some time the policy of the Enrique Creel regime encouraging privatization of agricultural and pastoral lands was recognized as a factor precipitating peasant participation during the revolution in Chihuahua (Wasserman 1980; Katz 1981), Lloyd advances several original points in her chapter that address issues beyond a particular region.

First, she demonstrates how this policy of the Chihuahuan state was linked to U.S. capitalization of land, and hence was an outcome of a phenomenon already under way during the *porfiriato,* since U.S. and Mexican investors had been consolidating enormous estates in Chihuahua for decades at the expense of the inhabitants of Chihuahua's peasant communities (on which see Hart 1987; Katz 1981:7–20; Nugent 1993:57–68; Orozco 1995). Second, she details the specific form of class differentiation in the region and the curious way it was related to revolutionary mobilization. Former free peasants were becoming *medieros,* or sharecroppers, on land which had in the past belonged to them; other agropastoralists, fortunate enough to retain some control over the land, became *rancheros*. But the circumstance that *rancheros* and *medieros*—whose respective sets of interests did not have a great deal in common structurally—succeeded in uniting against capitalism's invasion of what was conceived as communal land, and that this unity came about as a direct result of state policy, sheds an interesting light on popular mobilization in rural Mexico.

Just as the agrarian policy of Porfirio Díaz in the 1880s and 1890s failed to produce a new class of yeoman farmers but instead created a mass of landless peasants or an "indigent class of people,"[1] so too did the Municipal Land Law in Chihuahua fail to rationalize private holding of agricultural land and instead drove the dispossessed former peasants, whatever their "class character," to join the ranks of revolutionaries between 1905 and 1911. The unanticipated and surprisingly effective character of popular response to state policy in Mexico has continued into the 1990s. Thus, for example, President Carlos Salinas de Gortari's "reforms" to Article 27 of the Constitution of 1917 provided a major impulse to the organization of actions by the Ejército Zapatista de Liberación Nacional in the years immediately following the reforms (García de León 1995). As Gilly writes below: "Step by step [the governing elite] committed exactly the same error of failing to appreciate the consequences of their policy as had their modernizing ancestor, Chihuahua Governor Enrique Creel, almost a century earlier. And it would not be long in generating similar results."

Kearney's essay analyzes several of the ways in which ethnic identity among oppressed groups in the Mexican countryside may provide the catalyst for a transition from passive to active resistance when countering oppression. The interesting point that emerges from his discussion of the Mixtec in Oaxaca and in the Californias is that this self-conscious ethnic identity appears in its strongest form along the border, where the Mixtec work for large-scale capitalist farmers, rather than in their "native" sierra of Oaxaca (see also Kearney and Nagengast 1989; Nagengast and Kearney 1990). Kearney illustrates in a compelling fashion the complex character of the relationship between indigenous forms of self-identity and transnational capitalism (cf. Rouse 1991, 1995) while also taking account of the

---

1. Note Porfirio Díaz, according to whom dividing "the *ejidos* of the *pueblos* among the heads of families [would have] a very beneficial outcome for that indigent class of people, for it would assure them small private properties." CPD 1.41, Caja 7.16, fols. 170–72, 10 September 1889.

imbrication of class and ethnicity in rural revolts in Mexico (cf. Stern 1987:15–18).

María Teresa Koreck considers both *geographical* movement and *political* movement as well as their possible combinations in the north of Mexico. She discusses the role that nationalism played as an element of popular mobilization during the second half of the nineteenth century and throughout the revolution. While cognizant of continuities in particular forms of organization and resistance to the state and to foreign capitalism in Chihuahua from the 1880s through the revolution, and indeed to the 1980s, Koreck argues for a radical reconceptualization of the notions of "region" and "nation," or "nationalism" itself. Drawing on Benedict Anderson's (1983) study of nationalism and Philip Corrigan and Derek Sayer's (1985) investigation of state formation, Koreck writes: "The development of conceptions of national identity is linked to processes of state formation." Her essay explains why the distinctive conceptions of nation and locale which developed in eastern Chihuahua assumed the shape they did in relation to Mexican state formation and the revolution.

Gilbert Joseph examines two episodes in Yucatán's history during which North American influences conditioned rural mobilization in the peninsula: during the "Caste War" of the 1840s, and following the outbreak of the Madero rebellion of 1910. Joseph shows how what was perceived by the nineteenth-century Mayas as a fundamentally economic and agrarian conflict was recast by local elites such that "the struggle assumed a more savage and explicitly racial character." He also chronicles how the image of a "peasant rebellion" by "savages" figured in the horrified imagination of those same elites, even decades later. In other words, a conception of popular rural revolt was transformed through its recension in elite discourse. At the same time, shifting his focus between U.S. filibusterers and militarists, between Yucatecan elites and the popular classes in the countryside, Joseph demonstrates how internal relations within each of those groups conditioned their relationships to others. For example, "the immediate need to renew society [by August 1848] deprived the free Mayas of their main chance to retain their social integrity in the long run," while during the early twentieth century, "U.S. influences on the local agrarian society were mediated through regional elites," even as peasant villagers and many peons were able "to turn elite feuds to their own advantage"—again, phenomena manifest in southeastern Mexico in the 1990s.

How subaltern social groups take advantage of the confusion reigning in higher circles of power to advance popular interests is also addressed by Ana María Alonso. Her chapter explains why peasants in one of the most *villista* areas in Mexico turned against their former leader and actively collaborated with foreign military forces in an anti-*villista* campaign. She discusses nationalism and the Mexican revolution, focusing on the local leaders who were active in Namiquipa, Chihuahua, as well as the agrarian, political, economic, and cultural struggles in which the people of Namiquipa were involved. Alonso argues that what may appear as "antinationalist" and even "collaborationist" behavior by *namiquipenses* really provides evidence of a temporary convergence of localist and interventionist projects. But this short-lived Mexican peasant collaboration with the U.S. military was the contingent outcome of a particular historical and sociocultural conjuncture, not a function of the transparent reshaping of popular ideology by a hegemonic power from outside.

What each of the studies "from below" demonstrates are ways of understanding the relationships among peasant revolt, popular mobilization, and global structures of power; which is not very different from what is revealed by the studies "from above." Perhaps the unit of analysis, in each instance, is not very different. Indeed, that is one of the many prescient points driven home in Gilly's three-part essay, which carves out its own section in this book. Among other things, Gilly reminds us that the relation of domination/subordination is not a dyad but rather a triad: "For both parties, domination and subordination are active relations; between each, molding the one and the other, is interposed and exists a third term, *resistance,* the active part *par excellence,* the most of the time invisible element of the relation in its totality." Gilly's discussion of the rebellion as culture, his history of the EZLN and the desires and demands of the indigenous communities of Chiapas, his demonstration of the character of the language in which rebels speak of topics such as dignity, and the questions he poses about the tormented conscience of the modern world is a remarkable text. While wide-ranging reference is made to the work of anthropologists, historians, sociologists, and political activists in India or England, in Eastern Europe or the United States, as well as in Chihuahua, Morelos, or Chiapas, the focus of the argument never strays from the enchanted world of his title, a world represented in all its empirical density and experiential depth; an otherworld that locates itself in the territory of the possible.

Bringing the People Back In

How, in the most general manner, are the social and historical processes implicated in rural revolt connected to the world context? What is the character of the articulation of social groups at the local level vis-à-vis global structures of power? An important, if often neglected, feature of the concept of "articulation" as I am using it, is that it signifies at once "connection" *and* "giving expression to" (see Post 1978; Foster-Carter 1978:215; Nugent 1993:36–38, 152–53). These are not the same things.

Social groups such as the "peasantry" or the "rural working class," cultural practices such as revolt in the countryside of Mexico, and historical processes such as accommodation and resistance (see Calagione and Nugent 1992), do not exist in a social and historical vacuum. They are *connected* to global structures of power. At the same time, through the modalities of their own structure, they *give expression to* global structures of power. However, this "giving expression to" does not operate in one direction only. Rural revolt, for instance, also affects or is "expressed in" global structures of power; there is a multidirectional character to such articulation. The "expression" of rural revolt and forms of popular mobilization in global structures of power is as important a determinant of historical process as the more routinely recognized manner in which global structures of power are expressed in rural revolt. If the former expression is more opaque than the latter, I suspect the reason for that has more to do with the conventions, the bias, and the political project of liberal social science than it has with the inefficacy of those popular movements.

The basic idea of looking at the Mexican peasantry (especially) in relation to systems of power has been current for decades, and that idea found fertile ground in the work of Eric Wolf and Angel Palerm, among others (see, e.g., Wolf 1959, 1969, 1982; Palerm 1980; Glantz 1987). More recently, historical anthropologists such as Guillermo de la Peña have tackled the issues of local and regional power in Mexico over time both in ethnographic studies (de la Peña 1980) and in comparative, more theoretical investigations (de la Peña 1989; see also Wolf 1990). However, for every *Sons of the Shaking Earth* there is a boatload of "community studies" by anthropologists seemingly oblivious of the fact that the isolated and backward "Indian" or "peasant" "community" they study is also a dominated political space, situated within an embracing and very brutal organization of power, its residents the subjects of modes of governance that emerge out of routines and rituals of rule generated both within and without those only hypothetically isolated spaces. The circumstance that looking at local-level revolts in relation to power still seems "innovative" to some historians and anthropologists is indicative of the extent to which this "old-fashioned" position that we are attempting (still!) to advance has been taken much less seriously than it merits.

Nevertheless, it is possible to correct the view that sees rural revolt in Mexico as the result of exogenous or external forces, influences, and determinants operating on incompletely formed (or undeveloped or under-developed) social groups which have organized themselves only in relation to (or have been destroyed by) those external forces (cf. Chevalier 1983; G. Smith 1985, 1989; Turner 1986a, 1986b; Hobsbawm 1973, 1975; Corrigan 1975). Instead, we can discover the manner and the degree to which external forces, influences, and determinants are themselves shaped by the actions of people in the countryside, and thereby restore the peasantry to their place in world history and in global society. We must, in other words, examine the way "external forces are both mediated and transformed by internal structures" (Long 1984:2). In this connection, William Rose-berry's stimulating essays, "Americanization in the Americas" and "European History and the Construction of Anthropological Subjects" (in Roseberry 1989), point the way to a more nuanced analysis of the fate of the peasantry in twentieth-century Latin America generally. Following up such insights, the task for analysis becomes one of "uncover[ing] the complex relationships, the terms of a 'dialectic of articulation,' between the community [or subaltern groups and classes]—constituted, as John Coma-roff suggests, by an 'internal dialectic'—and the state as those relationships shift over time (Comaroff 1982:146)" (Nugent and Alonso 1994:214).

This is not to deny the effects of external influences on the process of rural revolt in Mexico. Indeed, the essays in this volume and many other studies as well demonstrate unequivocally how external forces such as periods of headlong capitalist development, economic booms and economic crises, changing immigration policy, drought, the development of extractive industries, the appearance of new labor regimes and of a new kind of work force, the formation of a capitalist state that called itself

"revolutionary" even in the late twentieth century, and unrelenting intervention by the United States have all been important in shaping rural
revolt in Mexico. However, such general and incontrovertible arguments
fail to deal fully with the human subjects of change (i.e., the Mexican
peasantry); the peasantry and urban and rural workers figure, when they
figure at all in such observations, as a *subjected* population, the passive
recipients of effects of power. That perspective leaves little room for understanding how the peasantry contends with this kind of subordination
subjectively.[2]

What is required is a model of social change where the unit of analysis
has been reformulated to include the Mexican people as instruments of
change. For, indeed, another point that these chapters demonstrate is that
the "external influences" have not exclusively been realizing their own
logic on or in Mexican society, but instead have been modified and transformed by popular resistance to what only seem to be inexorable realities.

One example of unanticipated peasant response to external influences
has to do with the transformation of Mexico's land from a subject of labor
for the rural masses into a commodity during the second half of the nineteenth century (cf. Cardoso 1980; Marx 1973 [1858]:471–72; Marx 1906
[1867]:784–805). This transformation in Mexico (also discussed in Nugent
1991, 1994) was realized in part as a latent or indirect consequence of North
American capitalization of land, agricultural production, and the production process generally. (For this formulation of the "latent" consequences
of capitalization, see Knight's essay below; for evidence of the actual extent
of U.S. capitalization in Mexican land, latent or manifest, see the Hart
essay.) But it was also mediated by specific policies of the Mexican state
during the same period (see Lloyd, below; Cardoso 1980). Ultimately, this
transformation had a curious consequence within rural Mexican society
very distant from the expectations of modernizing capitalists. Rather than
turning the rural masses—the peasants—into yeoman farmers and free
laborers, it motivated many to participate in "precursor revolts," in the

---

2. The last two sentences rely on the double sense of subjectivity (as a kind of subordination and as a kind of self-knowledge) formulated by Michel Foucault (1982:212;
1978). The point is rather less to unqualifiedly endorse a sort of Foucauldian discourse
analysis (see Nugent 1994:153) and rather more to argue for a historicization of the old
anthropological notion of "the native's point of view." See Cohn and Dirks (1988:227),
calling for linking "histories of power and anthropologies of culture," or the chapter by
Gilly below.

Mexican revolution, and in post-1920 popular mobilizations.[3] Attempts to effect a similar transformation of land from subject of labor into commodity—for instance, the 1991 reforms to Article 27 of the Mexican Constitution which effectively ended redistribution of agricultural land to peasant communities and sanctioned the privatization (or commodification) of existing ejidal plots—meet with resistance in the 1990s; witness again the EZLN uprising in Chiapas and the paltry number of petitions through PROCEDE to secure individual title to agricultural fields formerly in the *ejido* sector, potent reminders not of peasant recalcitrance but of active resistance (Subcomandante Marcos et al. 1995; Baitenmann 1994a, 1994b).

In other words, people in the countryside of Mexico have not simply been passive spectators to the destruction of the material and social bases of their lives, bearing mute witness to the effects of external forces they neither control nor comprehend. On the contrary, they have repeatedly acted upon those conditions and engaged those forces in such a way as to shape their own destiny. They have resisted and they have persisted. The peasantry and the popular classes in general have demanded and in large measure succeeded in eliciting a variety of responses by the Mexican state and the United States, ranging from the creation of official organizations and mobilizations (which putatively, and sometimes actually, advance the interests of the participants in revolts) to reform, co-optation, and repression. Yet if the defeats that peasants have suffered are many, that is not a consequence of their inherent lack of ability to formulate demands, but because their popular mobilizations, moving the site of struggle out of the "little community," became in turn objects of contention for dominant classes, for the state, and for foreign powers. But putting to the side this perennially indeterminate outcome (which brings to mind Mao Zedong's

3. "Precursor revolts" appears within quotation marks in order to highlight that the very conceptualization of pre-1910 rural revolts in Mexico as phenomena easily separated out and analyzed apart from the events of "the Mexican Revolution" is a scholastic artifact rather than a legacy of distinct and separate struggles. Moreover, the very expression reveals a tendency to study the pre-1910 period through the prism of "the Revolution" (cf. Joseph and Nugent 1994a). By way of contrast, there is much to be learned from an examination of the continuities between prerevolutionary, revolutionary, and postrevolutionary peasant mobilization: see especially Osorio, below; Orozco 1995; Nugent 1985, 1993, 1994; Hart, 1987; Bartra 1985. While the publication of Cockcroft's study of *magonismo* three decades ago popularized and put into circulation the "precursor" concept, the very point, it seems, was to underline the continuities just noted.

response to the question of what he thought of the French Revolution: "Ask me again in five hundred years"), we are still left with the issue that it remains difficult to "listen to the silence" of peasants, to uncover what James Scott (1990) characterized as the "hidden transcripts" of peasant resistance.

A decade ago I was convinced that that issue could be largely resolved by simply taking seriously the notion of a "domain of subaltern politics," a notion introduced to students of peasant mobilization in the work of Ranajit Guha, a social historian and the founding editor of *Subaltern Studies: Writings on South Asian History and Society* (Delhi: Oxford University Press, 1982 et seq.). My conviction in this regard has not altered over the past ten years, but in light of the more widespread dispersal of and discussion about the work of the *Subaltern Studies* group in recent years (e.g., Chakrabarty 1992; Mallon 1994; O'Hanlon 1988; Prakash 1990, 1994; Sivaramakrishnan 1995; Spivak 1988), a clarification of the theoretical and political reasons for drawing on the work of Guha and his collaborators here is in order.

In convoking the meeting where these chapters were first presented as working papers and in the introduction to an earlier edition of this book, I cannibalized from six paragraphs of Guha's essay "On Some Aspects of the Historiography of Colonial India" (1982)—a programmatic and methodological polemical statement that introduced *Subaltern Studies*, vol. 1— substituting "Mexico" for "India" and slightly altering certain passages while interpolating some others, though astonishingly few.[4] Rather than reproduce that exercise in searching-and-replacing (which indeed raises interesting questions about some striking parallels between peasant insurgency in Mexico and India, Latin America and South Asia; cf. Cooper et al. 1993, on Africa and Latin America), since the essay by Guha is now widely available I can simply refer the reader to it and draw attention to

4. At that time—in 1987—Guha's essay, like the first four volumes of *Subaltern Studies*, was largely unknown outside a small circle of South Asia scholars. It was only in 1988 that Oxford University Press in New York issued a trade paperback of *Selected Subaltern Studies*, edited by Guha and the famous literary theorist Gayatri Chakravorty Spivak with a foreword by Columbia University Professor Edward W. Said. I do not think it coincidental that, with Said and Spivak lending their names to the project, the work of the *Subaltern Studies* group received a more significant reception among Anglophone literary critics than among social historians (regardless of area of speciality) or anthropologists in the years immediately following (cf. Sivaramakrishnan 1995).

how what Guha set out there[5] is of value for understanding rural revolt in Mexico and, significantly, who the people are that are so revolting.

With a critique of various modalities of "elitist historiography" as his point of departure, Guha argues that what is absent in elite historiography is the relatively autonomous domain of the politics of the people. While elite mobilization tends to be vertical, subaltern or popular mobilization is horizontal. Further, the peasant uprising or rural revolt is a central feature of subaltern/popular politics. Popular ideology resists control by elites and by the center, but economistic and regionalistic splits can fracture horizontal alliances. Finally, accepting that we can "demarcate the domain of subaltern politics from that of elite politics" and acknowledge that there "were vast areas in the life and consciousness of the people that were never integrated into [the bourgeoisie's] hegemony" (Guha 1982:6), what is indicated is what Guha terms a "structural dichotomy"—elsewhere identified as an "ideological disjuncture" (Nugent 1987)—between popular and elite politics and consciousness, a widely recognized feature of social and class relations in Latin America. The lineaments of that structural dichotomy or ideological disjuncture are now somewhat clearer, both as a result of political action by Mexicans since 1988 (cf. EZLN 1994, 1995; Gilly 1989; Subcomandante Marcos et al. 1995) and owing to some of the "discussions about history" provoked by the events of the 1990s among writers and activists (Gilly, Subcomandante Marcos, and Ginzburg 1995).

This volume focuses on what Ranajit Guha calls "the domain of subaltern politics" or "the politics of the people." Such a focus need not, indeed should not, occlude consideration of international relations, or what could be called "elite politics on a global scale." Rather, we should be concerned to understand the articulation of these two domains of political action, evident in rural revolt in Mexico and in the forms of U.S. intervention, whether manifest or latent, visible or invisible but no less palpable. To analyze U.S. intervention and Mexican rural revolt requires a perspective that is neither "from the top down" nor exclusively "from the bottom up"; rather, it is now possible to combine *both* points of departure in a unified analysis, as is demonstrated in the essays that follow, and in much other work published over the past decade (e.g., Cohn 1996; Cooper and Stoler 1989, 1997; Dirks 1992; Gilly 1994; Gootenberg 1995; Joseph and

5. And elsewhere: e.g., Guha 1983a.

Nugent 1994a; Katz 1988a; Noriega Elío 1992; Prakash 1995; Roseberry and O'Brien 1991; Stocking 1991).

An important point to bear in mind is that the domains of subaltern and elite politics are precisely that: power domains. I emphasize this point because, in many of the commentaries about or efforts to extend the work of the *Subaltern Studies* group, it frequently goes neglected; the issue is recast as having to do with discourse rather than with material social practice (Nugent 1994:165–66). Gayatri Chakravorty Spivak writes of the *Subaltern Studies* collective that "they generally perceive their task as making a theory of consciousness or culture rather than specifically a theory of change" (Spivak 1985:331; 1988:4), by which I presume she means social change. She later asserts:

Because of this bestowal of a historical specificity to consciousness in the narrow sense, even as it implicitly operates as a metaphysical methodological presupposition in the general sense, there is always a counterpointing suggestion in the work of the group that subaltern consciousness is subject to the cathexis of the élite, that it is never fully recoverable, that it is always askew from its received signifiers, indeed that it is effaced even as it is disclosed, that *it is irreducibly discursive.* (Spivak 1985:339; 1988:11, emphasis added)

Neither is there a place for social change in those accounts in which, evidently, subaltern discourse is expected to take a back seat to the discourse of academics themselves. Gyan Prakash, for instance, appears to be calling for treatments of the resistance of the colonized "as theoretical events" (Prakash 1995:5). And in their "founding Statement," the Latin American Subaltern Studies Group identifies the subaltern "as a subject that emerges across, or at the intersections of, a spectrum of academic disciplines" (LASSG 1993:112), rather than, say, a historical and active subject of political history (Ahmad 1995:3–4).[6]

Notwithstanding the prominence of a certain type of discourse analysis—which draws in perhaps unequal parts on Roland Barthes and Michel Foucault—in the best of the work published in *Subaltern Studies* since 1982 (e.g., Guha 1983b), I would simply emphasize that, as K. Sivarama-

6. Assertions such as those just cited might serve as examples from the Americas of what David Harris characterized as "the effects of Gramscianism on cultural studies" in his pungent description of how a generation of academics in the United Kingdom used a particular reading of Antonio Gramsci to advance their own careers (Harris 1992).

krishnan demonstrates in his recent review essay, there are other currents and tendencies as well in what he calls the "*Subaltern Studies* project" (Sivaramakrishnan 1995). Rather than surrender to the insuperability of the "tensions between 'real social history' and the study of 'discursive effects'" (Sivaramakrishnan 1995:404), or between "bottom–up" and "top–down" perspectives, we should just get on with our work, uniting the two when the material being analyzed permits and, for the rest, remaining cognizant of the incomplete character of our historical and political understandings (which is similar to, though not isomorphic with, the centrality of contingency in historical process). We might even direct our investigations "to the study of the structures and meanings involved in the creation of systems of solidarity and authority and to what appear to be the unconscious systems of control which mark many modern societies" (Cohn 1987 [1980]:40).

The studies that follow are the initial steps of such an investigation and make no claim to provide the final word on rural revolt in Mexico and U.S. intervention. Indeed, they scarcely begin to explore that relationship; the Mexican-American war (1846–48), for instance, is barely mentioned. Neither do these chapters, all but one written a decade ago, provide much explicit discussion of state formation in Mexico, a topic addressed by myself and others in the years since (cf. Gilly, below; Mallon 1988; Nugent 1993:34–38, 150–65; Joseph and Nugent 1994b:12–23). The adoption of a "state formation approach," inspired or encouraged in large measure by the work of the late Philip Abrams (1988 [1977]) and Philip Corrigan and Derek Sayer (1985), has proven immensely valuable in investigations of revolutionary and postrevolutionary Mexico, examples of which are the empirical studies in *Everyday Forms of State Formation* (Joseph and Nugent 1994a). Terri Koreck was already drawing on this approach in her chapter below. What is thereby underlined is how these chapters do provide a provocative launching pad for other studies in the future.

Rather than directly address the issue of bourgeois state formation, most of the contributors below in fact focus instead on Mexican nationalism and the Mexican nation. The circumstance that the *nation* is the subject of more sophisticated conceptualization than the *state* in the chapters that follow raises the interesting question of what the relationship between state and nation in Mexico is. John Womack concluded his contribution to the *Cambridge History of Latin America* with the suggestion that the new state which emerged in Mexico in the 1920s would "serve as the nation's bourgeois party. Its function forecast its programme, a long series of reforms from above, to evade, divide, diminish and restrain threats to Mexican sovereignty and capitalism from abroad and from below" (Womack 1986:153). Womack's argument relies on distinguishing between the state and the nation in Mexico without precisely specifying what is meant by either term. What is clear, though, is the grim picture he paints of the relationships of domination and subordination between state and nation, and between the ruling and subaltern classes in Mexico.

In *Imagined Communities: Reflections on the Origin and Spread of Nationalism,* Benedict Anderson defined the nation as "an imagined political community" (1983:15). Many writers who cite that work tend to neglect the central word of the definition; perhaps it's enough to remember the book's title to know what a nation is. Such neglect is entirely unsuitable for understanding Mexico. As an instance of "the invention of tradition" (see Hobsbawm and Ranger 1985), the postrevolutionary Mexican nation may be viewed simultaneously as a sign of despair or of hope, as a successful "imagining of community," or as the past and future site of alternative and contested imaginings of community. Despair is signified through the violence directed at the Mexican people, through the defeats to which popular mobilizations have been subjected in the countryside and in the towns. Hope is signified by the fact that the popular imagining of community in Mexico remains a site from which challenges to the state are issued; the complete formation of the nation is still a *political* project, one that the people will continue to shape.

Popular Nationalism and Anti-Imperialism in the Mexican Countryside

ALAN KNIGHT

The United States and the Mexican Peasantry,

circa 1880–1940

While there have been many studies of U.S.-Mexican relations during the period 1880–1940 and, especially in recent years, many significant studies of peasant protest and rebellion, these two themes have rarely interacted. Indeed, they have tended to absorb the attention of quite distinct scholarly groups, who have followed contrasting approaches. People who are interested in peasants are not usually very interested in diplomats, and vice versa (Katz 1981 is a notable exception). By uniting these two themes, this volume offers certain new angles and may serve to show whether their previous mutual neglect was warranted by the intrinsic nature of the different problems or was merely the contingent outcome of conventional academic divisions—social history, agrarian history, diplomatic history, etc.

New angles do not necessarily come easy, however. My own analysis demands three initial disclaimers. First, unlike most of the other essays, it adopts a national rather than a local or regional viewpoint. Generalizations advanced at the national level are likely to face the objection that they are inapplicable in this or that specific case. This is a familiar enough historical problem, but one whose solution is far from straightforward. It involves distinguishing what is typical, or broadly representative, of certain trends/patterns/types from what is untypical or aberrant. Untypical cases of course deserve study, but they should not be elevated to the status of paradigms; there is a contrasting misapprehension—evident, for example, in some discussions of *zapatismo*—whereby the untypicality and exceptionality of the case is mistakenly stressed. Either way, it is important to try to locate case studies within some broader (national or international) comparative context. "What should they know of England who only England know?" is just as relevant for those who claim knowledge of Mexico, or even of Morelos.

If, from the national perspective, it is crucial to distinguish between "typical" and "untypical" local examples, such intellectual discrimination is notoriously hard to achieve. This introduces my second disclaimer. While "typicality" carries connotations of statistical incidence, it is rarely possible to achieve satisfying statistical data—not to mention satisfying theoretical criteria—whereby the typicality of cases may be judged. How many peasant rebels do we need to make a peasant revolution? How many nationalists to make a nationalist revolution? So familiar and recurrent (and recalcitrant) are such problems that, by way of excuse for the lack of "hard" numerical data presented here, I would quote a historian of quite different provenance:

> I particularly regret not having been able to offer more of those exact statistical data upon which the precise analysis of historical change must so often depend. Unfortunately, the sources seldom permit such computation. . . . [Hence] in my attempts to sketch the main outlines of the subject I have only too often had to fall back upon the historian's traditional method of presentation, by example and counterexample. (Thomas 1973:x)

Of course, such a method, even if unavoidable, can easily lead to critique and debate which are in turn based upon the further trading of examples and counterexamples—whether like goods in the market (i.e., to comparative advantage) or like blows in a prizefight.

My third and final caveat derives in part from this last consideration. Two main conclusions, relevant to the current discussion, emerged from my study of the Mexican Revolution, which focused on the years 1910–20 (Knight 1986a). The first, contentious for some but probably not for the contributors to this volume, was that the revisionist dismissal or demotion of the role of peasant groups and agrarian factors in the revolution had gone way too far; that while the old "agrarian-populist" notion of the revolution (espoused, for example, by Frank Tannenbaum) was highly simplistic and not a little romantic, it nevertheless contained truths and insights about the revolution which the revisionists had overlooked—or even brusquely dismissed—to the detriment of their interpretation. The revolution was clearly more than a simple confrontation of peasant and landlord, village and hacienda; but that confrontation, in its many variations and nuances, was central to the revolution and lent the revolution its markedly popular and agrarian character. Indeed, it seems likely I was sometimes overcautious in my reemphasis of the peasant/agrarian factor, especially in Chihuahua (cf. Alonso 1986).

A second conclusion, negative and therefore less eye-catching, also emerged from my research. Foreign interests did not figure as victims of the revolution to anything like the extent argued or assumed in many studies, "traditional" as well as "revisionist."[1] To put it at its simplest, the idea of a virulently nationalist popular revolution was largely a myth. Clearly, this conclusion is directly relevant to the present discussion, and it conflicts with the argument of other essays in this volume. The conflict may derive from contrasting evaluations of "typicality," as already suggested (what, for some, may be a revealingly typical "nationalist" outburst is, for me, a rare aberration); or, even more likely, it may depend upon contrasting interpretations of agreed "facts." We all know, for example, that American interests suffered damage during the Mexican Revolution; we may even be able to agree on some rough computation of these damages (though, when confronted by Claims Commission data, we should surely strive for the skepticism of insurance claims adjusters); but none of this affords straightforward evidence of motive, of the underlying grievances, pressures, and attitudes that gave rise to damages and claims. Only careful analysis of specific cases can reveal the context and thus the significance of supposedly "nationalist" or antiforeign actions. The subtleties of attitude and behavior can rarely be inferred from aggregate statistics (as cliometricians have learned to their cost in several encounters, apropos both European popular radicalism and North American slavery).

At the outset, therefore, it seems best to emphasize, rather than to obfuscate, the position taken here: the Mexican revolution (1910–20) was fundamentally—though not, of course, solely—popular, rural, and agrarian in character, and heavily dependent on peasant participation. The revolution was not, least of all in terms of its basic origins and popular manifestations, a nationalist, or anti-American, or anti-imperialist revolution. Central to this argument is a distinction between the latent and manifest role of American influence and American actors in Mexico.

The latent influence of the United States—especially of U.S. capital—

---

1. A stack of references could be given. For a good, recent synthesis which discerns a "strong nationalist feeling," sometimes xenophobic and "predominantly anti–North American," see Vázquez and Meyer 1982:2–3, 108, 115, 141; note also González N. 1969.

was profound, as I shall argue. At a very basic level it could be stated that the Mexican Revolution occurred because of the rapid incorporation of a large "traditional" peasantry within a dynamic, commercial, agrarian economy, a process that also necessarily involved a considerable extension of state power. The dynamism of this economy was to a significant degree the result of U.S. trade, enterprise, and investment. Of course, European demand and capital also figured; and, of course, other agrarian societies also experienced these broad processes during the same period. But nowhere else did so rapid and powerful a deployment of U.S. economic influence encounter so large and entrenched a peasantry, possessed of resources that made resistance possible.[2]

Elsewhere, the tide of American influence ran more slowly (e.g., in Peru, at least in this period); or, as in the case of Cuba, it washed over an agrarian society of radically different character, such that the response was—*pace* Eric Wolf—less a "peasant war" than middle-class nationalism and working-class syndicalism (Wolf 1973). In this very general sense, the Mexican Revolution—not just the first but, perhaps, the only major peasant (*sic*) revolution of Latin America—may be said to derive its distinctive character from the fortuitous juxtaposition, within North America, of the most dynamic representatives of twentieth-century capitalism alongside the still numerous and doughty carriers of the ancient Mesoamerican and Hispanic peasant tradition.[3]

Nevertheless, the *manifest* consequences of this *latent* American influence were another matter. Historians, like sociologists or psychologists, are familiar enough with this distinction. Spanish American silver may have caused—or contributed to—European price inflation in the sixteenth century, but the European victims of this trend did not share Bodin's sophisticated grasp of its causes. Mexican peasants may have suffered as a result of growing American trade and investment during the *porfiriato*, but that alone did not ensure an anti-American or nationalist response among the

---

2. By "resources" I mean not only the .30-30 hidden under the floor but also the ideological and organizational resources of communities who had resisted external challenges in the past and who, now facing a more serious challenge than ever before, would resist again, under "revolutionary" auspices (Knight 1986a, 1:159–65).

3. "Hispanic" because we are dealing not simply with "Indian" communities, direct descendants of Mesoamerican cultures, but also with those of *mestizo* composition, possessing strong Iberian traits. Both fall under the broad rubric "peasant" which is used here.

insurgent peasantry. No more did the impoverished artisans of the Bajío vent their ire against the Puebla, Veracruz, and Federal District industrialists who were responsible for their plight; rather, they concentrated on local targets: officials, merchants, moneylenders, and retailers.

American influence, then, could exert a powerful latent effect without necessarily incurring a manifest, targeted reaction. And "American influence" could, of course, embrace a range of elements. An initial task within this general analysis of the problem must therefore involve the disaggregation of the many elements covered by the umbrella term "American influence."[4] In particular, it is only by such an analytical disaggregation that we can appreciate what I have suggested is a central—and, at first sight, paradoxical—feature of the Mexican Revolution: U.S. capital (by far the most efficacious agent of American influence) laid the groundwork of the revolution, but the revolution was not directed against U.S. capital, especially not in its popular, peasant manifestations. U.S. capital, to put it differently, helped bring about significant, objective, structural changes in Mexican society, but these did not translate into comparably significant, subjective, conjunctural reactions.

To call U.S. capital the most efficacious agent of American influence is to imply some sort of sectoral breakdown of "influence." "Influence" may be defined according to type, agent, or recipient. *Types* of influence would include political, economic, cultural, ideological, etc. (each, to be sure, overlapping and intersecting). *Agents* would denote the actors, individual and institutional, who transmitted influence: governmental (politicians, diplomats); private (U.S. companies, churches); or social (e.g., the broad influence exerted by "American society," whether upon Mexican migrants or Mexican policymakers impressed by U.S. values). Finally, *recipients* could be found throughout Mexican society: peasants and landlords, middle and working classes, radicals and conservatives, Catholics and Protestants. Since our agreed focus is the peasantry, the range of recipient groups is, to that extent, formally limited. (However, given the definitionally subordinate position of the peasantry within society, it should be recognized that American influence acting upon nonpeasant groups—say,

4. Thus we may aim for some precision, and avoid making spurious connections, impelled, perhaps, by a natural desire to stress the importance of the subject in hand. Social historians, no less than biographers, have to guard against the perennial danger of inflating their subject's real significance.

Sonoran landlords or *magonista* intellectuals—could indirectly affect the peasantry too.)

American influence on the peasantry may therefore be analyzed by type or agent. (Needless to say, more precise limitations of time and space are possible and perhaps desirable; here, however, I attempt a national overview of this relationship throughout the "long" revolutionary period, c. 1880–1940.) And within this overview, it is the analysis of *agents* rather than of *types* of influence which is preferred—not least because major agents, such as the U.S. government, exercised a polyvalent influence, at once political, military, economic, and ideological. Though we may wish to isolate analytically such types of influence, it is the polyvalent actor—the U.S. government, U.S. capital, U.S. "society"—which should provide the starting point. Accordingly, I will start with the most visible and institutionally concrete actor, the U.S. government, and will then proceed to the more diffuse—but, I will argue, more powerful and pervasive—influence of U.S. capital and society.

The U.S. Government's Influence on the Mexican Peasantry

As regards the causes, character, and consequences of U.S. governmental influence during the *porfiriato* and the revolution I shall be brief, for four main reasons. First, these have already been the subject of considerable study and debate, even if no scholarly consensus has emerged (cf. Katz 1981; Haley 1970; Grieb 1969; Gilderhus 1977; Ulloa 1971). Second, as one participant in the debate has suggested, the study of U.S. policy toward Mexico, of its inputs and outcomes, reflects the policy itself, which was formed "on the basis of conjectures and amid great uncertainty" (Hoernel 1981:209). Hence the debate often hinges upon assumptions and inferences that are strongly resistant to empirical validation or falsification. Ostensible "facts"—U.S. official tolerance of Madero in 1910, opposition to Orozco in 1912, recognition of Carranza in 1915, repudiation of the new Constitution after 1917—can accommodate widely different interpretations, for each of which some supportive evidence can be found. Adjudicating between rival interpretations is difficult, since the balancing of evidence may depend less upon the intrinsic weight of this or that "fact" than upon divergent prior assumptions, according to which "facts" are assembled and arrayed.

A familiar historiographic dilemma, this problem is, I think, particularly acute in the analysis of Great Power policymaking. Charles Maier's observation concerning the celebrated debate over the origins of the Cold War bears repetition in this comparable, albeit narrower, context: "more than in most historiographical controversies, the questions about what happened are transformed into concealed debate about the nature of freedom and duress, exploitation and hegemony" (Maier 1978:24).[5] This is not to suggest that we give up and go home, but rather to recognize that, in a brief part of a brief essay, no very solid advances or conversions are likely to be made.

Instead, point three, I shall state my position: that U.S. governmental influence over the Mexican Revolution has often been exaggerated, especially for the period 1910–20. And, if post-1920 is a somewhat different story, it is not a story that primarily concerns the peasantry. That being the case, it seems (point four) much more profitable and interesting to focus on the unofficial, nongovernmental actors who impinged on Mexican society, not least Mexican peasant society, and who did so in important and often neglected ways. Such a focus will dominate the latter, more positive, sections of this essay.

However, if only briefly to substantiate the third point above, a word about U.S. policy is in order. Debates about the role of (official) U.S. intervention in the revolution are as old as the events they seek to explain. Did the U.S. government—acting, perhaps, in collusion with U.S. business—work for the ouster of Díaz? For the fall of Madero? For the elimination of, first, Villa, then Carranza? As regards the first case (1910–11), the empirical evidence does not seem to warrant a confident answer (cf. Calvert 1968:73–84; Wilkins 1971:129–30, 277). Nor do arguments based on the principle of *cui bono* lend much strength to the evidence. It is not clear

---

5. Maier's study benefits from being read in full. Another historian has observed, specifically of the Taft-Wilson period, that "in analyzing US policy a researcher has to overcome the superabundance of source materials. Sometimes it seems as if one can 'prove' anything one is predisposed to because in the mass of archival stuff just about everything that was said seems preserved and just about everything was said" (R. Abrams 1974:97).

that the Taft administration—or the U.S. economic interests it sought to represent—stood to gain from the ouster of Díaz, or that they rejoiced at his fall. Like most people, they were surprised by the turn of events in 1910–11. Even if U.S. tolerance of Madero's sojourn in the United States implied a degree of official connivance (which is open to question), it certainly cannot be inferred that this determined the victory of the 1910 revolution, or that the United States actively sought such a victory. As Braulio Hernández, who had no reason to love or to exonerate the United States, trenchantly remarked: "the truth of God is that the revolution [of 1910] was fought with the abnegation and hunger of Mexicans, with no more."[6]

In subsequent episodes, U.S. policy was more obviously positive, even "interventionist"; and, occasionally, it was moderately successful. But "intervention" covers a multitude of sins (on which, see Knight 1987), and the ostensible "successes" of U.S. policy—the defeat of Orozco in 1912, of Huerta in 1914—must be placed in their contemporary context. In these instances the United States aligned itself with powerful forces within Mexico making for these outcomes; hence, it would be a crude form of historiographic *dependismo* to stress overmuch the determining role of the United States, as some have done. Cases must be judged on their merits: the fall of Huerta was not analogous to the fall of (say) Arbenz. Furthermore, in other important instances U.S. policy signally failed. The U.S. government did not seek the triumph of Carranza in 1915; it grudgingly accepted that Carranza had won, that a cobbled-together compromise, though preferable, was unattainable, and that realpolitik made recognition unavoidable.[7]

What is more, in these several cases, covering 1910–15, it is far from clear how U.S. policy—even if assumed to be effective—affected peasant interests (e.g., peasant forces or agrarian reform movements). The ousters of Díaz and Huerta, which have been attributed to U.S. pressure, served peasant interests. The consequences of Madero's defeat of Orozco in 1912, or of Carranza's of Villa in 1915, are open to debate. In my view, the Carranza-Villa split did not reflect clear class or ideological differences; hence it cannot be confidently asserted that Carranza's triumph—even if it

6. USS 1920, 2:2520 (testimony of September 1912).
7. Robert Lansing, "Consideration and Outline of Policies, 11 July 1915" and "The Conference in Regard to Mexico, 10 Oct. 1915," Lansing Notes and Memoranda (Blue Box 2), LC, Ms. Section.

were the work of U.S. policy, which I doubt—represented an unqualified defeat for peasant interests (Knight 1986a, 2:263–302).

Subsequently, with the consolidation of the Carranza regime and the formulation of the new Constitution, U.S. policy became both more interventionist and more traditional in the sense that the United States intervened in pursuit of traditional ends: namely, the creation of conditions favorable to U.S. commercial and strategic interests. Wilsonian moralism, in other words, began to fade. In particular, with the most blatant and overt intervention of the revolutionary decade, the United States sought to use the Punitive Expedition as a lever whereby to remove the offensive radicalism of the 1917 Constitution. Yet here, with the first decisive American attempt to deradicalize the revolution—partly in the interests of U.S. landowners, thus implicitly to the disadvantage of the agrarian cause— U.S. policy roundly failed (Haley 1970:236–37; Katz 1981:577). Prior to 1917, we may say, the revolution was recurrently "intervened" by the United States, but it was not derailed; its course was broadly determined by endogenous forces, not least by the insurgent peasants themselves.[8]

Contrary to certain assumptions, however, the progressive establishment of a stable national regime in Mexico after 1917 tended to accentuate rather than to diminish official U.S. influence. The old quagmire of competing factions, into which so many U.S. policy initiatives had sunk without trace, now gave way to an established central government, solid enough to be levered—by the familiar instruments of U.S. recognition, credit, arms—but fragile enough to fear and thus to respond to such leverage. Furthermore, the ending of the First World War refocused American attention on Mexico just at the time when the radicalism of the new Constitution (a paper radicalism, in some respects, it is true) seemed to threaten U.S. interests, which included not only the oil companies but also American landowners. During the 1920s, therefore, U.S. influence was deployed, at least in part, to protect these landed interests, now threatened by possible expropriation under the agrarian reform program.

It is difficult to assess the strength or effectiveness of this influence. Certainly it would be wrong to jump to the easy conclusion that the (leisurely) pace of agrarian reform was chiefly the result of direct U.S.

8. "This fight is entirely a Mexican fight. . . . [I]t is their own family quarrel." U.S. Consul Hanna, Monterrey, to State Dept., 28 November 1913, SD, Record Group 59, Microcopy 274, 812.00/10301.

pressure. Obregón, desperate for recognition in 1920–23, may have stalled, curtailing the *agrarista* threat to American landed interests; but this represented an additional delay in a long, slow process, rather than any definitive defeat (Gruening 1928:606). By 1925–26 the pace of land distribution had quickened; compensation for expropriated landowners remained negligible; and, when Dwight Morrow arrived as ambassador in 1927, committed to restraining the agrarian reform, "his exhortations and protests . . . did not seem to achieve any effect." In 1929, in fact, Portes Gil pushed the figures of land distribution to a new high. And if the *reparto* abated under Ortiz Rubio, it revived spectacularly after 1933. "Morrow's influence," a reliable source concludes, "had no lasting effect," at least as regards the agrarian reform (L. Meyer 1978a:236). We may contrast this conclusion with the same writer's evaluation of the oil controversy, from which Mexico emerged a net loser in both 1923 and 1927 (and in which, therefore, U.S. pressure proved to be strenuous and broadly effective) (L. Meyer 1972:216, 273–75).

In general, Morrow operated by aligning himself with and deftly influencing existing currents within Mexican official opinion/policy. He sniffed the wind and trimmed his sails accordingly. In this respect, he departed from the practices of his disastrous predecessor, James Sheffield who, invoking the spirit of "Mother Yale," steered doggedly into the teeth of storms. Morrow did not therefore belong to that category of egregious U.S. ambassadors—Henry Lane Wilson, Mexico, 1913; Sumner Welles, Cuba, 1933; Spruille Braden, Argentina, 1945; Richard Patterson, Guatemala, 1948–51—who in their respective postings pursued policies that were aggressive, interventionist, even proconsular in character (Ross 1959:506–28; Blaiser 1976:59–60, 65–66). Morrow, in contrast, realized that dramatic U.S. initiatives would be received with suspicion, even hostility, and could thus prove counterproductive (Smith 1972). In the area of agrarian reform, therefore, Morrow's role is best seen as that of reinforcing certain powerful existing trends within Mexican political circles. Official U.S. resistance to the reform thus formed part—and not the greatest part—of a broad anti-*agrarista* coalition which embraced Mexican and foreign landlords, a good many clerics, the bulk of the national press, and many "revolutionaries," especially the recently enriched and the dominant northern "veterans" (Simpson 1937:87, 89, 112–18; Tobler 1971; L. Meyer 1978b:233–34).

The latter, epitomized by Calles, had by the late 1920s reached the conclusion that the agrarian reform was a costly mistake that had to be curtailed. In this, they were undoubtedly influenced by the American model among others; Calles was also negatively impressed by his acquaintance with French peasant agriculture. Prosperous family farms and large capitalist enterprises were the hallmarks of an American-style agrarian model that the "veterans" knew—often firsthand—admired, and sought to emulate. In more general terms, too, the American model of free-enterprise capitalism and *laissez-faire* financial orthodoxy was highly influential: state intervention had therefore to be limited; social engineering—outside the classroom—was to be avoided; nor should the public debt be swollen by wholesale agrarian expropriations. In all this Ambassador Morrow found plenty of ideological purchase; hence it made more sense for him to cajole than to bully. The approach was exemplified by Morrow's lengthy economic tutoring of Finance Minister Montes de Oca.[9]

This general, subtle, collaborationist influence did not—indeed, could not—involve strenuously effective defense of specific American landed interests on those occasions when they came under *agrarista* threat. Ever since 1910 American landowners, especially the smaller landowners, had felt that their government had systematically neglected them, choosing to deploy its influence on behalf of the large corporate interests, especially the oil companies. They had been left to sink or swim, and it was limited consolation that only a minority had in fact sunk (USS 1920, 1:830, 1422, 1432–33, 1713–14, 1770; USS 1920, 2:2368, 2406; Evans 1926:61, 207, 221, 240). During the 1930s, however, these feelings of abandonment were enhanced, and the limits of direct U.S. influence over the agrarian reform program were more fully revealed. With the brusque change in political and economic climate brought on by the Great Depression and the rise of *cardenismo*, American landed interests faced renewed threats and, in some cases, outright extinction. Once the old Sonoran model had been scrapped in favor of *cardenista* radicalism (a radicalism evident not only in the scale and speed of the reform, but also in the novel expropriation and collectivization of entire capitalist enterprises), the chief defense of American landed interests—namely, official Mexican adherence to broadly "orthodox" economic policies—was gravely weakened. Morrow's economic tu-

9. What Morrow did, individually, in the 1920s, Harvard and MIT have done institutionally since the 1940s (J. Meyer 1977:36).

torials were forgotten, at least for the time being. And official U.S. pressure proved a quite inadequate substitute: "US officials persistently protested the seizure of the property of US citizens and called for compensation, almost invariably without success or apparent effect on Cárdenas' land reform policies" (Blaiser 1976:84).

Indeed, as major American properties were affected—in Puebla, the Laguna, the Yaqui and Mexicali valleys, and elsewhere—so American landowners again alleged the indifference and incapacity of their domestic government. *Agrarista* fellow travelers were to be found even in the U.S. Embassy—for example, in the portly shape of Ambassador Josephus Daniels. American landowners, a close observer reported, "all consider Daniels worthless; in fact, a great detriment [*sic*]. He is for 'peace at any price.' He slobbers over the President who is robbing his nationals."[10] The observer, a British landowner, shared the sentiments of his American counterparts (Anglo-Saxon attitudes were broadly shared, just as Anglo-American material interests were often intertwined); lobbying in Washington in defense of the Laguna cotton estates, he concluded that the State Department were "pigs" and that "[President] Roosevelt and [Secretary of State] Cordell Hull would rather compensate their own expropriated nationals than demand it from Mexico."[11] Yet even in that old nest of reaction, the British Embassy in Mexico City, which had backed Huerta and doggedly—if neither very diplomatically nor very successfully—defended the interests of the embattled landowner Rosalie Evans in the 1920s, the winds of change were now blowing, bringing with them an acquiescence in, even a qualified approval of, the *cardenista* agrarian reform.[12]

The reasons for this growing Anglo-American tolerance—or feebleness, as it seemed to the landlord-victims—were several. First, as in the past, petroleum counted for more than real estate. Landowners again felt that they were being sacrificed on the altar of Standard Oil. Cárdenas, too, saw these issues as linked, though in a somewhat different way: for him, the land question served foreign interests as a mere tactical appendage of the

10. J. C. Tabor to R. Benson, 13 November 1936, Mexican Cotton Estates of Tlahualilo Papers, Kleinwort Benson Archive, Speen, Newbury, Berks., U.K.

11. Tabor to Benson, 12 August 1937, Tlahualilo Papers.

12. British Minister Murray applauded Cárdenas' honesty and sincerity and showed qualified sympathy for the administration's agrarian and *indigenista* programs; Consul Pegram, in Torreón, broadly concurred. FO reports, March–April 1936, FO 371/19792, A2862, A3895, A4142.

petroleum problem (González y González 1981:203). Either way, the real battle concerned oil, not land. In American official eyes, however, both questions were now subordinated to international strategic requirements; the Axis threat made détente with Mexico imperative. And if this militated against any major conflict over oil, it is hardly surprising that the lesser, landed interests received short shrift from the State Department.

The U.S. stake in Mexican real estate had always been small relative to other U.S. assets (it had represented perhaps 4 percent of total U.S. investment in Mexico in 1910), and it had shrunk since 1910. The armed revolution, we will note, had taken a toll, especially of smaller landed interests (more by virtue of incidental destruction and upheaval than of any targeted xenophobia). Colonists' numbers had fallen significantly. Larger interests, too, which had survived intact, had fallen appreciably in value: Hearst's massive Babicora estate in Chihuahua, hit hard by the collapse of the northern cattle industry during the revolution, was worth only one-third of its 1910 value a decade later.[13] During the 1920s, American interests had not borne the brunt of the agrarian reform: prior to 1928, one-eighth of the expropriated land had been taken from foreigners, who owned one-fifth of Mexican rural real estate; furthermore, Americans had got off more lightly than the Spaniards—a significant fact, as we will note. Figures vary, but one estimate puts total American losses from the agrarian reform prior to 1928 at scarcely 1 percent by area.[14] These figures illustrate the tangential impact of official land distribution on American landed assets prior to the 1930s. However, they fail to convey a true picture of the position and profitability of these assets. Territorial losses may have been small, but many estates never recovered the stability and profits of the Porfirian *belle*

13. Ciudad Juárez report, among consular replies to 12 November 1919 circular, SD 812.503/1. Marked declines in agricultural output and real-estate value were also reported from Tabasco, coastal Oaxaca, Guerrero, San Luis, and Colima. Sherwell (1929:46, 61–62) notes the "practical obliteration" of foreign stockraising in Mexico during the revolution, and further suggests that 75 percent of foreign, nonexporting, agricultural holdings were no longer profitable.

14. C. L. Jones and G. Wythe, "Economic Conditions in Mexico" (1928), SD 812.50/161, suggests that 711,000 hectares had been taken from foreign landholdings under the agrarian reform program; of this, Spaniards had yielded 52 percent, Americans 27 percent (190,000 has.). This is a widely accepted figure: Sterrett and Davis (1928:87, 96) put foreign landholding (pre-1910) at some 20 percent of total area. The U.S. share of this property is hard to establish: for differing figures, see Blasier 1976:75, 83; these put total U.S. losses at between 1 and 10 percent.

époque. Furthermore, many—chiefly in the export sector—were hit by recession after 1927, depression after 1929. By 1936, it was dolefully reported, "the agricultural real estate market all over the country is dead."[15] Some landlords now looked to cut their losses. The chief concern of the Tlahualilo Co., as it faced the Laguna *reparto,* was to extract itself from a fast-deteriorating situation to maximum monetary advantage.[16]

Now, as during the armed revolution, landlords placed little faith in diplomatic intervention and relied heavily on local contacts, deals, and maneuvers. They could not match the national clout of Standard Oil or Royal Dutch Shell, but they could still pull their weight locally. Battles against *agrarismo* were fought locally, not in embassy corridors in Mexico City. The Tlahualilo Co., highly successful in its local politicking until the mid-1930s, finally lost out; William Jenkins of Atencingo, however, cleverly finessed even the *cardenista* agrarian reform, shedding hectares while preserving his local economic supremacy and profitability (Ronfeldt 1973:chap. 2). Other American interests, too, rolled with the *agrarista* punch. They discovered—if they had not already foreseen—that they could switch from direct landowning to processing and marketing: a transition that became evident in several Latin American countries over time, Cuba being a good, early example (Martínez A. 1977:96, 100–101).

Agrarian reform, unless it was thorough, radical, and durable, did not therefore eliminate American agrarian interests; rather, it served to shift U.S. capital laterally within the agrarian sector. Before long, the Anderson Clayton Co. had established a profitable liaison with the Laguna *ejidatarios,* while the Yaqui Valley *ejidos* became parcelized and highly stratified appendages of a northwestern commercial economy tightly linked to that of the United States (Senior 1958:103–4; Hewitt de Alcántara 1985:126–30, 271–72). Some individual American enterprises lost out along the way— victims of revolutionary upheaval, agrarian reform, or economic depression (rarely of targeted popular xenophobia)—but the outcome, from the general perspective of U.S. business interests, was far from unfavorable. The broad proposition that Latin American land reforms have usually

15. Murray, Mexico City, to Eden, 11 March 1936, FO 371/19792, A2060.
16. "Owning a large agricultural property in Mexico is becoming a liability instead of an asset"; hence, "some such plan as selling Tlahualilo lock, stock, and barrel to the Government on any terms seems to be the best bet for the owners." Fairbairn to Benson, 13 August 1936; Holby to Benson, 19 August 1936 (Tlahualilo Papers).

served to stimulate rather than to arrest capitalist development—and, with it, U.S. investment—is certainly borne out by the case of Mexico since c. 1940 (de Janvry 1983:202ff.). This is not to say that U.S. government policy prior to 1940 was based on any such presumption; but it is to suggest that U.S. acquiescence in the Mexican agrarian reform proved, over time, to be justified in terms of American economic self-interest (and hence, perhaps, influenced subsequent policy; e.g., in Bolivia in the 1950s).

At the official level, therefore, U.S. policy toward the Mexican agrarian reform was of limited significance. U.S. policymakers disliked such social experiments, especially when they prejudiced American assets; but those assets were relatively small and could not quicken the political pulse in the way that, say, petroleum could. Thus it was not politically cost-effective to strive to halt the experiments at all costs. Some American observers even began to appreciate their domestic utility. In consequence, the post-1915 agrarian reform, which was crucial in the formation of the revolutionary state, society, and mythology, had far less impact on U.S.-Mexican relations than the oil dispute—which, conversely, affected a very reduced sector of Mexican society. Or, to put the same matters differently, "The structure of land tenure—in contrast to industrial structure—was a problem which basically affected national, and not foreign, interests" (L. Meyer 1978a:235). The United States could live with a measure of peasant mobilization and agrarian reform; many U.S. interests could live and prosper too. The same would prove true of Bolivia, but not of Guatemala or Cuba, where U.S. landholdings were proportionately larger, and where agrarian reforms were seen—or depicted—as lurid Red, hence deserving a strong strategic rather than a cautious diplomatic response.

The Influence of U.S. Capital on the Mexican Peasantry

If, viewed in the round, U.S. government policy toward the revolution did not exert a decisive impact upon peasant movements or the agrarian reform program, indirect American influence, mediated through private capital, was a different matter. It is generally recognized that the influx of U.S. investments into Mexico during the *porfiriato* had decisive consequences for Mexican society, urban and rural. Of course, U.S. investment and the trade that accompanied it formed part of a larger flow of capital from "center" to "periphery"; hence much of the following analysis, focusing on the role of private capital, could as well be related to British, German, French, or Canadian (though not, in the main, Spanish) capital. The specifically American component was distinguished by only two features: first, it emanated from the *coloso del norte*—an overmighty neighbor who posed a strategic threat, and whose capital could thus appear as an economic stalking-horse for territorial aggression; and, second, U.S. capital progressively outstripped its rivals in quantity—hence, roughly speaking, in socioeconomic impact.[17] Indeed, a paradoxical outcome of the supposedly "nationalist" revolution was an increase in U.S. direct investment during the 1920s.[18]

The consequences of this trend for rural Mexico and peasant society were profound, and they dwarfed the puny effects of official U.S. governmental intervention in the period 1880–1940. Nor is this contrast surprising, given the gross imbalance of the forces at work. First, the object of U.S. influence was not a small Caribbean republic; and even in small Caribbean republics, the U.S. government often found it difficult to control events. Mexico was a large, populous nation, possessed of strong notions of nationhood and old traditions of patriotic resistance. After 1910, Mexico was plunged into an intense social ferment which, again, made external—not to mention internal—control downright difficult. Americans who talked blithely of "Cuba-izing" Mexico were usually Americans quite out of touch with Mexican reality (Knight 1986a:153–56). And, second, the United States possessed powers of private initiative and influence that exceeded any official capacities. Recall that we are talking of a burgeoning capitalist system, still governed by a diminutive state, whose leaders were steeped in Jeffersonian ideals, wedded to *laissez-faire*, and, often enough (e.g., in the crucial periods 1913–21 and 1933–45), possessed of a democratic self-image that differentiated them from the militarist and

17. According to Luis Nicolau D'Olwer (1965:1154), U.S. direct investment stood at 1,233 million pesos (1911) out of a total foreign direct investment of 2,903 million (= 42%; cf. Britain, 907 million pesos = 31%; France, 581 million pesos = 20%). Other estimates put the U.S. share higher. An admittedly deficient consular estimate reckoned that the U.S. share of total foreign investment, direct and indirect, was 64 percent ($1,058 million). Letcher, Chihuahua, 15 June 1912, SD 812.501/1.

18. Between 1910 and 1929 U.S. investment in Mexico rose by some 50 percent, such that it constituted around 65 percent of total foreign investment. The U.S. share of Mexico's foreign trade also rose. See Krauze 1977:289–91 and R. F. Smith 1972:145–46.

imperialist elites of the Old World. Raymond Aron's "Imperial Repub-lic"—executive-dominated, militarily potent, globally interventionist—was still a generation away. Intimations of its birth came with 1917, but final parturition awaited the Second World War and Cold War. By then, the United States was engaged not only in global hostilities, but also in global alliances, intelligence gathering, and covert operations. By then, of course, the Mexican Revolution had run its course; other revolutions, other insurgent peasantries, would suffer the implacable gaze of the American eagle.

Prior to c. 1940, however, private U.S. influence in Mexico greatly outweighed official influence. This was still the era of "informal empire." Such private influence was pervasive and complex. By far the most important changes set in motion—significantly but not solely by U.S. capital—involved the quickening of economic activity and the growth of market production during the *porfiriato*. This, as is well known, depended on U.S. demand (for mineral and agricultural goods, including henequen, coffee, chicle, vanilla, rubber, and timber) and on U.S. capital (railways, mines, petroleum, real estate). Both had a marked impact, which extended beyond their immediate geographical locations.

Mexico—along with Cuba—was thus the first Latin American country to be drawn into the U.S. economic sphere.[19] Geographical proximity—exemplified by the pattern of the U.S.-Mexican railway system—as well as economic complementarity (the Yucatán-Midwest liaison is the best example; see Joseph, below) both contributed to this outcome. And the consequences were particularly dramatic, it may be suggested, because, following the major civil wars and upheavals of the mid-nineteenth century, Mexico's insertion into the world division of labor was belated—compared, that is, to Brazil's or Argentina's. U.S. trade and investment,

19. However, "the economic presence of hegemonic states within dependent states takes many forms": while U.S. investment in Cuba in the 1920s was less in absolute terms than that in Mexico ($1 billion compared to $1.5 billion), its impact was relatively greater, since it figured within a smaller economy, was coupled with a powerful political presence, and faced less competition from either domestic or other foreign capital (see J. R. Benjamin 1977:13–19). What is more, instead of coexisting with a large "traditional" peasantry and landlord class, it confronted a mass proletariat and a sizable, articulate rural middle class, the *colonos*. In Cuba, therefore, the twin threats of working-class radicalism and middle-class nationalism posed a much greater challenge than in Mexico, where both were correspondingly weaker.

surging into Mexico, thus acted like an antibiotic (or, if you prefer, a
bacillus) encountering a virginal organism. Investment, exports, and especially agricultural exports all recorded major gains from the 1880s to the
1900s.[20] Meanwhile, contrary to certain crude assumptions, export-led
growth was also associated with significant increases in production for the
domestic market. Agricultural raw materials, especially cotton, and consumer goods—coffee, sugar, pulque—flowed to the expanding cities.

Such a phase of marked expansion was not wholly novel for Mexico.
The late colony had experienced roughly analogous increases in population, urbanization, and market production (it had also witnessed roughly
analogous social trends: falling real wages, the expansion of commercial
agriculture, the erosion of peasant communities) (Van Young 1981). But
this process had been cut short by the insurgency. Furthermore, the process had lacked the inherent scale and dynamism of the Porfirian experience—first, because New Spain remained (imperfectly) locked within a
mercantilist empire; second, and more important, because the level of
demand, supply of capital, and available technology all served to limit the
process of economic expansion (which, indeed, showed signs of faltering
on the eve of the insurgency). Where the Bourbon boom depended upon
Spanish demand for bullion, coupled with Mexican demographic growth,
the Porfirian boom derived from the far more potent stimuli of a global—
though primarily North American—industrial economy, richly endowed
with capital and technology and greedy for industrial raw materials and
consumer goods. Domestic urbanization and industrialization complemented these external stimuli. And, together, with the added assistance of
the state, they began to achieve—for the first time—some form of real
regional and national economic integration within Mexico. Of course,
both forms of stimuli, external and internal, fluctuated with the business
cycle; and, at least by the 1900s, domestic demand was running up against
serious "structural" barriers. But these barriers, the product of falling real

20. Foreign investment in Mexico grew thirtyfold (at current peso values) during the
porfiriato. Meanwhile, between 1873–75 and 1910–11, Mexican exports grew from 29
million to 288 million pesos (i.e., tenfold; Argentine exports, 1880–1913, grew ninefold).
During the same period, furthermore, the Mexican population grew only some 62
percent, while the Argentine population tripled. The rate of growth of Mexican agricultural exports (6% per annum) paralleled that of total exports, in which nonprecious
minerals gained at the expense of the traditional precious metals. For a recent survey, see
Guerra 1985, 1:295–306.

wages, did not hit agrarian producers so much as they hit industrial manufacturers (above all, the textile interests). Engels' law afforded "traditional" (grain-producing) landlords some basic protection, which the tariff reinforced, while agrarian exporters enjoyed generally buoyant demand, despite intermittent crises like that of 1907.

The resulting impact on Mexican rural society was far more profound and extensive than had been the impact of Bourbon commercialization. While the Bourbon boom had chiefly affected the Bajío and Guadalajara regions (its impact on the populous Central Plateau was contrastingly muted), the Porfirian boom affected—albeit in different ways—all parts of the newly integrated economy: the dynamic, open, mining and pastoral north; the "traditional," densely populated hacienda/peasant society of central Mexico; and the recently "developed" plantation regions of the south. In the first and last of these zones, U.S. capital was heavily and directly involved; in the second, its impact was less marked and more indirect. Nevertheless, throughout the country the growth of foreign trade and investment tended to open up new, profitable opportunities for landowners, who now found that the perennial problem of constricted markets had been substantially alleviated. Demand, national and international, was more buoyant; the railways had slashed freight costs, especially for exporters; the regime facilitated landlord acquisition of land and water; peasant dispossession, coupled with population growth, ensured a supply of cheap labor, at least by the 1890s. Meanwhile, land prices rose even in the ample north, and conflict over finite resources became more acute.[21]

The broad impact of all this upon the peasantry is well known, though still subject to debate concerning its particular effects, which clearly varied from region to region: proletarianization in much of the Central Plateau, as well as in pockets of the hitherto "peasant" north (a proletarianization strenuously resisted not only by threatened villagers but also, if less dramatically, by hacienda peons who strove to cling to older, "precapitalist" benefits); the fluctuations of a more thoroughly commercialized economy in most of the north; a deterioration of tenancy and sharecropping terms in

21. Through the letters of William L. Purcell, Anita Purcell (1963) charts the change in the northern rural economy from a condition of ample land, poor transport, and low demand in 1880 to one of improved demand, transport, and market opportunity—hence land acquisition, speculation, and conflict—in 1882, 1883, and 1885. See Purcell 1963:49–50, 78, 80, 88.

the Bajío, Guerrero, and the central-north borderlands (e.g., in San Luis); a contrasting combination of incipient proletarianization and reinforced, often coercive, peonage in the south (cf. Soconusco and Yucatán).

The impact of foreign capital, U.S. capital in particular, thus varied according to its intensity (weaker in the center than in the north or south) and its consequences. Whereas in the north the growing U.S. presence tended to accelerate commercialization, market production, and proletarianization along what might be called conventional capitalist lines, elsewhere the outcome was more ambiguous, though by no means unusual for the period. In much of the center (and in Yucatán) market forces acted upon an established Mexican—or Spanish—landed elite who, out of choice or necessity, clung to "precapitalist" forms of labor that, in the circumstances, proved profitable (e.g., sharecropping and—a better example—peonage, both traditional and coercive).[22] Here, as in many places, market expansion and conventional proletarianization did not proceed hand in hand. And U.S. economic penetration, though profound, had divergent effects, dependent upon regional conditions.

These broad regional variations, which will reappear in my analysis shortly, were further compounded by specific local peculiarities. These become apparent as we start to focus on the role of U.S. enterprises in particular cases—as we enter, let us say, the *microhistoria* of the U.S.-Mexican liaison. It is here, too, that we begin the transition from latent to manifest influence, from an influence that—affecting demand, prices, wages—is pervasive but anonymous, to one that is locally situated, recognizable, and concrete. It is here, therefore, that one would expect to find examples of anti-Americanism or anti-imperialism, based on subjectively critical evaluations of American enterprises in the Mexican countryside. It is here that the insurgent peon or peasant should confront the embattled gringo landlord (or, perhaps, mine owner; for we cannot posit a neat urban/rural, industrial/agrarian dichotomy).

Many Mexicanists have indeed sketched such scenarios, as John Hart does, with his usual vigor, in this volume. A recent comparative study, stressing the Latin American export sector's capacity to determine both the character of national labor movements—broadly defined to include

22. On the deceptive variants of peonage, see Knight 1986b.

peasants and rural workers—and, in consequence, the structures of national politics, hypothesizes that "in Mexico one should expect to find a relatively developed sense of class and cultural autonomy within the early labor movement and a relatively greater propensity for multi-class alliances of the reformist, nationalist, and anti-imperialist kind" (Bergquist 1986:380). American domination of the export sector, to put it simply, should have led to a mass, nationalist, anti-imperialist revolution.

Certainly there are examples of popular protest directed against American enterprise. The initial process of railroad building, involving speculation and land grabs, spurred protest and revolt (Coatsworth 1974; Purcell 1963:79). American landowners incurred the wrath of peasant communities whom they confronted: in the Yaqui Valley, in the Huasteca and southern Tamaulipas, in Chihuahua. American planters were also alleged to maltreat their peons, in the south and in the Laguna. Hence, come the revolution, some paid the price. The colonists of the Yaqui Valley faced retribution; those of the Huasteca and Tamaulipas were "systematically robbed"; the Mormon colonies of Chihuahua were persecuted. In each case, the colonists' numbers shrank as a result of the revolution and, in some instances, whole enterprises foundered (Hewitt de Alcántara 1985:121–22; Whetten 1948:155–58; uss 1920, 1:979–87; uss 1920, 2:2460–64, 3397). Some planters, too, found their labor discipline and recruitment failing, partly because, even if the revolution did not immediately and entirely eliminate (coercive) peonage, it did substantially erode this important prop of southern agriculture (Knight 1986a:362–63). Finally we should note the impact upon U.S. enterprise of "working-class" mobilization—unionization, strikes, and political and military participation—at least where the mobilization involved semiproletarians ("hyphenated workers-peasants") and peasant migrants.

Reviewing these actors, have we found the cast for Bergquist's hypothetical—or Hart's actual—scenario of radical, class-conscious, export-sector nationalists? Not at all. In reviewing their numbers, actions, and historical significance, I am struck not by the depth of peasant anti-Americanism ("peasant" is used here as a portmanteau term for rural workers in general) but rather by its shallowness. Of course there are examples of peasants locked in combat with U.S. enterprises. But, in our quest for what is typical, representative, and significant, they must be seen as heavily outnumbered by cases of (*a*) peasant combat with non-American enterprises and (*b*) peasant collaboration with American enterprises ("collaboration" being defined as the maintenance of voluntary, supportive relations, whether as workers or suppliers).

The nub of the argument is this: along the wide spectrum of landlords whom Mexican peasants confronted, Americans constituted a minority. Furthermore, that minority tended to differ in important respects from the Mexican—and Spanish—landlord norm, and the differences were such as to mitigate, not to aggravate, conflict, as we shall see. Conversely, since American landholdings were greatly outweighed by other American investments (in railways, mines, petroleum, etc.), American enterprise more typically appeared in such industrial/extractive guises; or, in some circumstances, chiefly in the north, American enterprise combined such industrial/extractive activities with agricultural operations (e.g., William Greene's mining + railway + lumber + cattle empire). In short, the typical American entrepreneur was not a landlord, especially not a landlord *tout court*. In contrast, the typical Mexican entrepreneur was.

Central to this argument is the assumption that nationality per se was not a major factor in determining peasant opposition to Americans (in the relatively unusual instances where such opposition was manifested). Americans were not confronted qua Americans. They were confronted qua landlords who had appropriated peasant land, who had maltreated their workers, etc. The national factor might acquire a certain resonance when a dispute arose (it could be played upon in the hope of securing political backing), but it did not engender the dispute and, in the many instances where collaboration prevailed over conflict, it remained a dormant issue. There was no popular presumption of gringo malignity. If anything, there was a modest presumption of gringo beneficence. It should be stressed that these generalizations refer to popular/peasant attitudes, not to those of the educated, urban classes.

We may contrast the American experience with that of the Spaniards. For complex, deeply rooted historical reasons, Spanish identity carried strong negative connotations with the Mexican poor—and these were further accentuated by the economic vicissitudes of the *porfiriato* and the revolution. There was, therefore, a popular presumption of *gachupín* malignity, sanctioned by long-standing memory, tradition, folklore and—

most important of all—daily experience.[23] Furthermore, the "official" symbols and rhetoric of *mexicanidad*—dating back to 1810, if not before—tended to legitimize anti-*gachupín* sentiment. Official/elite notions conspired with popular prejudices; the "Great" and "Little" Traditions produced a powerful confluence of Hispanophobia. In consequence, the years of revolution were littered with examples of popular xenophobia directed against Spaniards: landlords, *mayordomos, administradores*, merchants, and moneylenders. Occupational hazards, one might say, were compounded by popular cultural stereotypes. In regions of agrarian insurgency, especially, Spaniards were prominent victims: Puebla, Morelos, Guerrero, Michoacán, the Laguna. And, as the institutional reform of the 1920s got under way, Spaniards suffered more than other foreigners.[24]

"*Yanquifobia*," in contrast, was the hallmark of a narrower, educated, predominantly urban upper and middle class. It had shallow popular roots; it depended on written sources and formal education; it could not quicken the popular pulse. It grew only as formal education expanded, chiefly after the revolution. And, by then, it was further stimulated by recurrent crises in U.S.-Mexican relations, some of them involving armed conflict: 1914, 1916, 1919, 1926, 1938. By the latter date, the groundwork had been laid for a broad display of popular nationalism, orchestrated by government, party, union, and school and directed against the Anglo-American oil companies. But that came nearly thirty years after the revolution began, and some twenty years after the Sonorans undertook their conscious project of *forjando patria*. Before and during the armed revolution, however, the formal "nationalizing" education or acculturation required to generate genuine popular anti-Americanism was lacking, especially in the countryside. Anti-Americanism—often of a somewhat cerebral kind—remained largely the preserve of big-city students, professionals, and intellectuals (many of them conservative and Catholic rather than radical and revolutionary).

23. Knight 1987 offers a résumé, and several examples are given in Knight 1986a; note also Menegus B. and Leal 1982:152, 160. It is finally worth citing a classic consular text: Bonney, San Luis, to State Dept., 28 May 1913, SD 812.00/7790.

24. Figures have been given in note 14 above. Evans (1926:198) notes, in typical style, how "all the Spaniards' places around me have been turned over to the agrarians and a sort of pandemonium reigns"; Sherwell (1929:43, 59) affords more sober evidence of the flight of Spanish capital and its replacement—for example, in the coffee sector—by U.S. and German capital.

Hence there were plenty of peasants who, in default of nationalist acculturation, entertained no marked preconceptions about the gringos. For
such peasants the United States was a distinct, intangible entity, and they
took Americans as they found them. And there were many who found
them "buen[os] amigos"; so, at least, intimated some Mayo Indians of
Sinaloa with reference to the American United Sugar Company (see
Knight 1986a, 1:103–4).

By way of explanation for this state of affairs—as regrettable to ardent
nationalists as to doctrinaire radicals—we should first note the pattern of
American investment, particularly in real estate. In general terms, American landholdings were concentrated in regions where peasant agrarianism
tended to be weak: the north and the south. True, there were strong
agrarian movements in the north, some of which confronted American
landed interests in parts of Chihuahua, the Laguna, and the Yaqui Valley,
for example. But in many other states and regions (Baja California, northern Sonora, most of Coahuila, Nuevo León, and the northeast more generally) large U.S. interests, operating in the relative absence of settled
peasant communities, escaped popular/agrarian retribution. In the south,
too, American (landed) capital was concentrated in nonrevolutionary
states such as Tabasco, Campeche, and Chiapas (where, though limited
revolutionary movements occurred, they were not usually agrarian in character). In simple terms, therefore, U.S. investment, especially investment
in land, did not correlate with agrarianism.

Conversely, hotbeds of *agrarismo* (Morelos, Puebla, Tlaxcala, parts of
Guerrero, Michoacán, San Luis) entertained few American enterprises
and were dominated by Mexican (and Spanish) landed elites. Hence,
Americans could afford to take a more tolerant view of the *zapatistas* ("just
humble peasants with guns in their hands") than could Mexican/Spanish
landlords, and not just those of Morelos (uss 1920, 1:822, 1775; quoted
words are of George Carothers). The institutional reform of the 1920s, too,
was concentrated in the Central Plateau (Morelos, Puebla, Hidalgo, Mexico State), Yucatán, and San Luis; hence the main victims were again
Mexican or Spanish landowners (Simpson 1937:174, 185, 614–15). Instances
of agrarian confrontation with—occasionally dispossession of—American
landowners occurred, but they were untypical, either of agrarian confrontation and dispossession on the one hand or of American-peasant
relations on the other. For every William Benton there were rather more

James Sheehans; that is, landowners whose losses were the indirect result of military campaigning and economic disruption rather than of any focused hostility (USS 1920, 2:2401–4). Needless to say, even such indirect losses could give rise to claims for indemnification: the fat files of the claims commissions are first and indubitably proof of claims; second, and probably, proof of losses; but third—and only hypothetically—proof of popular hostility/xenophobia/anti-imperialism. That third hypothesis must be substantiated by specific evidence relating to a range of cases.

It is also easy to find counterevidence of direct U.S.-peasant collaboration (and collaboration, moreover, with revolutionary peasants). The insurgent Mayos got on well with the United Sugar Co.; thus, an American landowner in Tamaulipas (who, he said, had been "received as a friend by all of the Mexican people with whom I came in contact") suffered sequestrations by revolutionary forces but "was glad to get off so cheaply in comparison to my Mexican neighbors, against whom the revolution was really directed" (USS 1920, 2:2465–68). The argument can be rendered even stronger if nonlanded American interests of rural location (chiefly mines) are also included in the analysis, as they probably should be. Again, for every confrontationist Cananea there was a collaborationist Cedral—or two.[25]

Collaboration, it should be stressed, did not imply any love for the *gringos,* nor yet did it indicate popular fears of American military retribution. Many examples were to be found far from the border or the coast, thus well out of reach of any retribution; and, while a more pervasive fear of the United States may have influenced national elites (without, of course, stopping them from defying the United States at many junctures), it is unlikely that insurgent peasants in, say, Zacatecas bridled their anti-Americanism for fear of compromising national sovereignty. "National sovereignty" was a somewhat abstract concept to set against the immediate exigencies of existence: witness the conduct of the peasants of Namiquipa in 1916 (in Alonso, below). Furthermore, it is often clear from the context that popular/rebel restraint was a matter of choice, not compulsion (and

25. When "revolutionaries attempted to interfere with the work [of the Cedral mine] . . . the women formed a protecting posse, declaring that he [the manager] had been the benefactor of the town." Bonney, San Luis, to State Dept. 30 August 1915, SD 812.00/16135. For a similar case from Chalchihuites, Zacatecas, see E. Turnball to J. Arkell, 8 June 1913, SD 812.00/8078.

the record of U.S. compulsion, in 1910–20, was hardly impressive anyway). That economic collaboration could proceed in the absence of affective ties (which is not to say that such ties were uniformly absent) is suggested by the experience of Mexican migrant workers in the United States who, while they complained that "the treatment that they got in Texas was very humiliating to them and they were called 'niggers' and 'greasers' . . . nevertheless they got good pay," which represented sufficient compensating incentive (USS 1920, 2:2328). Inside Mexico, too, the economic end justified the collaborationist means. These were primarily instrumental, not affective relations.

The instrumentality derived from the place U.S. interests occupied within the local economy. Most interests were welcomed, since they paid better wages and, indeed, pushed up local wage rates (sometimes to the disgust of Mexican employers) in the Laguna, Chihuahua, Veracruz, and elsewhere. Wage earners were therefore the chief beneficiaries, but Mexican merchants could also profit from enhanced demand (they could suffer, too, as we will note in a moment) and some peasants also benefited, as suppliers of goods as well as labor. (The evidence is ample and conclusive. Cf. USS 1920, 1:129, 235–36, 939–40; USS 1920, 2:2398, 2409; Wasserman 1984:52–53, 89; Lloyd 1983:122–23; O'Connor 1937:98; de Szyszlo 1913:276, 281; Harper 1910:61, 66–67.) Wages tended to rise because American enterprises sought labor by means of cash incentives rather than coercion—a crucial point to be developed in conclusion—and, in addition, they experimented with the payment of premiums, bonuses, and differential rates in order to secure and hold a reliable, productive work force. As one landowner put it: "we were willing to pay for a better class of person" (USS 1920, 2:2409). Companies also built houses, sometimes schools, and occasionally provided some basic medical services.

None of this should be exaggerated or misconstrued. Such benefits derived overwhelmingly from market calculation rather than charitable impulse. They informed part of a reciprocal (and unequal) bargain, in which both parties were guided by perceived self-interest. But they should not for that reason be overlooked, nor should they be judged by anachronistic criteria. In a harsh world—increasingly harsh in the 1900s and again after 1913—employment in American enterprises offered a lifeline for the poor, the dispossessed, the cash-starved. Such employment did not promise the good life, but at least a less harsh life. Hence—even critics agreed—this employment was eagerly sought and often keenly retained.[26]

One final topic deserves mention. A particular source of Mexican resentment—sometimes cited as an example of widespread popular nationalism/xenophobia—was the favoritism shown American employees in certain companies. This certainly caused resentment at Cananea and on the railways. We should note, however, that the ensuing protest focused on questions of wages, work conditions, and job opportunities, not on the question of foreign ownership. Companies that lacked a large foreign payroll, as most did, avoided such problems, which were peculiar to these untypical—though certainly important—enterprises. The latter, however, soon shed many of their higher-paid American workers; the American employees of the National Railways even struck in protest. In doing so, the companies went a long way toward meeting Mexican demands—which did not, therefore, feed into the popular revolution in a major way. Furthermore, the companies probably did themselves a favor at the same time. The promotion of qualified Mexicans—evident here in the cases of Cananea and the railways, later in the case of the oil industry—served company interests by cutting costs. The Mexican North-Western Railroad actively pursued such a policy without the stimulus of an industrial dispute (French n.d.; Knight 1986a, 1:145–49, 428–29). Companies were in Mexico to make a profit, not to dispense charity to their needy nationals. If the pursuit of profit meant offering promotion and incentives to Mexicans (as, in these cases, it did), what was served was market logic, not altruism. But companies thereby established durable collaborative relations with their labor forces, which enabled them to ride out the revolution with greater success than many more "traditional" Mexican landlords/employers.

Indeed, during the revolution, worker dependence on companies often increased, offsetting the effects of growing labor organization and militancy. Especially after 1913, as the economy slumped, major companies especially were often disposed to offer a basic subsistence in order to retain the work force they had built up, at some cost, during the *porfiriato*. And in

26. USS 1920, 1:129, 235–37, 503, 702; USS 1920 2:2397–98, 2409. On the North-Western Railway, in the rebel heartland of Chihuahua, "managers experienced few difficulties in securing and controlling Mexican labor," even (or especially?) during periods of revolutionary upheaval (see French n.d.).

this they were frequently successful. So long as work and subsistence were provided, there were few mass defections to the armed revolution. Successive authorities—Porfirian, Maderist, Huertist—expressed repeated fears that shutdowns would immediately boost rebel numbers. Occasionally, desperate rebel leaders sought to curtail business operations for precisely this reason, though it cannot be said that this was a widespread or effective strategy.

Of course, employees of U.S. enterprises *did* sometimes join the revolution—and not *faute de mieux* because they had lost their jobs. They did so, however, on an individual, not a collective basis. They did so in their capacity as individual political activists, victims of the authorities, committed liberals, members of oppositionist families—not as employees of U.S. companies or as rebellious collectivities. (Contrast, for example, the collective village rebellions evident elsewhere in revolutionary Mexico; or the collective armed insurgency of Bolivia's tin miners in the 1950s.) Given such motivation and organization, these individuals cannot be seen as armed anti-imperialists. This is proven by the fact that they rarely evinced any anticompany, anti-U.S. sentiment.

Anti-U.S. sentiment, where it did materialize, was the result not of some prior socioeconomic conditioning, but rather of immediate, political events: chiefly, U.S. interventions in the revolutionary process. The classic case is *orozquismo*, which is often invoked to illustrate revolutionary anti-Americanism. Yet *orozquista* anti-Americanism manifested itself only after and because the U.S. government gave vital support to the Madero regime, thus dooming the *orozquista* cause (summer 1912). *Magonista* radicalism no doubt played some part in fomenting these sentiments, but it cannot be ignored that they became broad and apparent only when the *orozquistas*—hitherto entirely responsible and reasonable in their treatment of U.S. interests—tasted the bitter pill of defeat, which they felt, understandably, had been administered to them by the United States. A similar, belated anti-Americanism affected *villismo* in 1915–16 (uss 1920, 2:2403; Knight 1986a, 1:149, 320; Knight 1986a, 2:342–45, 411–12.[27]

The clientelist relations evident during the revolution often endured beyond 1920, just as they had often existed before 1910. This need cause no surprise unless, again, there is a dogmatic assumption of popular anti-

---

27. Editor's Note: But compare Osorio, Alonso, and Katz in this volume.

Americanism. Revisionist scholarship has rightly stressed the staying power of the hacienda, especially in terms of its clientelist manipulation of resident workers.[28] The capacity for manipulation of U.S. companies was arguably greater, above all in material terms. Further, I would suggest, material rewards and security were, by this period, the crucial factors; affective, "paternalist" ties no longer supplied the chief glue holding hacienda communities together. The clearest cases are corporate giants like ASARCO (O'Connor 1937:337). But agrarian enterprises, too, successfully sustained collaborationist/clientelist relations with their workers, a relationship that could prove invaluable in fending off *agrarista* pressure. Tlahualilo's peons remained docile well into the 1930s; William Jenkins successfully mobilized his workers in order to deflect peasant challenges at Atencingo.[29]

American enterprises could sustain such relations over time because they provided coveted jobs in what was usually a buyer's labor market.[30] Dispossessed or land-hungry peasants welcomed the opportunity to earn cash wages: by temporary work, for example, or by sending family members who could remit their earnings. In certain respects, this was an ancient practice, as old as the colonial cash economy. Peasants and haciendas had established similar "symbiotic" relationships centuries earlier; the Yaquis had played off Spanish miners and landowners against the Jesuits, seeking—with some success—a degree of remuneration and independence for

28. E.g., Amerlinck de Bontempo 1982:188–90. Evans (1926:135–38, 146–47, 196, 214) continually distinguishes between "good" (i.e., peaceable, industrious) Indians and "wicked" Indians/communities (i.e., *agraristas*).

29. The Laguna peons, a report of 1896 stated, were "quiet, strong and industrious"; forty years later, as unionization proceeded and expropriation loomed, the Tlahualilo Co. was still congratulating itself on its hitherto harmonious labor relations: "we have always had good relations with our labour and it is most disturbing when these upsets occur." Report of J. M. Duane, 17 June 1896, and Colefax to Holby, 5 March 1936, Tlahualilo Papers. See also Ronfeldt 1973.

30. The question of labor supply—especially in the agrarian sector—is highly complex. Conditions of labor surplus, such as those which existed—certainly in central Mexico—by the 1900s, did not at all eliminate employers' complaints about labor shortages. These reflected (*a*) a refusal to pay the market rate (as, I am arguing, American employers more readily did) and (*b*) seasonal fluctuations, in particular, the high demand for labor, on the part of both landlords and peasants, during the rainy season. It was this last factor that U.S. companies had to combat with cash incentives (see O'Connor 1937:325)—which probably encouraged *hacendados* to cling to "traditional" peonage, even though real wages had fallen sharply (Knight, 1986b:65).

themselves (Tutino 1975; Hu-DeHart 1988). Wage labor was not an inherent evil—or, at least, it was a lesser evil than many.

Under Díaz the needs and incentives that elicited wage labor were all the greater. Hence a new symbiosis could be established, linking peasants to new American employers. Usually the link was forged with peasant labor, which implied a necessary degree of proletarianization. But there were also cases of peasant producers supplying American plantations—with sugar, for example, in a fashion reminiscent of the Cuban *colono* system.[31] And, though in conclusion I shall stress the proletarianizing function of American enterprise, it should be noted that some versions of this symbiosis *preserved* peasant communities—preserved "peasantness," it could be said. Migrant workers remitted cash earnings to peasant villages, thus boosting their resources and facilitating their survival. This pattern, familiar in Peru, was reproduced in Soconusco, Chiapas (where the wage-labor plantations were largely German); but American enterprises could also perform such a function, both within Mexico and, of course, within the United States, whence migrants' remittances poured back to peasant communities, especially in west-central Mexico.[32] Needless to say, such a symbiosis—or "articulation of modes of production"—made wage labor all the more attractive and tolerable.

In making this argument for a new symbiosis, I would not wish to restrict my examples simply to American landholding. Several of the best cases involve either nonagricultural American interests (e.g., mines) or non-American agricultural interests (e.g., the German *cafetales* of Chiapas). This apparent eclecticism is justified, since these various interests belonged to a common category of enterprise, to which U.S. capital made the biggest contribution and which was distinguished by its capital-

---

31. USS 1920, 2:2326–27 (sugar), 2699 (rubber). Note also the contrasting forms of labor contracting used by the foreign and Mexican tobacco planters of San Andrés Tuxtla: the foreigners preferring an incentive system whereby the *habilitado* (a rough equivalent of the Brazilian coffee *colono*) "has an interest in (performing) good work," the Mexicans operating a fixed-price system which "results in the habilitados taking no interest in the quality of production" (Karl Kaerger cited in Katz 1980a:78–79).

32. According to Thomas Benjamin (1981:88), "most indians signed on voluntarily and returned to the harvests year after year since wages were nearly twice as high in Soconusco as they were at home." Cf. Gamio 1971:30, 41. Amerlinck de Bontempo (1982:193) gives a good and more recent example of how *bracero* remittances serve to underpin *ejido* farming at home.

intensive character.[33] Such enterprises relied on cash incentives to lure labor from the villages, haciendas, and sierras and to create a dependable, voluntary work force, temporary or permanent. They did not rely heavily upon a monopoly of land—the trump card of the classic *latifundista*—still less did they depend upon outright ("extra-economic") coercion. Thus, they broadly fit Jeffery Paige's definition of plantations "dominated by upper classes whose wealth is based on financial or industrial capital," whose "economic success is ensured by the workings of the free market," and whose "commanding economic position . . . makes it less necessary for them to take a direct political role in restricting competition or expropriat-ing the lands of the peasantry" (Paige 1975:chap. 1). This form of enterprise contrasts with the "traditional" haciendas, heavily dependent upon landed monopoly (sometimes of ancient origin), upon coercive dispossession of the peasantry, and even upon forcible labor recruitment—all of which required substantial political (as against market) strength, a strength man-ifested in control of political offices, agrarian laws, tariffs, and taxation. We should note—even though this aspect of Paige's theory is more debatable—that the first type is deemed likely to produce labor protest of a reformist, trade-union kind, while the second (Paige's "commercial hacienda" or "sharecropping/migratory wage labor estate") may give rise to agrarian revolt or revolution.

The capital-intensive U.S. enterprises that fell into this second category were both agrarian and industrial/extractive; their reliance on capital, hence on the purchase of free labor in the market, was common to both, and both legitimately figure in this analysis because both consequently relied on the voluntary recruitment of peasant labor, according to the symbiotic relationship just described. Both, in contrast, differed not only from "traditional" Mexican haciendas, but also from those lesser, capital-deficient U.S. interests that were the principal focus of Mexican popular hostility: the smaller ranchers, farmers, colonists, traders, storekeepers. These appeared in Mexican rural society not as providers of jobs, but rather as competitors for land, water, or markets. Colonization schemes were labor-intensive, though with the labor by definition being imported from the United States. They lacked ample resources of capital and em-

---

33. "Capital-intensive" not by virtue of a heavy reliance on expensive technology, but by virtue of its ultimate dependence on capital resources, rather than resources of land or coercion.

ployed few Mexicans, but they sought good, cultivable land. Mature colonies, like those of the Mormons in Chihuahua, were tight, prosperous communities that also competed with Mexican producers and traders in local markets—and did so all too successfully (Lloyd 1983:127–29; USS 1920, 1:1466). In part, the hostility shown to the Mormons in 1912 was the contingent consequence of the *orozquistas'* defeat, already mentioned; in this respect, the Mormons happened to be in the wrong place at the wrong time. But it also reflected the distinctive role of the Mormons in the Chihuahuan society—a role that excited antagonism and lacked collaborative potential. The same was broadly true of the afflicted colonists of southern Tamaulipas. In many respects these American interests stood closer to the Spanish or Chinese model (of trading and truck farming, hence of retail competition and alleged price-gouging) than to the classic U.S.—and, one could add, "imperialist"—model of large, capital-intensive, job-providing mines and plantations. Hence the treatment they got resembled the treatment meted out to the Spaniards and Chinese during the revolution—treatment that was recurrently hostile, even brutal.

Such lesser U.S. interests were also unable or unwilling to encase themselves in a cocoon of local clientelism. They lacked the economic resources from which such cocoons were spun; they probably lacked, too, the worldly-wise expertise of old Mexico hands like, for example, the mining magnate John Hays Hammond (Hammond 1935:112, 160). Appeals to the U.S. government—or even to Senator Fall—were usually futile. Fall's correspondence, like his Senate subcommittee report, is full of their desperate plaints (M. Meyer 1965). Thus, such lesser interests became prime victims of the revolution. ASARCO, at the other extreme, boosted investment even during the years of upheaval (during which not a single American employee lost his life); the company bought out competitors, continued to recruit labor, and emerged in the 1920s more powerful than ever. This was achieved by virtue less of U.S. government backing than of ASARCO's own economic and sociopolitical resources, deployed on the ground in Mexico. ASARCO survived and prospered because Mexicans, high and low, wanted it to. And they wanted it to because it served their interests. The same was true of many other enterprises of comparable, capital-intensive character.

This character, I am arguing, differentiated them from many Mexican employers and propertyowners. The latter, conforming roughly to Paige's "commercial hacendados"—and practicing what Barrington Moore has referred to as "labor-repressive" agriculture—relied less on capital, more on a combination of landed monopoly and political muscle. In very simple terms, they depended upon coercion as much as cash (Paige 1975:18–25; Moore 1969 [1966]:434). Of course, these are ideal types, and reality was not so straightforward. There were American enterprises that used coercion (as we will note); there were "progressive" Mexican landlords who relied squarely on cash incentives (Katz 1980a:44; Margolies 1975:30). Such exceptions do not invalidate the broad distinction. Americans were much more likely to resort to voluntary labor recruitment, where Mexican landlords relied upon a range of extra-economic devices. The extremes of outright coercion were to be found in the Mexican—and often Spanish—plantations of Chiapas, Yucatán, Tabasco, and Oaxaca. Even in the free-labor north, a potentate like Terrazas could maintain a measure of peonage. Extensive dispossession of the peasantry in central Mexico ensured a supply of cheap labor (as well as an eventual agrarian uprising); the ensuing landed monopolies even obviated the need to pay cash wages—hence forms of (traditional) peonage and sharecropping throve in states like Tlaxcala and Guanajuato. Meanwhile, favorable grain tariffs kept global market pressures at bay, and political influence helped ensure that taxes—on land per se or on products like pulque—were disproportionately low. Finally, since "extra-economic coercion" is often assumed to involve an ideological element, the docility of the *peonaje* was instilled by the priest in the pulpit as well as the *rural* in the saddle (Wasserman 1984:51; Katz 1980a:35, 38, 67, 83–103; Gruening 1928:216–19; Friedrich 1970:48). There is no evidence that these "archaic" forms of labor, resistant to the rigorous logic of the market, were heading for extinction on the eve of the revolution. On the contrary, in some areas they were gaining strength.

American (as well as other foreign) capital-intensive enterprises generally opted for voluntary labor recruitment, mediated through the cash nexus. This they did not so much for any moralistic or ideological reasons, but rather because it worked. The timing and the manner of their entry into the Mexican economy made dispossession of peasants less imperative; they usually exported and had no need of tariffs; they lacked direct political influence (the climate of the *porfiriato* was benign, but American entrepreneurs did not sit in the statehouses and ministries of the Republic, as did Terrazas, Molina, Escandón, Diez Gutiérrez, etc.). Instead, they bid for labor in the market, offering—where necessary—wage raises, perks, and premiums. Workers concluded that "the Americans would give them a good deal"; Mexican landlords, on the other hand, believed that "contact with the US, and even with individual Americans, spoils the peons" (uss 1920, 1:129–30 and 2:2342; both comments made by "hostile" witnesses).

Conversely, Americans—and capital-intensive enterprises of whatever nationality—tended to avoid outright coercion. True, there were exceptions. J. K. Turner's prize exhibits (Yucatán and the Valle Nacional) concerned Mexican and Spanish planters, but there was also evidence of coercion on some American-owned properties in the south. Such evidence is patchy, though. American, British, and Canadian capital was involved—along with dominant Mexican and Spanish interests—in the notorious *monterías* of Chiapas, whose operations involved extensive coercion. It may be significant, however, that the huge Anglo-Canadian Agua Azul *montería* was reckoned—by the severe critic B. Traven—to be the only one that treated its workers like human beings, "as far as such a thing was possible in a *montería*" (Traven 1971:59).[34]

Other examples that have been cited elsewhere to illustrate American-inspired coercion are also ambiguous. Karena Shields is quoted to the effect that "freedom was only a meaningless technicality" on the plantations of Chiapas—Mexican, German, and American—in the 1900s. It is clear from the context, however, that this was a loose generalization, made by an indifferent reporter; her father's plantation (and he was American) involved none of the coercive and corrupt methods that, "Papa told us with anger and disgust," were practiced elsewhere (T. Benjamin 1981:102; Shields 1959:40). Similar doubts arise from the Fall Committee testimony of John Lind, who uses a single example to frame a general indictment—exceptions to which both he and his colleague William Cananda at once furnish (uss 1920, 2:2325–27, 2432–34; cf. Katz 1980a:27). It cannot be doubted—and it is not surprising—that American and other foreign enterprises did sometimes follow local coercive practices in their labor recruitment. But a norm cannot be established on the basis of these few, ambiguous cases, and they are insufficient to destroy the general hypothesis presented here.

If the hypothesis is broadly valid, one final significant conclusion might

34. It also paid better wages; in general "the worse the reputation of a *montería*, the lower the wages that were paid"; a classic inversion of market principles and a key indicator of prevailing coercive logic.

be teased out. The creation of a proletariat, urban or rural, is more than just a question of numbers. The dispossession of direct producers, the creation of a propertyless mass, are necessary but not sufficient preconditions. There must also be a process of long and difficult acculturation: the breaking of old habits, the inculcation of the "time and work discipline" of capitalism. This involves (*a*) the creation of a fluid and responsive labor market and (*b*) the instillation of the work ethic. It is well known that subsistence peasants (and this category may be said to include the "internal" as well as the "external" peasantry; i.e., traditional peons as well as free villagers) are refractory to this transformation (Thompson 1967; García D. 1981). Even entirely dispossessed landless peasants do not become model proletarians instantly. Hence the familiar complaints from employers, especially landlords, about peasant fecklessness and irresponsibility, absenteeism and lack of initiative, about the peasant's refusal to work, strive, save, and accumulate, characteristics that economists have abstracted in the form of the backward-sloping supply curve of labor.

Such complaints abounded during the *porfiriato*. Peons and peasants, being idle and recalcitrant, had to be coerced; but coercion, in turn, perpetuated idle and recalcitrant peons and peasants (Katz 1980a:87–91; Knight 1986a, 1:8; García D. 1981:46; Moats 1932:63; and Lumholtz 1903:418, which offers a distinctive version of perverse, premarket behavior as displayed by the Tarahumara, for whom "profit is no inducement . . . as they believe that their gods would be angry with them for charging an undue price" for goods). A deceitfully coercive debt-peonage system also constituted a major obstacle to the formation of a fluid free-labor market. Breaking out of this vicious circle was not easy. It had been attempted, with some success, in the context of the colonial mining industry (hence Mexico had no *mita*); but that had meant paying attractive wages and offering additional incentives (e.g., the *partida*, the "share"). Even there, however, further attempts to achieve full proletarianization—by abolishing the *partida*—had proved risky; furthermore, the demand for labor in the colonial mines could not compare with that which would prevail a century later, for reasons already suggested (Brading 1971:147–49, 277).

Massive dispossession of the peasantry, coupled with population growth, went some way toward solving the problem. Yet employers' complaints were still common. Traditional peons were "indolent and vice-ridden"; they took solace in drink and ran up debts, resisting proletarianization even where the "progressive" landlord sought to promote it. Temporary workers (*eventuales*) could not be trusted to come when they were needed or to stay until they were no longer needed. And most of the rural poor (peasants, day laborers, miners—all save a minority of docile *acasillados*) showed, like Weber's celebrated Prussian workers, a perverse list for independence, an itch to find alternatives to steady, unremitting and, above all, dependent toil. So they became squatters, sharecroppers, petty artisans, *gambusinos,* even—critics said—beggars (Katz 1980a:87; uss 1920, 1:1008, 1433; O'Connor 1937:98; Bendix 1977:22).

Coercion could not solve the problem, it compounded it. And Mexican landlords, locked into a system of generally low economic productivity, cheap (but feckless) labor, and ample politico-coercive powers, were not disposed to innovate. Foreign—especially U.S.—capital was relatively free of these constraints. By offering competitive wages, better conditions, and certain additional cash incentives, capital-intensive enterprises could attract and retain free labor. Thereby they contributed to the formation of regional and national labor markets. In addition, they may have disseminated certain technological knowledge, as well as fostering greater work commitment. An American who had spent $300,000 modernizing a massive Chihuahuan estate (initial value $350,000; labor force 350–400) offered better pay and conditions for those engaged in the laborious development work: "after we were working the first year on that, it became very apparent that the men whom [*sic*] we had on the development work were particularly anxious to be kept there, for the reason that they were better fed, better cared for, while working them harder and longer hours [*sic*], but they had better pay." Such major U.S. enterprises thus constituted poles of proletarianization—qualitative as well as quantitative. "The Mexican peons would say," the same entrepreneur ventured, "that they worked harder for us than they ever did previous to the time we became owners of the property, but they were better treated and better paid" (uss 1920, 2:2395–2410).

Similar arguments could be advanced (indeed, they were anticipated many years ago by Manuel Gamio) concerning Mexican migration to the United States itself.[35] It is well known that migration could have significant *political* consequences, particularly during the phase of "secondary"

35. Gamio (1971:37–38) draws a parallel between American employers in the United States and in Mexico, both of whom exemplify the principle that "when the pay is higher and the working day eight hours, the work is more productive."

peasant mobilization in the 1920s and 1930s. Primo Tapia may therefore stand as an exemplary case of a more general phenomenon embracing the *norteños* of Los Altos or the anticlerical faction of Cherán. It should not be assumed, however, that migration played a similarly significant role in pre-1920 peasant protest. Nor can an invariably radicalizing effect be assumed: Guanajuato, which supplied a vast contingent of migrants, was consistently Catholic and *sinarquista* rather than radical and agrarian. (Cf. Craig 1983:42–43, 178–82, esp. 179n4; Beals 1973:119–20; J. Meyer 1979:45–49.) Peasant protest clearly did not require prior migration, nor did migration guarantee radicalism. But it was clearly conducive to the formation of new attitudes and, hence, in the political sphere, to deviance and dissent. In the context of the present essay, however, it is the socioeconomic consequences that matter.

The "new ideas on the subject of a just standard of living" which migrants acquired had socioeconomic as well as political significance, by which distinction (admittedly somewhat artificial) I mean that they affected the labor market as well as the political system (Simpson 1937:44). The migrant, Gamio reckoned, "undoubtedly benefits economically by the change. He learns the discipline of modern labor. He specializes . . . he becomes a laborer of the modern type, much more efficient than before" (Gamio 1971:42, 49). Not surprisingly, returning migrants were reluctant to go back to traditional hacienda work; quiet economic dissent accompanied—perhaps exceeded—outspoken political dissent (Craig 1983:179–80). The "demonstration effect" of U.S. society, therefore, helped inculcate the work ethic as well as political radicalism. In the United States, one migrant noted, "everyone works." Furthermore, work was linked to thrift, savings, and self-improvement; migrants tended to be more literate, bringing books back from the United States, along with the usual furniture, utensils, bathtubs, and sewing machines (Craig 1983:180; Gamio 1971:68–69). The limited good was perceived not to be so limited after all.

For these migratory influences to endure, however, conditions in Mexico also had to permit their development; some forms of migration-induced acculturation—e.g., in the sphere of religion—proved vulnerable once migrants returned to their hostile home environment. Capitalist enterprises in Mexico thus performed an important acculturating role, one that was arguably more profound and pervasive, if less obvious and dramatic, than that performed by the fields and factories of *el norte*. And it was a role that accorded well with the prevailing philosophy of the Sonoran elite of the 1920s, ardent developmentalists and admirers of the U.S. economic system who were somewhat stymied when it came to imitating that system south of the border. For were not *laisser-faire* principles—prescribing a weak government and a powerful private sector—a hallmark of that system? To exercise state power in pursuit of economic development—to build a form of state capitalism—as risky and contradictory; yet to rely on the autonomous forces of Mexican society (especially southern, rural, Catholic society) was to postpone development indefinitely. So the Sonorans reasoned.

For some, education was the answer. Here was an area where governmental intervention was licit, benign, and effective. Vasconcelos' rural schools would create not only model citizens but also hardworking producers: reading Plato would turn pulque-sodden peons into industrious proletarians (not a fictitious example: Simpson 1937:107–8). If these were the limits of Sonoran social engineering, it is not surprising that it largely failed. Fortunately for the Sonorans, however, the forces of private capital—more efficacious according to their philosophy anyway—were lending a hidden hand. U.S. capital (indeed, *any* foreign capital—the United States simply happened to be the biggest supplier) was a powerful instrument not only for developing the material resources of the country, but also for inculcating desired economic values and practices. What the mines and plantations of the 1880s and 1890s had pioneered, the factories of Ford and General Motors would continue in the 1920s and 1930s. And the intervening revolution, by undermining without totally destroying the traditional hacienda, significantly accelerated the process (Knight 1985a:17–26).

As for the migrants and U.S. employees themselves, they readily combined an admixture of radicalism (sometimes stimulated by American example), a growing propensity for unionization (recall Paige's theoretical presumption), and a commitment to the new work ethic and discipline (which they shared with their Sonoran rulers). If the combination appears contradictory, it should nevertheless be recognized as a common working-class ensemble. It formed part of the making of the Mexican working class as it did of the English. The inculcation of the work ethnic—the qualitative as well as quantitative creation of a proletariat—was necessary for Mexico's capitalist development, even if, at the same time, it carried certain radical implications (E. P. Thompson 1967:65–66). The stable, organized working class which underpinned such development could also underpin militant unions (in the 1930s particularly); potentially, it could underpin radical parties.

It is in this general realm of social and economic change that American capital had its epochal impact on Mexico, and on the Mexican rural population in particular: namely, by accelerating the sluggish transition from peasant to proletarian, not so much in the obvious and negative sense of dispossessing the peasantry (that was the work of traditional Mexican landowners, who paid the price in terms of agrarian revolution), but more discretely and positively by molding—within Mexico and the United States—the new mass proletariat of the twentieth century. Given the size and tenacity of Mexico's historical peasantry—and considering the protracted difficulties encountered elsewhere in pursuit of full-scale proletarianization—this was a major task. It was a task requiring capital, enterprise, and incentive. Neither private coercion nor official exhortation were sufficient. It was a task, too, that had to proceed gradually, in subtle, subterranean fashion. For this reason it did not, as I have argued, excite strenuous popular resentment. And for this reason, too, it is easily overlooked. Yet it was a task—and, to some extent, an accomplishment—that dwarfed the vaunted yet limited and frequently ineffective efforts of the U.S. government to mold Mexican society to its will.

JOHN H. COATSWORTH

Measuring Influence: The United States and

the Mexican Peasantry

In this chapter I argue that the United States exerted enormous casual influence on the outbreak, development, immediate outcome, and long-term consequences of the Mexican Revolution. I do so by taking a new look at a number of substantive and methodological issues that have long perplexed historians of nineteenth- and twentieth-century Mexico.

Since Alan Knight's clear and judicious analysis of U.S. influence in this volume and elsewhere[1] provided the inspiration for these reflections, I want to begin by acknowledging his many and penetrating contributions to the historiography of the Mexican Revolution. Three major points elaborated in Knight's chapter above are especially worth recalling. The first is his insistence on the significance of proletarianization as a conse-quence of the dependent modernization of the Porfirian era and as a major factor in precipitating rural discontent. The second is his effort to restore "peasant groups and agrarian factors" to a central place in the historiogra-phy of the revolution. Finally, there is Knight's recognition of the impor-tance of uniting the external and internal historiographies of the revolu-tion, an approach pioneered by Friedrich Katz (1981). On all three of these points, Knight's work provides convincing logic and evidence.

Nonetheless, I believe that Knight may have underestimated the per-sistence and depth of the North American impact on Mexico's historical development, and thus on the peasantry. Knight's notion that the United States did not exercise much influence over the development of the Mexi-can Revolution rests on the unquestionable fact of U.S. restraint and on the equally unchallengeable importance of the revolution's internal dyna-mism. The absence of massive overt intervention and the Wilson admin-istration's serial dissatisfaction with successive revolutionary factions lim-

---

1. In addition to his two-volume study of the Mexican Revolution (Knight, 1986a), see, e.g., Knight 1985a, 1985b, 1987.

ited the direct U.S. impact on events and outcomes. But this is true only in the most literal (and therefore least interesting) sense.

Recall for a moment the statistical distinction between the value of an independent variable, the size of its regression coefficient, and the magnitude of the correlation between the independent and dependent variables. The independent variable in this case is the behavior of the United States toward Mexico. During the Mexican Revolution, as Knight reminds us, the United States, for various reasons (ideological, strategic, political) intervened only modestly and inconsistently. The value of the variable was small. Nonetheless, the parameter that measures the effect on Mexico of a unit increase (or decrease) in American intervention might well have been quite large. That is to say, the structure of the relationship cannot be measured by the value of the independent variable (degree of U.S. intervention), but rather by the coefficient that shows the (potential) multiplier effect of changes in this variable on the dependent variable (Mexico). Moreover, the correlation between U.S. behavior and Mexican outcomes might also have been quite strong; that is, each alteration in the degree of U.S. intervention might well have produced highly predictable effects on Mexican outcomes.

In short, do we say that U.S. policy had *little effect* on the Mexican Revolution because the United States failed to intervene more forcefully, or do we say that the U.S. policy had a *major impact* on the Mexican Revolution because it failed to intervene more forcefully? Knight's explicit analysis embraces the former proposition: his analytical framework suggests the latter one. I prefer the implicitly structuralist Knight to the explicitly empiricist one.

Perhaps an overly schematic exercise in comparative counterfactualism will make this distinction clear. As Friedrich Katz pointed out some time ago, the radicalization of such major upheavals as the French and Russian revolutions occurred in response to foreign interventions (Katz 1978a). Mobilizing resistance against foreign aggression pushed revolutionary regimes to embrace more sweeping demands for social change or strengthened the more militant and radical factions of revolutionary movements. Massive foreign intervention did not occur during the Mexican Revolution and, in part as a result, neither did the radicalization. Zapata's peasant followers and Villa's more heterogeneous but nonetheless "populist" armies suffered defeat on the battlefield: the Constitutionalist victors even turned on their own *agrarista* and working-class supporters as soon as it was safe to do so. What, however, would have occurred had the United States—perhaps more committed to its hemispheric isolation under a Republican president, or after the 1918 armistice with a stricken Wilson unable to resist the pressures of the oil lobby—decided to occupy (rather than merely to wander through) a major portion of northern Mexico or the oil fields along the Gulf?

The major historiographic puzzle of the Mexican Revolution continues to revolve around the inexplicable "delay" of nearly two decades between the consolidation of the "revolutionary" regime after 1917 and the implementation of the massive land redistributions and other reforms of the Cárdenas era (see Knight chapter, above; and Knight 1985a, 1987). Either the revolution was not so revolutionary after all ("interrupted," merely a "rebellion," or indeed "defeated")—in which case the Cárdenas reforms become inexplicable—or the revolution succeeded in some sense that makes the delay problematic. Perhaps the missing variable is the United States, or some set of theoretically relevant factors for which the United States may stand as a convenient proxy.

The revolution clearly succeeded in displacing the *porfirista* political leadership, with its close links to the country's recently revitalized class of great landowners. The impact of agrarian movements, land seizures, and continuous conflict ruined many large estates and provoked a displacement of labor and capital from the countryside to the cities. With the notable exception of certain (mostly northern) regions, Mexico's landowners no longer wielded sufficient political and economic power to defend their interests against the new regimes. In fact, by the 1920s it had become altogether clear that the new order had more to fear from Catholic peasants than from the old landowners, many of whom had either abandoned their estates, sold them to raise funds for more profitable opportunities in commerce, industry, and public "service," or simply resigned themselves to a lesser role in their country's economic progress. What, then, prevented the major agrarian reform that the Constitution of 1917 had already legitimated?

A full discussion of this question has yet to take place among historians of Mexico, but when it does, the role of the United States is likely to reemerge as crucial. The United States failed to induce the radicalization that a timely and massive intervention could have produced. Moreover, the escalating demand for Mexican mineral and agricultural exports (at rising prices) provoked by the outbreak of the war in Europe added another, external factor that weighed in against radical reform of any kind. The gains to be reaped through a quick consolidation short of drastic reforms were evident for all to see. Indeed, despite all the turmoil and disruption occasioned by years of bitter fighting, no Mexican regime that controlled the country's major ports and northern railroad junctions ever faced the kind of economic catastrophes that other revolutions have historically had to confront.[2] Fiscal revenues suffered and, for a year or so, the value of the country's exports declined modestly. But collapse never came. Any faction capable of imposing reasonable order and willing to respect the property rights of private producers (including foreigners) had a reasonable chance of raising the revenues needed to consolidate its power. As it turned out, only the Constitutionalists were willing and able to exploit this opportunity. The externally induced boom conditions of the war years, along with U.S. restraint, played a major role in shaping the outcome of the Mexican Revolution.

The opportunity costs of radical reform shifted dramatically with the depression. By 1934, no Mexican regime, no matter how conservative, could have restored the country's export markets or induced foreign banks and enterprises to renew the flow of capital into the country. Mexico, in effect, had already suffered all of the economic costs that an earlier radicalization would have imposed. Thus, the external inducement to conservative social policies finally disappeared, years after the revolution had removed the major domestic impediments to agrarian reform. Moreover, the character of the U.S. administration, and the U.S. strategic position in Latin America, had also changed; the major political cost of a radical turn—U.S. intervention—was now less likely. Why, then, did agrarian reform (and the support for labor organization, mainly in the foreign-owned sector of the economy, and the nationalizations of the railroads and the petroleum industry) wait until Cárdenas? Perhaps because the United States and international economic conditions were not ready until then to tolerate them without imposing heavy costs.

Let us now return to the revolution itself and to the problem of its

2. The *villista* collapse provides negative confirmation of this point. When Villa found himself cut off from sources of export earnings, fiscal revenues, and finance, his paper currency lost value, inflation soared, and popular discontent in the areas under his control led to widespread disaffection (see Katz 1981:285–86).

structural and contingent causes. The United States, I believe, played four important roles in creating the conditions that produced the revolution whose outcomes it so powerfully affected. First, there is the unexplained but powerful tradition of peasant militancy and assertiveness of which Knight's work has so convincingly reminded us. In comparison with the peasantries of the other Latin American countries, Mexico's has a unique history of precocious politicization and aggressiveness beginning in the early nineteenth century. This historical fabric was woven of many fibers, but as I have argued elsewhere, the Texas War in 1836–37 and especially the North American invasion of 1846–47 appear to have had a profound effect (Coatsworth 1988). These disasters destroyed all possibility of political consensus, weakened national political authority beyond repair, mobilized and armed tens of thousands of peasants in the center of the country, and left the surviving veterans to return to their villages and farms to lead the innumerable movements, large and small, that wracked the Mexican countryside from the 1840s to the 1880s. Clearly the French invasion in the 1860s played an important role, as did U.S. support for the *juaristas* who eventually restored the Republic. Without the intensified political strife and social upheavals that followed the U.S. war, however, the French and their Austrian archduke would not have had an opportunity to seize upon. In short, the unique tradition of rebelliousness in the Mexican countryside that the Díaz regime had only recently managed to smother or conceal owes its development in large part to the United States.

The second role the United States played in fostering the conditions that led to the Mexican Revolution was economic in nature. As Knight points out, the rapid and disruptive commercialization of agriculture that occurred in Mexico beginning in the 1870s and that resulted in the proletarianization of many peasants and villagers during the *porfiriato* was induced by the construction of railroads and the export-led economic growth of this era.[3] Many of the grievances that pushed rural people to revolt as the Porfirian regime collapsed were the inadvertent consequence of an economic transformation in which U.S. capital and U.S. markets played a central role.

3. Recent work has tended, however, to cast some doubt on some elements of this view. See, for example, Robert H. Holden's nearly exhaustive review of the infamous survey companies, challenging the widely held view that these enterprises undermined peasant landholding (Holden 1986).

Third, the regime that collapsed in 1911 owed its fragility in part to the conditions that had allowed it to flourish. The product of a reactionary alliance of landlords and merchants facing a temporarily defeated peasantry and a tiny and unorganized working class, the Porfirian regime could not, for all its superficial similarities to the simultaneous top–down modernizations of Japan and Germany, control the process over which it presided; it simply lacked the political and economic resources to do so. Mexico's was ultimately a modernization from without, not from above (see Coatsworth 1975).

In the consolidation of the Díaz regime, the United States played both a direct and an indirect role—direct in its willingness to recognize the Díaz regime while the European powers continued their efforts to isolate Mexico and force it to recognize the huge debts incurred by the Second Empire, and indirect because the economic success that cemented the Pax Porfiriana stemmed initially and in large part from the flow of U.S. capital and the demand on the part of U.S. consumers and industries for Mexico's exports. The resources required for modernization came from abroad, eventually from all of the industrializing powers. The economic policies required to maintain this flow of resources, as the regime understood matters, emphasized balanced budgets and low levels of taxation. Government spending as a percentage of GDP fell from nearly 12 to just over 7 percent between 1877 and 1910 (Coatsworth 1985:43).

When the economy turned sour and protests multiplied, especially after 1905, the Díaz regime found that it commanded neither the economic resources or policy instruments needed to stimulate growth nor the fiscal or political resources required to co-opt discontent. Díaz could not have played Bismarck, even if he had understood the game and wished to do so. The regime turned, in its dotage, to repression. Nothing, as Mexico's tiny bands of would-be revolutionaries discovered to their amazement (and to that of the regime as well), is quite so ripe for destruction as a regime that is both weak and repressive at the same time. And nothing accounts for this peculiar ripeness in Mexico at the end of the first decade of the twentieth century more than the effects of the economic trajectory that the Porfirian regime pursued so successfully with the indispensable aid of U.S. (and other foreign) capital and markets.

Fourth, again as Katz has pointed out, even this mixture—peasants armed with a rebellious tradition, resentful and bitter at the loss of their access to land, and facing a weak and repressive regime—might now have been enough had it not been for the transformation of the U.S.-Mexican frontier into a border region capable of supplying and sustaining revolutionary armies (Katz 1981:7–18). Additional elements, like the influence of North American Protestantism or trade unionism (concentrated disproportionately in the border area) might also be cited in this connection.[4]

A final point, which returns us to the gap between fact and interpretation, concerns the "nationalism," or lack of it, of the Mexican peasantry during the revolution. Knight's essay in this volume rightly points to the notable lack of xenophobic anti-Americanism among all of the revolutionary factions, including the peasantry. The more interesting question, however, is whether we should take the lack of peasant nationalism as a literal fact, as it was, or pursue the matter further.

In rebelling against the Porfirian regime, Mexico's peasants (and their many, if feckless, allies) called into question all that imperialism had accomplished in their country, and did so in a way that U.S. business interests and the U.S. government correctly perceived as prejudicial. Peasants did not have to lay siege to U.S.-owned properties to lay them waste: they needed merely to assert at gunpoint a different vision of what their country was about to unsettle business, increase risks, disrupt transportation, pressure governments into unpredictable turnovers and policy shifts, and in general to wreak havoc upon the investment "climate." Bankruptcies and defaults followed as predictably as they would have had the peasants and their allies stormed the banks and factories directly.[5] Moreover, turning again to the longer run, the seeds of that agrarian and explicitly "socialist" vision with which Cárdenas and his lieutenants sought to remake Mexico in the 1930s were sown by the peasant movements of the 1910s and 1920s. If they did not turn on foreign interests more directly or more often or with greater consistency, that was no doubt because they preferred to take aim at more important targets. Does the militant assertion of social aims contrary

4. On Protestantism, see Baldwin 1979; on the effects of U.S. trade unionism (esp. the IWW), see Hart 1978.

5. As Knight points out, the paradoxical effect of the revolution's impact on business was to enhance the position of the larger U.S. firms (against that of their Mexican and European competitors). But this effect assumes the triumph of Constitutionalist conservatism as well as the repatriation of European assets after the outbreak of World War I; agrarian radicals largely opposed the first of these developments and had nothing to do with the second.

to foreign interests, in flagrant disregard of foreign pressures, and in reaction against a foreign-financed "modernization" constitute a "nationalist" movement?

If, then, the United States played a key role in creating conditions that produced Mexico's unique tradition of peasant rebelliousness in the early nineteenth century, led to the expropriation of peasant freeholds and village lands later in the same century, rendered the Porfirian regime both weak and repressive after 1905, gave revolutionaries a border for gunrunning and escape, favored "moderate" over more radical, agrarian factions in the revolution, and promoted reform rather than orthodoxy during the 1930s, what is there in the modern agrarian history of Mexico that the United States (or the external economic world) has not shaped or conditioned? Perhaps it is only that vision of a just society of free producers freely cooperating—that profoundly national (if not negatively nationalist or antiforeign) utopia—which persists even amid the smog and rhetoric of a different era.

JOHN MASON HART

Social Unrest, Nationalism, and American Capital in the Mexican Countryside, 1876–1920

During the Mexican Revolution of 1910, peasant and local elites, independent of outside control, erupted in violence across the countryside. They rose up against the Porfirian latifundia complex of intrusive commercial agricultural estates.[1] In doing so they focused on their *hacendado* rivals and, as a part of the revolutionary process, landholders came under attack.

Mexican elites owned the vast majority of the estates, but recently arrived American landowners owned about 27 percent, or 130 million acres, of the nation's surface. Fewer than a hundred American interests held nearly 90 million of those acres in tracts larger than 100,000 acres. Perhaps 15,000 Americans held smaller properties that made up the remainder. In the southwestern quarter of Durango, American estate owners held some 70 percent of the land. A handful of American and Mexican great-estate owners also dominated western and northern Chihuahua.

The growth of large rural estates had been part of a slowly evolving yet stress- and conflict-laden process of economic, social, political, and cultural transformation that began late in the seventeenth century. In the last third of the nineteenth century, however, the estates began to develop more rapidly, encroaching with unprecedented intensity upon peasant agriculture.[2] The growing capitalization of the estates and the destabilization of rural society began to intensify between 1867 and 1883, when new markets, technologies, and state intervention on behalf of agricultural commercialization stimulated the reorganization, development, and expansion of properties nationwide.

1. For the purposes of this essay, peasants will be defined as those who control the production of a plot of land and whose productivity is oriented toward self-sufficiency.

2. For the survival of Indian customs and society, and the limits on rural violence in the colonial era, see Wasserstrom 1983; Aguirre Beltrán 1967; McLeod and Wasserstrom 1983; Jones 1977; and Taylor 1979.

At first the increasingly uneven competition for land and water rights led to peasant revolts, which were put down by the army. Those struggles assumed critical importance between 1906 and 1914 because of an agricultural downturn and growing public outrage. A deepening elite crisis developed in those years and compromised the state's repressive apparatus. Between 1909 and 1920, peasant and rural working-class violence directed first against the domestically owned great estates and then against the foreigners swept Mexico. The provincial elites terminated the uprisings by militarily defeating the larger lower-class-led rural forces with a controlled mobilization of other peasant contingents and industrial workers and a co-optive program of land redistribution.

After Porfirio Díaz became president in 1876, he had intensified the process of expropriating peasant and communal holdings with the aim of land commercialization and made the expropriations national in scope. By 1910 127,111,824 acres of land had been expropriated, leaving 98 percent of the rural working class landless while creating a small class of some 7,000 *hacendados* along with 45,000 *rancheros* or middle holders. Beginning in the late 1890s, Díaz increased his efforts to attract powerful foreign capitalists who might invest in Mexican lands. The newcomers often bought the land of Mexican provincial elites in competition with other locally prominent Mexicans.

The North Americans became a part of the Porfirian land-tenure system as their enterprises spread across the southwestern United States during the second half of the nineteenth century and then crossed the border. They capitalized their holdings on a scale unprecedented in Mexico, creating plantations and ranches associated with the ports of Salina Cruz, Acapulco, Manzanillo, Mazatlán, Guaymas, Campeche, Puerto México, Veracruz, Tuxpam, and Tampico, and with the entrepôts of El Paso, Brownsville, Eagle Pass, and Laredo. Those cities linked the enterprises directly with foreign markets at New Orleans, New York, Galveston, San Antonio, Houston, Los Angeles, and San Francisco. Pioneers for profit, the Americans produced rubber, cotton, henequen, timber, livestock, sugar, coffee, and bananas. In the process they erected fences and canceled land-rent and labor contracts traditionally maintained between the Mexican owners and *campesinos*. Fences meant less access for the peasants to firewood and water, and were in violation of accepted practices. The Mexican countryside, along with Cuba, became the first foreign region exploited systematically by U.S. investors in a process of economic expansion that rapidly became global.[3]

Until 1895 the Americans in Mexico, through their land development and railroad construction companies, focused on government-owned properties which were often intact lands claimed by the peasantry. For the rural working classes, at first, the Americans were a secondary factor in their displacement from long-claimed lands, in the cancellation of or increase in rents, in boundary disputes, and in lost local political power. After 1895, however, the Americans increased their purchases of Mexican livestock, mining and timber haciendas, and plantations. They rapidly capitalized these operations, creating a strong foreign economic and cultural presence. After 1905, as the value of the peso declined and land prices soared, Mexican rural elites lost their ability to compete with the Americans in real estate and began to join the peasants in their protests.

Regional differences accounted for the wide range of responses from the rural working class once the revolutionary crisis began. In the north the land developers encountered a *pueblo* citizenry that differed from that of the south-central region and most coastal areas. The communities of the northern frontier had been established by the Spanish Crown and succeeding Mexican governments as a military and demographic buffer against the incursions of Texans and Comanche or Apache Indians. Land grants had induced migration to the frontier among army veterans, Seminoles and blacks from Florida, Kickapoo Indians, and *mestizos* from central Mexico. Northerners developed considerable military potential relative to their counterparts in other areas of Mexico.

Their differences from coastal and southern groups were important for the later development of large-scale revolutionary forces. Northerners were more experienced in military self-defense, geographically remote, better armed, and more mobile. They were often far removed from the discipline and authority of provincial elites. They had more experience in the commercial economy of the United States than their counterparts of the south, and they enjoyed access to arms at the border. The northern villages resembled those of the south-central region in their desire to regain lost land and the status of autonomous municipalities.

3. The records of many of the American companies and interests in Mexico are contained in the archives of the United States–Mexican Claims Commissions, Record Group 76, WNRC.

In the coastal areas and in much of the south, the rural communities had been subdued during violent struggles between 1690 and the late 1840s and then, during the rest of the nineteenth century, were more gradually integrated with the commercial economy.[4] By 1910 the majority of the rural poor on the coasts and in the south had long since been transformed into plantation and hacienda laborers. But, in the south, the remaining peasantry still disputed Porfirian land seizures and maintained a shaken *pueblo* authority structure.[5]

During the *porfiriato* the rural areas of Coahuila, Chihuahua, Sonora, and Durango underwent commercial transformation. American-owned oil, railroad, timber, mining, livestock, and agricultural companies joined Mexican *latifundistas* and forged strong economic ties with the United States. After 1901, the propertyowning local and provincial elites of the north lost heavily and became disgruntled with the centralist regime during the droughts, crop failures, and financial crises (except in Tamaulipas, where oil investments were creating new wealth).

In Chihuahua and Durango the massive acquisitions by American interests—including Cargill, the Corallitos, Hearst, Huller, International Lumber, the MacManus Land Company, Southwestern Land and Cattle, Rio Bravo Land and Cattle, and the Riverside Ranch—overwhelmed all but the most powerful among their Mexican neighbors. Some Mexican elites such as the Terrazas-Creel interests also expanded. Meanwhile, *pueblos* like Janos, Casas Grandes, and Cuencame faced landlessness. The Mexican *latifundistas* and American companies offered overwhelming competition for most local elites. In Coahuila the same conditions prevailed among the Seminole/black, *mestizo,* and Kickapoo *pueblos* versus Eagle Pass Lumber, Jennings-Blocker, Magnum, Ord, and various Texan holdings nearer the border, while at La Laguna Mexican farmers lost heavily owing to the intrusion of the Noble and McClellan, Potter, Rockefeller, and Brown Brothers interests.

In Sonora the Mexican government drove the Yaqui and Mayo Indians from their river valley farming enclaves. Local and provincial elites looked on with ambivalence as the Compañía Constructora Richardson acquired

4. For an examination of these struggles, see Hart forthcoming; Tutino 1976.

5. A *pueblo* is a legally incorporated rural settlement without jurisdiction over other de jure established rural communities. A *villa,* or village, is a legally endowed community with authority over designated *pueblos* and is the site of a regional marketplace.

993,650 acres, extending from just south of Guaymas to the Mayo River and eighty miles inland. The railroad holdings of E. H. Harriman and his associates James Stillman and William Rockefeller of the National City Bank (who controlled the Southern Pacific railroad) extended the length of the state. Other holdings included R. H. Vick's Compañía de Terrenos y Ganados with 1,500,000 acres. In the timber and mining regions of the Sonoran interior, the same situation prevailed. Phelps Dodge held 350,000 acres, and the Wheeler Land Company, owned by Chicago and Rockport capitalists, held 1,450,000 acres, extending from the Richardson properties eastward to those of Hearst and other Americans in Chihuahua. The Cananea Copper Company held 346,000 acres, while the Phelps Dodge holdings were even greater. The Americans joined a still powerful and prosperous Mexican oligarchy in the state.

By 1910 American holdings in the south were equally impressive. In Chiapas, the Chacamax Land Development, Esperanza Timber, Kansas and Chiapas, Coapa Development, Mexican Rubber, Castilloa Rubber, Casa de Arroyo, Mexico Land Securities, Chiapas Land and Stock, Edward Hartman, Pennsylvania Plantation, Soconusco Development, Real Estate Company of Mexico, and others established highly capitalized operations. In Quintana Roo the Mengel Company held a 3,500,000-acre timber concession, while Adams Gum also held a large grant. In Campeche, International Lumber and Development owned 300,000 acres; Probst and Company, 1,020,000 acres; Mexico Gulf Land and Lumber, 610,000 acres; Laguna Corporation, 1,350,000 acres; and Hearst, 500,000 acres. The Sakahal and Bailey holdings were also enormous. Equally prominent Americans held similar estates in Coahuila, Colima, Guerrero, Oaxaca, San Luis Potosí, Sinaloa, Tamaulipas, and Zacatecas.

By 1910, too, most of the largest properties along the coasts and frontiers were in American hands. The total landholding for all foreigners totaled at least 145,000,000 acres. These lands included much of the nation's most valuable timber, mining, and agricultural properties. Falling prices for produce and stock crushed any residual rural Mexican ability to buy land, while American property purchases compounded the problem by inflating costs.

Then the Americans took the final step, placing themselves in the face of a growing rural fury and helping it become nationalistic. The U.S. land-development companies recruited thousands of American "pioneers," "boomers," and "colonists." Brandishing property titles and rifles, these 15,000 Americans poured across the border and off of ships, displacing tens of thousands of Mexican peasants and *rancheros*.[6] They put up fences and hired *campesino* laborers, attempting to utilize an inexpensive agrarian work force. Their actions contributed to the transformation of independent Mexican land users into transients who crowded the towns and cities in a futile search for employment.

Despite the desperate alienation of the rural working class, it was unable to assert itself successfully until the dissent of the provincial elites helped to precipitate the 1910 revolution. Its limited access to weapons, lack of adequate military and political leadership, and isolation effectively neutralized most incidents of *campesino* violence. Provincial elite and local *pequeña burgués* revolutionary leadership emerged in the early 1900s, striking out against the government, and against Mexican and foreign landholding elites.[7]

In late 1910 and early 1911, five areas of generalized lower-class violence developed: the Gulf and Pacific coasts, the far south and north, and the state of Morelos, where Spanish and Mexico City estate owners had enclosed most of the village lands. By early 1911, two relatively developed rural lower-class uprisings emerged from the wider violence. One surfaced in Durango and western Chihuahua. In Chihuahua, military settlement colonists had forged a *ranchero* economy in relative isolation at the urging of the national government. The northerners—unlike their equally overwhelmed coastal and extreme southern counterparts, but like the villagers of the south-central region—still lived in intact, locally ruled communities and enjoyed geographical remoteness. In addition to their own firearms they had access to war materials from the United States. They could sustain a protracted struggle.

Alienation among the northern provincial elites, though, was the key to the beginning of revolution in Coahuila and Sonora. In the late nineteenth century, technological breakthroughs in transportation and communications had strengthened the power of entrepreneurs and government officials in Mexico City to extend their authority and interests to previously

6. The term *ranchero* has many regional meanings. In this essay it will refer to the owner of a holding that was "middle-sized" relative to the local land-tenure regime.

7. *Pequeña burgués* refers to small business operators, such as ranchers and shopkeepers, and to white-collar workers (e.g., intellectuals, schoolteachers, and lawyers).

remote areas. Government functionaries in the provinces now sought career advantages by pleasing the national government, rather than the state
and local elites. The routes and tariffs of the foreign-controlled transportation system served the needs of large American companies in the north
and south and of Spanish land developers like Iñigo Noriega in the center-
south, rather than the commerce of remote regions on the "periphery."

A deep hostility developed between the provincial elites and what they
saw as an alliance of the national regime and foreign entrepreneurs that ran
the political economy from Mexico City. Enmity toward the metropolitan
elites became extremely intense among the *hacendados* and industrialists of
Coahuila and Sonora, who competed with the foreign companies. Beginning in 1906 the displaced provincial elites tried to rally the populace; first
they attempted to oppose bossism in peaceful elections, but when the Díaz
regime denied them that alternative, the once remote northern elites led an
armed insurrection in defense of semiautonomous home rule.[8]

In Coahuila and Sonora important elements of the provincial elites
rebelled, led by Francisco Madero. In Chihuahua and Durango, where the
oligarchy was integrated both nationally to the political regime and inter-
nationally with the economic regime, the elites stood fast with Díaz.
There, rural lower-class leadership, personified by Pascual Orozco, Francisco Villa, and Prisciliano Silva, emerged and rallied large-scale rural
working-class participation. In the south-central region the provincial
elites, despite their alienation, proved too close to the metropolitan regime
both geographically and politically to take the giant step from electoral
resistance to revolutionary violence. Instead, they stood with the government against the still intact and contentious *pueblo* hierarchies that led the
uprisings. The result was a grassroots movement that defined agrarian
revolutionary goals.

The uprising in the south centered on Morelos, where the estate owners
controlled Mexico's most productive sugar haciendas. The owners of
expansive sugar estates competed directly with local landholders, merchants, communal village peasantry, and hacienda field workers. When
massive layoffs began in 1907, the *hacendados* clashed with disgruntled
field-workers in the nation's most densely populated rural area. Despite its

8. For extended analyses of the prerevolutionary crisis in the countryside and the
nation at large, see Hart 1987; Katz 1981.

numbers, the Morelos rural working class controlled only 2 percent of the farmland. In a diverse immigrant and industrial setting, 20 percent of the population still spoke Nahuatl, and some of the village citizenry still claimed pre-Columbian landholding traditions. Like the northerners, some of the Morelos citizenry lived in autonomous communities.

Morelos, the southern portions of the state of Mexico including Chalco and Sultepec, western Puebla, and much of Guerrero had been sites of protracted struggle against outside intruders. *Pueblos* in these areas had rebelled against the conquistadors, the *encomenderos,* and the intrusions of the *hacendados* in the eighteenth and nineteenth centuries. In Morelos the American invasion of the 1840s and the final consolidation of landholding during the early years of the Díaz regime reinforced that experience. In the last third of the nineteenth century these areas were introduced to revolutionary ideology by immigrants, including anarchists, from Mexico City.[9]

In his attempt to build a wide base of support, Madero offered incentives to the peasants that had not been in evidence during his presidential campaign. These incentives imbued the already restless rural working classes with expectations of change. Lower-class revolutionism continued to grow outward from its base in Chihuahua and Durango. Clause 3 of Madero's Plan de San Luis Potosí promised to return peasant lands: "those who acquired them in such an immoral way, or their heirs, will be required to return them to the original owners."[10] Madero stimulated support throughout rural Mexico.

With Madero's promises serving as a catalyst, the successful armed struggles of 1911 encouraged the formation of what became the mass-based agrarian working-class movements of the revolution. The crisis between the elites of the metropolis and the periphery paralyzed the state's repressive apparatus, providing the opportunity for the rural masses to act on a national rather than a local basis. The revolution of the rural lower classes produced most of the violence of the next ten years.

The rural revolutionaries in the north coalesced under the leadership of Pascual Orozco and Francisco Villa. The western Chihuahua, Durango, and La Laguna insurgency came from long-restive farmers, agricultural

---

9. For the origins of the *zapatista* revolt, see Womack 1970:9–37. Otilio Montaño, who is credited with drafting the *zapatista* Plan de Ayala, attended school in Ajusco where the anarchist Plotino Rhodakanaty served as a teacher.

10. Quoted in Womack 1969:70.

workers, and miners, whose resistance against the Porfirian latifundia system included the alien intruders. The Americans owned 50 percent of the
land surface in the region, and exercised a degree of power that rivaled the
Spaniards in Morelos.

The rural populace primarily fought for the restoration of landholding,
but water rights and municipal autonomy were also important. By 1910
most of the available water in southwestern Coahuila, Chihuahua, and
Durango had been allocated to commercial operations, threatening the
very maintenance of life in the *pueblos*. By May of 1911 Madero had 5,000
armed supporters in the irrigated Laguna region near Torreón, many of
them displaced agriculturalists who had lost access to the waters of the
Nazas River. Between November 1910 and May 1911 formidable rebel
forces emerged in Durango. The rebels, many of them displaced village
farmers who had been ruined by the Díaz government's massive water
reallocation program, supported the agrarian provisions in the Plan of San
Luis Potosí.

During the spring of 1911 farmers and field-workers in the north, and
their less well armed counterparts along the Gulf coast, in Campeche, the
Isthmus of Tehuantepec, the Pacific coast of Chiapas, and in the south-
central areas attacked and devastated commercial agricultural properties.
These were regions where foreign landholding was especially strong. With
the exception of Morelos, the great majority of the alien landowners were
North Americans. In Durango, Chihuahua, and Morelos structured revolutionary forces formed, based on leadership from the town and *pueblo*
elites, the peasantry, and rural working classes. These insurgents stood
apart from the provincial and local elite-controlled revolutionary structure
originally conceived by Madero and his advisers.

The better-organized revolutionaries in the north won significant victories in Chihuahua, Coahuila, and Durango. Their southern counterparts
had successes in Morelos and Guerrero, while myriad smaller and independent rural working-class groups in Baja California, Campeche, Jalisco,
Puebla, San Luis Potosí, Sonora, Sinaloa, Tabasco, Tamaulipas, Veracruz,
Zacatecas, and the Isthmus of Tehuantepec attacked the landed estates of
Mexicans and foreigners, making commercial transportation risky. Independent groups of rural, lower-class-led revolutionaries began to take the
lead in a growing wave of violence against domestic and foreign-owned
commercial estates. They dynamited and raided many American-owned

mines in the north, burned the big houses and rubber fields in the south and on the coasts, tore down fences, carried away livestock, shot owners and managers. The Mexican *hacendados* fled; when some American colonists did not, the revolutionaries warned them to get out. *Pueblo* citizens and hacienda workers occupied hundreds of hastily abandoned properties.[11]

On 20 May 1911, 4,000 *zapatista campesinos* entered Cuautla, the road and rail hub of eastern Morelos. To the west, federal forces fled Cuernavaca, the state capital, conceding *zapatista* hegemony over the region immediately south of Mexico City. By then, the *zapatistas* constituted a rural populace in arms, led by members of the remnant village society and displaced hacienda workers. The *morlense* hacienda workers and village populations supported the revolution en masse, and the alienation of the plantation workers led to the collectivization of the *ingenios* when the revolution matured.[12]

Locally led *zapatistas* near Puebla and in Veracruz endangered the railroad artery between Mexico City and the port. In the north, Durango, Torreón, and Hermosillo fell, giving the rebels—none of whom were controlled by Madero—power in part of the northwest. The fall of Tehuacán, between Puebla and Veracruz, further threatened Mexico City's Veracruz lifeline. By May, peasant land seizures had taken place in Chihuahua, Durango, Coahuila, Sonora, and throughout the center of the country. The rising tide of lower-class revolution spurred the elite to compromise on their differences in order to end the turmoil. The negotiators in Ciudad Juárez, representatives of the provincial elites and the Díaz regime, reached a rapid accord. On 25 May 1911 Díaz resigned, and Madero became president later that year.

However, in November 1911 the *zapatistas* declared revolution against

---

11. The papers of the Mixed Claims Commission record dozens of assaults by armed revolutionaries against American properties from 1910 until May 1911. For examples, see Agency nos. 216, 289, 943, 1399, 1426, 1524, 1553, 1703, 1733, 1740, 1922, 2343, 2346, 2603, 2606, 5811, and 5820, Entry 125, Record Group 76, Mixed Claims Commission, WNRC. For other assaults against American properties, see the lengthy report on the attack upon and occupation of the Corralitos hacienda in the Corralitos Papers, BLAC, or the duplicates in my possession. See also the Rascon Hacienda Records, Townsend-Stanton Family Papers, HTML, and the Northwestern Railroad Archive, BLAC.

12. In Morelos the term *ingenio* referred to an engine-powered mill, usually for sugar processing, as opposed to the smaller, animal-powered *trapiches*.

Madero for "bloody treason" and for failing to deliver the land back to the *pueblos.* In rejecting Madero as a member of Mexico's landholding elite, Otilio E. Montaño, a rural schoolteacher from Ayala, and the other rural intellectuals that helped write the *zapatistas'* revolutionary Plan de Ayala transcended the usual provincialism of peasant movements seeking national alliances. *Zapatismo* became a part of a wider grassroots peasants' war that embraced two-thirds of the country, from Sonora and Tamaulipas to Chiapas and Campeche.[13]

By mid-1912 a growing wave of rural violence against the Porfirian latifundia system, often nationalistic and sometimes anti-American, swept the country. Independent rebellions and strikes broke out among the agricultural laborers on the estates of the American-owned rubber, timber, and henequen companies in Campeche. Those properties, controlled by New York, Philadelphia, and Chicago banking interests, were part of more than 6,500,000 acres of American-controlled lands in the Yucatán peninsula.[14]

The most serious rural challenge to Madero in the north came from the adherents of Pascual Orozco, whose March 1912 rebellion merged with already widespread violence among the rural population. By then the Indians and *campesinos* of the north could see that there was virtually no program for land redistribution. Madero's plan called for the purchase by the government of "Bienes Nacionales" at a later date, and distributed only to those who demanded their original properties back immediately.

In 1912, independently led rural rebels began dividing up great-estate holdings in Durango, western Chihuahua, and La Laguna, but the *orozquistas* carried matters further. They threatened American settlers and singled out U.S. economic installations for nationalistic attacks across the breadth of northern Mexico. A few even carried out raids north of the river in the Lower Rio Grande Valley of Texas. They attacked American mines as far south as Jalisco, occupied the U.S.-owned 1,400,000-acre Rascon hacienda in San Luis Potosí and the 1,200,000-acre San Antonio de las Rusias hacienda in Tamaulipas, and raided the numerous American rural

13. For a concise statement of *zapatista* goals, see Emiliano Zapata, Yautepec, Morelos, to Woodrow Wilson, Washington, D.C., 23 August 1914, Box 653, Josephus Daniels Papers, LC.

14. For examples of the assaults on the American properties in Campeche and the Yucatán peninsula, see Agency nos. 1391 and 1396, Entry 125, Record Group 76, Mixed Claims Commission, WNRC.

settlements in Tamaulipas, San Luis Potosí, Sinaloa, Sonora, Chihuahua, and elsewhere as far south as the Isthmus of Tehuantepec near Salina Cruz. They repeatedly warned the Americans to "get out."

An emissary from President Taft, sent on board the Army Transport Ship *Buford*, reported on the evacuation of American refugees along the Pacific coast: "Twenty-eight refugees on board the *Buford* at Manzanillo. . . . In Colima . . . there is an anti-American sentiment . . . [even] more serious in its possible consequences. . . . It has been unconsciously engendered by the American investors and lumber companies in that state."[15] In Salina Cruz another 130 desperate American refugees boarded the ship. A total of 364 Americans fled Mexico on the *Buford*, leaving their property and possessions behind.

The *orozquistas* helped engender local nationalistic attacks on American property by their example. Therefore, the U.S. government placed an embargo at the border in order to deny the anti-American rebels arms and ammunition, forcing the *orozquistas* to fight major engagements while severely underarmed and undersupplied. In Sonora, Yaqui and Mayo Indians joined the *orozquista* ranks. In Chihuahua, Coahuila, and Sonora a multiclass front of supporters rallied to the revolt, but the American government embargoed them while *maderista* commanders received U.S. arms. The *maderistas* defeated the *orozquistas*, and safeguarded American company properties.[16]

But the endemic rural violence increased. In the spring and summer of 1912, bands of men and women calling themselves "zapatistas," but actually independent of outside affiliation, surfaced as far north as Sinaloa and Tamaulipas. Led by hacienda workers, tenant farmers, miners, *pueblo* elites, artisans, and *rancheros*, they attacked American-owned mines, mills, and landed properties, including again the Rascon and San Antonio de las Rusias haciendas, as well as the United Sugar Company holdings along the Río Fuerte in Sinaloa. The nationwide *campesino* violence against Americans ruined the U.S. government's confidence in Madero.

15. Claude E. Guyant, Consul on Special Detail, on Board the *Buford*, to Secretary of State, Washington, D.C., 14 June 1912, Department of State Decimal File 312.11/635, NARA.

16. For the *orozquistas* in Sonora, see Aguilar Camín 1977:208–61. The best general treatment of the *orozquista* revolt is M. Meyer 1967. On the protection of American properties, see the U.S. Army Intelligence Reports, U.S. Adjutant General, "Villa's Revolution," Collection no. 2212358, Record Group 92, NARA.

In the south, independently led *campesino* revolutionaries raided Mexican-elite and foreign-owned great estates from coast to coast. The nation experienced so much armed conflict that commerce and industry came to a near standstill. The uprisings and concomitant banditry directed against large landholdings (including the American properties) became so widespread that the army's manpower was too spread out to maintain control. The countryside erupted in a crazy quilt of antagonisms: class-based actions by *pueblo* citizens and rural workers against *hacendados,* nationalists versus foreigners, hacienda workers seizing estate properties. Bands of *campesinos* invaded towns and burned the municipal property records.

The basic political and economic institutions of the Mexican "ancien régime" began to break down. The residents of American colonies and the general managers and employees of the most powerful companies in the United States looked on in shock. They complained to their government and employers while gangs of *campesinos,* operating outside any external authority, invaded dozens of huge, American-owned establishments: the Corralitos hacienda near Casas Grandes; the Rascon hacienda and the Atascador and San Dieguito colonies in San Luis Potosí; the Mengel Company, Laguna Corporation, and Gulf Coast Land and Lumber Company properties in the Yucatán; the San Antonio de la Rusias hacienda and the Blaylock and La Palma colonies in Tamaulipas; the Piedra Blanca hacienda and Tlahualilo Estates in Coahuila; the Buena Fe mine in Jalisco; the Richardson Construction Company, Rockefeller, and Dodge properties in Sonora; the Colima Lumber Company in Colima; the Motzorongo plantation in Veracruz; the Medina colony in Oaxaca; the Zacualapa-Hidalgo Rubber Plantation in Chiapas; the Mormon colonies in Chihuahua and Sonora; the secular colonies in Tamaulipas, San Luis Potosí, Oaxaca, and Chiapas; and the 1,750,000-acre Aldrich-Baruch-Guggenheim-owned Cedros hacienda in Zacatecas. Many of the owners were well connected in the U.S. government. The Americans identified their assailants as former employees, neighboring "squatters" and villagers, and sometimes as local *rancheros* and petty officials.[17]

17. The violent attacks against Mexican-elite and American-owned estates, and against the properties of American colonists, by Mexican revolutionaries grew dramatically in intensity and scope during 1912. These innumerable assaults are recorded in the archives of the Mixed Claims Commission. For examples, see Agency nos. 289, 331, 334, 436, 1315, 1316, 1318, 1341, 1343, 1396, 1399, 1524, 1553, 1568, 1700, 1737, 1740, 1921, 2343, 2346,

Beginning in late 1913 and intensifying during 1914, a *campesino* guerrilla war spread across the region extending from Morelos to the Isthmus of Tehuantepec in the south to Michoacán and Hidalgo in central Mexico. Villages that had participated in what were often ethnic-related uprisings from the late seventeenth to the late nineteenth centuries now united around *zapatismo* and related banners. They frequently regarded the *hacendados* as "españoles," or foreigners. The planters, alarmed by *villista* victories in the north and growing *zapatista* strength in the south, fled to Veracruz—especially after the U.S. government offered them refuge there following the invasion of April 1914.[18]

The *villista* main forces coalesced into the largest fighting force in the revolution, the División del Norte, formed largely from rural workers and artisans in the wake of the *golpe de estado* of Victoriano Huerta. Many of the countless rebel groups in the northern countryside affiliated with the *villista* forces, but most operated independently from outside authority. They obtained arms and supplies through capture, raids on armories, and purchases at the border with monies made by confiscating livestock and seizing crops from Mexican estates and Americans. The higher-ranking *villistas* attempted to maintain good relations with the U.S. government by safeguarding American properties while taking over and administering Mexican holdings, but they could not always control local groups.[19]

During 1914 in Chihuahua, Jalisco, Morelos, San Luis Potosí, Zacatecas, the Isthmus of Tehuantepec, along the Pacific coast from Sonora to Chiapas, and along the Gulf coast from Tamaulipas to Campeche, local nationalistic insurrectionists sacked the commercial estates and American

---

2381, 2450, 2452, 2606, 4486, 5817, and 5820, Entry 125, Record Group 76, Mixed Claims Commission, WNRC. See also the Department of State Decimal Files, especially the 312.11 collection, NARA. For examples, see the report by Guyant, Consul on Special Detail, 14 June 1912, 312.11/635, or the reports numbered 312.115M574/3 and 312.115T541/1, NARA. The latter file treats the armed invasion of the Tlahualilo Estates on the Nazas River by armed rebels calling themselves "Maderistas" (15 February 1912).

18. The Mixed Claims Commission records contain the complaints of more than 3,200 American companies and individuals who experienced losses from violence between 20 November 1910 and 31 May 1920. Other complaints for the period January 1912–February 1913 can be found in myriad company archives and in the Department of State Decimal Files, some of which have been cited above. My book-length study treating these issues is forthcoming.

19. The details of the relationship between American arms dealers and manufacturers and the División del Norte are contained in the Lázaro de la Garza Papers, BLAC.

colonies in intensified assaults. The *campesinos* broadened their attacks to include more than a thousand additional properties, shot dozens of Americans, and warned others to leave the country. The giant American properties in Campeche were again attacked by field hands "who had rebellion in their eyes."[20]

The *zapatista* high command, consistent with the rural working-class revolution, carried out wholesale land redistributions. Venustiano Carranza, the provincial-elite leader of the Constitutionalist movement and a man openly hostile to the *campesino* insurrection, defended the *hacendados*, insisting that they had property rights that could not be violated in order "to give land to those who had no rights." Then, while local rural working-class groups carried out unauthorized land seizures against the Mexican-, American-, and other foreign-owned properties, the *villista* high command began to nationalize the Mexican-owned estates of the north. In September 1914 the *villistas* demanded that Carranza immediately "approve measures for the redistribution of the land." They rejected Carranza as the leader of the revolution because he failed to support their agrarian plan and was unrepresentative of the "people's" will. Villa's actions outraged John Lind, President Wilson's emissary to Mexico and a Carranza supporter, who called Villa a "traitor."[21]

---

20. See Gilly 1971:106–9; Katz 1981:260–62. For examples of the countless land seizures and violent attacks against American-owned commercial estates during this period by lower-class groups outside the authority of the revolutionary elites, see Docket no. 78 and Agency nos. 88, 89, 90, 135, 136, 170, 226, 236, 296, 435, 437, 438, 520, 1344, 1391, 1396, 1428, 1524, 1568, 1572, 1701, 1721, 1726, 1733, 1737, 1740, 1751, 1752, 1804, 1913, 1914, 1920, 1921, 1922, 2336, 2346, 2350, 2381, 2605, 2606, 2607, 2608, 2618, 2691, 2692, 4493, 4978, 5104, 5820, and 5830, Entry 125 and others, Record Group 76, Mixed Claims Commission, WNRC. At this time, the revolutionaries devastated many of the largest American-owned estates in Coahuila, Chihuahua, San Luis Potosí, Campeche, Chiapas, Durango, Sinaloa, Tamaulipas, Oaxaca, and Veracruz. See the Department of State Decimal Files 312.115M5712/2 and 312.1150C3/6, NARA; the Townsend-Stanton Family Papers, HTML; the Kirby Papers, Houston Metropolitan Research Center, Houston; and the Corralitos Papers and Northwestern Railroad Papers, BLAC.

21. For the *villistas'* agrarian reform plans, see Katz, below; Katz 1981:280–87; and Córdova 1973:155–72, 465–70. Silliman, the U.S. chargé to Mexico, despised Villa and jubilantly followed the reports regarding the progress of what he labeled "our boys" (i.e., the Constitutionalist forces) at the critical battle of Celaya, which was the turning point of the revolution. See the report of John Lind to Robert Lansing, Washington, D.C., Folder 2321, Box 70, House Papers, Yale University Library. Lind was later accused of serving as Carranza's attorney.

Carranza depended on the army of the provincial-elite leader Alvaro Obregón Salido in order to defeat the rural, lower-class-led *zapatistas* and *villistas* and the myriad localized rural insurgencies. The Americans supported Carranza. To the benefit of Carranza and Obregón Salido's army, they turned the Veracruz port area into a marshaling yard for an enormous stockpile of modern armaments. That equipment, combined with military training for thousands of raw, working-class recruits (including 7,000 men and women from the urban working class of greater Mexico City), helped forge a new army 20,000 strong.

By 1916 the Constitutionalists were gaining control of the nation. They had defeated the *villista* main forces, and the *zapatistas* had demonstrated their incapacity to sustain a strategic threat. However, from 1909 to 1916 hundreds of independent and often nationalistic *campesino* groups occupied American hacienda, development company, and colony lands in every part of the nation, demanding that the Americans leave. They attacked and seized property from the most powerful businessmen in the United States and from thousands of the 15,000 American "colonists." They killed more than 250 Americans. Insurgents occupied the best lands of the American-owned estates. Overwhelmingly, they acted on their own initiative.

The Constitutionalist government's search for social peace was predicated on the need to placate the demands of the mobilized peasantry. Thus the new government stalled the complaining Mexican and American landholders while legitimizing many of the land occupations with property titles, placating the rebellious local rural working class and isolating the *zapatista* and *villista* main forces. In the short run, this strategy pacified the rural insurgency through a mix of agrarian reform and force. In the long run, the government and its Constitution of 1917 confronted the Americans with a legitimized agrarian nationalism. The great-estate owners were presented with a long-term program of land redistribution. Then the government went much further. It prohibited foreign ownership of properties on the frontiers and coastlines where the Americans were strongest. The *zapatistas* called the new Constitution of 1917 a "farce," but it did address Mexico's political realities, calling for national unity against the foreign intruder, and ultimately it delivered control over all forces to the government.

Because the Constitutionalists defeated the peasant- and worker-led forces, the rural working-class demands for autonomous local control over production and government were not realized. However, during the period 1920–1940 the nation regained ownership over most of its real estate and natural resources from the foreign intruders. The core elements of the American properties were crushed during the revolution and returned to Mexican ownership during the 1930s, when the government carried out intensive agrarian reform and the oil industry and railroads were nationalized. Of the well over 100,000,000 acres that have been seized and redistributed since 1916, most have gone to placate the social group that caused all the disturbance: the rural working class.

The sustained and massive scale of revolutionary violence by the locally led rural working class successfully checked the spread of American-owned commercial estates and American economic hegemony in the Mexican countryside until the end of the twentieth century. In that respect, the Mexican revolutionaries exceeded the nationalist achievements of many of their Third World counterparts.

RUBÉN OSORIO

Villismo: Nationalism and Popular Mobilization in Northern Mexico

The Mexican Revolution, one of the most violent and complex historical processes of the first half of the twentieth century, was a popular social movement that peaked between 1910 and 1920 but never succeeded in becoming a generalized effort by the Mexican people to liberate themselves from their oppressors. The revolution officially began in 1910; however, for reasons I shall give below it is possible to argue that it really began in Chihuahua almost twenty years earlier, with the rebellion in Tomóchic. Moreover, it did not end in 1917, as official history tells us, but in 1920, when Francisco Villa, accompanied only by cowhands and peasants, signed a peace treaty with the Mexican government in Sabinas.[1]

Dissatisfaction with the dictatorship of Porfirio Díaz, already evident throughout Mexico by the late nineteenth century, developed unevenly in various states. There were various plots to topple the Díaz dictatorship, an outstanding example being the one planned by Catarino de la Garza during 1891 in Tamaulipas.[2] Another example is the 1893–94 uprising led by Víctor Ochoa.[3] But it was only in the state of Chihuahua that popular rural movements organized an armed opposition to the Porfirian regime and went into action during the last decade of the nineteenth century.

In the wake of the celebrated and tragic rebellion of Tomóchic in 1891–92, for instance, there was an armed uprising in Cruces, Municipio de

1. The remarks of General Felipe Angeles on the occasion of his being sentenced to death in 1919 are pertinent in this regard: "I recall that once when we arrived in a village, Villa said, 'General Angeles, well now you see that only the cowhands (*vaqueritos*) are still with us; so we'll have a government of just cowhands.' I replied, 'That would be good, a government like that would be just divine.'" In a copy of the written transcript of the Consejo de Guerra "El proceso del gral. Felipe Angeles," p. 15, ARO.

2. For the complete text of his "Plan Revolucionario," see file on Catarino de la Garza in AHSRE, exp. 11-10-44.

3. For the Ochoa uprising, see Almada 1968:446.

Namiquipa, Chihuahua, on 1 April 1893 led by Simón Amaya and Celso Anaya, who "wished to depose the Supreme Power of the Nation."[4] The bloody rebellions of Tomóchic and Cruces in 1891 and 1893 were savagely crushed by the Díaz government, leaving a trail of death and destruction affecting hundreds of households in the state. The abuses, the brutal repressions, and the murders carried out by the Mexican army, especially in the Guerrero district,[5] left a painful imprint in the collective memory of the people, and resistance to those actions provided a clear precedent for popular struggle.[6]

An interesting and important example was the "Plan Restaurador y Reformista de la Constitución," drafted in the home of Teresa Urrea (the "Santa de Cabora," then living in exile in the United States), circulating in southern Arizona in 1896, and similar to the earlier plan of Víctor Ochoa. This was an explicit plan to overthrow Díaz and was followed by armed incidents in Chihuahua that gained international attention.[7] Bearing the signatures of seven women and sixteen men, the "Plan Restaurador" was designated (symbolically, one may presume) as emanating from "Tomóchic, Chihuahua." This plan of the *teresistas* (followers of Teresita, La Santa de Cabora) consisted of eighteen points, some of which address social problems in Mexico in a much more advanced way than even the early plans of the PLM (Partido Liberal Mexicano, or *magonistas*) at the start of this century.[8]

4. For the rebellion of Tomóchic, see Almada 1938; Chavez C. 1964; Osorio n.d.; for the Cruces uprising, see Almada 1938:117.

5. See the correspondence from Julio Irigoyen to José Vicente Salinas (archbishop of Durango), Temósachic, Chihuahua, 12 and 16 May 1893, ACD, 1893 file of letters. In his letters, Irigoyen, the priest of Temósachic, paints a vivid picture of the army's savage repression in Chihuahua. Irigoyen's description of the massacre at Santo Tomás (which marked the end of the Cruces uprising) suggests that it surpassed in brutality what happened in Tomóchic, and includes the remark that the towns were devastated since "the Federal troops shot whomever they felt like shooting."

6. A detailed description of the social, political, economic, religious, health, and military problems in the Sierra Madre during the last quarter of the nineteenth century is provided in Osorio n.d.

7. See communication from the Graham County, Arizona, prosecutor W. Jones to Chihuahua governor Miguel Ahumada, informing the latter of the proposed revolution to overthrow the Díaz regime, sent from Solomonville, Arizona, 26 February 1896. AHSRE, exp. L-E 7301.

8. The complete text of the "Plan Restaurador" is in one of the files on "Lauro Aguirre y Manuel Flores Chapa, Movimiento Revolucionario," AHSRE, exp. L-E 7301.

From these initial rumblings of rebellion in the Sierra Madre Occidental there emerged a highly regarded popular leader, Santana Pérez. A brave and renowned Apache-fighter since his youth, Pérez preceded Francisco Villa by fifteen years as an expert in guerrilla warfare. Issuing a manifesto in 1894 in which he accused Porfirio Díaz of murder and extortion and of selling the country to foreigners, Pérez left no doubt about the peasant origins of his movement and its determination to topple the Díaz regime. Further, accompanied by a small group of *serranos* from Chihuahua, he set out to harass the Mexican army in the sierra of Chihuahua; since he knew the region like the back of his hand, the task was an easy one. On one occasion he humiliated the army by defeating them with the Apache stratagem of stoning the enemy. The people of the Guerrero district still celebrate this memorable event in a short poem:

Ese don Santana Pérez	That Santana Pérez,
Lleva dos guerras ganadas.	Already two wars has he won.
Una la ganó a balazos	One victory he achieved shooting bullets,
Y otra la ganó a pedradas	And the other he won throwing stones.[9]

The people of Chihuahua, crippled by the army's assaults of the 1880s and 1890s, were waiting for a chance to even the score. The Madero movement in 1910 provided them with just such an opportunity.

In short, *maderismo,* particularly in western Chihuahua, did not appear in a vacuum, but rather secured a following among an already resentful population looking to avenge itself against the state. This fact, which some historians of the revolution have tended to underestimate, explains the powerful popular mobilization in Chihuahua, first in 1910 with Madero and later in 1913 under Villa. The mantle of leadership of this mobilization had passed from Cruz and Manuel Chávez, Celso Anaya, and Simón Amaya—killed by the army in the 1890s—to Pascual Orozco, Francisco Villa, Toribio Ortega, Trinidad Rodríguez, and others who applied to the federal army the biblical law "An eye for an eye, a tooth for a tooth." That a

9. Santana Pérez took away the soldiers' documents, arms, ammunition, and clothing, sending them back to their barracks practically naked. In 1910 Pérez declined an invitation to join the Madero movement [he had been arrested in 1908 in Casas Grandes, Chihuahua, along with some other members of the PLM who planned an armed uprising in that year—ED.] because of his advanced age. He died in December of the same year in Yepómera, Chihuahua (Candelario Pérez, interview held at Ejido Pancho Villa, Chihuahua, 20 July 1979, CHOCH).

revolutionary movement of such extreme violence unleashed itself in Chihuahua in response to the army's repressive measures in the decades preceding the revolution is not at all surprising.

The causes of the Madero movement are well known; it drew its strength from "the discontent produced by social and economic inequalities, exacerbated by the middle class's hatred of a dictatorship that restricted liberty and upward political, social, and economic mobility, and this class's opposition to the increasing influence of foreigners in all aspects of Mexican life" (Katz 1979a:28). During the *maderista* period of the revolution—which ended with Huerta's counterrevolution and the assassination of Madero in February 1913—Villa stands out as a northern military leader of great talent. But he is still of secondary importance; properly speaking, *villismo* did not yet exist. The general consensus is that during the *maderista* period—and for years after—Villa remained unwaveringly loyal to Madero. I do not totally agree with that judgment, for reasons that emerge in a verbal exchange between Generals Felipe Angeles and Villa in 1919 in the desert of Chihuahua. The conversation throws new light on the ideology of each participant.[10]

One evening while arguing about some aspect of the revolution, Villa called Madero a "fool" for having signed the peace treaty at Ciudad Juárez in 1911 and for not having executed Felipe Díaz in Veracruz. Raising his voice, Angeles responded: "Don't call Madero a fool for those reasons. In Juárez he acted as a patriot and in Veracruz he respected individual rights." "Yes, General," Villa responded bitterly, "and look at what happened to him and what is happening to all of us." Villa went on:

Listen, General, I'm going to tell you the prophesy I made to "Maderito"[11] during the banquet that took place in the customshouse in Ciudad Juárez in 1911 at the moment of the revolution's triumph; I attended because he asked me to, but already I felt a deadly hatred for all those elegant dandies (*perfumados*). They had started in with the "espiches" [Spanglish in original], and that bunch of politicians

10. A description of this exchange may be found in Jaurrieta n.d.:235–37. For the text of Angeles' reference to Villa's characterization of Madero quoted in the next paragraph, see "El proceso de gral. Felipe Angeles," p. 15.

11. Villa often used the diminutive suffix "ito" to express special affection for close friends, for example in Trillito, Pinoncito, or as above in *vaqueritos*. But using it here to refer to Francisco Madero is clearly meant to be derogatory.

talked endlessly. Then Madero said to me, "And you, Pancho, what do you think? The war is over; aren't you happy? Give us a few words." I didn't want to say anything, but Gustavo Madero, who was sitting at my side, nudged me, saying, "Go ahead, chief, say something." So I stood up and said to [Francisco] Madero, "You, sir, have destroyed the revolution." He demanded to know why, so I answered, "It's simple: this bunch of dandies has made a fool of you, and this will eventually cost us our necks, yours included." Madero kept on questioning me. "Fine, Pancho, but tell me, what do you think should be done?" I answered, "Allow me to hang this roomful of politicians and then let the revolution continue." Well, seeing the astonishment on the faces of those elegant followers, Madero replied, "You are a barbarian, Pancho, sit down, sit down."

Witnessing this exchange between Villa and Angeles was José María Jaurrieta, Villa's secretary and aide-de-camp. Jaurrieta commented that it was General Angeles (seated by the fire listening to Villa) who had the surprised look one would have expected to see on Madero's face. On this point there would be no meeting of the minds: Angeles was peaceable and conciliatory; Villa, pitiless and aggressive.

Any consideration of nationalism and popular mobilization during the *villista* period requires a preliminary understanding or definition of *villismo* itself. What was it and what did it represent? Richard Estrada has defined the movement with great clarity:

In February 1913 the revolution was dealt a severe blow by the counterrevolution in Mexico City. Among the conservative contenders for power was General Huerta who, fearing that the deposed Madero would regain power, ordered or at least acquiesced to his assassination. This violence against the *maderista* leadership soon reached Chihuahua where Abrahám González, the *maderista* governor, was assassinated on March 7th. These violent events unleashed an equally profound popular reaction that was strongest in the North. At the beginning of March the governor of Coahuila, Venustiano Carranza, assembled the funding and following to initiate his military movement. In Sonora, Alvaro Obregón was named head of military operations. And in Chihuahua at approximately the very hour that Abrahám González was assassinated, Francisco Villa reentered the ranks of the revolution. While there is no denying that the revolution in the North had very complex social, political and economic causes and that Villa's influence was not singularly responsible for the movement that broke loose during the Spring of 1913, it is equally evident that in Chihuahua, especially along the border region near El Paso and Ciudad Juárez, Francisco Villa was certainly the magnetic force that attracted thousands of revolutionaries who were fiercely loyal to his cause. (Estrada 1975:112–13)

In order to deal with nationalism, popular mobilization, and *villismo,* I will divide Villa's military career into three well-defined periods. The first, Villa's Constitutionalist period, began when Villa crossed the U.S.-Mexico border with eight men in March 1913 to initiate, in alliance with Carranza, the ultimately successful struggle against Huerta. The second period commences in mid-1914, after Huerta's fall, when Villa as commanding general of the army of the Convention of Aguascalientes undertook the defeat of Carranza; this is the so-called Conventionist period of *villismo.* Last is the guerrilla period, which began with the dissolution of the Conventionist army in Chihuahua in December 1915 and continued until the signing of the peace treaty with the government of Adolfo de la Huerta at Sabinas, Coahuila.

Before we turn to the themes of popular ideology and U.S. intervention in rural revolt in Mexico, a note about Villa's contradictory nature is in order. Sixty-five years after his death, Villa continues to be the most controversial figure of the Mexican Revolution. Above all in the state of Chihuahua, the mere mention of his name still incites stormy arguments. Although there is no universal agreement about other leaders such as Zapata, Obregón, or Carranza, they can be discussed calmly; no such calm prevails in regard to Villa, despite his recognition as a national hero by both the Mexican national government and the Chihuahua state government.[12] The controversy in Mexico about Villa's character reached its zenith in a recent television program provocatively entitled "Villa: Hero or Bandit?" The intense gut reaction that Villa's name elicits extends beyond the Mexican border as well; when former President José López Portillo donated an equestrian statue of Villa to a city in the southwestern United States, the

12. In 1967 Francisco Villa's name was inscribed in gold letters in the Chamber of Deputies in Mexico City, and on November 20 of the same year an equestrian statue of Villa was placed at the intersection of Universidad and División del Norte in Mexico City. Nine years later to the day, Villa's remains [minus his head—ED.] were transferred from Ciudad Chihuahua to the Monument of the Revolution in Mexico City. His name appears on the walls of the State Congress in Ciudad Chihuahua, and his statue adorns the principal thoroughfare of that city.

gesture set loose a local torrent of protest. Similarly heated disputes erupt sporadically in academic circles in the United States and Mexico.[13]

Some of the questions regarding the extraordinarily complex nature of Villa, his ideology, and the ideology of his movement are discussed in Friedrich Katz's prologue to *Pancho Villa, ese desconocido* (Osorio 1990), in which Katz, an expert on Pancho Villa, proffers the following questions:

—Did Villa have a revolutionary ideology, or was he simply an outlaw who fought for wealth and personal power?

—Was his behavior rational, or did he kill indiscriminately?

—Was he merely an opportunist, who did the bidding of the United States between 1913 and 1915 without regard for Mexico's sovereignty? And when he took up arms and invaded the United States in 1916, was he motivated, not by interest in Mexican independence and sovereignty, but rather by a sense of abandonment over U.S. recognition of Carranza as head of the Mexican government in lieu of Villa?

—While in power in Mexico, did he institute social reforms, or did he become just another *caudillo,* indistinguishable from the local and regional bosses that dominated Mexico and the better part of Latin America throughout the nineteenth century?

—Was his opposition to Carranza—which plunged Mexico into a bloody and devastating civil war—driven by ideological differences?

—Who supported him during the early years when he fought against Huerta? And later, when his power was at its peak? Who supported him in the final years, in his guerrilla warfare against Carranza's Constitutionalist state?

—Why did he continue this bloody guerrilla struggle when he could easily have left Mexico at the end of 1915, taking with him most of the money belonging to the División del Norte? (Osorio 1990:xi)[14]

Of the innumerable questions that we could add to this list, two relate directly to the topics addressed in the present volume: (1) Precisely when

13. For an example from the United States, see Katz 1979a, and the subsequent exchange of letters between Katz and James Sandos in the *American Historical Review* 84, no. 1 (February 1979): 304–7.

14. Villa controlled significant sums of money while head of the División del Norte. Cotton exports through El Paso were valued at $2,152,373 in 1914 and $2,733,392 in 1915. Sales of Chihuahuan cattle brought in $2,455,106 in 1914 and $2,353,942 in 1915. During fiscal year 1914–15, imports through El Paso of supplies, arms, and ammunition may have reached $3,000,000 (see Estrada 1975:120–24).

and for what reasons did President Wilson turn his back on Villa? In October 1915, when he officially recognized Carranza, or earlier, when U.S. troops withdrew from Veracruz? (2) When U.S. troops departed Mexico in 1914, did they leave arms and ammunition behind in Veracruz with which Carranza could continue the battle against Villa?

Answering these questions may help us address the issues of ideology and intervention. But they can be answered only in light of an account of the social groups or forces that constituted *villismo* in March 1913. In other words, was *villismo* a truly popular movement in Chihuahua?[15] According to the information at hand, the answer to this final question is that between 1913 and 1915 *villismo* was a coalition of three different forces and had arisen from widespread popular mobilization. Included in its ranks were members of a distinctive frontier peasantry, a working class involved primarily in extractive and transport industries and, finally, a regional bour-

15. In seeking to answer these questions, I have made use of many little-known or heretofore unknown sources. They include the following. First of all, there is the correspondence of Villa from 1911 to 1923, including letters and telegrams to and from major revolutionary leaders such as Madero, Zapata, Carranza, and Obregón, and other important actors such as González, Calles, and de la Huerta. In 1986 I published a selection of 103 letters and telegrams from this correspondence. Second, I have examined four manifestos signed by Villa in Chihuahua, Sonora, and Durango between September 1914 and August 1920. The complete texts of Villa's first three manifestos (September 1914, Cd. Chihuahua, Chihuahua; 5 November 1915, Naco, Sonora; October 1916, San Andrés, Chihuahua) are reproduced in Delgado 1975:144–82. A photocopy of the complete text of Villa's "Manifesto a la Nación" issued in Tlahualilo, Durango, 3 August 1920, is in the ARO. Third, we have the unpublished memoirs of José María Jaurrieta, Villa's personal secretary during the guerrilla phrase against Carranza (Jaurrieta n.d.). Fourth, I have benefited from the recollections of Francisco Piñón, Villa's adopted son and one of his closest collaborators in Canutillo from 1920 to 1923. These represent the most extensive entry in the CHOCH, for I have had the opportunity to interview Piñón at length many times between 1976 and 1979. He provided a firsthand account of his experiences with Villa during the revolution, conversations they had at Canutillo, and his life on the hacienda until Villa's assassination in July 1923. Fifth, an interview given by Villa to the U.S. press was published in the *El Paso Morning Times* on 9 October 1915. And finally, there is a collection of tape recordings and interview notes, compiled during several years of fieldwork in various parts of Chihuahua, that constitute an oral history of the state. This source (CHOCH) includes declarations from a variety of people, belonging to different social and ideological groups, who lived in Chihuahua State during the revolution. The majority knew Villa personally; some were his supporters, others fought against him, and some did both. Their statements shed much light on the extraordinarily complex nature of Villa and of the movement he headed. Some of the CHOCH interviews appear in Osorio 1990.

geoisie drawn from Chihuahua's cities and countryside. As one Chihua-huan remembered, "Well, my grandfather and four of my uncles were all *villistas*. Thing is, at the time, who wasn't?"[16]

How was it possible to achieve such a coalition of social forces in this state? At the outset, the uprising or rebel movement in Chihuahua was very different from those in other parts of Mexico. For example, there is a marked contrast between events in Morelos and in Chihuahua, and this contrast relates to the respective types of social differentiation present in each state prior to the revolution. In Morelos, the revolution was a move-ment of the peasantry and had relatively little contact with other social classes. In Chihuahua the various social classes that united against the Díaz regime in 1910 had existed as identifiable social entities since the nineteenth century, and each had experienced its own formation in op-position to the state.

The first of these were Chihuahua's peasants, whose demographic insig-nificance was counterbalanced by the social and political significance they assumed by occupying and working land throughout the state. Chihua-hua's peasants were well organized, much more so than their counterparts in southern Mexico. This peasant class had come into being under very special conditions during the colonial period, as settler-soldiers, or literally as an armed peasantry living in presidios constructed by the Spanish gov-ernment as protection against the "barbarous Indians."[17] The construction of railroads to connect Chihuahua with the southwestern United States and the interior of Mexico precipitated a social disequilibrium within the peasantry. In combination, railroad construction and capitalist develop-ment engendered an export-oriented economy, provoked a sudden in-

16. Maurilio Chávez, resident of Ejido Francisco I. Madero, Municipio Bachiniva, Chihuahua interview on 28 January 1987, CHOCH. Approximately 95 percent of the people with whom I have spoken at the Seguro Social hospital in Ciudad Chihuahua say their relatives were *villistas*.

17. There is a persisting oral tradition relating to the Apache Wars in *pueblos* such as Ascención, Janos, Casas Grandes, San Lorenzo, Namiquipa, San Andrés, Santa Isabel, Satevó, Pilar de Conchos, Ciudad Guerrero, and all the villages of the Papigochic Basin. Yepómera, for example, was totally destroyed in 1852 and all its inhabitants killed, leaving the town completely uninhabited for twenty years. The people of Chihuahua remember the Apache Wars as savage battles in which prisoners were never taken. Women were kidnapped, as were children, by both sides, and all the men, white or Indian, were scalped or burnt alive. For two centuries the whites and the Apaches were equally ferocious in the conduct of these wars.

crease in property values all along the border and the railroad lines, and led to underhanded dealings such as those of Limantour in the Guerrero district to expropriate land from the Chihuahuan peasantry and *indígenas*.[18]

The second group within Chihuahua's coalition was the north's more highly developed, better-organized, and pugnacious working class; these characteristics antedate the *magonista* (PLM) movement, which arose in the border area and affected the U.S. mining companies in both Mexico and the United States at the start of the twentieth century. The special nature of Chihuahua's working class first manifested itself during a workers' protest against the Pinos Altos Bullion Company, an English mining company in the Sierra Madre, in 1883, three years prior to the Haymarket police riot in Chicago. After a work action at Pinos Altos, during which the company manager John Buchanan Hepburn died, the first five martyrs of the workers' struggle in Mexico were shot down, events that have been systematically overlooked by Mexican historians.[19]

The third component was an urban and rural middle class that demanded greater participation in the exercise of political power in a state then controlled by the Terrazas-Creel clan. Heading this political opposition group were Silvestre Terrazas, who persistently attacked his relative Luis Terrazas in the pages of the newspaper *El Correo de Chihuahua* from 1906 onward, and Abrahám González, member of a once-influential upper-middle-class family from Ciudad Guerrero which had shared control of the state during the nineteenth century but subsequently lost it to the Terrazases.

Two remaining factors, political and economic, help explain the polarization of the local opposition against the state. The first relates to the Terrazas-Creel clan's total control of political power in the state, a gift to the clan from *gran cacique* Don Porfirio at the beginning of the twentieth century. In combination with the family's already vast economic power in Chihuahua, their political control made the Terrazas-Creels the most influential family in the country and sole masters of state. This total con-

18. "Convenio ortorgado entre el Sr. Ingeniero Don Manuel Fernández Leal y el Sr. Licenciado José Ives Limantour por sí y como representante de su hermano Don Julio M. Limantour," Escritura no. 46, 25 February 1919, AGN DTN.

19. The workers executed in Pinos Altos on 21 January 1883 (by order of the Consejo de Guerra headed by Carlos Conant, *presidente municipal* of Ocampo and member of the Sonoran bourgeoisie) were Cruz Baca, Francisco Campos, Ramón Mena, Juan Valenzuela, and Blas Venegas.

centration of power united disparate social forces in opposition.[20] The second factor is the economic crisis of 1907, during which a large number of now unemployed workers returned to Mexico from the United States following the collapse of numerous businesses and companies, especially in the mining sector. This crisis coincided with a decrease in agricultural production, poor harvests, inflation, and a shortage of basic foodstuffs [see Lloyd 1983—ED.].

After the revolution finally broke out in 1910, its trajectory in Chihuahua was totally different from the trajectories followed in Sonora and Coahuila, where large landowners assumed important leadership positions. In Chihuahua no *hacendados* figured prominently during the revolution except as enemies of the insurgents. But neither was Chihuahuan leadership strongly peasant-based, as could be argued for Morelos. Rebel troops in Chihuahua formed a coalition of three different social classes. Although their first leaders—Orozco and González—were middle class, both disappeared from the revolutionary scene in the north after Madero became president of the Republic. Orozco first sold out to the Chihuahuan oligarchy to direct the counterrevolution, later joined Huerta after the coup d'état in 1913, and was finally assassinated by Texas Rangers near El Paso. González was pitilessly murdered in early March 1913, immediately after Madero met the same fate in Mexico City.

The absence of *hacendados* from Chihuahua's leadership and the removal of Orozco and González from the stage left a military and political vacuum that was filled by commanders such as Villa, Calixto Contreras, and other men of humble origin. In March 1913, when *villismo* was born, the middle class was much weaker than it had been previously, and less influential than its counterparts in Sonora and Coahuila. In this profoundly revolutionary state, the preeminence of popular leadership in Chihuahua's revolutionary movement served to distinguish *villismo* from mobilizations elsewhere in northern Mexico.

Questions remain: Was nationalism an important element of *villismo?* Were Villa and the *villistas* patriots, or just a horde of bandits oppor-

20. "First Luis Terrazas, later his son-in-law Enrique Creel, and later still [Luis' son] Alberto Terrazas were governors of Chihuahua, and they behaved as though they were managing a family business" (Friedrich Katz, in Katz et al. 1977:ix–xii). For a detailed study of the enormous wealth controlled by the Terrazas-Creel clan in Chihuahua, see Wasserman 1984.

tunistically taking advantage of the confusion and violence to secure wealth for themselves? What did intervention mean to them, and whom did they identify as interventionists? In addressing these questions I will restrict my comments to an interpretation based on the substance of Villa's four manifestos (see note 12 above).

The "Manifiesto al pueblo mexicano"

Issued in Chihuahua in September 1914, this first manifesto is a compilation of grievances expressed by Villa and the leaders of the División del Norte regarding the corrupt manner through which Carranza guaranteed his own power in the revolutionary movement. The manifesto concludes with Villa encouraging the Mexican people to disavow the self-proclaimed "First Chief" (Carranza) in order that the revolution might realize its ideals. Should they fail to take action, he warns, "all the revolutionary work [so far accomplished] will collapse, and we will have destroyed one dictatorship only to replace it with another."

"To My Compatriots, to the People, and to the Government of the United States"

Signed by Villa in Naco, Sonora, on 5 November 1915, the second document was written after Villa and his troops suffered a brutal defeat at the hands of *carrancista* soldiers outside Agua Prieta, Sonora, thanks to *carrancista* reinforcements from the U.S. side of the border sent with the complicity and approval of the Wilson administration. Villa's bitterness in the face of this unexpected and devastating defeat is clearly evident in a letter to Zapata in which Villa fulminated against Carranza, "who rules the destiny of people in much of the Republic with the illegal support of foreign powers," thanks to "betrayal and intrigue, evil and envy, his contemptible baseness, the hypocrisy of the technocrats, and Wilson's Machiavellian maneuvers."[21] As if that were not enough, Villa unambiguously accused Carranza of betraying Mexico and handing the country to the *yanquis*.

21. This letter of 8 January 1916 from Villa to Zapata, written in San Gerónimo, Chihuahua, appears in Osorio 1986.

In the Naco statement, after attacking his domestic enemy, Villa turned to his foreign enemy, U.S. imperialism:

The *yanquis* have permitted *carrancista* troops to pass through their territory, in a favor bestowed upon our country's new Santa Anna. And will Mexicans stand by passively and accept this? Could foreigners, especially the *yanquis,* maintain the illusion that in the future they shall effortlessly exploit Mexico's natural resources "in peace and by the Grace of God"? [As for President Wilson, Villa declares,] we had never presumed that this evangelical president was a corruptible bourgeois poseur (*tartufo*), that he would destroy the notion of fundamental human rights and try to impose a government of his will on an independent country jealous of its sovereignty, thus further enflaming the civil war in Mexico under the hypocritical pretext of pacifying the country.

Finally, Villa clearly identified the agents of intervention and defined his position vis-à-vis the people of the United States:

I hold no animosity toward the North American people in general, whom I respect and admire for their marvelous traditions, their steadfastness and frugality, and their determination to progress. The people of the United States are not one with the illicit traffickers and adventurers who violate the rights of other people and carry piracy into the sphere of diplomacy. . . . I decline all responsibility for what may happen [between our two peoples] in the future. . . . History shall define those responsibilities. . . . The generations that succeed us will judge the actions of a man [i.e., Wilson] who, under the pretext of a love for humanity, vents his rage against the actions of a weak but valiant and noble people.

The "Manifiesto a la Nación" of October 1916

Signed by Villa in San Andrés, Chihuahua in October 1916, after the Columbus raid and while the U.S. Army occupied parts of the state, the third manifesto is probably the most patriotic of all Villa's pronouncements. Its nationalistic and openly anti-imperialist tone may explain why it is also one of his least-known statements. Drafted by Villa himself without the coaching of any of the revolution's intellectual supporters—at the time none were at his side, only peasants, *rancheros,* and workers from the Chihuahuan countryside—it comprises sixteen basic points of the revolutionary plan. The most salient of those points are these:

I. The revolutionary government will convene popular, free elections for president of the Republic, and "any who attempt to tamper with election results will be condemned to death."

III. Elections will also be held for congressional deputies, who will be charged with the most difficult tasks of governance, "as well as with [responsibility for] controlling any presidential excesses.

IV. The deputies and senators "should be honorable men who concern themselves with the well-being of those they represent and should not be involved in activities beyond their designated duties, such as securing concessions for themselves which prejudice the interests of the masses; should they fail in this respect, their penalty will be death by execution."

VIII. To achieve its goals, the revolution requires both foreign and domestic resources; however, "NO DEBTS WILL BE HONORED," even those owed to foreigners.

IX. With the exception of those who have been naturalized citizens for a minimum of twenty-five years, no foreigner will be allowed to purchase property in Mexico. To cover the costs of war, "all foreign investments and property will be confiscated and ownership will revert to the nation."

X. Neither North Americans—"who are in great measure responsible for our national disaster—nor the Chinese will be allowed to purchase real estate in Mexico under any circumstances."

XI, XII. The Mexican government will nationalize railroads and mining interests.

XIII. To encourage industrial development in the country and improve the quality of nationally produced goods, "all types of commercial transactions with the United States will be suspended and telegraph and railroad service will not operate within eighteen leagues of the border."

The third manifesto concludes with a battle cry that clearly reflects Villa's nationalist spirit: "To war against the traitors—MEXICO FOR THE MEXICANS!"

The "Manifiesto a la Nación" of 31 August 1920

Signed by Villa in Tlahualilo, Durango, the fourth document gives us a clear idea of Villa's notion of nationalism: "Therefore we lay down our arms and declare before the nation and the world that from this day forward the soldiers, officers, and leaders of the Army of National Reconstruction will return to private life and promise never to bear arms again, save in the event of a foreign intervention."

There is a great temptation to conclude this essay with a synthetic statement regarding nationalism and popular mobilization as it developed within the Villa movement between 1913 and 1920. Instead I will quote from what is certainly the most important interview Villa gave to the North American press. These words, spoken shortly before his Sonora campaign, provide an excellent description of how the original *villista* viewed these issues:

I am here in Juárez, but I shall never go further north. Mexico is my country and I shall never leave her. Here I have lived and here I have fought; the cause for which I have fought will live on. They may kill me in the battlefield or assassinate me in the mountains or as I sleep, but the cause for which I fought for twenty-two years will endure because it is the cause of liberty and justice, so long denied us and so much hoped for by my long-suffering countrymen. I want nothing for myself; what matters to me are the fifteen million Mexicans who have been enslaved, living in the most abject poverty, oppressed and buffeted by their old and wealthy exploiters.

When the reporter asked Villa to comment on the U.S. government's recognition of Carranza, Villa said:

In his speech at Indianapolis, President Wilson guaranteed that while he was in the White House, the United States would not use force to intervene in Mexico. Well, there are many types of force, my friend, and many types of intervention. The United States can intervene with men or with money, with arms or with gold. The means differ but the outcome is the same. The cause of liberty can die just as easily under the big guns of Washington, London, or Berlin, as from an artillery based in Mexico City.[22]

22. *El Paso Morning Times*, 9 October 1915, p. 1.

II *Class, Ethnicity, and Space in*

Mexican Rural Revolts

JANE-DALE LLOYD

Rancheros and Rebellion: The Case of Northwestern Chihuahua, 1905–1909

This essay analyzes the sociopolitical consequences of the 1905 law for the surveying, expropriation, and sale of municipal land in Chihuahua decreed by Governor Enrique Creel.[1] Here, particular attention is paid to what happened in the Galeana district in northwestern Chihuahua, which comprises the municipalities of San Buenaventura, Galeana, Casas Grandes, Janos, and Ascensión. Bounded by the Sierra Madre Occidental, the U.S.-Mexico border, the Río Bravo, and the desert plains of northwestern Chihuahua, the area already displayed a precarious balance between land and population prior to 1905. The implementation of the new law brought social polarization in the towns to an explosive point and was a determining factor in the process of social mobilization in this region from 1905 to 1913.

Considering the effects of this law on the popular classes, we find a direct correlation between the implementation of the law and the rise of *magonismo* (an anarchist movement founded by Ricardo and Enrique Flores Magón) in the region. Individuals and social classes in Casas Grandes, Janos, Ascensión, and elsewhere who were most directly affected by the law through dispossession were precisely those who became members of the armed groups that began forming in 1905. Almost without exception, the local leaders involved in contesting and refuting the law were those who later led the local and regional revolutionary movement.

The years from 1905 to 1909, then, mark a qualitative change in the level of dissension in the towns, from latent resistance to open antagonism toward the state and toward foreign landlords. Opposition political parties were formed, and the radical wing of the Partido Liberal Mexicano (i.e., the *magonistas*) organized several armed uprisings against the Porfirian regime.

On the other hand, for the dominant classes in the region, the law

1. "Ley sobre medida y enajenación de Terrenos Municipales," POCH, no. 9, 4 March 1905, pp. 7–12.

represented the legal culmination of the modernization movement. Since first gaining power in 1866, the Chihuahuan oligarchy had fought for capitalist modernization along the lines of the liberal model for development being implemented throughout Mexico as a whole. The intention of the Municipal Land Law was to place in private hands the collectively held municipal and town property that remained despite the successive disentailments of the peasantry carried out under liberal governments. This late-Porfirian phenomenon, documented here for Chihuahua, may have been more generalized throughout Mexico than was previously thought. Recent regional studies, such as those of Horacio Crespo and Salvador Rueda on the state of Morelos, suggest that Chihuahua's 1905 Municipal Land Law was not atypical, but rather *symptomatic* of agrarian legislation during the latter years of the Díaz regime. It is not coincidental that this type of legislation was promulgated in precisely those states such as Morelos and Chihuahua which were considered models of the modernization process fostered by the Díaz government, states in which capitalism was most prevalent and most deeply rooted. Nor should it be surprising that Chihuahua and Morelos became important bases for the revolutionary movements that swept the country from 1910 to 1920.

The 1905 law spotlighted the power relations and alliances among rich merchants, Mormons, local and regional authorities, and the regional oligarchy in the Galeana district, and the law's implementation served as a catalyst for regional discontent. The popular reaction to the law is evidence for the increasing social polarization in the *pueblos*. This new consciousness of socioeconomic differences promoted popular awareness of the privileged role assumed by local elites in their political and economic domination of the region; thus, the social struggle in the region from 1905 to 1913 was one between poor and rich, between original settlers who fought for their territorial and social rights and newcomers who tried to usurp them.

Terminology

The terms *medieros* and *rancheros* will be used throughout this essay to define two distinct social groups that existed during the last years of the *porfiriato* in northwestern Chihuahua. *Rancheros* are rural farmers controlling both crops and livestock, small-scale landowners who engage in agricultural production for local, national, and even international markets. Although they adopt technological innovations whenever possible, they work and administer their own property primarily to increase family resources rather than to accumulate capital as such. And while *rancheros* rarely hire outside labor, they frequently recruit from among their poorer relatives. The *ranchero,* in other words, maximizes his productive capacity by maximizing human resources through such culturally accepted mechanisms as exercising parental authority and mobilizing close and binding ties established by religious customs such as baptisms, weddings, first communions, and *compadrazgo. Rancheros* are frequently carpenters or blacksmiths as well, as were their fathers and grandfathers before them; but they practice these trades only when they do not interfere with agricultural work. *Rancheros* can read, write, and do basic arithmetic. Culturally and socially the *ranchero* is immersed in a range of direct, face-to-face relationships with his extended family and the community, participating actively in the ceremonial life of his immediate neighbors and the community.

As used here, the term *mediero* describes a more impoverished rural farmer who works to provide for family consumption. He participates in the regional and local market on a small scale and owns his own farm implements. He may own a small plot of land; more likely, the *mediero* enjoys access or usufruct to land through relations of kinship or *compadrazgo.* In addition to cultivating land, he may or may not be involved in wage labor such as cowhand, mining, or railroad work, but he has no permanent salary that supplements household income. To varying degrees all family members play a role in the family economy. Male members' off-farm activities respond to the need to improve the family's economic situation. Social relations are direct, face-to-face; the basic unit of social organization is the extended family. The *mediero* uses traditional farming practices and generally does not adopt technological innovations. He is immersed in a community ceremonial life that reinforces family ties and reaffirms cultural identity. He is usually illiterate and has not learned a trade.

Background on the 1905 Law

Both tradition and laws in effect since colonial times granted the *rancheros* and *medieros* of the Galeana district usufruct rights to vast unpopulated areas of pastureland.[2] When the liberal laws distributing uncultivated lands to surveying companies and other new purchasers were implemented in the late nineteenth century, these vast unpopulated areas in Galeana were surveyed, declared vacant, and sold to foreign companies and settlers or allotted to the largest landowners of the Chihuahua oligarchy. By the end of the nineteenth century, the region's five towns had lost most of their pasture.

Beginning in 1883, companies began surveying the region, and large parts of traditional communal lands (called *ejidos*) which had their origin in colonial laws were transferred to government ownership and put up for sale. Companies controlled by Ignacio Gómez del Campo, Mauricio and Telésforo García, and Luis García Teruel were authorized to survey those *ejidos*.[3] In accord with the 1883 law, the surveying companies limited the *ejidos* to an area of 28,080 hectares for pasturing livestock, whereas the original agreements granted these towns a total of 112,359 hectares of pasture.[4] Thus, the surveying carried out under the 1883 law reduced the *ejidos* to a quarter of their original size; the remaining 84,279 hectares were declared to be vacant or national lands and were transferred to private individuals.[5]

Between 1881 and 1898, 96 percent of the total land surface in the district—approximately 4,069,905 hectares—were transferred in this manner (Lloyd 1987). During this same period, a single town lost 90 percent of its original *ejido* land.[6] Despite these dramatic losses, at the end of the nine-

2. These rights derive from their having descended from colonial-period settlers of the region. On 15 November 1778, Teodoro de Croix, governor and commander general of the Provincias Internas, had ordered the establishment of five presidial towns at the most important sites on the northern frontier. These towns were to minimize hostilities in the region, provide work and property for people who had neither, and expand commerce, encourage agriculture, and bring knowledge of industry to the region. In other words, the settlers were to fight the Apache. In return, each of the towns was given sixty-four *sitios de ganado mayor* (112,000 hectares) for *ejidos*, for common use, and for agricultural plots that the settlers would be obligated to develop. Five towns were established through this order, known as the Bando de Teodoro de Croix: Namiquipa, Cruces, Galeana, Casas Grandes, and Janos. The latter three sites are all in the Galeana district (cf. Katz 1981:8–9; Nugent 1988:84ff.).

3. POCH, no. 19, 10 May 1924; Cossío 1911:98; Almada 1958:340.

4. POCH, no. 69, 13 April 1889.

5. POCH, no. 36, 4 September 1924.

6. POCH, no. 36, 4 September 1926, p. 6. The data come from the official transcript of the *Dictamen de la Comisión Nacional Agraria*, 27 March 1923 (which restored the land to the Galeana township), AEL.

teenth century the towns of northwestern Chihuahua still held on to some of their original land, since the portion set aside for house lots and for the town itself (called the *fundo legal*) was untouched by the 1883 and 1894 laws. Such land for common use as remained in the control of the *pueblos* had already been subdivided into private or family plots or was maintained as municipal land that the local government rented out—usually to local *rancheros* and *medieros* for grazing or cultivation—to help defray municipal expenses.

The drastic reduction in *ejidal* land occurred at a time of low population density and relative economic prosperity. Further, beginning in 1885, at the conclusion of the Apache Wars, large investments of local (oligarchical) and foreign (especially U.S.) capital provided new work opportunities for the former colonists and diversified economic activities in northwestern Chihuahua. This infusion of capital fostered the development of local and regional business and promoted a boom in small- and medium-scale commercial agricultural production supplying the basic needs of the mining enclaves, the railroad companies and, to a lesser extent, the large cattle haciendas. This economic diversification minimized the discontent generated by the loss of land, since it also created better alternatives for well-paying jobs and capital accumulation than had traditional economic activities.

In short, although the territorial limits of the towns were seriously encroached upon between 1883 and 1905, the survival of the *ranchero* and the *mediero* was still possible since, by cultivating their own land or renting and cultivating the municipal land still available, they were able to participate in what was an expanding regional market. But to sustain this process, local control of the *pueblos'* municipal lands (now reduced to between 10 and 25 percent of their former size) was essential. This was especially true for small *rancheros* and *medieros* who, during the boom in commercial agriculture and the speculation caused by the appearance of the Rio Grande, Sierra Madre, and Pacific Railroad in 1897, had sold or mortgaged their small family plots and then lost them after a series of bad harvests. The municipal land, legally outside the bounds of agrarian legislation at the time, provided a refuge for small *rancheros* and *medieros*, guaranteeing them access to arable land and usufruct on a limited area.

While maintaining their right to the little land they still held, the *rancheros* and *medieros* found themselves increasingly dependent on the

permanent range of alternative sources of work. *Rancheros* tended to de-
vote their time to small-scale commercial production, while *medieros*
stocked up on essential consumer goods that, when sold, complemented
the household income and provided a degree of self-sufficiency.

However, the surveying and expropriation of municipal land initiated
under the 25 February 1905 law eliminated access to basic resources in the
area and exacerbated the already precarious ratio of population to land.
This process, combined with the crisis of 1907–9, revealed the problems
inherent in the accelerated process of modernization that had begun in
1885 and contributed to the social mobilization that began in the Galeana
district in 1906 (see Lloyd 1983; Wasserman 1980). Using as an example the
land subdivision in Janos, let's now analyze the 1905 law and its application
in the Galeana district between 1905 and 1910.

Provisions of the Law

On 25 February 1905 Chihuahua's governor, Enrique Creel, decreed the
law for the survey, expropriation, and sale of municipal land which set the
pueblos' boundaries and specified that all municipal land in the state was to
be subdivided and sold to those who could afford to purchase it. Towns
most directly and profoundly affected by the law were those whose male
inhabitants later contributed most to the process of social mobilization in
the region. By analyzing the law and its effects on the region we can
determine to what extent the law served as a spark to ignite the flame of
discontent in northwestern Chihuahua (Wasserman 1980:31–34).

According to Governor Creel, the intention of the law was, first, to
promote the formation of a dynamic group of small landowners in the
state, an old dream of the Mexican liberals. Concurrently the law was
supposed to diminish the abuses by wealthy landowners who seized reportedly fallow and national land in order to expand their large cattle
haciendas. A second intention of the law was to increase municipal revenues, since proceeds from the sale of municipal lands went to local, not
state, treasuries. By this means, local governments could secure a certain
degree of autonomy from the state in budgetary matters, while also financing a series of public improvement programs (secondary roads, telegraph

service, etc.)[7] that were destined to facilitate the process of capitalist modernization, thus relieving the state government from this financial burden.

As the governor pointed out in his 1905 annual address, this law represented the final attempt by the oligarchy of Chihuahua to modernize the structure of land tenure in the state (Creel 1905:21). Its implementation would affect what was left of the colonial *ejidos,* as well as municipal land, and would convert what remained of the *fundos legales* into merchandise to be placed on the market, promoting land speculation in those areas of the state where livestock and agricultural production were most developed.[8]

Scarce revenues and increasing deficits[9] in municipal treasuries appear to have been important factors in the local government's acceptance of the law. Such was the case throughout the Galeana district; only through the sale of municipal land were municipal governments able to balance their budgets. However, it should be noted that this penury which preceded 1905 derived from the concentration of basic resources in the hands of a few families and from the fact that the *pueblo* of Galeana, for example, did not enjoy the extensive commercial development of Casas Grandes, nor did it have working mines nearby from which it could collect taxes. But of still greater importance in determining certain municipal authorities' acceptance of the decree was the opportunity that the law offered them to expand their own holdings or those of their relatives, followers, and supporters.

The law authorized the subdivision of three types of land: urban house lots, pastureland, and agricultural plots. The last type had been part of the municipal land that was traditionally rented to the townspeople and in some cases included pasture designated for communal use.

Galeana was one of the first districts affected by the decree. Beginning in April 1905, on orders from the local *jefe político,* surveying of municipal

7. AMCG CJP 1905, of. [oficio] 575, fols. 140–49, 15 March 1905 (Informe del jefe político, 1905); AMCG CJP 1906, of. 2783, fols. 389–94, 15 October 1906 (announcing the increase in municipal taxes to finance public works).

8. The districts with the greatest number of *denuncias* of municipal lands were Iturbide, Guerrero, Bravos, Parral, and Galeana, the state's most developed zones, where commercial agricultural enterprises had secured their strongest footing. Not coincidentally, two of these districts (Iturbide and Galeana) enjoyed most of the investments of the oligarchy. See AE 1905.

9. AMCG CJP 1905, of. 575, fols. 140–42, 15 March 1905.

land commenced in the *pueblos* of Galeana and Casas Grandes. But the pace of the surveying, subdivision, and sale of municipal lands varied widely throughout the state and within the Galeana district itself. Thanks to the opposition of its municipal government, Janos succeeded in delaying the subdivision of its *ejidos* until mid-1909 (Creel 1909). Ascensión and San Buenaventura were not seriously affected by the law for several reasons, in part because their "municipal lands" were much less extensive than those of Janos, Galeana, and Casas Grandes.[10] In addition, Ascensión declared that since 1883 its lands had all been private, not municipal, property, and that consequently the law did not apply.[11] In San Buenaventura, the municipal government's opposition to implementation of the law effectively curbed the subdivision of its municipal land. According to data on the number of *denuncias* of municipal lands in *municipios* throughout Chihuahua (AE), the concentration of municipal land after 1905 was of less consequence in San Buenaventura than in Galeana, Casas Grandes, and Janos, where the number of claims was significantly greater.

The state government fixed the sale price of the subdivided lots at between 50 and 68 pesos per hectare,[12] and the earnings were earmarked as municipal funds. While the sale price was high for some social groups, such as *rancheros* and *medieros*, for merchants and others a fixed-maximum sale price constituted a kind of subsidy, since it eliminated the practice of auctioning municipal land to the highest bidder. This latter practice, which had been the norm from 1886 to 1905, tended to increase the sale price to an artificially high level, higher even than the price of land on the free market. Thus, speculation has led to land being concentrated in the hands of the richest rancher-merchants of Galeana and Casas Grandes, who, not coincidentally, were members of the Municipal Council when the law was decreed. After 1905 they could purchase municipal land at what were, for them, bargain-basement prices.

But the Municipal Land Law not only authorized the subdivision of

10. Galeana, Casas Grandes, and Janos had been, like Namiquipa and Cruces in the Guerrero district, the sites of colonial-period presidios, and consequently their inhabitants were heirs to the extensive land grants donated to the eighteenth-century soldier/ farmer settlers.

11. POCh, no. 11, 6 February 1908.

12. AMCG CJP 1905, of. 2574, fol. 273, 24 October 1905; AMCG CJP 1907, of. 2740, fol. 314, 19 October 1907.

uncultivated and uninhabited municipal land, it also allowed for the sub-division of residential lots within the *fundo legal*, as well as almost all the communal land that had been worked for generations by the original settlers in these towns. With no warning, many small farmers found that they now had to pay to legalize titles to house lots and arable land[13] that had historically been theirs by right of possession. Many did not have the money required to buy these property rights and overnight found them-selves without land to cultivate or a house of their own. Thus, between 1905 and 1907, when most municipal land was sold in Galeana and Casas Grandes, many small farmers became *medieros*.

The agrarian dispossession that occurred in the town of Galeana was even more acute in Casas Grandes,[14] a commercial center in the moun-tainous zone between Chihuahua and Sonora. Its level of economic de-velopment had attracted immigrants from other parts of Chihuahua and from within the Galeana district itself, resulting in an apparent scarcity of housing. In response, several of the municipality's most astute merchants placed claims to house lots and called in the debts of some small farmers. From 1907 forward, small farmers were victims of the general economic crisis in the region; lacking sufficient cash, they had to settle their debts by handing over their houses or by selling them well below market value.[15]

Consequently, the law failed to foster the development of a strong stra-tum of small-farmer property owners; to the contrary, it facilitated and promoted speculation in municipal land by the rancher-merchants, who bought up the greater part of the town's pasturage and arable lands, thus tightening their political and economic control. The law stripped *rancheros* of their ancestral lands and encouraged concentration of land in the hands

13. "Ley sobre medida y enajenación de Terrenos Municipales," poch, no. 9, 4 March 1905, pp. 7–12.

14. Casas Grandes had the greatest number of *denuncias* in the entire state, followed closely by Galeana. poch, no. 24, 22 March 1908, pp. 6–7; no. 18, 1 March 1908, p. 5; no. 22, 15 March 1908, p. 5; no. 21, 12 March 1908, pp. 6–7; no. 19, 5 March 1908, pp. 2–3; no. 87, 20 October 1908, pp. 10–11; no. 41, 21 March 1908, p. 13; no. 17, 27 February 1908, p. 5; no. 84, 20 October 1907, p. 8; no. 87, 31 October 1907, p. 11; no. 89, 7 November 1907, pp. 4–5. Also see amcg cjp for the years 1905–9.

15. Interviews with María Orozco (ninety-one-year-old niece of Manuel Orozco), Casas Grandes, Chihuahua, 3 May 1979; and Juana Miranda (merchant), Casas Grandes, Chihuahua, 30 October 1977.

of those who could pay the costs of legal land titles. This phenomenon was not limited to the Galeana district (see AE, especially regarding Namiquipa and Cruces in the Guerrero district).

Through a decree issued on 24 September 1906, Governor Creel tried to restrain this tendency toward land concentration by setting a limit to the number of claims that an individual could make.[16] Nevertheless, even after that date, multiple family members (wife, children, cousins, etc.) would present individual claims and the consolidated land would be worked as a single unit. Moreover, after 1906 the names of individuals who already owned plots of newly acquired municipal lands continued to appear on the list of titles to land recently expedited.[17] Individuals whose claims to multiple plots of land went unchallenged included distinguished members of the oligarchy, such as Luis Terrazas, as well as important regional rancher-merchants.[18] District and local authorities were frequently (and accurately) accused of favoring certain groups and prominent figures. As Francisco Mateus, *jefe político* of the Galeana district, noted in 1907,

Some municipal office employees give preference to certain individuals who make claims or provide information to persons they favor so that they can substantiate their claims while denying the claims of others. Moreover, it appears that those same employees, directly or through third parties, have claimed land, prejudicing the poor who have been deprived of the benefits that the law entitled them to receive.[19]

16. AMCG CJP 1907, of. 2740, fol. 314, 19 October 1907; Circular no. 9, from the Secretaría del Gobierno del Estado, Ramo de Fomento, 24 October 1907. This circular published the complete text of the Decree of 24 September 1906, allowing adult individuals to present a maximum of three *denuncias:* one for a house lot (*solar*) within the *fundo legal;* another for a plot of agricultural land; a third for pasturage. "Having exercised this right," it was made clear "[the individual] may not acquire by *denuncia* any other municipal lands."

17. AE 1906:223. General Luis Terrazas denounced a good number of plots in the Iturbide district on 30 June 1906. In 1907 he denounced several plots near Casas Grandes and in 1908 returned to denounce other plots in the same zone, without their being rejected for having been in violation of the stipulations of the law of 24 September 1906. Apparently those stipulations were not written for members of the oligarchy. See POCH, no. 19, 5 March 1908; and no. 96, 1 December 1907, p. 4.

18. EDITOR'S NOTE: The situation was very similar in Namiquipa (Guerrero district), where the Comaduran and Corral families acquired multiple, contiguous plots of municipal land. AE 1905–9.

19. AMCG CJP 1907, of. 3032, fol. 445, 10 November 1907.

In other words, a person's status in the region and relations to kinship, friendship, and *compradrazgo* to municipal employees was instrumental in acquiring municipal lands.[20]

The concentration of municipal land in the hands of small and influential groups is an important factor in the social polarization of Galeana, Casas Grandes, and Janos. It is not surprising, then, that in mid-1905, a few months after their municipal lands had been surveyed and subdivided (though not yet sold), the residents of these three towns formed the first groups of the Partido Liberal Mexicano in the region, as implementation of the law caused regional discontent to reach a breaking point. A more detailed analysis of the subdivision of municipal land in Janos will elucidate this point and also demonstrate how this process was affected by U.S. investment and influence in the region.[21]

Effects of the Law on Internal Power Relations in Janos

As previously mentioned, the municipalities of Janos and San Buenaventura vigorously protested when the 1905 law was approved, and their municipal administrators moved to obstruct the implementation of the law. Janos provides the clearest demonstration of the manner in which protest against the 1905 law led to social polarization and acted as a catalyst for the subsequent social movement.

From 1905 to 1911 a militant rejection of the subdivision of municipal land in Janos was organized by Porfirio Talamantes, who later became an important revolutionary figure in the *villista* ranks. A *ranchero*, Talamantes owned irrigated land where he planted corn, beans, and wheat; dairy cattle; and some fine horses.[22] He was a bachelor and a relative of Juan Aguilar, a small-scale *ranchero* from Casas Grandes.[23]

20. On the other hand, it appears that opposition to the subdivision and expropriation of municipal land by certain members of the Municipal Council of San Buenaventura slowed the application of the law in that town.

21. Janos, the northernmost (i.e., closest to the United States) of the *pueblos* affected by the law, also had lost some of its colonial land grant to North American landlords.

22. Interview with Narzario Prieto (farmer), Janos, Chihuahua, 5 June 1979.

23. Interview with Manuel Almeida (*presidente municipal* of Casas Grandes, born in Janos, farmer), Casas Grandes, Chihuahua, 31 May 1979.

Talamantes had been named *juez menor* in Janos in 1905, but he was removed from that post in 1908 by order of the governor. The governor also ordered that Talamantes no longer be permitted to serve as president of the Municipal Council,[24] this in response to the fact that the Municipal Council had opposed the survey of municipal lands in Janos in 1905 and had sent Talamantes to Mexico City to protest against the law.

In 1907, recognizing their powerlessness to prevent the subdivision of the *ejidos* by appealing to state-level authorities or by registering their protests in Mexico City, the council gave Talamantes power of attorney to return to the capital—this time to petition the Ministry of Economic Development for the free division of municipal lands among the most impoverished members of the community,[25] who had previously rented the land now being sold off to outsiders. During the first few months of 1908 the petition was declared inadmissible by both the ministry and the state government,[26] and the expropriation, subdivision, and sale of the municipal land proceeded according to the law. But in October of the same year, the Municipal Council successfully suspended the claims process, according to the *jefe político* because no authority had yet clearly distinguished what was to be the area for communal use *after* subdivision.[27] The outcome of the lawsuit by the people of Janos was decided through the direct intervention of the governor, who personally authorized that the surveying proceed.[28] At the end of the year, when the *magonista* plot in Casas Grandes was discovered, Talamantes was accused of being a participant.[29] His friend Ruperto Verduzco was accused of cattle rustling and was thrown in jail in Casas Grandes.[30]

Fleeing to Ascensión, Talamantes hid on the farm of a friend, from where he managed to cross the border into the United States. It is rumored that while he was in hiding in Ascensión he wrote a letter to President Díaz, denying his involvement in the *magonista* plot but insisting all the

24. AMCG CJP 1908, of. 1260, fol. 22, 18 April 1908.

25. AMCG CJP 1908, of. 522, fol. 974, 22 February 1908.

26. AMCG CJP 1908, of. 1260, fol. 22, 18 April 1908; of. 522, fol. 974, 22 February 1908.

27. AMCG CJP 1908, of. 3120, fol. 213, 21 October 1908.

28. AMCG CJP 1908, of. 3120, fol. 213, 21 October 1908.

29. Interview with eighty-three-year-old María Verduzco, Janos, Chihuahua, 5 June 1979.

30. Verduzco interview; AMCG CJP 1910, of. 11, fol. 219, 1 January 1910.

same on the justice of his position in defense of the *ejido*.[31] Talamantes' problems did not end there, even though he was in exile. Another of his closest collaborators was jailed and, subsequently, was forcibly drafted into the federal army, while Guadalupe Zozaya, *jefe municipal* of Janos, systematically persecuted Talamantes' followers.[32]

Thus, as of November 1908, the Chihuahuan state set in motion the subdivision of Janos's municipal land, especially grazing land, and control passed into the hands of the town's wealthy. The Mápula and Zozaya families headed the list, but it was the latter, particularly Guadalupe Zozaya, who most assiduously engineered the division and redistribution of the *pueblo*'s lands at the local level.

The Mápula family had already seized much of the territory that comprised the colonial-period land grant to the settlers of Janos in the decades before 1905. Implementation of the 1905 Municipal Land Law permitted them to extend their control of Janos's land. This family, which owned small and medium-size properties in the region, were merchants with close ties to the regional oligarchy. Donaciano Mápula owned a hacienda encompassing 7,885 hectares (the equivalent of five *sitios de ganado mayor*)[33] which was within the original *ejido* of Janos.[34] Donaciano had claimed the land in 1886 while serving as *jefe político*.[35] In 1898 he bought another 49,052 hectares of pasture from the Banco Minero, whose director at the time was Enrique Creel. This land had also been part of Janos' colonial-period land grant and was used communally as grazing land before the García Teruel Surveying Company acquired it as a concession in 1891.[36]

When the *ejido* in Janos was surveyed, part of another plot of land belonging to Donaciano ended up inside the *fundo legal* of the town, which assumed control of that insignificant portion of the Mápula properties.[37] However, in 1904 Donaciano Mápula requested other land in exchange for

31. Interview with eighty-four-year-old merchant and *ranchero* Rubén Fernández, Ascensión, Chihuahua, 12 June 1979.

32. AMCG CJP 1910, of. 11, fol. 219, 1 January 1910.

33. POCH, no. 5, 29 January 1927, p. 6.

34. POCH, no. 113, 15 December 1886; POCH, no. 12, 25 March 1882.

35. POCH, no. 5, 29 January 1927, p. 6 (publication of the presidential resolution proclaiming the restitution of lands to the municipality of Janos).

36. AMCG CJP 1905, of. 1209, fols. 336–39, 25 May 1905.

37. AMCG CJP 1905, of. 1209, fol. 339, 25 May 1905.

what had been expropriated, and he was awarded some agricultural plots in an area called San José.[38] This land, which had previously been rented to sharecroppers and small *rancheros*,[39] had a spring[40] which was one of the few water sources in the municipality.[41] After Mápula's seizure of the spring in San José, the townspeople had only one remaining water source, the Janos River, water rights to which were already rented out by the municipality to *medieros* and small *rancheros*.[42] Those affected by this legal decision sent their protest to the state authorities and refused to move from San José. Although he did not secure legal title to the land for another four years, Donaciano began evicting the *rancheros* at the end of 1905.[43] In other words, the Mápula family had assumed control of much of the best *ejido* land in Janos with the blessing of the regional authorities in the decades *before* the Municipal Land Law was passed.

In addition to his haciendas, Donaciano owned a wholesale-retail store.[44] He served as a local representative to Congress on several occasions during the years of General Terrazas' governorship in Chihuahua; and during 1882 and for many years previously, he had functioned as *jefe político* of the Iturbide district.[45] North of Janos, his brothers Joaquín, José María, and Francisco jointly owned another small hacienda of about 5,265 hectares (three *sitios de ganado mayor*).[46] This hacienda, located within the original boundaries of the Janos *ejido* (i.e., the colonial-period land grant),[47] encompassed sizable extensions of hilly, uncultivable land (*monte*) which the town's inhabitants had traditionally shared communally, and where they had cut their firewood.[48] Under Mápula family ownership, cutting firewood was prohibited.[49] According to oral accounts, the Mápula family

38. AMCG CJP 1909, of. 3411, fol. 31, 22 September 1909.
39. AMCG CJP 1909, of. 3411, fol. 31, 22 September 1909; of. [unnumbered], fol. 133, 24 May 1905.
40. AMCG CJP 1910, of. 579, fol. 303, 7 and 8 February 1910.
41. See note 38 above.
42. AMCG CJP 1905, of. 1209, fol. 337, 25 March 1905.
43. AMCG CJP 1905, of. 1209, fols. 337–39, 25 March 1905.
44. AE 1910:114.
45. AMCG CJP 1905, of. 1208, fol. 33, undated; POCH, no. 61, 16 February 1889, p. 1; POCH, no. 12, 25 March 1882; POCH, no. 64, 21 September 1905.
46. AE 1908:223.
47. POCH, no. 5, 29 January 1927, p. 6.
48. AMCG CJP 1911, of. 747, fol. 303, 6 December 1911.
49. AMCG CJP 1911, of. 747, fol. 303, 6 December 1911.

originally rented their arable land to *medieros.*[50] Some evidence suggests that the family undertook direct cultivation of the land sometime around 1905–6, when they began raising cereal grains.[51] When the market for cereal grains dropped off in 1908, the family switched to cotton. Because cotton requires more water, the family probably increased their use of the little water available.[52]

In fact, Janos and Ascensión receive less rainfall than other *municipios* in the district. This lack of rain and a scarcity of permanent water sources seriously limited agricultural production, dependent as it was on the few permanent sources of water in the area.[53] During the summer of 1904, drought brought a high death toll among livestock in both municipalities and seriously reduced grain production.[54] *Rancheros* were particularly hard hit by these two events, since their lands lacked irrigation. But in the same year, thanks to the San José spring, Donaciano Mápula increased the amount of cultivated land on his hacienda, planting alfalfa, wheat, and other grains.[55] During the 1907 drought, whole stretches of the Janos River dried up, seriously affecting the *rancheros* who were totally dependent on the river for irrigating their plots. Again in 1909, there was little rainfall and the frosts came earlier than usual. Northwest of Janos, in the *colonia* of Fernández Leal, where the majority of the population were poor tenant farmers, almost all the crops were lost. The situation was little better in Janos itself.[56]

In short, by 1905 the Mápulas (Donaciano and his brothers Joaquín, José María, and Francisco) controlled considerable properties around Janos and operated stores in Janos and Casas Grandes. They had acquired those properties through their political connections with the regional oligarchy. After passage of the 1905 law, they and their first cousins Jesús and Ascensión Mápula assumed control of numerous plots of municipal land,[57]

50. Interviews with Narzario Prieto and María Verduzco (notes 22 and 29 above).

51. AMCG CJP 1905, of. 72, fols. 17–28 (report of the *jefe político*), 16 January 1905.

52. Interview with María Verduzco (note 29 above); AMCG CJP 1905, of. 1208, fol. 333, 24 March 1905.

53. AMCG CJP 1905, of. [unnumbered], fol. 333, undated.

54. AMCG CJP 1905, of. 72, fol. 26 (report of the *jefe político* on agricultural production in 1904), 16 January 1905.

55. AMCG CJP 1905, of. 72, fol. 27.

56. AMCG CJP 1910, of. 518, fol. 297, 4 February 1910.

57. AE 1905:112; AMCG CJP 1910, of. [unnumbered], fol. 277, undated.

thereby expanding their cattle haciendas to the north and northeast of Janos.

But the Mápulas were not the only family to purchase multiple lots of municipal land, thereby benefiting directly from this new law of Enrique Creel's Chihuahua. One of the principal families to take advantage of the claims process under the 1905 law was Anastasio Azcarate and his sons, Francisco and Santiago, all prominent local rancher-merchants. Anastasio owned the two largest stores in Janos, where he frequently bought the *rancheros'* harvests and exchanged merchandise for the crops or traded on account.[58] He also had good land that he rented to local *medieros* and in 1910 was considered by the *jefe municipal* to be one of the most important local farmers.[59] But the importance of the Azcarate family was not predicated solely on their exploitative relations with *rancheros* and *medieros;* they also cultivated relationships with the Mápulas, to whom they were related by ties of kinship. In 1902 Francisco and Santiago Azcarate sold the property "La Virgen" (1,755 hectares, or one *sitio de ganado mayor*) to Donaciano Mápula.[60] All of the Azcarates' properties were within the original *ejido* of Janos.[61]

The Azcarates, related as kinsmen both to the Mápula and the Zozaya families, held important municipal and district posts over many years.[62] Among them, the three families almost completely dominated local commerce and speculation, as well as most of the land that was cultivated or used in livestock production. Together, the Mápulas and the Azcarates controlled 94,669 hectares, about 84 percent of the original *ejido* of Janos. The 1905 law allowed these families to take control of even more land, and by the end of 1908 Anastasio Azcarate, his two sons, daughters-in-law, and other close relatives had initiated the claims process on a large share of the town's communal pastureland.[63]

But the names that appear most often as purchasers of municipal land in Janos were Guadalupe and Francisco Zozaya. Their claims to agricultural

58. AE 1905:81, 114; interview with María Verduzco (note 29 above).

59. AMCG CJP 1910, of. [unnumbered], fol. 277, undated (report of the *jefe político*).

60. AE 1906:220.

61. POCh, no. 5, 29 January 1927, pp. 6–7.

62. AMCG CJP 1908, of. 3471, fol. 389, 18 November 1908.

63. AMCG CJP 1908, of. 3386, fols. 351–57, 11 November 1908; of. 3423, fol. 368, 13 November 1908; of. 3764, fol. 473, 30 November 1908.

and grazing land provoked numerous lawsuits related to unjust or illegal dispossession of the previous users or tenants (or owners, if untitled). Guadalupe was the proprietor of a wholesale-retail store in Janos and, like Anastasio Azcarate, a moneylender who allowed his clients to pay interest or alternatively to borrow against their harvests.[64] In 1910 Guadalupe Zozaya was one of Janos' most important farmers;[65] that same year he was also accused several times of having taken control of subdivided land and of having extended his own cultivation for commercial purposes at the expense of *medieros* who for generations had worked the municipal land on the southeast side of town. That land had been surveyed and expropriated under the 1905 law.[66]

As the *jefe político* described the situation in 1905, the majority of the *rancheros* in Janos did not hold title to the land they were working.[67] Very few private properties existed within the *fundo legal* and other *ejido* land. By tradition, members of the community had the right to rent land, and it appears that since the colonial period the townspeople had enjoyed usufruct to the land of the colonial *ejido*.[68]

In 1908, as *jefe municipal*, Zozaya ordered subdivision of the *ejidal* land and evicted the townspeople who had been renting their parcels.[69] It was not coincidental that those plots passed into the hands of Guadalupe Zozaya and other members of his family.[70] Those most affected were small-scale *rancheros* and renters who were dependent on access to rented municipal land to supplement what other lands they might have cultivated. And *medieros* with no land of their own were left without any land at all to cultivate. Again it was Porfirio Talamantes who brought the protests of tenant farmers before district and state authorities; the latter responded by fining the farmers for failing to respect the local authorities (in Janos, the Zozayas, precisely the same people who were dispossessing the peasants).

64. AE 1908:114; interviews with Narzario Prieto and María Verduzco (notes 22 and 29 above).

65. AE 1908:114; Prieto and Verduzco interviews.

66. AMCG CJP 1910, of. [unnumbered], fol. 277, undated.

67. AMCG CJP 1905, of. 1208, fol. 332, 24 May 1905.

68. AMCG CJP 1910, of. 192, fols. 257–60, 16 January 1910.

69. AMCG CJP 1908, of. 3208, fols. 240–42, 26 October 1908.

70. AMCG CJP 1908, of. 3208, fols. 240–42, 26 October 1908; AMCG CJP 1910, of. 192, fols. 257–60, 16 January 1910.

The Zozaya takeover of land in the immediate vicinity of the *pueblo* shifted the dispossessed farmers toward the rain-fed areas of the traditional *ejido* land, where the possibility of a yearly harvest was slight. One such area, San Francisco, depended on the river's rising for successful harvests. In 1909, a year after the farmers were dispossessed, large stretches of river dried up and a good percentage of rain-fed crops were lost.[71]

Beginning in 1908, to the end of securing incomes for their families, a sizable number of those severely affected by the Mápula and Zozaya expropriations began to look for off-farm employment more frequently and for longer periods. They worked as cowhands and herders on the nearby livestock haciendas, especially those that were foreign-owned, such as "Nogales." Since these were temporary jobs, workers could return to care for their own crops or work as *medieros* for local landholders. But usually the younger members of the families of small-scale *rancheros* left for longer periods of time.

Among the residents of Janos who suffered from the Zozaya land takeover were Simón Rentería, an artisan and farmer who made and repaired shoes,[72] and his brothers Angel, Amado, Jesús, Ambrosio, and Abrahám, who were owners of small rain-fed plots in San Francisco.[73] Another of the dispossessed was Ruperto Verduzco, who owned five hectares in the same area and a team of burros. Ruperto was a faithful follower of Talamantes, accompanying him whenever he presented the small farmers' protests and negotiated their demands. His brothers, Cristóbal, Tartolo, Luis, and Cirilo, worked as cowhands on nearby haciendas and also tilled small plots.[74] Cornelio and Anastasio Madrid, *medieros* with no land of their own, also worked as cowhands during roundups on the foreign-owned cattle ranches in the region.[75] Martín and Alejandro Echeribel were owners of small agricultural plots; the former also owned the only cantina in the region.[76] Pablo and Alejandro López, Paulino Flores, Anselmo, Florencio, Marco, and José María Pacheco, who lived in San Francisco, were

71. Interview with María Verduzco (note 29 above); Creel 1910.

72. AE 1909:147; Verduzco interview.

73. Verduzco interview.

74. Verduzco interview.

75. Interview with eighty-four-year-old Pedro Torres Madrid, Janos, Chihuahua, 5 June 1979.

76. AE 1909:114; AMCG CJP 1910, of. [unnumbered], fol. 277, undated.

all small-scale farmers who rented municipal land and, along with others, signed the letter of protest against the subdivision of the town's municipal lands.[77]

Given the poor quality and limited amount of the agricultural land in the town, most of the claims and awards of municipal land were for grazing land, more desirable because it was of better quality. Almost all the small-scale *rancheros* of the municipality were also small-scale dairy farmers who sold their products locally or in the border towns of New Mexico. The poor quality and scarcity of land for agriculture, when combined with the increasing commercialization of regional cattle production and the takeover of pastureland in Janos by the Mápula, Azcarate, and Zozaya families, threatened these *rancheros* with ruin. The lands that had not been awarded to the three families on the basis of government concessions stipulated in the law of 1883 now passed into their hands during the post-1905 subdivision and sale of municipal lands.[78]

Thus, by 1908 the majority of the *rancheros* in Janos had no pasturage for their animals. In order to feed their livestock they either rented small grazing areas or purchased plots of pastureland from the municipality.[79] Among those choosing the latter option were Porfirio Talamantes' brother, Jesús, the *cantinero* Martín Echeribel, and others who allied themselves with the dispossessed *rancheros* and *medieros*.

The subdivision of municipal land in Janos appears to have encouraged polarization of the town's different groups and to have catalyzed the latent discontent, this despite the fact that a few *rancheros* used the stipulations of the 1905 law to secure properties for themselves. On one side, the Zozayas allied themselves with the two wealthiest families, the Azcarates and Mápulas, who were obvious beneficiaries of the subdivision and were supported in their seizure of municipal land by Francisco Mateus, the *jefe político* of Galeana. But Talamantes simultaneously gained the support of the majority of the small-scale *rancheros* and *medieros*, all of whom objected

77. AMCG CJP 1910, of. 579, fol. 303, 7 February 1910; of. 589 and 590, 8 February 1910; of. 192, fols. 257 and 260, 16 January 1908; of. 3208, fols. 240–42, 26 October 1908.

78. POCH, no. 5, 29 January 1927, pp. 6–7.

79. AMCG CJP 1905, of. 1209, fol. 338, 25 May 1905; AE 1905:81; AE 1909:114; AMCG CJP 1908, of. 347, fol. 389, 18 November 1908; interviews with María Verduzco (note 29 above) and Ventura Chávez, Janos, Chihuahua, 11 June 1979.

to the subdivision of municipal land and to the seizure of *ejidal* lands by outsiders.

The years between 1905 and 1908 witnessed a struggle within the Janos Municipal Council that pitted elected council members, who represented the interests of small-scale *rancheros,* against council members—led by Zozaya—who had been directly appointed by district authorities. The *jefe municipal* defended the interests of the large landowners and the important local merchants, and Guadalupe Zozaya took advantage of this support to enlarge his own property holdings and those of his family. Since the majority of those adversely affected by the subdivision were unable to buy land, they were left with no irrigated land within the town.

The struggle for land was closely linked to the battle against the corruption and favoritism of local authorities, who used the political and economic system—created and sustained by the northern oligarchy—to defend the interests of local landlords. With the beginning of revolutionary activity in the area, a sizable number of small-scale *rancheros* joined either the *magonista* forces in Casas Grandes and Ascensión or Madero's troops, headed by Porfirio Talamantes.

The aim of the small-scale *rancheros, medieros,* and locals who rented land in Janos—viz., to maintain the integrity of the municipal land as it was before the 1905 law—responds to a history of land grabs in the area; since 1895, owners of several local livestock haciendas had begun a slow takeover of the colonial *ejido.* Although the Mápulas and Azcarates took over the major part of the original land, foreign companies and other hacienda owners who were prominent members of the regional oligarchy also acquired significant portions of the *ejido.* The Corralitos Land and Cattle Company's holdings encompassed *ejido* land to the south and southeast of Janos. On 29 December 1884, Manuel González, then president of Mexico, issued the company a title to property equivalent to eighty *sitios de ganado mayor* in the same area. This concession, just a portion of the Corralitos Land and Cattle Company's holdings in northwest Chihuahua, invaded the communal pasture of the Janos *ejido.*[80] The hacienda "Ojo de Federico," owned by Pedro Prieto, invaded land of the Janos *ejido.*[81] Pedro Prieto's wife acquired 28,000 hectares northeast of Janos, and by 1905–6

---

80. POCH, no. 5, 29 January 1927, pp. 6–7.
81. POCH, no. 5, 29 January 1927, pp. 6–7.

Pedro and his brothers were among the most important ranchers in the district.[82]

Before the small-scale *rancheros* and poor farmers of Janos began their fight against the 25 February 1905 law, the original *ejido* had already lost a significant amount of land, especially pasture that had been incorporated into regional livestock haciendas prior to 1905. The legal battle waged by the ordinary citizens against subdivision of the remaining areas of the *ejido* was their last attempt to defend their land against the frontal attack of the *hacendados* and the speculation in and takeover of land by the most powerful merchant-ranchers of Janos.

Conclusions

The 1905 law had significant repercussions throughout the Galeana district: it exacerbated the already precarious balance between land and population and significantly increased social polarization in the region. With the stroke of a pen, it deprived communities of popular control over basic resources while it legalized the individual parceling of agricultural land and pasture and converted communal land into merchandise to be sold in an expanding market. The law subjected control of the land to changes in family fortunes and inclement weather, putting the farmers in debt, forcing them to sell their property, and imperiling their future.

From an agrarian perspective, the law eliminated traditional rental of *ejido* land. This seriously affected local small-scale *rancheros* and *medieros* who had taken refuge in the *ejido* zones when the hacienda owners had begun their land takeover during the last third of the nineteenth century. The law also encouraged the privatization of extensive areas of what had previously been communal land, shifting small-scale *rancheros* to less productive, usually rain-fed areas, thus making their situation still more precarious.

One fascinating contradiction in the law is its stated intention to provide legal title to individual plots of land and house lots located within the *fundo legal.* However, many families were in fact evicted from their homes as a result of the law. Land was concentrated in fewer hands, and its control

82. AE 1906:223; AE 1905:81.

was monopolized by the wealthiest families in the region. Merchants benefited most from the law since they were able to advance the most claims.

Thanks to the region's economic development, begun in 1885, there was
significant growth in the tertiary sector, and a small segment of the population dedicated to commerce was able to accumulate capital rapidly.
These merchants' favorable position allowed them to increase their property holdings under the 1905 law. Moreover, many merchants exercised
considerable local power; they contributed an overwhelming number of
jefes municipales in the district and monopolized other less important municipal jobs and posts. They formed a majority on the municipal councils,
the bodies that supposedly made decisions at the local level. This control
gave them immediate access to information about the surveying of municipal land; armed with this information, they could claim the best land
before other members of the community did. And once in power, they
favored members of their own group and their allies, a policy detrimental
to the small-scale *rancheros* and *medieros* of the town.

Not coincidentally, the Municipal Land Law was pronounced just when
the Galeana district was becoming Chihuahua's most important livestock
area and one of its major areas of agricultural production. The speculation
in pasture is easily understood in the context of livestock's importance in
the regional economy. The law actually functioned to guarantee a kind of
subsidy for small- and medium-scale livestock ranchers, allowing the most
important merchants to make inroads into a new and lucrative business
area, while others with livestock and crops, like the Mápulas and the
Azcarates, were able to increase their landholdings and consolidate a
regional-level group able to influence developments throughout the district. Finally, the law reinforced the implicit pact between the most important local merchants and the regional oligarchy.

In Casas Grandes the most important merchants—such as the Mirandas
and the Galaz brothers, allies of municipal authorities and of important
hacienda owners like the Bookers and the Terrazas—actively supported
the subdivision of municipal land. The *rancheros* and *medieros* from the
barrios of San José and Guadalupe in Casas Grandes, on the other hand,
who were forced off their land and threatened with imminent dispossession, organized in opposition to the subdivision. In the face of open conflict, what appeared at the outset as a hegemonic group of rancher-

merchants in Casas Grandes now split apart, some of them joining the *rancheros* and *medieros* in their protest.

The presence of the Mormons who had settled on *ejido* land after 1885 made the situation in Casas Grandes even more complex. Mormons took advantage of the 1905 law to increase the size of their already flourishing communities of Dublan and Juárez. Colonizing members of this foreign religious group added one more to the set of factors destabilizing the precarious balance between population and land in Casas Grandes and undermining popular control of the lands, already threatened by important members of the regional oligarchy like General Luis Terrazas, foreign owners of cattle haciendas, and local merchant-ranchers.

In Galeana, as in Casas Grandes, the rancher-merchant group split into two camps. The first, comprising *rancheros, medieros,* and small-scale merchants allied with the wealthy Ponce family, opposed the subdivision, in direct conflict with the municipal authorities and their supporters. At the end of 1905, after the subdivision of land began, this opposition formed the first *magonista* group in Galeana. The second group, those who supported subdivision, formed armed groups in support of the Porfirio Díaz regime.

In Ascensión, *magonista* groups formed in early 1908 when the effects of subdivision began to be felt and when a group of *rancheros* initiated a lawsuit against some local Mormons who had invaded land. In Ascensión, in contrast to other nearby towns, some of the most important merchants joined the *magonista* forces, for the Mormons' takeover of land and their increasing control of small business in the region encroached on Mexican interests and control of the regional and local market.

In Janos, people who had in the past rented municipal land allied themselves with small *rancheros* such as the Talamantes and Verduzcos in opposition to the most important rancher-merchants in the town. The latter group, allied with municipal authorities and other powerful families such as the Mápulas, supported and imposed municipal subdivision. The Talamantes-Verduzco group joined the revolutionary forces in 1910 after having lost their lawsuit to obstruct implementation of the law.

The endogenous process of land takeover and accumulation already under way in the Galeana district by the late nineteenth century had tended to polarize social groups, to exacerbate existing social differences, to increase social tension, and to provoke confrontation between social classes. Thus, the implementation of the 1905 law only accelerated the pace of social differentiation and polarization in the area and spotlighted the economic and political monopoly exercised by local and district-level merchants in alliance with the regional oligarchy managed by the Terrazas-Creel clan. In response, the merchant groups turned in on themselves; their social relations became increasingly horizontal, exclusive, and classist. This new orientation broke the area's social tradition, which during the nineteenth century had been one of solidarity and strong, vertical intergroup relations.

On the other hand, the *rancheros* and *medieros,* too, began to relate more strongly to each other and to form alliances among themselves. After 1905 the *medieros* who had no land and who could no longer rent municipal land strengthened their relationships with those *rancheros* related through kinship or *compadrazgo* who did own land. This process concretized vertical alliances within the lower strata through which the *medieros* again became dependent on the *rancheros* from whom they rented land. At the same time, though, the *rancheros* were able to strengthen their ties with the *medieros,* and these relationships had the effect of encouraging a new kind of horizontal solidarity among what were now the least privileged segments of local society.

Thus, from 1906 to 1908, two different socioeconomic blocs formed in the *pueblos* of the Galeana district. The wealthy rancher-merchants allied with the regional oligarchy, which exercised power throughout the state, while the small-scale *rancheros* and *medieros* of the region forged a new alliance united in opposition to the more powerful group. During this period the differences between these two social groups became so accentuated that they developed different kinds of leisure activities. While the wealthy ranchers and merchants attended formal dances organized by the "distinguished and elegant *jefe político* of the district, Francisco Mateus" or by the foreign groups in the region, the small-scale *rancheros* and *medieros* endeavored to revive the traditional ceremonial life of the *pueblos* in which the local parish became the center of social life, "no matter the priest's wishes." Baptisms, first communions, and marriages became memorable neighborhood celebrations, reinforced the bonds of solidarity between *rancheros* and *medieros* and, by establishing relationships of marriages and *compadrazgo* among group members, created new social spaces. A new popular culture arose, in which *rancheros* and *medieros* were able to reinforce their collective self-identity and simultaneously differentiate them-selves from the wealthier people of the region.

Eventually, group association came to define where the men of the town would gather socially. The favorite retreat of the wealthy ranchers and merchants was the billiard parlor, where there was heavy betting and beer drinking. The *rancheros* and *medieros* frequented the bars, cantinas, and *sotol* outlets. These sold *aguardiente* made from sugarcane and locally pro-duced *sotol,* made from agave specific to the region, which the people preferred to beer. Relations among equals were encouraged while social relations between the two groups diminished sharply, deepening the social polarization that had begun with the economic development dating from 1885.

There were exceptions to the rule: Enrique Portilla, a rancher and son of the municipal tax collector in Casas Grandes (Genevevo Portilla Chávez), joined the town's radical group of *rancheros* and *medieros* in 1907. Later, in 1910, he became one of the town's most notable revolutionary leaders even though he belonged by birth to the wealthy group and had still enjoyed their social acceptance prior to the revolution. But perhaps this is less an exception that proves the rule than it is an example of the mobilization of an older structure of relationships. Enrique Portilla was related on his mother's side to a family of *rancheros* and *medieros* named Chávez, and it was these same Chávezes who sponsored Portilla's membership by *com-padrazgo* in the "los de abajo" group. Such a relationship was a throwback to the not too distant past of the Apache Wars, when vertical intergroup social relationships were the rule and were synonymous with daily survival. Where this tradition lapsed, the horizontal alliances within the two groups became the rule and brought with them the possibility of violent inter-group confrontation.

These profound social changes combined with ecological and economic conditions between 1906 and 1909—droughts, crop failures, a commercial and industrial crisis, and high unemployment—to exacerbate an already precarious situation. The Galeana district was like a lighted stick of dyna-mite, and the explosion came in 1907 when a large number of *rancheros* and *medieros* joined the Partido Liberal Mexicano and took part in an unsuc-cessful armed uprising.

The participation of *rancheros* and *medieros* of the Galeana district in the armed insurrections carried out by members of the PLM from 1906 to 1908 marked a qualitative change in what had been a process of latent resistance from 1886 to 1905. During the prior period, the region's residents reacted against capitalist modernization and the devastating effects of large-scale agribusiness. The *rancheros* formed agrarian commissions, petitioned the Ministry of Economic Development, and traveled to Mexico City to present their grievances directly to the Government Palace or to the president of the Republic himself. On other occasions, such as the riot in Ascensión in 1891, they reacted violently to the appointment of an outsider as municipal judge or to excessive taxation. In the former case they killed the judge; in the latter, they destroyed the tax records.

There was also latent resistance to the Mormon colonies in the area. This Protestant sect, whose members began settling in the region in 1886, provoked a process of cultural reawakening in which the locals rejected the Mormon presence on a day-to-day basis. Reinforcing their own Catholicism, traditions, local customs, monogamy, and incipient communal culture provided them an identity with which to oppose the Anglo-Saxon culture brought by the Mormons.

This almost imperceptible resistance sometimes erupted in violence; after 1902 the intrusion of the wealthy Mormons in economic areas traditionally controlled by the *rancheros* made patent the political competition between the two groups. At the beginning of this century, it was a commonplace event for Mormon women to be insulted in the streets of these towns. Many times between 1902 and 1905 Mormon men were insulted and attacked on these streets, although they were never robbed. The irrigation system constructed by the Mormon-owned Compañía Mexicana de Agricultura e Irrigación was sabotaged, and the culprits were never brought to justice. All these actions were clear manifestations of the fact that the *rancheros* in the region had identified the Mormons as their enemies.

Also, with the implementation of the law of 1905, the judicial records showed increasing but apparently isolated acts of violence against important merchant-moneylenders. Poor *rancheros* and *medieros* who had suffered from the moneylenders' voracity were the perpetrators of most of these attacks. This violence shattered even the traditional ties of kinship and *compadrazgo* that had in the past held the poor citizens' vengeful impulses in check.

This general situation reveals many (if not all) of the characteristics of a struggle between rich and poor. The community solidarity typical of the region since the first settlers had arrived and banded together to protect themselves from the attacks of the Apache Indians disintegrated during the first decade of the twentieth century. After 1905 the *rancheros* fought to expropriate Mormon properties, to refute the local elites allied with the oligarchy headed by Terrazas, and to appropriate the haciendas owned by the regional oligarchs.

MICHAEL KEARNEY

Mixtec Political Consciousness:

From Passive to Active Resistance

This chapter speaks to the bewildering complexity of the Mexican countryside and its political landscape. It focuses on the Mixteca region of
western Oaxaca, a region that is underrepresented in the literature on
agrarian issues and is in many ways anomalous with respect to rural Mexico. Its study may well prove of use when reconsidering the current debates
about the interrelationships between ideology and political action, and
the historical, national, and geopolitical conditions that influence their
expression.

In what follows I shall examine these issues with respect to the Mixteca
at large, drawing on my ethnographic work among residents and migrants
from the town of San Jerónimo Progreso, in the district of Silacayoapan.
Like the term "region," "the Mixteca at large" may have several meanings,
for today there are tens of thousands of identifiably "Mixtec" people concentrated in areas far from the sierra of western Oaxaca, in particular in the
cities and countryside of Baja California and in the United States. Here I
analyze the changing contours of Mixtec political consciousness—and the
movement from passive to active resistance that these changes entail—by
contrasting descriptions of Mixtec political consciousness in Oaxaca and
in three contexts near the border where the Mixtecs are subject to distinct
sets of influences and are politically engaged in a manner that has never
been seen in Oaxaca.

Some working definitions are necessary before turning to the consideration of Mixtec political thought and action. I take *politics* in the context of
the Mixteca and the Mixtec diaspora to be based on the struggle for *value*
derived from land and labor, including agricultural production for use,
for wages, and for profit. Value can also be accumulated from market activity including nonagricultural labor markets and commodity markets. *Repression* is herein defined as any economic, political, social, or cultural-

ideological condition or practice that furthers the extraction of net value from the Mixteca or from sectors of its dispersed population located elsewhere in Mexico or in the United States. Conversely, *resistance* is defined as activities and social forms—and the sentiments, culture, and consciousness cohering with them—that impede the extraction of value from the Mixteca or, to put it another way, that enable low-income Mixtecs to retain value that would otherwise be extracted from them.

The form that resistance takes, whether passive or active, rebellious or revolutionary, is shaped in part by the forms of repression. These range from direct, immediate, and highly visible forms of repression (of which the most dramatic is appropriation of land) to much more subtle ones such as the payment of a few cents to have one's shoes shined by someone who shines shoes for a living because his parents or grandparents lost their land. When we say that resistance in the face of repression is *active*, this implies that it is conscious, as for example in the attempts of farmworkers to form unions. While such currents are sporadically present among the Mixtecs, passive resistance is pervasive. *Passive* resistance is informed by a less articulate political consciousness, embodied in cultural forms and contents that are usually called "traditional" or "indigenous."

Repression and Passive Resistance: A "Primitive" Identification of Ethnicity

In the first hundred years of the conquest, the population of the Mixteca declined by some 90 percent. Also annihilated in this human catastrophe was the greater part of pre-Columbian Mixtec culture. But in a seeming paradox, the Mixteca today, three hundred years later, is still remarkably "Indian" in appearance. Communities such as San Jerónimo are wrapped in what appear at first glance to be "indigenous" cultural and social forms, presumably survivals of its pre-Columbian past. But what is it that survives? In the first century of Spanish control, the economy and society of the Mixteca were profoundly transformed by the introduction of Spanish agricultural technology and commercial production. Much of the largely dispersed population was concentrated into planned settlements for more effective governance, conversion, and extraction of wealth (Spores 1967, 1984). These new communities were constituted as communes with considerable internal autonomy, but also with enhanced vulnerability to extraction by interests in the greater colonial society. Each commune became a social and cultural world of its own, in which local tradition was invented by processes of local mutation interacting with the tutelage of Catholic priests who oversaw the indoctrination of the Indians within the administrative structure of colonial society.

The presence of the commune as a legal basis of land tenure and community distinguishes areas of "Indian" Mexico from *mestizo* communities of *pequeños proprietarios* and *ejidatarios* in central and northern Mexico. The Indian commune, Eric Wolf's "closed corporate peasant community," is today an anachronism that took shape as the main Hispanic contenders competed for the spoils of New Spain.

In colonial times, as today, the communes insulated the indigenous communities from the most direct forms of accumulation by outside interests. While tribute and taxes siphoned off wealth from these communities, they did not completely destroy their capacity to reproduce themselves autonomously (Diskin 1986). Inside these reserves, the semicaptive inhabitants seized upon the cultural resources of their pre-Columbian heritage, and the not so different forms of Spanish colonial culture, to establish a hybrid *bricolage* that defined their collective identity vis-à-vis the predatory forces encircling their community. This dialectic of inside and outside generated the continued invention and reinvention of locally distinctive social forms and symbolic systems, the most notable of which are the civil-religious ceremonial complexes that form the backbone of community organization and identity.

In these communes there developed a colonial Indian society and culture, hybrid in some ways but better thought of as new forms that diverged from the equally emergent *mestizo* society with which they contrast today. In communities such as San Jerónimo, the most genuine survival is the pre-Columbian language, which invests all other indigenous traits with an apparent authenticity.

Land disputes, endemic causes of armed conflict in the Mixteca as in Oaxaca generally, are (with the exception of sporadic land grabs by *caciques*) typically not between local communes and outside interests, but between neighboring communes themselves (Dennis 1976). These perennial tensions have reinforced the enclavement of these communities to a degree equal to if not greater than the threat of penetration by non-Indian interests. The society and culture of the reserves are thus doubly determined: first by the colonial and postcolonial administrative policies, and by corresponding geopolitical conditions, and second by the internecine conflict among neighboring reserves. This perpetuation of local identity makes possible a collective closing of ranks against the outside and, as such, is the main form of "passive" resistance. Thus, although their pre-Columbian authenticity is largely spurious, these local traditions together constitute a viable identity that is conspicuously distinct from mainstream Mexican culture and society. As a form of passive resistance, this invented tradition is both salvation and damnation. For just as it strengthens the Indian community, so also does it become a stigma of the oppressed—which marks the Mixteca native as prey for his enemies.

The situation of the Mixteca within the increasingly internationalized world economy is thus somewhat paradoxical. Unlike central and northern Mexico, where there have been and still are rather direct connections between penetration of foreign capital and revolutionary activity (Goldfrank 1979), there is at present very little direct penetration of either national or international capital into the Mixteca. In this regard its insularity is assured by its rugged mountainous terrain. Having no extensive commercially exploitable natural resources, the region has been abandoned to the "Indians," who themselves are unable to scratch out even a minimal livelihood from the increasingly deteriorating landscape and who are therefore forced in massive numbers to migrate and emigrate from their homeland in search of supplemental income. The Mixteca thus has become indirectly internationalized with respect to labor, given that large and growing numbers of Mixtecan migrants work in Mexican commercial-agricultural and other enterprises that are themselves highly internationalized. Furthermore, large and increasing numbers of migrants from the Mixteca are directly internationalized as they stream into the United States in search of work.

While there is today little direct intervention by the state in the region, the Mixteca has a long history of extraction of value. Formerly via pre-Columbian tributary obligations and colonial *caciques* and haciendas, extraction is now mainly via migration and emigration, indirect forms of extraction that correspond to the general quiescence of the Mixteca. There are, to be sure, current instances of active rebellion among the Triques of the Mixteca Alta in response to land seizures and gross human-rights violations by local *caciques* (Amnesty International 1986); and in the northern Mixteca of Guerrero, the revolutionary sentiments that arose in the 1960s, when Lucio Cabañas led guerrilla forces in the area, are still alive. But aside from these sporadic rebellions and revolutionary currents, the Mixteca at large is best characterized as permeated with varying types and degrees of passive resistance expressed in the social and cultural forms of the indigenous communes.

The perpetuation of the commune as a collectivity, and efforts by individuals to remain a member of it, stem from a desire to avert total proletarianization and the likely impoverishment and misery that accompany it. The commune is thus both an economic defense against proletarianization and a source of psychological security for the migrants in the distant north.

From Passive to Active Resistance:
The Emergence of Ethnicity as an Idiom of Popular Politics

Mixtec migration has scattered individuals and families to the four winds. One might expect that these experiences would dilute any sense of "Indianness" or collective identity. Since this is not the case, the Mixtecs provide an interesting case study for exploring recent post-Leninist theories of peasant-worker consciousness. Nash (1979), Taussig (1980), and Archila (n.d.), among others, have argued that resistance can be informed significantly by forms of consciousness that draw upon non-Western social and cultural resources, and that the ensuing resistance may assume correspondingly nonstandard forms.

Owing largely to the survival of the Mixtec Indian nobility well into the colonial period and to the relatively small number of Spanish and *mestizo* settlers in the region even today, the Indian versus non-Indian caste relations typical of Chiapas and Guatemala have not developed in the Mixteca. Consequently one wears one's Indianness casually in the Mixteca, and it is constructed as such (as I have discussed above) more vis-à-vis other Indian communities than vis-à-vis *mestizos*. In the north, this Indian-versus-Indian opposition is relaxed, and the Mixtecs find themselves to be a minority indigenous group. This latent ethnicity, which in the Mixteca serves as a form of passive resistance, in the north becomes the raw material of a self-conscious ethnicity serving the cultural and ideological needs of a people awakening to active forms of resistance.

There are three distinct northern contexts in which Mixtec ethnicity is being so reconstituted; and in each of these, Mixtec experience is anchored in the Indian communes of Oaxaca. These northern contexts are (1) farm-work for transnational agribusiness corporations, (2) urban shantytowns, and (3) semi-underground undocumented life in communities and diverse secondary labor markets throughout California. In the following pages I examine the Mixtec experience in these three milieux and show how they have set in motion oppositions between "Mixtec" and "non-Mixtec" that are promoting the emergence of a conscious Mixtec identity, both as a target of repression and as a basis for active resistance. This examination of the dialectic of emergent Mixtec ethnicity provides the terms for a critical commentary on prevalent theories of popular mobilization in rural Mexico.

MIXTEC FARMWORKERS AND THE STATE

Subsistence and Commercial Agriculture. As recent empirical and theoretical work demonstrates (see Kearney 1980), modern commercial agriculture and so-called subsistence agriculture are but components of a highly integrated system of production that spans national boundaries. The most advanced modern agronomy and the most wretchedly poor villagers are incorporated into one distorted agrarian system. Rather than being two distinct systems of production, subsistence and corporate agriculture are but two sides of the same coin. Champions of the "Green Revolution" maintain the myth of the separateness of these hypostatized "sectors" by focusing on their technological differences; they fail to mention the human and economic links between them.

The most important of these links are people, farm laborers who are born and reproduce in the subsistence sector but who are employed in the commercial sector. Corporate commercial agriculture has destroyed subsistence cultivation by accumulating land and national and international resources that might otherwise have been devoted to more-balanced agrarian developmental policies. It also perpetuates and indeed exacerbates rural poverty by providing less than living wages for the so-called subsistence cultivators who are in its employ, virtually all of whom are more accurately referred to as "infrasubsistence cultivators."

Thus, each year tens of thousands of these small, part-time Mixtec farmers are forced into the distant farm-labor markets of Sinaloa and the Californias. But here they are only partially absorbed by corporations that hire them as temporary field-workers. And although there is a growing, fully proletarianized, floating Mixtec-farmworker population, the majority are sporadically thrown back onto their village economies.

Peasants and Proletarians. The deconstruction of the mythic duality of commercial and subsistence agriculture entails the collapse of certain social categories based on it, especially the idealized distinction between "peasant" and "proletarian." The category of pure peasantry has generally been inappropriate for most of Latin America. It is, however, constantly reified by *campesinista* populists and by romantic anthropologists who attempt to resurrect A. V. Chayanov, the anti-Soviet champion of the Narodniks. Whereas Stalin was unwilling to accept the essential non-kulak peasantness of the rural Soviet small farmers, some modern-day populists are unwilling to accept the essentially proletarian character of the contemporary Mexican rural masses; they ascribe to them a "traditional peasant" nature and propose the conservation or the resurrection of the "small family farm" as a solution to the problems of the countryside.

The situation of the Mixtecs is similar to that which Laite (1981) has demonstrated in the case of migrant Peruvian mine workers. Their partial proletarianization is an insufficient condition for the formation of a working-class consciousness, while at the same time this split existence undermines agrarian consciousness. But other cultural and historical forces also intrude.

A case in point: some 40,000 Mixtecs migrate to work in the tomato fields of the San Quintín Valley of Baja California.[1] They enter these industrial settings—which Carey McWilliams (1939) appositely described decades ago as "factories in the fields"—carrying with them the non-capitalist culture of their indigenous homeland. In recent years the Mixtec

1. This situation is a spin-off of similar conditions in Sinaloa, where essentially the same analysis elaborated here also applies.

leadership of the independent national farmworkers' union, the CIOAC (Central Independiente de Obreros Agrícolas y Campesinos), has been attempting to organize this work force in the face of well-orchestrated repression leveled by the combined forces of the growers and the government at the state and federal level. Given the ethnic background of the work force, this confrontation has taken on the dimensions of a conflict of *los mixtecos* against the growers and various representatives of the state. The state and the growers not only have a major labor problem on their hands, but they also find to their chagrin that they have *un problema indígena* in what is perhaps the most *mestizo* corner of Mexico. The quasi-organized Mixtecs are embarrassing the state by repudiating any allegiance to the PRI and the CTM[2] into which the grower-state alliance is attempting to incorporate them, with the immediate objective of breaking the CIOAC and defusing the labor conflict.

Less than living wages and abysmally bad living and working conditions are the grievances of these farmworkers and the focus of classic working-class demands, voiced by cadres from the CIOAC and the PSUM (Partido Socialista Unificado de México), which supports the farmworker union. Thus, both the material and the semantic milieux are affecting class consciousness to some degree. But the internal dialogue within the work force is being elaborated as a struggle between *nosotros los mixtecos* and *los patrones*. For their part, the state and the growers are opposing the Mixtecs qua Mixtecs and, in so doing, are also collaborating in the objectification of what would otherwise be a latent ethnic identity. In the Mixteca, Mixtec identity is not salient, for there is no direct non-Mixtec opposition against which to define it. In the tomato fields and labor camps of Baja California, though, it is emerging as a major and conscious theme. With respect to class consciousness, then, these itinerant Mixtec farmworkers are arguably far from constituting a "class in itself"; they are, however, rapidly becoming an ethnic group *for* itself. This unanticipated development of Mixtec political consciousness is also evolving in the other principal northern Mixtec settings, in the urban shantytowns of the border and in the United States.

2. The PRI (Partido Revolucionario Institucional, or Institutional Revolutionary Party), the dominant political party in Mexico, is virtually synonymous with the state. The CTM (Confederación de Trabajadores Mexicanos, or Confederation of Mexican Workers) is effectively controlled by the PRI.

URBAN MIXTECS AND THE STATE

As migrants to the border cities of northwestern Mexico and in California, Mixtecs tend to form enclaves in which they replicate village society and culture. As in Oaxaca, these enclaves become bastions, more or less protecting one and all from outside dangers. But here the immediate external threat is not equally land-poor neighboring indigenous communities but, rather, predatory and dangerous forces of the city: urban crime and violence, labor exploitation, and police extortion and harassment. These are conditions common to all the shantytown dwellers of the border area, but the experiences of the urban Mixtecs are unique in that they are targeted for and experience these abuses as *indios,* often referred to by the epithet *los oaxacas* and, increasingly, as *los mixtecos.* In Tijuana, Mexicali, Tecate, Ensenada, and Nogales—all cities that essentially have been ethnically homogeneous—"racial" discrimination now poisons public spaces. Ironically, the castelike relations between Indians and *mestizos,* of which the Mixteca is relatively free, are highly manifest in Mexico's northwestern cities. Here, as in Sinaloa and in the San Quintín Valley, Mixtecs 2,000 kilometers from their homeland are forced into an awareness of their status as *un pueblo indígena.*

The dialogue of confrontation with the state that is being played out in the border cities has parallels with the confrontation occurring in San Quintín. An example: two years ago, several emerging urban-Mixtec spokespersons and their middle-class allies confronted municipal authorities over police extortion from Mixtec women street venders in Tijuana. As a result of extensive media coverage of these events on both sides of the border, a police commander was removed from office and abuse of the women was reduced. Heartened by these victories, the Mixtecs formed the Asociación de los Mixtecos Residentes en Tijuana (ASMIRT).

The association is modeled on the indigenous democratic town councils found in the Indian communes of the Mixteca, with two important differences: first, the association was conceived as open to members of *any* Mixtec community who happened to be residing in Tijuana (clearly a vision of pan-Mixtec identity); and second, unlike the town councils of the communes, women were encouraged to be officers and otherwise to take active roles in the association. These two innovations—the vision of a pan-

Mixtec identity and the emergence of women as political participants—are indicators of the progressive currents that were emerging. Moreover, this association vociferously asserted its independence from all political parties and soon began to form cooperative links with the CIOAC in the San Quintín Valley, while simultaneously developing close links with the PSUM. With increasing frequency, no doubt in large part because of the novel Mixtec presence in the border cities, the international print and electronic media (especially those papers in opposition to the government) began to cover what quickly developed as the "Mixtec story."

Although lacking the large numbers of the San Quintín population—where the CIOAC was able to turn out between 8,000 and 10,000 marchers—the urban Mixtecs were able to rally about 1,000 Mixtecs and their supporters for street demonstrations. On several occasions they confronted Baja California's governor in what were widely regarded as embarrassments for the PRI. During one of these events, officers of the ASMIRT publicly presented the governor with a copy of the Mexican Constitution, presumably so that he might read it; and on another public occasion they presented him with a jar of Oaxacan *mole,* to remind him of the presence of the Mixtecs. In all of these confrontations the presence of the Mixtecs as Indians from Oaxaca was affirmed, not only for the public at large but for the urban Mixtecs themselves. As in the San Quintín Valley, the sense of a pan-Mixtec identity was strengthened and defined for the urban Mixtecs, primarily in opposition to the state in its various guises. Formal and informal linkages and solidarity between the urban association and the CIOAC continued to flourish, and the public discourse of the urban Mixtecs began to manifest language to the *left* of the left wing of the PRI.

The adamant political independence of these two groups—urban dwellers and farmworkers—vis-à-vis the government and the PRI was both their greatest strength and, in retrospect, their greatest liability. For just as the transnational agribusiness firms and the state have been able to frustrate the efforts of the CIOAC, so too have outside interests (apparently emanating from the government, but in any event politically aligned with it) intervened internally in the ASMIRT to neutralize it as an independent popular organization and to bring it officially, and with much fanfare, into the fold of the PRI. Although the association is now in disarray, ironically the government—by attempting to crush independent Mixtec political opposition—is objectifying what until recently has been a nonexistent pan-Mixtec identity. And in so doing, it is preparing the ground for new phrases of the "Indian problem."

It is important to underscore the symbolic significance of *el indio* in Mexican nationalism and the embarrassment to the state of having *indígenas* in Tijuana and in San Quintín denouncing what they claim are abuses by the state. Furthermore, these denunciations are not occurring in the remote mountains of Oaxaca but on Mexico's northern border—in the spotlight of international public opinion. Although the state finds this situation intolerable, its attempts to resolve the problem have served only to exacerbate it, unwittingly arousing and reifying Mixtec identity.

MIXTECS IN THE UNITED STATES: EFFECTS OF IMMIGRATION POLICY

The third northern context in which pan-Mixtec identity is being nurtured is among the undocumented Mixtecs residing in California. As the Mexican peso and the material bases for existence in the Mixteca continue to decline, incentives for residing in California increase. Concurrently, the maturation of migration networks that support the binational migrants facilitate such relocation. Needless to say, such *ilegales* feel very insecure about any long-range residence in the United States, and uncertainty regarding the new U.S. immigration law has elevated their anxiety. One major liability of long-term residence in the north is the potential for loss of membership in one's natal commune. For this reason, both temporary and long-term sojourners make constant efforts to reaffirm their commune membership. These efforts include the remittance of assessments and returning to fulfill ceremonial and civil duties (or hiring someone as a stand-in). The amount of money expended by migrants on ceremonial and civil obligations in towns of the Mixteca has grown recently, in particular as a result of northern wages and dollar income. The civil-religious ceremonial complexes have been enhanced as a result, and the construction of migrant-subsidized public works has boomed. Thus, although Mixtecs are being expelled from their homeland at high and increasing rates, and to ever greater distances, the effect of this diaspora is a revitalization of the most important symbols and collective expressions of Mixtec identity.

Conclusions

These, then, are several of the contexts and dynamics that are nurturing the emergence of Mixtec ethnicity. Mixtec culture and society persist in the Mixteca as a form of passive resistance. In the north, however, they are becoming mobilized as a form of active resistance, as individuals and groups of Mixtecs are consciously and intentionally elaborating that resistance. This elaboration is derivative of the village-based passive ethnicity of the Mixteca; but, in contrast, this northern expression is pan-Mixtec in conception and influenced by a leftist agenda. The oppositional basis of ethnicity in the Mixteca lies in the conflicts between a particular community and the "enemy" communities that surround it and with which it feuds. In the north, however, this opposition is distant, not an immediate basis for differences. Instead, the more immediate oppositional relationships in the north, where the Mixtecs are fish out of water, are not "Mixtec versus Mixtec," but "Mixtec versus non-Mixtec" and, most especially, "Mixtec versus the state."

It is perhaps not an exaggeration to say that the current "Mixtec problem" is the major political issue in Baja California, and that the Mixtecs there are the most troublesome thorn in the side of the federal government and a number of its agencies. The response to this Mixtec problem—i.e., the reactions and policies of the PRI, the government of Baja California, and various state and federal agencies—has been an unwitting reaction to the Mixtecs as an "indigenous people." A dialectic of confrontation is being acted out: by responding to the Mixtecs qua Mixtecs, the state objectifies what is otherwise a vaguely defined identity. As the dialogue between the state and what was formerly a dispersed, nonidentifiable constituency becomes increasingly a dialogue between the state and a well-delineated ethnic group, the state concretizes Mixtecs as a group. And this definition becomes a powerful basis for the emergence of a Mixtec consciousness, which in turn is the basis for the activation of Mixtec political action—in opposition to that same state and its various national and international allies. The role of the news media in this process should not be underestimated. The ability of Mixtec leaders to call press conferences and the regular appearance of Mixtec voices and images on radio and television, on both sides of the border, are instances of news engendering news; this reportage gives substance to the emergent consciousness that it reports.

There is, to be sure, a primary conflict between the Mixtec communes and the forces of capitalist society that surround them. But this conflict is not, as in most of rural Mexico, the immediate struggle for land and its natural resources per se. Instead, the struggle for land in the Mixteca is replaced by a struggle for a product of that land: namely, the value-producing human labor power that is reproduced within the partial insularity of the commune. The Mixteca is a mosaic of such semiautonomous communities locked into age-old feuds with their neighbors, feuds that engender but also dissipate resistance. In the north, the terms of conflict are restructured, the repression is more immediate, and the resistance to it is more conscious and therefore more active.

MARÍA TERESA KORECK

Space and Revolution in Northeastern Chihuahua

I pondered all these things, and how men fight and lose the battle, and the thing that they fought for comes about in spite of their defeat, and when it comes turns out not to be what they meant, and other men have to fight for what they meant under another name. WILLIAM MORRIS, 1886[1]

In this essay I argue that the ascendancy of local and regional forms of consciousness over an incipient national consciousness may be accounted for in terms of identifiable social and political processes, rather than in terms of a "prepolitical" peasant mentality or an innate peasant parochialism. Forms of consciousness are enmeshed in historical processes and linked to particular territorial spaces, but they also have historical consequences, particularly to the degree that they orient the behavior of people acting within those spaces. The focus of this essay is the historical configuration of forms of collective identity that gained ascendancy during the 1910 revolutionary uprising in a particular area of the U.S.-Mexican border: the northeastern section of the state of Chihuahua, across the Río Bravo from the Texas counties of Presidio and Brewster, site of the Big Bend. To comprehend how forms of consciousness have informed social action, I analyze the materially and ideologically significant sociopolitical and territorial relationships that linked the rural groups mobilized on a part of the U.S.-Mexican border with a myriad of Mexican and U.S. social and political forces.

Popular participation in the 1910 revolutionary uprising by inhabitants of the Chihuahua countryside may be understood as the expression and the historical outcome of an ideological discontinuity in the articulation

This essay is based on ethnographic and archival research conducted from November 1982 through May 1984 in the village of Cuchillo Parado, Chihuahua, the state archives of Chihuahua, and the Mexican national archives located in Mexico City. The research was supported by dissertation research grants from the Social Science Research Council and the Inter-American Foundation. I am grateful to these institutions for their support.

1. Quoted in E. P. Thompson 1978:88.

between (*a*) local or regional spaces inhabited by rural groups and (*b*) national spheres of action and sentiment. This discontinuity stems from the tension between alternative styles of "imagining community" (Anderson 1983) and the personal, social, and political practices through which these different ways of imagining community could sustain historically constituted subjectivities, identities, and aspirations.

Marginalized both physically and culturally from the political nation, the rural groups that joined the revolution in northeastern Chihuahua found relevant modes of expressing alternative forms of social identification in the context of a semiautonomous political space. For the purposes of my analysis, the boundaries of this space are identified as coterminous with the material and ideological boundaries of a regional system of social relations. The distinctiveness of this regional system derived from the fact that it contained within itself "transnational" relations. That is to say, the border between Mexico and the United States did not operate as a boundary between two political nations but was itself embedded in a regional system of relations that crosscut national identities. In the analysis that follows, the most important contrast is not between "Mexico" and "the United States," but between this regional system of social relations and the Mexican nation.

Imagination and Destiny of the Chihuahuan Frontier

Benedict Anderson argues that "all communities larger than primordial villages of face-to-face contact (and perhaps even these) are imagined" (1983:15). What defines nations as political communities is that they are imagined as limited and sovereign. Anderson further observes that *nationalist* ideologies have come into being out of the transformation of two preceding cultural systems: the religious community and the dynastic realm (p. 20). Thus, for nationalism to develop, "what was required was a transformation of fatality into continuity, contingency into meaning.... It is the magic of nationalism to turn chance into destiny" (p. 19).

The development of conceptions of national identity is linked to processes of state formation. State activity is objectified in a repertoire of institutional practices that simultaneously define socially relevant events, practices, and relations as well as the seemingly unified "public sphere" which, besides its single sites, "exists as a shared social horizon for the members of a society" (Bommes and Wright 1982:260). This "public sphere" is legitimized as the civic sense; it is "disinterested" and nonpartisan:

What the civic sense more than anything else seems to involve is a definite concept of the public as a separate and distinct body and an attendant notion of genuine public interest, which though not necessarily superior to, is independent of and at times even in conflict with, both private and other sorts of collective interest. (Geertz 1963:156)

It would be misleading and inaccurate, however, to interpret the popular disaffection expressed in the revolution as the outcome of a confrontation between pristine and isolated social orders and the institutional forms and seemingly impersonal agencies that make it possible to "think the nation."[2] To do so would amount to assuming that local social orders—e.g., "the village community," on the one hand, and "the nation" and "the state" on the other—are in essence entities ontologically opposed to each other and that each independently contains the dynamics of its own explanation.

Relationships of a symbiotic or contradictory character between the local/regional spaces inhabited by rural groups and encompassing sociopolitical structures are anchored in historical and social processes. The military and civilian colonies established along the northern frontier throughout the nineteenth century, and their colonial predecessors, the presidios, were located on what at that time were regarded as the geographical and political fringes of Mexico. The creation of these colonies was the outcome of state activity; therefore, they were the genuine outposts of a nascent civic society. The inhabitants of these settlements internalized and embodied the ideological propositions that defined the "public interest."

These ideological propositions which established the categorical distinctions that regulated social relations, shaping identities and loyalties, were objectified in the settlement policies enacted by the Mexican state in the northern "fringes." In the nineteenth century, the inhospitable and dangerous frontier was to be settled with "Mexican nationals"[3] who had necessarily to be encouraged to become "a warrior people" (*un pueblo*

2. The expression "think the nation" is from Anderson 1983:28.
3. See Mexico 1848:11; also AGN, Ramo Gobernación Rep[ública] Mexicana Correspondencia, 1874 (2°874[2]1).

guerrero),[4] able to defend themselves against the incursions and attacks of alien "others," be these the Apaches or unidentified "barbarous hordes." It was through the military and defensive duties performed vis-à-vis this alien "other" that these settlers were to participate, albeit at the fringes, in a civic society that legitimated certain forms of claim through which these settlers won tacit recognition of their rights to local autonomy and freedom from outside interference, and explicit recognition of their rights to land (see Katz 1979a:30).

Under these conditions, the northern colonists willingly sought the recognition and ratification of their social identities by that distant authority, the central government. In the nineteenth century, local settlements addressed petitions and requests for land to the central authorities, who, in turn, usually replied by issuing land grants. These land grants fulfilled a twofold purpose: on the one hand, they were the institutionalized forms whereby the state recognized and legitimized the existence of these communities as collective entities and welcomed the inhabitants as Mexican "citizens."[5] On the other hand, this act of recognition provided the settlers with the material means of production, and thus their own reproduction, and also materially and ideologically mediated their self-sufficiency and autonomy as a community.[6] In fact, what accounted politically for the considerable autonomy granted "from above" to the northern settlements was the inconsistent, uneven, and somewhat unreliable presence that the "center" enjoyed with respect to the affairs of the "periphery."

The reciprocal relationship established between the settlers and the state (see A. Alonso 1986), therefore, was sustained by an ideological framework that organized social relationships on the frontier vis-à-vis the presence of alien "others"—which made possible the appeal to a hegemonic unified "public interest"—and by granting settlers access to land and assuring their

4. See AGN, Ramo Gobernación Rep. Mexicana Indios Bárbaros, 1852 (2°852[1]3); also AGN, Ramo Gobernación sin Sección Indios Bárbaros, 1852, Caja 402.

5. The inhabitants of Cuchillo Parado, for example, calling themselves "citizen colonists," requested formal ratification of their claims to land in the 1860s (see ATN, exp. 1.29[06]E.274).

6. Other powerful official implications were attached to the granting of lands. Land was expected to mediate the "conversion" of the idle classes with neither property nor occupation into "hardworking propertyholders" (see Mexico 1848:12). This secular conversion evokes the Franciscan missionary efforts in the same area during the eighteenth century.

local autonomy. At this historical conjuncture, the prevailing social and institutional arrangements sustained by this hegemonic ideological frame-work resonated both with the experiential realities of the local social orders as collectivities and with the identities and aspirations of their inhabitants.

At times, however, the "public interest" collided with other emerging interests, which were "private" (although collective) and which guided the practices of the northern settlers. The latter set of interests was itself the historical outcome of contingent and contradictory frontier experiences. In 1851, for example, government records report on "the vile and treach-erous conduct of the frontier settlers," noting that "the *immorality* of those populations has reached the point that their customs have become con-fused with those of the barbarians." This conduct led the authorities to "judge as traitors to the motherland those settlers who would buy their [the barbarians'] loot and who would protect or assist them in any way."[7]

By the late 1870s and early 1880s, it was the settlers who expressed their bitter disappointment with an aloof and disengaged central government that had failed to provide assistance to fend off Indian attacks. In a moving complaint to the authorities, the settlers claimed that

the Government had abandoned them to their own *destiny* . . . that they contrib-uted their lives and arms to rescue the institutions and now that they need the help of their fellow citizens, the protection of the Government for whom they have shed their blood . . . [they seem to be unable] to stir the spirit of those in charge to grant them assurances and guarantees.[8]

This incident raises the issue of the meaning of the word "destiny" (*destino*) in Spanish and the implications of its use by the colonists. The Spanish word *destino* has a twofold meaning. On the one hand it refers to one's "fate," and in this sense it coincides with the English meaning. On

---

7. AGN, Ramo Gobernación sin Sección Indios Bárbaros, 1851, Caja 391, Communica-tion between Ministerio de Guerra y Marina, Mexico City, and Comandante General de Chihuahua (my translation, interpolation, and emphasis). David Weber made the interesting observation that on the Mexican frontier categorical distinctions defined a "way of being": "To be an 'indio,' for example, meant to dress, act, and speak like an Indian. Thus nomadic Apaches who raided Mexican settlements in Arizona continued to be regarded as Indians, but Apaches who assimilated began to lose their ethnic and racial identity 'and are regarded by the Mexicans as Mexicans'" (Weber 1982:214).

8. AHSRE XIX 2-1-1771 7/8/1878, Chihuahua to Gobernación, Mexico (my transla-tion, interpolation, and emphasis).

the other hand, the word also carries certain meanings that in English are conveyed by the word "destination," as in "the purpose for which something or someone is destined" and/or "the place toward which one is going or sent." Consequently, its use by the settlers themselves provides an insight into the unfolding estrangement between the central authorities and the northern communities, and the impending shift in the focus of political loyalty. The so-called magic of nationalism had been shattered.

Revolution in Space: Reidentification of the "Other"

The fragmentation of the symbiotic relationship that had existed between the state, the northern communities, and their local allies—such as the *hacendados* and *rancheros*—and that had created and sustained an incipient national consciousness in the northern "fringes" resulted in drastic transformations in the countryside, leading to the eventual expression of popular disaffection. An explanation of this popular disaffection must be sought, therefore, in the redefinition of the "public interest" and its effects on the lives of the northern settlers. Katz has characterized the historical conditions that in the 1880s made possible the process referred to as the "transformation of the frontier into the border" (1981:7–18).[9] The political and economic consequences of this transformation for the former colonies were the loss of municipal autonomies, precipitated by an unprecedented process of political centralization, and the loss of lands (Katz 1981:3, 21).

The redefinition of the "public interest" that occurred with the transformation of the border was followed by drastic changes in the modalities, agencies, and institutional forms that mediated the relationships between the "center" and the "periphery." The effects of this redefinition were manifested in the reconstitution of the social relationships that had organized life on the frontier. The same settlers who as "citizens" had been empowered by and had embodied a nation-state that depended upon their presence on the "fringes" to assert its own sovereignty were now confronted by a process that attached entirely new and conflicting meanings to

9. These conditions were the defeat of the Apache Indians in the 1880s in conjunction with the completion of the railways linking northern Mexico with central Mexico and with the United States, conditions that increased the potential for exploitation of the lands occupied by the military colonists (see Katz 1981:7–18; Wasserman 1984:105–12).

that original organization of consent. The three core elements that had sustained the framework of social relationships and organized consent—the alien "other," the granting of lands, the recognition of local autonomies—underwent a racial reevaluation.

The defeat of the alien "other"—whose presence had in the past organized a morally binding framework of social relationships and legitimized a "warrior people" paradigm—reoriented the focus of the "public interest." Previously defined by contrast to the foreignness of enemies, the public interest now turned inward, toward policies and institutions defined from within the confines of a sovereign social and territorial space; that is, a nation-state "imagined" anew. During the Porfirian regime regional oligarchies, and eventually municipal and local state authorities, replaced the northern settlers as the new consenting partners of the nation-state (see Knight 1986a, 1:17, 21).

From the perspective of the state, two paradigms guided the policies that affected the parallel processes of political centralization and agrarian dispossession. One such paradigm was represented by the principle of *nonintervention*. The repeated requests and pleas for intervention that the northern colonists addressed to the central government during the second half of the nineteenth century were met with unresponsiveness and aloofness. For example, between 1898 and 1903, the *junta directiva* of the Agricultural Society of Cuchillo Parado addressed a series of pleas to the central government, requesting protection for their lands and even requesting notarized testimony of the village's original land grant (see Koreck n.d. 1 and n.d. 2). The state's refusal to respond attests to the modus operandi of nonintervention. These requests and pleas "from below" also attest to the colonists' twofold attempt to appeal to prior alliances and elicit an act of recognition from the "center," on the one hand, and to circumvent the now evident existence of regional oligarchies and (later) of municipal and local state authorities, on the other. It is in the context of the state's noninterventionist modus operandi that informal processes of land dispossession occurred and were tacitly condoned.[10] The second paradigm,

10. The timing of agrarian dispossession in Cuchillo Parado between 1881 and 1904, and the local resistance the process engendered, clearly did not correlate with the advent of a formalized apparatus of political centralization (see Koreck n.d. 1 and n.d. 2). Also see Wasserman 1980:29 for an enumeration of the rebellions that occurred throughout the state of Chihuahua long before the 1910 *maderista* uprising. Nugent's suggestion for

that of state *intervention*, is an explicit one, represented by the development of a political and legal apparatus that directly mediated political centralization and land expropriation.[11]

The issue of land and the implications of its ownership by the 1880s, then, becomes a privileged analytical domain for the study of the redefinition of the "public interest." Along with the changes at the level of social relations there was a change in the relationship between people and the land. Land, which had symbolized individual self-sufficiency and mediated communal autonomy from outside interference for the long-established settlers, became the object of commercial speculation. Land was turned into a commodity by the *hacendados* and by legal provisions that permitted commercial interests such as the *compañías deslindadoras* (development companies that surveyed "vacant" public lands) to redefine the significance of land and its relationship to people.

The perceived arbitrariness of the new circumstances that fueled popular disaffection and moral outrage after the 1880s (see Knight 1986a, 1:165–66) stemmed from the lack of coincidence between "national" and "local" projects. These coincidences, which had existed previously, no longer obtained, nor did the material and ideological conditions that had sustained them. To use popular rhetoric, we may think of this discontinuity as the outcome of a fractured "destiny." Moral outrage indeed fueled popular mobilization. However, to attribute the armed uprising to a sudden emergence on the local and regional stage of a previously unknown political authority, conditioned by a process of state formation that had acquired a more explicit character, cannot portray the depth of the moral alienation inflicted by the nation-state (*el gobierno*) on the Chihuahuan peasantry, not to mention the perplexity that this alienation still evokes.

The marginalization of these rural groups from the political nation, a marginalization effected by the redefinition of the "public interest," led to the ascendancy of alternative modes of collective and individual identifica-

---

"a radical revision of the periodization of the revolution in Namiquipa" should obviously be broadened to include the whole state of Chihuahua (Nugent 1985:81; also see Osorio's essay above).

11. See Almada 1964 on the development of this legal and political apparatus. Processes of land dispossession in the villages of San Carlos, La Mula, and El Mulato were clearly associated with the apparatus of political centralization (Koreck n.d. 1 and n.d. 2).

tion. The reorientation of the loyalties that claimed the lives and actions of the frontier settlers, and of the ideological boundaries that sustained social relations, has been eloquently expressed by a participant in the popular mobilization of 1910. "We didn't yet have a definite idea of what government was; rather we wanted this or that chief, this or that leader—as we used to call him in that time—our chief."[12] This statement explicitly portrays the changes that had occurred with respect to the focus of political loyalty. While the self-sacrifice of the "warrior" had been conceived of as "public"—that is, offering oneself up for a territory or for an idea of the "nation-state" such as "the government" (*el gobierno*)—that of the "revolutionary" was "personal and individual," offering oneself up for the *patria chica* represented by a chief or leader.[13]

Revolution in Space: *Maderismo* and *Villismo*

Elsewhere I have addressed the historical and social configuration of identities and interests at the local and regional level in northeastern Chihuahua before and during the revolution (see Koreck n.d. 2). Local and regional details offer insight into the organization of popular revolutionary movements and their relationship to encompassing social and political processes. It is in the context of regional details that several relationships will be addressed: What were the contours of the *patria chica*? How were the social and territorial boundaries of revolutionary struggle defined? And how did the different experiences and aspirations of marginalized rural groups find relevant forms of expression?

The concept of region used here does not refer to a politically defined area or one whose boundaries are only naturally determined. Rather, the region is created by the system of social relationships that obtain within it; that is to say, by the exchange of goods, wives, husbands, priests, horses, harvests, arms, and such intangibles as the communication of knowledge, experiences, and events. Distinctive and characteristic patterns of social exchange have existed in the Río Conchos region over the past two hun-

12. My translation; quoted in E. Meyer 1978:34.

13. For a provocative discussion of the development of the concept of *patria* in medieval political thought, see Kantorowicz 1951, which distinguishes between "public" and "personal and individual" political sacrifices.

dred years, as is attested in Spanish colonial and Mexican national documents.[14] It is in this sense that the riverine settlements along the Conchos River developed over time into a region.

Similar historical and social continuities, reflected in accounts of daily experiences, developed across the border through the mutual involvement of Mexicans and Americans before the revolution (c. 1880s–1910) (see Hawley 1964; Langford and Gipson 1952; Smithers 1981 and n.d. 1; Tyler 1975b). This symbiotic relationship was described by an inhabitant of the Big Bend: "in that period the Rio Grande divided only the two nations, not the people" (Smithers 1981:15). Large ranches and small farms, mining and wax-making operations, and American trading posts, which depended on trade from the Mexican side, were all located on the Big Bend side of the border (Smithers n.d. 1). Barter and Mexican money, which circulated freely along the border, regulated most of the exchanges (Hawley 1964). The American trading posts, through which all transactions seem to have taken place, sold merchandise (sewing material, canned goods, coffee, sugar, and other items) and also purchased products (wood, furs, chino grass, ropes, etc.) from their customers (Smithers n.d. 1). Thus, regular patterns and objects of exchange, as well as regulated forms of social relationships, had been established along and across the border before the revolutionary uprising.

This system of social relationships, encompassing Mexican settlements along the Río Conchos and American settlements across the Rio Grande, was the geographical and social space within which emerged regional and personal loyalties that cut across national identities. In this context, the inhabitants of the region developed forms of social relationship and exchange that expressed joint interests contingent on the inhabitants' positions within the socioeconomic and political structures. During the revolution, this regional system of relationships became mobilized as a semi-autonomous political space.

An examination of the motives for revolt reveals that there existed common experiences and unifying grievances concerning land dispossession and political arbitrariness, giving rise to shared interpretations among the rural groups that articulated the significance of these events at the local and

14. See Hackett 1923–37; Kelley 1952a, 1952b; AHSRE, exp. 1/2/488, 1 February 1782; Parish Archives of Ojinaga, 1775–1850.

regional level. Popular grievances were directed against the abuses by Mexican nationals (*caciques, hacendados,* municipal authorities), and in most instances the abuses tied land dispossession to political arbitrariness (see Koreck n.d. 2). Available documents mention only one incident involving an American intrusion, yet the intruder is not even identified as "American." A complaint from the villagers of La Mula describes how their fields (*labores*) and houses were burnt by Ciro Amarillas, the Porfirian *jefe político* of Ojinaga, who is said to have been sent to claim their lands "for a certain foreigner."[15] That foreigner, whose national identity is neither revealed nor emphasized in the complaint, happened in fact to be one William Randolph Hearst.[16]

At the time of the revolution, this region contained no easily identifiable American-owned enterprises (e.g., mines, stores, haciendas) within Mexican territory, with the exception of a hacienda owned by Davis and Co.[17] This hacienda was the target of what seems to have been the only incident directed against American-owned property. In February 1911, Inés Salazar and a band of thirty revolutionaries surrounded the ranch of Lamar Davis, an American in San Antonio, Chihuahua, "demanding provisions, guns and ammunition, horses and saddles" (Tyler 1975a:272). This incident, however, could well have been motivated by factional disputes within the revolutionary leadership.[18]

The relationships and exchanges that sustained rebel activities from 1910 to 1915 resembled the routinized tactics of the region, based on reciprocally negotiated exchanges, that had emerged during the years preceding the revolution. After 1915, though, the organization of a social and territorial space as "habitat" encompassing both sides of the border no longer enjoyed the same character. The relationships established across the Rio Grande were no longer reciprocally negotiated; instead they were mainly organized through military campaigns and raids, demonstrated, for exam-

15. ATN, exp. 1.29(06)E.150, July 1908.

16. Information concerning Mr. Hearst's involvement in this case was made available to me by Carlos Gonzáles Herrera in a personal communication.

17. For information on enterprises in the district of Iturbide, Chihuahua, see Kalms 1905; POCH 1912–13.

18. The dispute may have involved Inés Salazar and José de la Cruz Sánchez, leader of the uprising in the Ojinaga region. Sánchez is said to have been conducting "personal arrangements" and privately benefiting from his business relationship with Mr. Davis (see AHSRE LE-757, leg. 9, 9 December 1912).

ple, by rebels' strategic use of "the other side" or the more direct manner in which "resources" were brought back to Mexico.

At the outset of the revolution, rebels found a receptive audience for their cause across the border. The positive disposition toward the rebel cause remained steady throughout the *maderista* struggle. Such receptivity encouraged at least one of the *maderista* men—Braulio Hernández—to issue a bitter accusation against the Porfirian regime in both English and Spanish. This lengthy manifesto, dated January 1911 in Cuchillo Parado, Chihuahua, states: "He [Porfirio Díaz] has deceived the people of the United States by fostering riots against Americans, so that the anti-reelection party [the *maderistas*] might be blamed for an anti-race feeling which does not exist among Mexicans."[19]

Widespread sympathy for the *maderista* rebels was evident along and across the border, and American openness toward the rebels was expressed in several ways. According to a message sent by the U.S. acting secretary of war to the secretary of state on 23 February 1911, "80% of the Mexican population on both sides of the river and the majority of the Americans sympathized with the rebels."[20] From Presidio, Texas, directly across the Río Bravo from Ojinaga, Chihuahua, reports stated that "almost the entire citizenship of the town are in sympathy with the insurrectionists. . . . The insurrectionists especially are courteous and offer to furnish every protection to any American coming in contact with them."[21]

The myriad resources available to rebels on the frontier during the revolution is an example of the semiautonomous characteristics of this regional space. A systematic account of these resources would include first and foremost the rebels' use of U.S. territory as a base from which they could organize, purchase arms, recruit men, and launch armed attacks against federal positions across the border. For example, in late 1910 the *maderista* leader Abrahám González prepared the attack on Ojinaga from Presidio and Shafter, Texas, spending more than a month there purchasing arms and ammunition and recruiting men.[22] Furthermore, the use of roads,

19. AHSRE LE-R-677, leg. 2, fol. 85.

20. Hall and Coerver forthcoming; see also ADN, exp. XI/481.5/60, Caja 13, 12 January 1911.

21. *New Era*, 17 December 1912.

22. AHSRE LE-620, 28 December 1910. See also AHSRE LE-620, 26 December 1920; AHSRE LE-623, 12 January 1911; ADN, exp. XI/481.5/63, Caja 20.

telephones, and postal services located on the American side of the border improved the rebels' ability to control and coordinate their actions (see Smithers n.d. 1).

U.S. territory also became a "sanctuary" (see Katz 1981:20), a place of refuge for revolutionaries when their own positions were threatened or attacked by enemy troops. During an *orozquista* attack on Ojinaga, for example, Colonel Sánchez and other *maderista* leaders fled across the border to Presidio, Texas.[23] At times of greater upheaval, leading to the breakdown of local economies and the paralysis of productive activities, U.S. territory served as a sanctuary not only for the rebels but also for displaced *pacíficos* and their families.[24] Further, the chosen place of residence for some revolutionary leaders was the United States. Ojinaga's local leader, José de la Cruz Sánchez, it was reported, "lives in American territory, having a house constantly occupied by his family in Presidio, Texas."[25] The territory of the United States was also considered a "neutral" meeting place for competing revolutionary leaders attempting to settle their differences. A series of such meetings took place on "the other side" between Torbio Ortega and José de la Cruz Sánchez in 1913.[26]

Proximity to the United States also provided the rebels with access to a disaffected population composed of Texans of Mexican descent and Mexican nationals who were permanent residents on the American side of the border. Several reports mention recruitment activities carried out by the rebels and their apparent success in enrolling a large number of recruits from Texas to join the ongoing revolutionary struggle in Mexican territory.[27] Luther T. Ellsworth, a U.S. representative for the Departments of State and Justice and American consul at Ciudad Porfirio Díaz, commenting on the siege of Ojinaga, was quoted as follows: "There are fully 10,000 Mexicans possessing modern arms who are ready at the least chance, should they gain confidence in a rebel leader, to cross the border and flock

23. AHSRE LE-744, leg. 3, 14 September 1912.

24. For examples of these occurrences, see AHSRE LE-661, 10 May 1911; AHSRE LE-744, leg. 3, 2 September 1912; AHSRE LE-767, leg. 7, 19 March 1913; AHSRE LE-757, leg. 4, May 1913.

25. My translation; AHSRE LE-757, leg. 9, 9 December 1912.

26. See AHSRE LE-757, leg. 8, 20 March 1913.

27. E.g., AHSRE LE-611, leg. 3, 17 and 18 November 1910; AHSRE LE-620, 22 December 1910; AHSRE LE-757, leg. 9, 16 July 1912; ADN, exp. XI/481.5/59, fol. 103, 28 November 1910.

to the aid of the men who have already rebelled."[28] An insight into the identities of these men who were ready to join the rebel cause is provided in another report, which mentions "the exodus of Mexicans employed in ranches throughout Texas to join the rebels who are active in the Ojinaga region."[29]

In contrast to the rural Chihuahuans from this region, the Texans of Mexican descent and Mexican nationals living in the United States who participated in the revolution were motivated by anti-Americanism and resentment toward "things American." The latter group had been the "victims of [American] prejudice and contempt" (Cumberland 1954:286). In the late nineteenth century, a newcomer to western Texas noticed the prevailing prejudice of the time and quoted an American lawyer as saying: "In this state [Texas] we have one set of laws for white people and one for Mexicans, all in the same words and in the same books" (Hawley 1964:9).

For the Mexicans living in Mexico, however, access to American supplies throughout the revolution (i.e., essential items such as arms, ammunition, and food; and items that can be categorized as "nonessential," such as gamecocks or Texas-style hats) proved to be crucial to the sustenance of rebel factions as well as federal troops stationed along the border. At different points in time all such supplies were under some form of regulated exchange imposed by a variety of agents. The most obvious formal regulations officially imposed "from above" were those curtailing the trade in arms, ammunition, and other war matériel. These were established through the enactment of U.S. neutrality laws and arms embargoes which were imposed and lifted to suit current U.S. foreign policy and to influence events in Mexico (see Katz 1981; Hall and Coerver forthcoming).

However, the selective enforcement of American regulations and neutrality laws affecting the trade in arms and ammunition ultimately rested upon decisions made by local U.S. officers and customs inspectors. American public sympathy for the rebels during the initial *maderista* uprising of 1910–11 was expressed in a lack of interest in enforcing such laws and regulations and led, consequently, to the success of the rebels in acquiring American supplies.[30] Later, throughout the year 1913, for example, a series of reports from the Ojinaga region give evidence of the role of "personal

28. *El Paso Times*, 16 December 1910.
29. My translation; AHSRE LE-678, leg. 2, 24 December 1910.
30. E.g., AHSRE LE-620, 26 and 28 December 1910; AHSRE LE-623, 12 January 1911.

sympathies" on the part of U.S. officers toward the Constitutionalist rebels, and the subsequent "selective" enforcement of neutrality laws and regulations against military officers of the Huerta government stationed in Ojinaga.[31] Yet the largest merchant and arms dealer in Presidio, Texas, I. Kleinman, supplied arms and ammunition to federal troops and to different revolutionary factions alike throughout the revolution.[32]

Livestock was the most valuable resource on the Mexican side of the border and was used by the Chihuahuan revolutionaries to finance the revolution (see Katz 1981:127; also Hall and Coerver forthcoming). Its role was meaningful only in the context of the border's political economy. Revolutionary control over the disposition of livestock through interboundary trading served to secure the loyalty of American and Mexican ranchers alike to the revolutionary leaders. One report mentions that José de la Cruz Sánchez, the local revolutionary leader in Ojinaga, "is well liked by the ranchers of this county [Marfa, Texas] because through him they are furnished with all kinds of facilities for the purchase of livestock."[33]

The proximity of the United States allowed the revolutionaries to purchase essential food items and provisions during collapses in the local economies. In March 1914, for example, Francisco Villa requested Lázaro de la Garza, one of his purchasing agents in the United States, to acquire "the elements of first necessity: coffee, sugar, rice, and lard," which were to be distributed among the distraught civilian population (Hall and Coerver forthcoming). Access to food supplies was of such importance that a complaint addressed to the Mexican president in March 1911 by the federal troops stationed in Ojinaga does *not* mention arms, but instead cites the fact that *maderista* rebels, and not federal troops, enjoyed access to the American bakery located across the border in Presidio, Texas.[34]

The relationships, practices, and exchanges portrayed in the preceding paragraphs express the discontinuity between "regional" and "national" spaces and provide evidence of the extent to which the former—a semi-

31. See AHSRE LE-757, leg. 2, 28 March 1913; AHSRE LE-767, leg. 8, 12 April and 11 August 1913. Also see ADN, exp. XI/481.5/69, Caja 27, fol. 326, 11 April 1913; fol. 327, 18 April 1913; fol. 286, 9 May 1913; fol. 289, 16 May 1913.

32. See AHSRE LE-611, leg. 3, 17 November 1910; AHSRE LE-757, leg. 9, 16 October 1912; AHSRE LE-722, 9 October 1916; AVC 12331, 25 December 1916.

33. My translation; AHSRE LE-757, leg. 9, 9 December 1912. For other examples, see AHSRE LE-767, leg. 8, 9 April 1913; AHSRE LE-806, leg. 1, 24 May 1913.

34. AHSRE LE-644, 28 March 1911.

autonomous political space—operated in the interstices of official U.S. and Mexican domestic policies and international diplomacy. However, the distinctiveness of this regional space resided not only in the availability of resources and the modalities of their acquisition, but was also informed by the objects themselves (clothing, food, livestock, uniforms purchased in the United States, etc.). This distinctiveness, expressed in certain symbols and cultural forms, was described by a former revolutionary:

> General Villa had lived in contact with the people of the north, who as you will be able to observe, even nowadays, are a little more civilized than the people of the south; they have a higher standard of living: they dress better, wear shoes, that is, everybody in the north. . . . That was General Villa's world, very different from the precarious one from which General Zapata came in the south.[35]

Another *villista* soldier recalls: "Villa gave us our uniforms. We were given a khaki trouser . . . and a [felt] Texan hat."[36]

The display and manipulation of this repertoire of objects conveyed a regional identity within a national space, giving expression to alternative modes of collective and individual identification. These items also had a regional significance, organizing the expression of the social distinctions that had emerged on the border during the revolution. An insight into these distinctions is provided in the account of an American expedition launched to pursue a band of raiders after 1915, when raiding and looting had become additional strategies for the popular acquisition of resources:

> I saw a dozen men watering their horses. For several minutes I examined them with great care through my glasses, for fear of shooting up a group of harmless *pacíficos* or a detachment of Carranzista [*sic*] soldiers. I ascertained that [emphasis added] *the men were carrying rifles, and were wearing bandoliers of ammunition over their shoulders; they also wore white shirts and felt hats—the former circumstance indicated that they were not regular soldiers, and the latter that they were bandits, for the* pacífico *always wears a big straw sombrero.* (Cramer 1916:219)

The so-called time of "the border troubles" (Smithers n.d. 2) refers to the pattern of interboundary raiding that was established in 1915 (see Cumberland 1954:285) and that lasted well into 1918. During these years, four major raids against American-owned properties occurred in and

---

35. My translation; quoted in E. Meyer 1978:21.
36. My translation and interpolation; E. Meyer 1978:28.

around the Big Bend area of Texas: On 5 May 1916 a simultaneous opera-
tion conducted by two raiding parties looted a wax factory located in
Glenn Springs and the general store at Boquillas, Texas (Cramer 1916;
Tyler 1975b; Smithers n.d. 2; Wood 1963). Later, on 25 December 1917
the Brite ranch was raided and looted, as was the Neville ranch on 23–
24 January 1918 (Smithers 1981 and n.d. 2). The fact that looting and
plundering—the inverse of routine trading—had replaced previously established commercial modes and paths for the acquisition of resources,
and that the spoils acquired in these raids were selectively chosen, endows
these incidents with special significance.

In all four events, the raiders not only wanted horses and cattle, "but
they particularly wanted the merchandise that the ranchmen stocked in
the commissaries." In three of the four incidents they took everything
except the food, emptying sacks of flour, beans, and corn onto the floor. In
all cases, the items looted from the general stores had the quality of being
"nonessential" or "luxury" goods. During the Brite ranch raid, "the bandits looted the store of the best merchandise, such as shoes, clothes, and
other more costly items. They dressed themselves in new clothes and
shoes." The general store at Boquillas, Texas "carried many items in stock
that could not be purchased in Mexico, this was the merchandise the
raiders wanted" (Smithers n.d. 2, 71–76). When the American troops who
pursued the raiders into Mexico recovered the loot, Lieutenant Cramer
found "a number of new Stetson hats, several pairs of new shoes, and
quantities of original packages of underclothing, socks, etc. Also at least
a dozen new Ingersoll watches, in boxes" (Cramer 1916:222). At Glenn
Springs, "the general store had been thoroughly looted and stripped of
post office and other funds, plus clothing and canned goods. Merchandise
such as flour and corn, was left" (Wood 1963:69).

The raiders selectively chose as spoils those objects which articulated a
regional distinctiveness linked to the categorical framework organizing the
social distinctions that emerged on the border during the revolution. According to Lieutenant Cramer's 1916 account (see quotation above) these
social categories were *pacíficos,* regular soldiers, and bandits. In the context
of these distinctions at this historical juncture, it is apparent that the
"resources" pursued and acquired during the raids were those associated
with the identity of the "bandits." The negative reciprocity implied in
looting—a reversal of reciprocal trading and commercial modes of acquisi-

tion deployed earlier—is integral to the appropriation of the items looted as objects of "the other." Furthermore, banditry, as a way of being, entailed a dissociation from the discipline of the army to which the regular soldier was subjected, and from that of the agricultural production to which the *pacífico* was tied. Therefore, the appropriation of these objects of "the other," and their display in local contexts, articulated an ideology of difference that contested the signs of domination and incorporation. The raiding and looting incidents embodied and exhibited historically grounded cultural forms. As cultural performances, these events evoked the images of "barbarous" attacks perpetrated against frontier settlements. The raiders, not surprisingly, were all men of northern extraction.

The members of the raiding parties that attacked Glenn Springs and Boquillas were identified as "men that came from the Laguna district. Added to them were others that lived right on the border on both sides."[37] The men who raided the Brite and Neville ranches were also of northern extraction and came from the villages of Pilares and Coyame, Chihuahua.[38]

With respect to contending revolutionary factions, the affiliations of the leaders of each of the raiding parties are known for each incident. The Boquillas raid was led by Natividad Alvarez, identified as a *villista* lieutenant colonel.[39] The three other raiding parties were all said to have been directed by *carrancista* officers or soldiers.[40] Furthermore, two minor raids that occurred in the area—the Petit raid in May 1918 and the Bill Russell raid in April 1918—were also attributed to *carrancista* soldiers.[41] The involvement of *carrancista* soldiers in raiding incidents against American-owned property was at odds with the standing of these revolutionary forces vis-à-vis the United States. In October 1915 the U.S. government had in fact extended de facto recognition to the movement led by Venustiano Carranza.

37. uss 1919–20, testimony of Col. Langhorne, p. 1630.

38. The aggregation of information from several sources made it possible to determine the northern extraction and villages of origin of these men. The sources used are the following: ahsre LE-807, leg. 4(1); Smithers n.d. 1, 79; Hinkle 1967; uss 1919–20, testimony of Capt. Matlack.

39. See Cramer 1916:205; Tyler 1975a:282; Smithers n.d. 2, 72.

40. See Smithers 1981:33, 35; uss 1919–20: testimony of O. G. Compton, p. 1059; testimony of W. E. Vann, p. 1253; testimony of E. W. Neville, p. 1510; testimony of Capt. C. D. Wood, p. 1517; testimony of G. Webb, p. 1526; testimony of S. H. Neill, p. 1540.

41. See Coerver and Hall 1984:124; uss 1919–20, testimony of C. Taylor, p. 1521.

A similar schism between rank-and-file and leadership was occurring within the *villista* movement. A considerable *villista* resurgence was noticed throughout the Ojinaga region during the years 1917, 1918, and 1919, while the *carrancista* troops were engaged in raiding and looting.[42] One report mentions that in Ojinaga there was a "tolerant attitude" on the part of some American authorities toward the *villista* movement.[43] Furthermore, during the taking of Ojinaga from the *carrancistas* by *villista* forces in November 1917, the *villistas* reportedly "committed no depredations as long as they were there."[44] This situation, which portrays the *villista* rank-and-file receiving American and popular support, stands in sharp contrast with the predicament and activities of the movement's leadership and the American and popular responses to it. On 9 March 1916, a *villista* contingent led by Villa himself had attacked Columbus, New Mexico. The attack was prompted by Villa's belief that the Carranza administration was compromising Mexican national sovereignty through its dealings with the United States and the government of Woodrow Wilson (see Katz 1978b). The United States' reprisal consisted of the punitive expedition led by General Pershing, which remained in Mexican territory from March 1916 through February 1917 (Katz 1978b; see also Alonso, below).

The apparent schism between the rank-and-file of both contending revolutionary factions—*carrancistas* and *villistas* alike—and their respective leaderships can be explained in the context of the character of the "new regime" in the region. The revolution had come full circle. A letter dated June 1919 in Presidio, Texas, written by a priest, Manuel Roux, portrays the arbitrary character of the *carrancista* administration in the Ojinaga region and the popular fear created by the *carrancista* troops. Roux portrays the *carrancista* administration in Ojinaga as resembling that of an old hacienda (i.e., the *carrancista* commander, Colonel Ceballos, monopolized all commerce and bars, conducted all the affairs of the municipal government, controlled the affairs of the church, and was hated throughout the region, even by his troops). Roux goes on jokingly to describe how in the village of

42. For reports on the *villista* resurgence in the Ojinaga region see ADN, exp. XI/481.5/76, Caja 29, fols. 11–12, 28 January 1917; AHSRE 17-8-133, 12 June 1917; AHSRE LE-858, leg. 4, 11 July 1917; AHSRE LE-807, leg. 1, 26 November 1918; AHSRE LE-839, leg. 9, 15 January and 5 February 1919; *El Paso Times*, 17 July 1919.

43. See AHSRE 17-8-133, 12 June 1917, report from Mexican Secret Service in El Paso, Texas, to Foreign Relations, Mexico.

44. See USS 1919–20, testimony of Col. Langhorne, p. 1629.

Cuchillo Parado the inhabitants had trained their dogs to protect and hide other animals, such as their chickens, from marauding *carrancista changos;* the exemplary part of the story concludes with the observation that "even the animals know who their enemy is."[45]

In this context, the *villista* resurgence in the Ojinaga region during these years, expressing the unmet aspirations of most segments of the rural population, can be explained by at least two related factors: on the one hand, by the profound popular disapproval of and hatred for the depredations and overall conduct of the *carrancista* leadership and troops in the area; on the other, by the fact that American tolerance toward *villista* activities endowed this movement with a degree of political legitimacy. Furthermore, an analysis of the raiding and looting incidents previously described reveals that the *carrancista* soldiers resorted to the appropriation and manipulation of the same objects that articulated a regional distinctiveness. They did so in order to establish alternative modes of identity and self-definition, thereby reversing their own subjection to the movement's regional leadership.

Conclusions

Ironically, the same objects pursued by disenchanted *carrancista* soldiers seventy years ago are currently appropriated and manipulated in local contexts. These objects of "the other" and alternative forms of "symbolic capital" such as "participation in the revolution" are engaged to remind us of the plurality and diversity of movements embodied in what is officially known as *"the* Mexican Revolution."

On the morning of 14 November 1983 the inhabitants of Cuchillo Parado[46] paraded through the streets of their village and gathered in its plaza

45. My translation; STC, letter from Manuel Roux, Presidio, Texas, to Silvestre Terrazas, El Paso, Texas, 29 June 1919.

46. Located on the east bank of the Conchos River, in the northeastern desertic section of the state of Chihuahua, approximately fifty kilometers from Presidio, Texas, the village of Cuchillo Parado currently has a population of about 600 inhabitants, whose livelihood depends on small-scale irrigation agriculture, cattle raising, wax making, and wage labor in the United States. The principal cash crops are wheat and cotton, while beans and maize are usually grown for domestic consumption and local exchange. Politically, Cuchillo Parado is a municipal section (*sección municipal*) of the village of

to commemorate yet another anniversary of "the revolution." The date on which the celebration occurs year after year honors with historical accuracy the village's early involvement in the *maderista* uprising of 1910. Cuchillo Parado rose up in arms on November 14, six days in advance of Madero's call to arms for the 20th of November, a circumstance influenced by developments and struggles occurring at the regional level (see Koreck n.d. 1 and n.d. 2). After the *maderista* uprising, Cuchillo Parado assumed a major role as a stronghold of the *villista* movement in northeastern Chihuahua during the revolutionary years. The persistent commitment and involvement of the inhabitants of the village in the *villista* cause prompted the *carrancista* federal army, as late as 1917, to consider the complete destruction of the village.[47]

I would like to reflect on the historical and political implications of the date on which the celebration occurs, and on the social and territorial spaces delimited by and associated with this celebration. By its reenactment of the original chronological sequence, the November 14 commemoration in Cuchillo Parado reflects the regional dynamics of the original armed uprising. These aspects of the commemoration give evidence to the obstinate refusal on the part of the community of Cuchillo Parado to partake of the "imagined linkages," "community in anonymity," and "simultaneity" of wills that are implied and enacted in national celebrations.[48]

The commemoration begins with a celebration in Cuchillo Parado on

Coyame, the seat of the municipality (*cabecera municipal*) which is located approximately thirty kilometers away.

Colonial records first mention the evidence of Cuchillo Parado as an inhabited settlement in 1715. The present-day inhabitants of Cuchillo Parado, however, link the "origins" of the community to a land grant received in 1865 from the government of Benito Juárez. During the 1920s Cuchillo Parado "became" an *ejido*, and the agrarian records pertaining to the village lands are kept in state and national agrarian archives under the name of Ejido "25 de Marzo." This name was imposed on the village by the state legislature of Chihuahua in 1904; however, it has since been used only in official records, and never in records originated in the village.

47. ADN, exp. XI/481.5/76. Letter from Col. Martínez Ruiz, in charge of federal troops in Ojinaga, to Gen. Francisco Murguía, army commander in the state of Chihuahua, 10 December 1917.

48. Anderson (1983:40) identifies the emergence of a "community in anonymity" as the hallmark of modern nations. National celebrations provide the occasion for "physical realization of the imagined community" (p. 132); that is, for the experience of the simultaneity of a multitude of wills through their anonymous, synchronically organized performances.

the 14th, the place and date the revolution began; it then moves to the surrounding villages that joined in the uprising during the days following November 14. The commemoration culminates on November 20 in the *cabecera municipal,* the village of Coyame, with an official gathering of municipal authorities. The intersection and contradictions between local, regional, and national histories are expressed and reaffirmed in the social and territorial spaces encompassed by the dynamics of this commemorative sequence. The relationship between these contrasting yet intimately related histories is dramatized by the fact that Coyame—the only locality in the region that remained faithful to the Porfirian regime in 1910, and Cuchillo Parado's archrival for land and municipal political hegemony in the late nineteenth and early twentieth centuries (see Koreck n.d. 1 and n.d. 2)—is the legitimate and official site for the celebration of "the Mexican Revolution."

The *pueblo* of Cuchillo Parado, on the other hand, enacts its own celebration of what is locally referred to as "the revolution," not as "the Mexican Revolution." In so doing, it chooses to distinguish itself and its history from the homogeneous and all-encompassing history of the nation. The deployment of this "rhetoric of contrast"[49] draws attention to what Corrigan and Sayer described as, "the active securing of assent; marginalizing, localizing, parochializing, sectionalizing expressions of the realities of difference [of the subordinated] in the face of the monolithic idealized unities of official discourse" (1985:198). Furthermore, the *cuchillenses'* representation of history portrayed in this celebration embodies a twofold quality both cognitive/descriptive in character and moral/evaluative (see Corrigan and Sayer 1985:6); it simultaneously portrays and evaluates the world (Comaroff and Comaroff 1987:193).

Beneath this evaluation of the social world lie implicit ambivalence and contradictions. Although the local festivity rejects the totalizing and unifying attributes of an official discourse and contests the resting place officially assigned to a historical process (i.e., "the Mexican Revolution"),[50] it

49. The concept "rhetoric of contrast" is taken from Comaroff and Comaroff (1987:200), who in a provocative discussion on the connection between consciousness, culture, and representation observe that the rhetorical use of contrast arises from the experiences of a contradictory social order.

50. Nowadays, the revolution is conceived by Mexico's governing party as an ongoing and permanent process that has settled all disputes and ended all differences. This

simultaneously makes explicit a desire to identify and acknowledge local participation in the process. The social identity conferred upon individuals and villages by the category of "revolutionary," while rejected as a unifying device, becomes desirable as an individualizing one. The ambivalence and contradictions involved stem from the fact that the officially legitimized and appropriated categories, which are contested as such, simultaneously resonate and coincide with the local and popular construction of subjectivities and identities.[51]

Furthermore, not only does this celebration—in all of its contradictoriness—devalue national ties, but the local rendition of the festivity displays obvious "international" liaisons and cosmopolitan overtones as well. The village's daily routines come to a halt, and the festive mood expressed in the parade is further reinforced by the arrival and temporary presence in the village of its "native sons" who have migrated to "the other side" (*el otro lado*), i.e., the United States. They come from towns across Texas through the border town of Ojinaga, some forty-five kilometers from Cuchillo Parado. They proudly roam the streets in American pickup trucks (*trocas*) identifiable by their U.S. license plates. From these trucks come the sounds of *corridos norteños*, telling stories about U.S. immigration agents (*la migra*). Meanwhile, the residents of the village display their own "luxury" items from across the border: Stetson hats, Levi jeans, and Texan leather boots and cowboy shirts.

This celebration portrays the *cuchillenses'* understanding and consciousness of their own history. But it also exposes a disparity between the unifying representations espoused "from above" (i.e., "the Mexican Revolution") and their own differential understanding "from below" (i.e., "the revolution"). This contemporary rhetoric of contrasts expresses an ideological discontinuity between (*a*) social groups occupying local/regional spaces and (*b*) prevailing ideological and institutional arrangements.

---

ideology has reigned since the creation in 1929 of Mexico's official party—the PRI, or Institutional Revolutionary Party—which appropriated "the Mexican Revolution" and declared itself its heir. However, to concede the overall hegemony of this party is ultimately to endow the historical process of revolution with a unity it did not possess.

51. The category "revolutionary" resonates with popular consciousness because the revolutionary Mexican state that emerged after the popular mobilization has been "parasitic upon the wider *conscience collective*, which it conversely regulates" (Corrigan and Sayer 1985:6).

In this essay I have presented a collage of historically discontinuous configurations of relations that have gained ascendancy at different moments as local, regional, and national histories have intersected. My critical aim is to spotlight the differential popular understandings so often masked by the unifying representations espoused by the very groups and/or apparatuses that define the domains, practices, and representations of a publicly shared social horizon. The contours of the *patria chica* and the semi-autonomous political spaces of rural Mexico need not be conceptualized as ontologically prepolitical or parochial. Rather, we should seek to denaturalize this viewpoint through historically and socially grounded analyses of competing aspirations and moralities.

III *U.S. Intervention*

and Popular Ideology

GILBERT M. JOSEPH

The United States, Feuding Elites, and

Rural Revolt in Yucatán, 1836–1915

In 1923, at the ripe age of forty-eight, Governor of Yucatán Felipe Carrillo Puerto began intensive tutoring in English. Why was the man who proudly proclaimed his administration "the first socialist government in the Americas" suddenly learning the language of the gringo?[1] Certainly more was involved here than his recently kindled romance with the North American journalist Alma Reed (who, after all, was fluent in Spanish). In fact, in the revolutionary Yucatán of the early twenties mastery of English was almost as important to the governor—though for quite different reasons—as the knowledge of Maya that enabled him to communicate so effectively with Yucatán's *campesinos*. A variety of structural and conjunctural factors tied Carrillo Puerto's political career and the fortunes of Yucatán's nascent socialist experiment to the United States.[2]

Most important, the exaggerated dependence of Yucatán's declining henequen monoculture on an increasingly unfavorable North American market (dominated by the powerful International Harvester Company) diminished planters' profits, worsened the *campesinos'* plight, and underscored the need for agrarian reform and agricultural diversification for Carrillo's Socialist Party of the Southeast (PSS). At the same time, Yucatán's subordinate position in the henequen market made agrarian expropriation immediately impractical. It also posed significant problems for an effective grassroots mobilization of the *campesinado* and generally impeded a socialist transition. Ironically, to a greater extent than his more moderate predecessor, General Salvador Alvarado (who had governed the region

1. Carrillo Puerto, quoted in Paoli and Montalvo 1977:90. Carrillo Puerto was tutored by Professor Alejandro Aguilar, who had earlier been trained in English and physical education in New York City and would head the government's new Departamento de Cultura Física. Interview with Mario Menéndez Romero, 31 December 1986.

2. I examine this relationship in some detail in Joseph 1982:chaps. 7–9.

in boom times [1915–18]), Governor Carrillo, a Marxist, found himself obliged to cultivate the goodwill of his North American class enemies— International Harvester and the cordage manufacturers—in order to negotiate the best prices in a buyer's market.³ In an extensive English-language section of *El Agricultor,* the official newspaper of the state-controlled henequen export commission, Governor Carrillo repeatedly publicized his desire to "harmonize . . . the relationship between Yucatecan production and North American consumption."⁴

Interestingly, much of the ideological inspiration of Carrillo Puerto's socialist regime also bespoke a North American connection. The Marxist leader's rudimentary political education owed much to the tutelage of Robert Haberman, the Rumanian-American socialist who advised the PSS in the late 1910s, and to the periods of exile that Carrillo Puerto spent in New Orleans during the same decade, when he worked on the docks and fraternized with militant North American workers (Joseph 1982:200– 204).

Perhaps it was during these brief stays that Carrillo Puerto deepened his fondness for *béisbol,* which had already taken root in Yucatán and would constitute a significant component of Carrillo's strategy of rural mobilization during his governorship (1922–23).⁵ In addition to the "national pastime," which subsequently became the Yucatecan regional pastime, Carrillo Puerto would import North American archaeologists from the prestigious Carnegie Institution of Washington to restore the classical Maya ruins of Chichén Itzá and Uxmal. In this manner, North American social science would help the PSS to instill in the historically exploited and culturally despised *campesinado* a sense of ethnic (and, by extension, class) pride in the great cultural tradition to which they were heir (Joseph 1982:222–24; also see Brunhouse 1971:chap. 9). Carrillo also disseminated progressive, modern-day North American notions of birth control, sex

3. General Alvarado's rather stormy relationship with the North American cordage interests (and with the U.S. government, which was frequently lobbied to act in their behalf, and which on one occasion during World War I actually sent a gunboat into Yucatecan waters) is explored in Joseph 1982:chaps. 4–6.

4. E.g., see *El Agricultor* for the year 1923; cf. *El Popular,* 14 August 1922.

5. Baseball was brought to Yucatán by Cuban immigrants in the early 1890s; thirty years earlier, U.S. merchant seamen had introduced the game to Cuban cargo handlers and it had quickly flourished among the popular classes. For baseball's origins in Yucatán and Carrillo Puerto's propagation of the sport "hasta los pueblitos," see Joseph 1988.

education, and divorce (e.g., translating and distributing in the public schools and marriage registries Dr. Margaret Sanger's controversial pamphlet on contraception). Armed with these ideological weapons, Carrillo Puerto and the PSS turned the entire area of women's rights and male–female relations into a symbolic front in the Socialists' struggle with the propertied class that ruled Yucatán's traditional, characteristically macho society (Joseph 1982:216–19).

In short, during the Carrillo Puerto regime, a variety of North American influences worked in a contradictory manner, both to promote the Socialists' revolutionary drive (which was essentially a strategy of agrarian mobilization from the top down) and to limit its potential outcomes. Indeed, much of Yucatán's modern agrarian history illustrates this fundamental theme: since independence, the region has experienced diverse forms of North American political-economic, cultural, and ideological penetration, advanced through the agency of private capital, dependencies of the U.S. state (often working indirectly through the Mexican national state), and representatives of the North American left. These diverse North American agents have, at certain pivotal national and international conjunctures, stimulated local- and regional-level responses and mobilizations, within which groups of Yucatecan *campesinos* have been able to advance their own agendas and causes, if only temporarily.[6] Moreover, in attempting to make their own history, such local subaltern groups have in reciprocal fashion occasionally registered a significant impact on regional and global structures of power.[7] In the mid-nineteenth century, the revolt of these *campesinos* threatened the hegemony and very survival of Yucatecan elites. More recently, *campesino* mobilizations have posed difficult challenges for the commercial agricultural expansion that regional elites have attempted in collaboration with U.S. capital.

After a brief historical overview of the contours of Yucatecan political economy, the remainder of this essay will examine two of the three episodes in the region's modern history during which North American influences conditioned rural mobilizations in the peninsula: (1) the apocalyptic peasant rebellion of 1847, more commonly (but perhaps misleadingly)

---

6. For incisive analyses of how "international relationships of power" can condition social revolutions and rural insurgencies, see Skocpol 1979; Skocpol 1982:351–75; Goldfrank 1979:135–63; and Tilly 1975:483–555.

7. Cf. the work of the Indian social theorist Ranajit Guha (Guha 1982).

known as the Caste War of Yucatán; and (2) the waves of rural insurgency that swept the Yucatecan countryside for several years following the outbreak of the *maderista* rebellion in 1910. (I have dealt at length elsewhere with the third episode, that involving the connection between the United States and the agrarian mobilizations from above that characterized both the bourgeois revolutionary regime of Constitutionalist General Salvador Alvarado and the short-lived and abortive socialist transition of Felipe Carrillo Puerto and the PSS [Joseph 1982; Joseph 1986:chap. 5].) In the analysis of each agrarian episode I will attempt to articulate macro- and micro-level processes and structures, examining catalysts and constraints on rural mobilization and revolt in terms of a set of intersecting political and economic relationships encompassing the United States, Mexico City, Mérida, and the Yucatecan countryside. The reader will come to appreciate the unique character of Yucatán's agrarian history, owing in large part to the peninsula's peripheral location and "special" orientation toward the Gulf and the North American mainland, an orientation that had profound socioeconomic and cultural consequences. At the same time, the Yucatecan case further illustrates the multifaceted, complex, and often subtle connection between the United States and rural revolt in regional Mexico.

The Historical Contours of Yucatecan Political Economy

Jutting out into the Gulf of Mexico, washed by the Caribbean on its eastern shore, and separated from Mexico proper by an almost unbroken succession of swamps and rain forests, Yucatán has always been more naturally oriented toward the United States, Central America, and the Caribbean islands than toward the remainder of the Mexican Republic.[8] Yucatán's communication by sea with the Mexican port of Veracruz had been inefficient, and it was not until the middle of the twentieth century that adequate rail and road links with central Mexico were established. Indeed, it appears that the federal government resigned itself rather early to the inevitability of Yucatán's geographical isolation and formulated political and economic policies that further marginalized the region within the national political structure. For much of the first half of the nineteenth

8. For a fuller treatment of the themes addressed in this section, see Joseph 1986:chaps. 3–5.

century, Yucatán was regarded as a foreign country for tax purposes and was forced to pay discriminatory duties on its exports.

Such policies severely strained center–periphery relations and only accentuated Yucatán's pronounced geographical affinity for the United States and Cuba, which over time would translate into a tradition of close commercial and cultural relationships. Already during the colonial period, the proprietors of Yucatán's corn and cattle estates had marketed their meat and hides in Cuba. When independence from Spain cut off Yucatán from its protected Havana market and deprived the peninsula of its traditional source of sugar and rum, *yucatecos* responded by diverting their capital into sugar production on the state's fertile southeastern frontier. In the 1840s, when their cane plantations were devastated by the frontier's insurgent Maya peasantry (whose traditional way of life had been threatened by sugar's expansion), Yucatán's *hacendados* turned their full attention to cultivating henequen in the old hacienda zone of the northwest.

Whereas sugar had been produced mostly for domestic consumption, henequen fiber was shipped abroad to meet an ever increasing demand for cordage, principally binder twine for North American mechanized agriculture. In return, Yucatán's planter class purchased necessary provisions and luxury goods. Beginning in the 1870s, they arranged for ever greater amounts of investment capital—which Mexican merchants either could not deliver or were not prepared to provide on such good terms as their North American counterparts. In the decades ahead, local henequen planters became increasingly dependent upon U.S. capital, loaned first by bankers and subsequently by cordage brokers and manufacturers, most notably International Harvester. In consideration for these credits, the North Americans (working through powerful Yucatecan *casas exportadoras*) demanded to be paid back in raw fiber rather than in cash, and at the market price prevailing at the moment of repayment.

The *yucatecos* would soon learn how onerous this lien arrangement could be. Recent scholarship has linked the brutal, regressive nature of the labor regime in Yucatán during the late *porfiriato* to the planters' pressing need for capital and their increasingly precarious position in the henequen marketing structure. Each of the rural mobilizations that took place in Yucatán during the early revolutionary era (1910–13) sought in one way or another to break the stranglehold on the regional political economy that North American corporate capital (i.e., International Harvester and its satellites) had established, in close partnership with the most powerful faction of the planter class. Yet while this transnational "collaborator mechanism" provoked intense opposition at all levels of regional society, it also underwrote a strain of dependent capitalism that would seriously impede popular participation and limit the effectiveness of the later revolutionary process (1915–24).

The Peasant Rebellion of 1847

Despite a resurgence of scholarly interest in the "Caste War," particularly its agrarian origins, the rebel Mayas' own perceptions of the conflict, and the political and cultural milieu of the renegade Maya states that emerged from it,[9] few studies have examined the significance of the North American role.[10] Nevertheless, although questions of causality are complex, U.S. influences appear to have played a part, first in the timing of the outbreak of peasant insurgency and then in assisting Yucatecan elites to mount a counteroffensive against the Mayas, thereby limiting the scope of the rebellion. While this discussion (based on the existing secondary literature as well as on some little-used U.S. archival sources) is not meant to be definitive, it does suggest the various dimensions of North American and other foreign involvement in the rebellion and its aftermath.

In spite of Yucatán's remoteness from Mexico proper, all the major problems of the early Republic, particularly the elite-based power struggles and foreign-relations debacles, were worked out at the regional level, with serious repercussions. Accustomed to exercising local rule, Yucatecan elites were outspoken advocates of federalism and liberalism following independence. Based either in Mérida, the state capital, or Campeche, its political and economic rival, these local merchants and *hacendados* competed fiercely among themselves for political office and the attendant com-

9. For a review of recent contributions to the Caste War literature, see Joseph 1985, and Joseph 1986:chap. 3.

10. The generally reliable standard treatments of the period, like the accounts of contemporary participants, tend to present the North American dimension of the conflict almost entirely within the context of traditional diplomatic history: e.g., Williams 1929; Chapman 1967; Manno 1963. Somewhat more suggestive for an appreciation of U.S. (and central Mexican) influences on the origins and outcome of the peasant insurrection of 1847 are Cline 1958; N. Reed 1964; and, more recently, Richmond 1985.

mercial privileges, but they remained united in the face of intrusions by the national state into regional affairs. Such intrusions multiplied with the onset of Santa Anna's Centralist Republic in 1835. Mexico City outlawed Yucatán's protective tariffs, ruining Campeche's shipping and endangering the new sugar industry on the southeastern frontier. Federal soldiers were garrisoned in the peninsula at the expense of the Yucatecan treasury. In 1836, regionalist sympathies were further inflamed when twenty-five hundred *yucatecos* were conscripted to fight overseas against the Texas Lone Star Republic, with no provision made for their passage home. In all, Yucatán would be made to pay 17 percent of the cost of Mexico's war with Texas, a war that most Yucatecan elites regarded as blatant intervention in the affairs of fellow liberals in another peripheral region. (Significantly, when the Texans opted for independence in 1835, they elected as their vice-president Yucatán's noted liberal ideologue Lorenzo de Zavala [Richmond 1985; Cline 1958:67; N. Reed 1964:26–27].)

It was only a matter of time before Yucatán would contest its own sovereignty with the Mexican Republic. During the turbulent decade or so that witnessed Mexico's crushing defeat in both the War for Texas Independence and its sequel, the Mexican-American War (1836–48), Yucatán withdrew from the Republic on several occasions, regional ports experienced naval blockade and occupation by the U.S. Home Squadron, and *meridano* and *campechano* elites became sharply divided over the question of what relationship their state should maintain with both Mexico and the United States. Even as they feuded with each other throughout the chaotic decade, these rival elites were determined to protect their traditional commercial privileges and markets with Mexico and the United States, as well as to preserve their social hegemony over the region's Maya *campesinado*. Yet out of this bickering intraclass rivalry, and the climate of international conflict that fed it, emerged the very conditions for a massive peasant insurrection that came close to extinguishing white rule in Yucatán. Let us rehearse the salient political events involving regional, national, and international actors that, when combined with oppressive social conditions and a tactically mobile Maya peasantry, triggered the "Caste War" of 1847.

Yucatecan elites first challenged Mexican centralism in May of 1839, when Santiago Imán, a captain in the state militia, pronounced against Mexico in the remote interior town of Tizimín, appealed for support, and then fled into the bush. Reinforcements arrived as troops from his old

battalion seized the boat that was taking them north to attempt a recon-
quest of Texas. After guerrilla tactics against the authorities produced little
result, Imán conceived a bold strategy that would have enormous future
consequences: the recruitment of the interior Mayas. Long forbidden to
bear arms under the colony, *indios* had recently been drafted by the Mexican Republic. Legion in number, they dreaded overseas military service in
Texas. An additional incentive—Imán's promise to discharge them from
mandatory payment of church obventions—persuaded the Mayas to join
the *dzul*'s (white señor's) battle in Yucatán against even more distant
foreigners. Thousands of new Maya recruits helped him take the interior
city of Valladolid, whereupon *meridanos* and *campechanos* alike affirmed
their commitment to rid the state of centralist rule. In June 1840, Yucatecan
battalions drove Mexican troops from their last stronghold in Campeche,
and local elites vowed to remain independent, or at least autonomous, until
the Republic returned to its senses and embraced federalism. To give point
to their decision, they promulgated an extremely liberal constitution and
established formal relations with the Lone Star Republic.[11]

Santa Anna immediately sought to negotiate with the *yucatecos*. An
agreement was hammered out, stipulating among other things that the
state could control its internal affairs, enjoy favorable tariffs and the free
passage of its goods to all Mexican ports, and preserve autonomy in military matters (an attempt to deal with regional fears of overseas duty).
Apparently, however, the Mexican *caudillo* had little intention of abiding
by the agreement. First, he refused to seat the Yucatecan representatives to
his provisional *junta* until Yucatán severed relations with Texas. Then he
banned all Yucatecan products from Mexican ports and declared Yucatecan ships to be pirates. Finally, in 1843, Santa Anna dispatched a large
Mexican army to invade Yucatán.

The Yucatecans were ready for the Mexican expeditionary force. They
were aided by the timely loan of the Lone Star Republic's small fleet—
three ships hired for 5,000 pesos per month—which patrolled the sea lanes
between Veracruz and the peninsula and protected Yucatecan shipping.
Texas' support and a series of logistical delays suffered by the Mexican

11. For Imán's revolt and Yucatán's first secession, see N. Reed 1964:27–29; Williams
1929; and Chapman 1967.

troops gave regional elites time to raise an army of 6,000 men—again, mostly interior Maya peasants—who were once more promised a reduction in the church tax and, more important, lands that had been lost to sugar expansion. When the fighting came, the Mexicans were outnumbered and outmaneuvered, surrendering after only a brief skirmish. The Mérida government deferred its promise to distribute land to the Maya recruits—a decision it would come to regret.[12]

Yucatán's ruling elites used their strengthened bargaining position to dictate the terms of the region's reincorporation into the Mexican Republic. They insisted that Mexico honor the substance of the ephemeral 1841 agreement, now codified in the *convenios* of 14 December 1843. Although they would be exempt from overseas duty, the *yucatecos* did agree that, in the event of a war, they would place their port facilities and naval forces at the Republic's disposal. This was no small point since, after Texas' independence, relations between the United States and Mexico had deteriorated and conflict seemed increasingly likely (Richmond 1985).

The national state's record of compliance with the December *convenios* would be a critical issue in the calculation of loyalties by rival Yucatecan-elite factions during the Mexican-American War. And prior to the outbreak of hostilities between the two nations in May 1846, Mexico City's record of compliance was poor. Yucatán was losing by executive fiat what it had gained in battle, particularly in the area of trade. Only two months after the *convenios* were signed, Santa Anna again banned the entry of all Yucatecan goods from Mexican ports. When his successors repeatedly refused to accept the *convenios*, Yucatán's elites, losing revenues from the closing of Mexico's ports, again opted for independence in December 1845. After their declaration of sovereignty, the *yucatecos* made it known that they would reunite if the *convenios* were respected. Yet even after the outbreak of war with the United States, the central government refused to sanction the 1843 *convenios*.[13]

The impasse ended in dramatic fashion in September 1846. In May,

12. The best accounts of Santa Anna's campaign against Yucatán and of the *yucatecos'* defeat of the invading Mexican force are N. Reed 1964:29–33; and Chapman 1967:21–69.

13. Drawing extensively on the proceedings and debates of the Yucatecan legislature, Richmond (1985) provides a detailed account of Yucatán's unremitting efforts to secure Mexican compliance with the *convenios*.

Santa Anna, who had been overthrown and exiled earlier in the year, was invited back by the Mexican army.[14] In order to galvanize mass support, he decreed a return to the original Federal Constitution of 1824. In late May, following quickly upon the announcement of his successful Plan de Guadalajara, Santa Anna met Governor of Yucatán Miguel Barbachano at the port of Sisal and agreed to support the *convenios* if Yucatán would incorporate itself into the new Federal Republic and provide limited assistance against the United States. After a heated debate in the Yucatecan legislature, where regional elites were bitterly divided over questions of trade, security, and patriotism, Yucatán agreed to reunite with Mexico. Most at issue was the questionable wisdom of supporting a national *caudillo* who had repeatedly betrayed them, and of initiating hostilities with the United States, Mexico's formidable foe but increasingly a valuable commercial ally of Yucatán. On 24 September 1846, Mexico City declared that Yucatán was officially "revindicated" and reincorporated into the federation.[15]

Yet the arrangement would not sit well in Campeche, where swift, heavily armed side-wheelers from the U.S. Home Squadron already lay menacingly off the Gulf ports of Ciudad del Carmen and Laguna de Términos. As a result of Yucatán's reunification with Mexico, these U.S. warships had begun a blockade of Laguna and Carmen (the principal channels of Campeche's entrepôt trade with Mexico) and would later occupy them. *Campechanos* had predicted the loss of their bread-and-butter trade and customs revenues but had been voted down by the *meridanos*, whose interests lay more in commercial agriculture for the internal market and, to a lesser extent, in trade with the United States and Cuba (Manno 1963; N. Reed 1964:15, 33–34; Cline 1958).

The United States fully intended to play upon the factionalism of regional elites to secure its strategic objectives in the war: (1) the pacification of the Gulf in advance of landings at Veracruz and Tampico, and (2) the

14. A number of writers have argued, plausibly, that the United States allowed Santa Anna, who had been in Cuban exile, to slip through its naval blockade and land in Veracruz. They suggest that the North Americans believed Santa Anna's return would have a destabilizing effect on Mexican politics that would undermine the war effort and ultimately force the *caudillo* to settle on terms favorable to the United States. Nelson Reed (1964:32–33) goes too far in stating that North American agents smuggled Santa Anna into the country for the purpose of losing a mock battle that would end the war.

15. *El Siglo XIX*, no. 819, October 1846; Richmond 1985; N. Reed 1964:33.

assurance that no supplies from southern Mexico would be sent to Veracruz and the Central Plateau. At one point early in the war, the U.S. State Department toyed with the idea of seizing the Isthmus of Tehuantepec in order to support any faction on the peninsula that would break definitively with Mexico.[16] On several occasions, Secretary of the Navy Bancroft advised the commander of the U.S. fleet, Commodore David Connor, to do all in his power to promote neutrality in Yucatán, playing upon the region's historical differences with Mexico and friendly relations with the United States.[17] As early as 4 June 1846, U.S. warships steamed into the port of Campeche, gave the Yucatecan flag a twenty-one-gun salute, then pressed Campeche's authorities to define their position on neutrality.[18] The show of force was not lost on the *campechanos*. The local press had already voiced widespread fear about the damage the U.S. Navy might visit on local ports. No sooner had war broken out in May than it became apparent that vocal sentiment for neutrality (or even for siding with the North Americans) existed on the west coast of the peninsula, around Campeche.[19]

Elite *campechanos* had numerous grievances with their rivals from Mérida. Now war, blockade, and a complicated choice of enemies exacerbated tensions. Despite its claim to liberalism and federalism, the Mérida-dominated state legislature had tightened its control over Campeche in 1846, appropriating municipal funds for the state treasury, raising import duties, and arbitrarily removing from public office followers of Santiago Méndez, Governor Barbachano's *campechano* rival. In the context of larger, weightier issues, such blatant *personalismo* was particularly galling (Richmond 1985; González N. 1970:50, 72; N. Reed 1964:15–16, 33–34).

Early in December 1846, as the North American blockade strangled

16. NARA, *Correspondence of the United States Department of State, Miscellaneous Letters, July 1–Dec. 20, 1846,* Microcopy 179, roll III, frames 89–90; Manno 1963; Richmond 1985.

17. NARA, NR, Record Group 45, Confidential Letters Sent, 1813–22, 1840, and 1843–79 (vol. 1), Secretary Bancroft to Commodore Connor, 19 May and 10 June 1846, pp. 197–98; 16 June 1846, p. 200; 1 August 1946, p. 290.

18. NR, Letters from Officers Commanding Squadrons, 1841–86, Home Squadron, Voyage of Commodore David Connor, Commander D. N. Ingraham to Consul J. F. McGregor, 4 June 1846. Cf. NR, Letter Books of Officers of the United States Navy, 1778–1908, Letters of Commodore David Connor, Connor to Ingraham, 20 May 1846.

19. NR, Home Squadron, Voyage of Commodore David Connor, Ingraham to Connor, 18 June 1846, and Connor to Bancroft, 30 June 1846; *El Siglo XIX,* 26 March 1846; Richmond 1985.

campechano coastal shipping and as local merchants speculated about the seizure or destruction of their vessels by the Home Squadron, Campeche revolted against Mexico (and Mérida). Declaring for an independent Yucatán that would restore the 1841 state constitution and remain unconditionally neutral in the war with the United States, Domingo Barret (formerly *primer alcalde* of Campeche) and other local leaders mobilized the Mayas along the frontier with old promises and new arms (Cline 1958:esp. 621–22; Richmond 1985). Yet while the *dzules* might debate fine points of tariff policy, federalism, and neutrality, the Mayas found the continued offer of tax reduction and the availability of guns and ammunition more compelling. This time, they were told the enemies were from Mérida, not from distant lands. Allowed to form their own battalions under their own leaders, the frontier Mayas routed the Mérida *dzules* in engagements at southeastern towns such as Tekax, Peto, and Valladolid. In the process, they came to recognize their collective power and, as we know, then brought it terribly and effectively to bear against their real enemy, the dominant white society whose sugar plantations were wreaking havoc with the life of their southeastern subsistence communities. The elite *campechano* revolt triumphed quickly—by January 1847—but in the process detonated what would become Latin America's most successful indigenous-peasant rebellion (N. Reed 1964:33–34, 46–49).[20]

A comprehensive analysis of the agrarian conditions on Yucatán's southeastern frontier that provided the rebel Mayas with both a concrete social agenda and the tactical mobility to revolt is beyond the scope of this essay and appears elsewhere.[21] We should note that in the rebel Mayas' own account of the rebellion, which has only recently been pieced together from oral tradition and the correspondence of the rebellion's leaders, it is clear that the 1847 insurgency assumed the dimensions of a social revolution against the encroachment of commercial agriculture, although it was

20. Cf. Aguilar C. 1977; Spicer 1980; and Hu-DeHart 1984 on the Yaquis, who fought for rival Sonoran *caudillos* but took advantage of periods of elite political instability to eject whites who had encroached on their lands.

21. For a review of the literature on the agrarian origins of the rebellion, see Joseph 1986:25–36. The important concept of "tactical mobility," which takes into consideration peasants' communal solidarity, their freedom from tight landlord control, and their relative freedom from state repression—often owing to their "marginal" geopolitical location—is developed in Wolf 1969.

triggered by a series of white factional disputes that conveniently put guns into Maya hands. The Mayas were quite explicit about the societal effects of the sugar estate's expansion: increased taxation on peasant agriculture; debt peonage, coerced labor (*fagina*) and physical abuse on the great estate; and the loss of accustomed access to *milpa* (Bricker 1981:87–118). Thus the great rebellion is best explained as a matter of free Maya villagers on the frontier seizing the day in an action based on their own self-realization—and *not* as a residuum of elite factional conflict and confusion, fanned by U.S. pressure. To be sure, the latter pressure on the *campechano* elite did bring matters to a boil. But while the United States figured *conjuncturally* in the revolt's outbreak, the *structural causes* lay within Yucatecan agrarian society.

Moreover, the Mayas are very clear regarding the "caste" nature of the war. A dominant theme in the communications of the Indian leaders is that laws should apply to all peoples, whatever their ethnic background. The burden of taxation should be borne by all racial categories, land should be available to everyone (and "the forest should not be purchasable"), and no ethnic group should have the right to abuse another physically with impunity. In this sense, the free Mayas clearly made a social revolution to erase caste distinctions. On the other hand, it appears that the fearful, skittish white elites must bear major responsibility for redefining a social conflict into a brutal race war. Central here was the *dzules'* costly decision during the earliest days of the rebellion not to honor the distinction that then existed between rich Indian *caciques*, or *hidalgos* as they were then called, and the majority of poor, landless Indians. Many of these educated, politically powerful Mayas had connections in, and identified closely with, white society. Like Creole *hacendados*, they seem to have obtained their wealth by exploiting Indian labor. By persecuting and actually lynching members of this privileged class, the whites forced such *caciques* as Jacinto Pat and Cecilio Chi to identify as Indians and contribute their leadership abilities to the rebel movement (Bricker 1981:93–99).

Finally, the Mayas' own perceptions of the conflict reinforce the recent findings of agrarian historians who are bringing greater precision to the question of the revolt's structural causation (see Joseph 1986:25–36 for a discussion of these findings). It is not enough to argue that the underlying cause of the rebellion was a lengthy heritage of "bad treatment," manifested in feudal-like forms of bondage dating back to Montejo the Conqueror. On the contrary, the Mayas' sociocultural adaptation to white domination in the northwestern corn and cattle zone had been a gradual process over generations, and by the end of the colonial period it had produced a stable, at least outwardly compliant labor force. Only on the frontier, where strong market conditions for sugar and other cash crops produced an increased demand for workers, did armed resistance occur.[22] This demand for labor necessitated the rapid (but far from complete) subordination of a previously isolated peasant population to a different and harsher labor regime that was now backed by the power of the state. Although the dominant white society viewed the rebellion in racial terms from its inception, it was only after negotiations of their land and labor grievances irreparably broke down in 1848 that the rebels' economic and agrarian perception of the conflict receded and the struggle assumed a more savage and explicitly racial character.

Nevertheless, it is likely that Yucatán's white elites would never have withstood the rebel Maya onslaught, let alone have successfully counterattacked, had it not been for the support—or at least the acquiescence—of the northwestern Maya *acasillados* who had long been attached to haciendas. Not only did these peons grow food and provide necessary auxiliary services, in some cases they were tenacious fighters, forcing the free Mayas to contend with Indian as well as white armed resistance. It is precisely this participation of a significant segment of the Maya population on the Creole side that prompts many recent scholars to argue that the "War of the Castes" is badly named.[23]

Another factor that contributed to the white recovery was the receipt of foreign (principally U.S.) assistance. If the specter of North American intervention had figured prominently in the elite factional disputes that created conditions facilitating the 1847 rebellion's outbreak, the U.S. government, as well as private actors, also had a hand in rescuing the dominant white society and in limiting the scope of the revolt. The following

22. Cf. Jane-Dale Lloyd's essay above on northwestern Chihuahua, suggesting that the revolt there was also facilitated by an unstable frontier where the local populace resisted subordination to a new agrarian regime.

23. E.g., Patch 1976:39–40. Conversely, white and *mestizo* regulars in the Creole army occasionally defected to the Indian side and, in some cases, actually led the rebel Mayas or instructed them in military tactics (Reina 1980:365–66).

discussion reconstructs the rather complex role that U.S. and other foreign agents played in promoting a white counteroffensive against the rebel Mayas, then assesses the impact that foreign agents had on the rebellion.

In the spring of 1848, charitable institutions in New Orleans arranged for the delivery of several hundred thousand pounds of corn, as well as gifts of money, to the *yucatecos* besieged in Mérida, Campeche, and the other Gulf ports—the last redoubts of Creole society in a peninsula otherwise under free-Maya control. In March, 2,000 rifles, several artillery pieces, and basic foodstuffs arrived from the Spanish government and the sizable Yucatecan colony in Havana (N. Reed 1964:103; Manno 1963:65–67).

Yet in mid-1848, it appeared to the commanders of the U.S. fleet, to the remaining members of the foreign colony, and to the Creoles themselves that these emergency supplies would not be enough to save "civilized society" from the "cruel depredations of ferocious savages."[24] The ships of several nations waited off the ports of Sisal, Campeche, Carmen, and Laguna de Términos to evacuate a steady stream of refugees.[25] As the Mayas moved within only a few kilometers of Mérida, Governor Méndez and the U.S. consul appealed to the new commander of the Home Squadron, Commodore Matthew Perry, for immediate military assistance.[26] Months earlier, in March, Perry had determined to make a show of force, hoping it would impress the rebels sufficiently to arrange an armistice with the Yucatecan government. He assembled a task force of side-wheelers and gunboats at Laguna, then traveled to Campeche where the flag was shown and extensive maneuvers were conducted. The Mayas continued to advance.[27]

Perry could not promise much more assistance to Governor Méndez without further instructions from the Department of the Navy. Moreover, he told the *yucatecos* that even with new orders from Washington, his fleet could at present commit only 538 marines and the stationary cannons

24. NR, Home Squadron, Voyage of Commodore Matthew C. Perry, McBlair to Perry, 10 May 1848.

25. NR, Home Squadron, Voyage of Perry, French Consul de Villeveque to Perry, 9 May 1848; N. Reed 1964:97.

26. NR, Home Squadron, Voyage of Perry, Consul McGregor to Captain Bigelow, 22 March 1848; Perry to Mason, 13 March 1848.

27. NR, Confidential Letters Sent (vol. 1), Mason to Perry, 8 March 1848, pp. 410–11; NR, Home Squadron, Voyage of Perry, Perry to Mason, 13 March and 18 May 1848; N. Reed 1964:85.

aboard his ships. Nevertheless Perry did what he could. Working with the U.S. military governor of occupied Veracruz, he arranged for guns and powder that had been taken from captured Mexican troops to be distributed to the defenders of Mérida and Campeche. Earlier the commodore had arranged for a warship to carry the Yucatecan special envoy Justo Sierra O'Reilly to Veracruz and the United States.[28]

The young *campechano* intellectual, who was Méndez' son-in-law, began his mission in November 1847 with the intention of securing full recognition of Yucatán as a neutral in the Mexican-American War as well as the removal of U.S. troops and tariffs from Ciudad del Carmen and Laguna. Then, as the Mayas tightened the noose on Campeche and Mérida, Sierra mounted a one-man lobby on Capitol Hill and in the North American press for direct military assistance and, finally, for a U.S. protectorate over Yucatán. Simultaneously, the envoy made the same offer—Yucatecan sovereignty in return for assistance in defeating the Mayas—to Britain, France, and Spain.[29]

Democratic President James Polk, whose blatant provocation of the war with Mexico in 1846 testified to a firm belief in America's "Manifest Destiny," granted Sierra a personal interview in early May. The president expressed his willingness to aid Yucatán militarily and to deliberate on Sierra's offer of annexation. At a minimum, Polk believed that a commitment of U.S. troops might prevent further bloodshed and preempt designs by foreign powers in the region—most notably the British, who were already selling arms and provisions to the *rebeldes* from Belize. A week later, however, when Polk took his Bill for the Relief of Yucatán before Congress, he had abandoned the idea of a U.S. protectorate. Instead, he invoked the Monroe Doctrine and asked for a commitment of naval forces already in the Caribbean.[30] In the Senate, Sam Houston of Texas spoke eloquently for the bill, displaying great sympathy for the *yucatecos'* plight.[31] Meanwhile, however, the issue had gained notoriety in the press, with the

28. N. Reed 1964:85.

29. See Sierra O'Reilly's own account of the mission in Sierra O'R. 1938 [1848]; cf. Richmond 1985 and N. Reed 1964:85–87.

30. Sierra O'R. 1938 [1848]:33–50; Williams 1929:138–41; N. Reed 1964:86. Commodore Perry had reported on British gunrunning to the rebels in January 1848. See NR, Home Squadron, Voyage of Perry, Perry to Mason, 30 January 1848.

31. Samuel Houston, "Speech of Samuel Houston of Texas on the Bill for the Relief of Yucatán," LC Washington, D.C., 1848.

nonsoft-interventionist Whig opposition and many journalists portraying the Caste War (accurately!) as an uprising of the oppressed Indian majority. In language reminiscent of speeches about more recent U.S. involvements, the Whigs (who had earlier opposed the invasion of Mexico as an immoral act) criticized the notion of a temporary occupation, pointing out that such operations had a way of becoming permanent. In mid-June, when word of Governor Barbachano's treaty negotiations with the rebel *cacique* Jacinto Pat reached Washington, the bill was abandoned by its Democratic supporters as having no purpose. The negotiations later broke down, but the lag in communications resulted in the demise of Polk's bill (N. Reed 1964:86–87; Richmond 1985; Manno 1963:69–70). Sierra's lobby did prompt almost a thousand volunteers and soldiers of fortune from the U.S. eastern and southern states to offer their services against the Mayas. Mostly recent veterans of the Mexican-American War who preferred adventure south of the border to the routine of civilian life, they were "the first of the American filibusters." After battling the Mayas in the interior bush for a year and taking heavy casualties, they straggled home (N. Reed 1964:86, 110–14).

Ultimately, it was the Mexican state that bailed out the *yucatecos*. President Polk had effectively deterred the European powers by invoking the Monroe Doctrine. Before new entreaties could be made to the North Americans, the Treaty of Guadalupe Hidalgo had been signed and the Yucatecans were again forced to deal with the "huaches"[32] in Mexico City. Barbachano suggested reunification on the basis of the old *convenios*. He accepted it without regional autonomy, the only stipulation being that the central government help Yucatán turn the tide against the *rebeldes*. One of the first acts of the new president, José Herrera, was to earmark 150,000 pesos for Yucatecan relief. Ironically, the money came from the $3 million indemnity that the United States had paid for Mexico's northern provinces, and the guns for Yucatán were bought from departing North American troops. By mid-July, the Mexican government had already sent five ships to Campeche, loaded with rifles, bullets, gunpowder, and provisions, and promised the rest of the money in monthly installments of 15,000 pesos worth of military supplies. On 17 August 1848, with all U.S. warships

---

32. *Huach* is a derogatory term that has been used for some time in Yucatán to designate people from the interior of Mexico. It is not a Mayan word.

removed from Yucatecan waters and the Maya threat to Mérida and Campeche lifted, Yucatán again joined Mexico.[33]

Yet how pivotal really were these arms shipments and other foreign factors in enabling Yucatán's white elites to break the siege, to limit the sphere of the rebellion and, ultimately, to subordinate the free Mayas? Certainly outside assistance, particularly the U.S. arms that were funneled through the Mexican state, played a role in turning the tide of battle. Nevertheless, neither foreign assistance nor *acasillado* support adequately explains why the masses of rebels, only a few kilometers from the gates of Mérida and Campeche and seemingly poised to drive the heavily outnumbered *dzules* from the peninsula in June and July, halted their advance and melted away almost overnight.

Although no relevant letters from Indian leaders explain the rebels' failure to pursue their advantage, oral tradition recorded several generations after the event suggests that the military campaign was interrupted by the beginning of the planting season. Perhaps more threatening to the Mayas than Commodore Perry's cannons and shiploads of military supplies was the prospect of a season without planting. Indian ritual and the peasant economy demanded that the rebels return to their *milpa*.[34] Ironically then, the immediate need to renew society deprived the free Mayas of their main chance to retain their social integrity in the long run. Although the siege of Mérida was not broken by a massive display of outside force, in the months and years ahead preponderant state force would reduce the scope of the rebellion and ultimately seal its fate.

In 1858, the *campechanos* split off from Yucatán to pursue a commercial future linked more closely to central Mexico, and *meridano* elites rebuilt the regional economy around henequen in the northwestern quadrant of the peninsula. Only gradually were Yucatecan elites able to pacify and reclaim the southeastern frontier from the rebel Mayas. Yet while the *dzules* ultimately recovered their hegemony, the sugar industry was lost forever. In that sense, the great rebellion ended with a bang. For although the rebel Mayas failed to take Mérida, suffered severe losses, and never "won" the Caste War, at least temporarily they accomplished their funda-

33. NR, Confidential Letters Sent (vol. 1), Mason to Perry, 15 June 1848, pp. 448–50; Richmond 1985; N. Reed 1964:103–4.

34. Bricker 1981:102; N. Reed 1964:98–100. The oral tradition was originally presented in E. H. Thompson 1932:70–71.

mental objective: they put a halt to the expansion of Creole commercial agriculture on the frontier.[35]

In the remote expanses outside the henequen zone, either by truce or by military stalemate, the war's conclusion signaled "the beginning of a process of decolonization . . . producing a reintegration of Indian culture in economic, social, political, and religious terms" (Bojórquez U. 1978:20). That the rebel Mayas managed to resist and preserve their autonomy around Chan Santa Cruz until 1901 no doubt owed greatly to their revitalization cult of the Talking Cross, the "psychological centrum around which [they] rallied themselves in the fight for their very lives" (Dumond 1977:127). But the independence of these *cruzob* also turned on their commercial relations with British merchants and munitions dealers in Belize— yet another illustration of the contradictory relationship between foreign influence and rural revolt in Yucatán.[36]

Summer of Discontent, Seasons of Upheaval: 1902–1915

The free Mayas' rebellion also provided some of the conditions that hastened the rise of henequen monoculture in later decades. Although southeastern agriculture was obliterated in the fighting, the estates in the northwest, around Mérida, suffered only temporarily and benefited ultimately by a dramatic alteration in the peninsula's demographic balance. For once, the north had been cleared of rebels. The *hacendados* lobbied successfully for the use of their former peons, who were discharged from military service. More important, these former workers were joined by significant numbers of refugees from the war-torn zones of the southeast. As the tide of war turned against the rebel Mayas, many opted for the food and relative security of the plantations in the northwest rather than a renegade life on the Quintana Roo frontier. Thus the Caste War firmly established the center of gravity of the henequen plantation in the northwest, fashioning the base of a dependent labor force that would power the ever expanding henequen estates in subsequent decades. Just as commercial sugar

35. For a discussion of the rebellion's short- and long-term consequences, see Joseph 1986:36–52.

36. For the British role in sustaining the *cruzob* state, see Jones 1971:415–21; N. Reed 1964:124–25, 170–73, 181–89, 201–5, 226–28.

expansion had shaped the possibilities for rural revolt, so the great re-bellion in turn had helped give rise to possibilities for subsequent commercial agricultural expansion.[37]

It was not until the 1870s, however, that the modern henequen estate really emerged. The growth of merchant marines in the nineteenth century had stimulated a need for rope and cordage. As demand for henequen continued to rise at midcentury, Yucatán's traditional northwestern corn and cattle haciendas gradually began their metamorphosis into export-oriented henequen plantations. The transition could not be effected at once, primarily owing to the significant cost of capitalizing an average-size plantation and maintaining it for seven years until the first harvest—about $130,000. After the Caste War, moreover, capital was in short supply owing to the devastation of the sugar industry. Because most planters preferred to shift piecemeal from old to new plantation techniques and crops, using existing fields to finance new *henequenales,* demand continued to outrun supply. However, when the invention of the mechanical knotting device for the McCormick binder (1878) began to revolutionize the North American grain industry and demand grew exponentially, Yucatecan planters were forced to seek greater and greater amounts of U.S. capital.[38]

North American economic influence, mediated privately and indirectly through U.S. capital and exercised in the context of a burgeoning and dynamic market, came to exercise a far greater impact on regional agrarian society than had the kind of direct official pressure that the U.S. government applied at midcentury.[39] Like so much of regional Mexico, Yucatán was thoroughly transformed by the requirements of North American industrial capitalism and governed by its fluctuating rhythms during the last quarter of the nineteenth century. The production of henequen increased furiously during the *porfiriato* as annual exports rose from 40,000 bales of raw fiber to more than 600,000 bales. By the turn of the century, green cornfields and idly grazing cows had been replaced by endless rectilinear

37. The most complete examination of the impact of the Caste War on the rise of henequen monoculture is Remmers 1981:esp. 299–835. The literature on the subject is reviewed in Joseph 1986:40–44.

38. Joseph and Wells 1982:69–99, esp. 73–74. The following discussion of the growth of the regional henequen industry and its reliance on North American capital draws heavily on this article as well as on Joseph 1982:chaps. 1–3; and Wells 1985.

39. This argument is persuasively developed in Alan Knight's essay above.

rows of bluish-gray spines and agricultural factories-in-the-field. Recently laid railroad tracks extended in every direction from Mérida, and over them passed convoy after convoy of boxcars stuffed with bales of fiber. Their destination was the United States, where manufacturers would convert the fiber into binder twine for the grain farmers of North America.

Mérida was transformed from the overgrown village it had been prior to the boom. Now the Republic's "White City," the "Paris of Mexico," it was spotless and modern, an appropriate seat for Yucatán's newly minted henequen millionaires. Yet the rise of henequen monoculture also dramatically changed the lives of tens of thousands of Maya workers who comprised the labor force. The indebted peon underwrote the planter's profits even under difficult market conditions, laboring on the plantations under miserable circumstances, often for less than 50 centavos a day.

The henequen estate differed from the classical pattern of late-nineteenth-century plantation agriculture in several important respects. Land tenure and ownership of the means of production were almost exclusively in Yucatecan hands. There was no major influx of technology from abroad. Indeed, Europeans and North Americans had failed miserably to invent the machinery required to make henequen processing economical on a commercial scale. Nor was management brought in from the outside; it, too, was completely Yucatecan. And finally, while capital was ultimately imported from the United States, it was made available and distributed on a local basis.

But Yucatán's relatively small planter elite of three or four hundred families were not independent actors. A much smaller, more cohesive group of about twenty to thirty families constituted a hegemonic oligarchical *camarilla* (or "divine caste," as they were called and came to call themselves early in the century). This ruling faction (based upon the Molina-Montes *parentesco*) had homogeneous interests, a relatively closed membership, and—owing in part to its collaboration with the principal buyer of raw fiber, the International Harvester Company (IHC)—such control over the economic and political levers of power in the region that it was able to thwart the opportunities of rival planter groups in late Porfirian society.

Prior to 1902, a truly exclusive and powerful collaborator mechanism had never characterized the Yucatecan henequen industry. Although loan capital had been extended to local *casas exportadoras* like Eusebio Escalante

e Hijo, Manuel Dondé y Cía., and Molina y Cía., North American cordage manufacturers had experienced only intermittent success in controlling the hard-fiber market. The fiber trade had fluctuated wildly throughout the quarter-century following the introduction of the McCormick
reaper-binder. Yet a secret agreement, consummated between IHC and
Molina y Cía. late in 1902, dramatically transformed the political economy of Yucatán by weeding out competitors and forcing down the price
of fiber.

The clout of the partners in this collaboration cannot be minimized.
The 1902 merger of Cyrus McCormick's Harvesting Machine Company
with several rivals to form International Harvester, with an initial capitalization of $120 million, eliminated the bulk of existing competition within
the U.S. farm implements and twine industries and placed at the manufac-
turer's disposal organizational and financial resources that had never before
existed. Harvester's chosen agents in Mérida, Olegario Molina y Cía.,
even prior to its collaboration with IHC represented a force in regional
affairs substantially more powerful than any of its nineteenth-century
predecessors.

The economic leverage afforded by the partnership had a complemen-
tary ripple effect in the political arena. Olegario Molina was not only
governor of Yucatán during the first decade of the century, but his family
relations and associates filled the upper echelons of the state's bureaucratic
machine. As was typically the case throughout Porfirian Mexico, the ruling oligarchical clique was subsequently incorporated into the national
superstructure. In 1907, following his first term as governor of Yucatán,
Molina himself joined Díaz' cabinet as minister of development.

Henequen's North American connection has been the subject of a continuing historiographic debate. Some North American scholars have recently argued that, despite the fact that U.S. corporations—principally
IHC—tried on occasion to control and manipulate the fiber market, they
never earned the spectacular profits that presumably would be the object of
such control. Rather, these writers have adduced less-visible macroeco-
nomic variables, such as changing conditions in the international hard-
fiber market and the combined devaluating trend of two global business
recessions and Mexico's 1905 monetary reform, to account fully for the
dramatic drop in the local price of fiber during the late *porfiriato* (Ben-

jamin 1977; Brannon and Baklanoff 1983; Cartensen and Roazen-Parrillo 1983). Nevertheless, I contend with Allen Wells and most Mexican writers that International Harvester's ever increasing control of local fiber production, its ever tightening grasp on the North American binder-twine market, and the *magnitude and duration* of the drop in price from 1903 to 1911 compel one to look beyond the natural play of the market. Moreover, we would argue that basic to an appreciation of International Harvester's role and impact on the regional economy is an understanding of the network of power relationships *within* Yucatán that affected the structure and control of production.[40]

If Yucatecan planters collectively constituted one of the wealthiest classes in Porfirian Mexico, their economic condition was among the least secure. In most cases these planters were not only big spenders but speculators, constantly seeking new ways to maximize profits amid the problematic fluctuations of the export economy, often overextending themselves in the process. For every genuine success story, many more planters existed in a perpetual state of indebtedness and fiscal instability that periodically led to bankruptcy. With increasing frequency throughout the period from 1902 to 1915, such members of the planter-merchant bourgeoisie became indebted to Molina's "divine caste" and were forced to advance their future product at slightly less than the current market price to cover present obligations. Moreover, it was access to foreign capital and International Harvester's capacity to funnel large amounts of it at critical

40. Joseph and Wells 1982 and 1983. The lively debate over corporate control of the Yucatecan political economy, which was played out over two years in the *Latin American Research Review,* has now been published as a small volume in Spanish (see Joseph, Wells et al. 1986). In her doctoral dissertation (1984), Diane Roazen-Parrillo argues provocatively that perhaps Molina's role in the partnership with IHC has been underestimated. She contends that if there was an "informal empire" in Yucatán, it was Molina and not Harvester who was the main protagonist, powerful enough to dictate the terms of the collaboration. Questions remain, however, regarding who supplied the capital and whether Molina's commissions from Harvester rose as the price declined and Molina's share of the business increased. Yet, as we shall see, subordinate factions of the planter elite were much less concerned with who was the senior partner; they bitterly resented the collusion itself, which they perceived to be the cause of shrinking prices and profits. In time, this bitterness (and the absence of other options) would impel these factions to organize multiclass coalitions and promote rural insurgencies against the *molinista* oligarchy.

junctures that helped Molina and his oligarchical faction to acquire mort-
gages, purchase estates outright, and consolidate their hold on regional
communications, infrastructure, and banking—all of which guaranteed
control of local fiber production and generally worked to depress the
price.[41]

Indeed, despite the fabulous wealth generated by the *auge henequenero,*
the first decade of this century was a veritable "summer of discontent" for
the vast majority of regional producers, merchants, workers, and *campesinos,* who found themselves subordinated to Molina's and Montes' oligarchy. Depressed fiber prices throughout the decade served to heighten
tensions within the regional elite and crystallized the belief among most
planters that the *molinista camarilla* was unwilling to countenance any loss
of economic control in the peninsula. By 1909, accommodation no longer
seemed possible. Political activity, and rebellion if necessary, were increasingly perceived as the only means to restore a more equitable reappor-
tionment of the spoils of the henequen economy.[42]

The national liberal reform movement of Francisco Madero, with its
democratic rhetoric, emboldened subordinate factions of the planter class
and their middle-sector allies to challenge Yucatán's ruling oligarchy. Just
as Madero's national coalition would topple Díaz' oligarchy (the *cien-
tíficos*), so these local planters now hoped to break the stranglehold of
Molina's and Montes' *casta divina.*

41. Backed by a substantial supply of foreign capital, Molina and Montes were able to
invest even when the economy was depressed and prices were low, precisely when most
planters and merchants faced capital shortages. This strategic position enabled them to
buy when most investors were compelled to sell out their interests at rock-bottom prices
merely to escape financial ruin (e.g., during the panic of 1907–8). Then, when fiber
prices rose and local property values increased, the Molinas had the option of selling
their newly acquired assets for a whopping profit or adding them to their expanding
empire.

42. Between January 1907 and December 1914 alone, fifty-five articles, either directly
or indirectly concerned with the role of IHC in the henequen market, were found in a
single local publication—*El Agricultor,* then the propaganda arm of the Cámara Agrícola, a planters' association created late in 1906 for the purpose of challenging *molinista*
hegemony. See T. Benjamin 1977:4n1. Cf. the stinging indictment of the trust by the
muckraking Yucatecan journalist Carlos P. Escoffié Zetina in the newspaper *El Padre
Clarencio* in 1909. The severe economic contradictions embedded in Yucatán's prerevolutionary order, the grievances these fostered among subordinate factions of the planter
elite, and the strategies they came to adopt are examined in Joseph and Wells 1986;
Joseph and Wells 1985. The following discussion draws upon these articles.

Yet unlike Sonora, Chihuahua, and much of the north from which so many of the middle-class leaders of Mexico's revolutionary bourgeois state would eventually come, monocultural Yucatán had a small, weak, middle class (only 3 to 5 percent of the population) and did not generate insurgent coalitions led by middle-sector or petty-bourgeois elements.[43] Instead, two rival parties led by disgruntled factions of the planter elite moved onto center stage as soon as political space opened up during the *maderista* period. These two parties were known popularly as "morenistas" and "pinistas" after their respective standard bearers, Delio Moreno Cantón and José María Pino Suárez, who were journalists. But they were financed by their planter supporters, and each rapidly attempted to construct alliances reaching into the middle-class intelligentsia, the small urban working and artisan class and, perhaps most important but until now not fully explained, the Maya *campesinado.*[44]

By late 1909, both the *morenista* and the *pinista* party attacked the Harvester-Molina-Montes combination, blaming it for the weakened fiber market, and each included an antimonopoly plank in its political platform.[45] When oligarchical repression foreclosed the electoral road to them, *morenistas* and *pinistas* alike rebelled against the government. But whereas in many other parts of the Republic episodes of local revolt built to a crescendo and toppled the ancien régime, in Yucatán these *maderista*-era rebellions occurred in fits and starts and never shook the foundations of the oligarchical order.[46]

Several explanations may be adduced for Yucatán's not being swept up in the early revolutionary tide. First, the peninsula's location on the far periphery made communication with revolutionary leaders in Mexico's core

43. Joseph 1982:chap. 3. Yucatecan society during the *porfiriato* had much in common with the colonial plantation and slave societies of an earlier period of Latin American history. An enormous chasm separated the two extremes on the social scale: the tiny minority of planters and the great majority of slaves and peons. Social infrastructure between these extremes was limited by an insignificant level of industrialization, owing to monoculture and the failure of an internal market. For a comparative perspective on the role of the middle sectors in the revolutionary process, see Katz 1976; Carr 1980.

44. Allen Wells and I analyze this mobilization in detail, from the perspective of elites as well as popular classes, in our forthcoming new book *Summer of Discontent, Seasons of Upheaval: Elite Politics and Rural Rebellion in Yucatán, 1890–1915.* For a preliminary statement, see Joseph and Wells 1985.

45. On the *morenista* and *pinista* platforms, see González R. 1984.

46. See the chapters above by John Hart and Alan Knight.

difficult and coordination of joint campaigns virtually impossible. Second, Yucatán's local *motines* and *sublevaciones* were often poorly armed and logistically isolated, in large measure owing to the inability of competing *morenista* and *pinista* elites to set aside their differences and unite against the ruling oligarchical faction. This organizational failure gave authorities the respite they needed to regroup, seal off troublesome areas, and prevent the spread of rebellion to peaceful zones. Third, and perhaps most important, the haunting specter of another caste war gave Yucatecan elites second thoughts about a full-scale mobilization of railway and dock workers, let alone Maya villagers and peons.

Morenista and *pinista* planters had grown up with their families' bitter memories of how similar internecine political disputes during the 1840s had led to the arming of Maya *campesinos* and their emergence as an independent hostile force. Few could forget a war that had reduced the peninsula's population by more than half and razed the profitable sugar industry on the southeastern frontier. Thus, although many planters itched to defeat Molina's *camarilla* in 1910, the majority feared that arming the rural masses would destabilize the elaborate mechanisms of control that were fashioned in the wake of the Caste War and that had so successfully underwritten the henequen boom.[47]

The expansion of the monocultural henequen estate throughout the peninsula's northwestern quadrant and beyond had alienated most peasants from their land base, disrupting their communities and forcing them onto the factory-like plantations. Once pulled into the large estate's sphere, the *campesino* became subject to the full weight of its political, economic, and social control. The monopoly of force that the planters exercised in the region through federal, state, and private police forces, reinforced by a monopoly of all political and judicial offices, made resistance and escape difficult. Bounty hunters responding to advertisements in the local press and "security agents" on retainer tracked down runaways. Identification papers became required for peons temporarily leaving their estates. In 1901, when the independent Maya state in Quintana Roo (which had given asylum to plantation runaways) was conquered by the Mexican army, the last avenue of escape was closed.

47. The following discussion of social control draws upon Joseph and Wells 1985; and Wells 1985:chap. 6.

Yet the planters took still other precautions. Whenever possible, they made sure that their work forces were heterogeneous groups, combining, for example, Maya *campesinos,* Yaqui deportees, indentured oriental immigrants, and central Mexican *enganchados.* The constant influx of outsiders and the extraordinarily high deathrate among laborers disrupted collective relationships among immigrants and Mayas alike. By intensifying the labor regime, then replenishing his work force with new arrivals, the *hacendado* accomplished a dual purpose: he combatted the chronic labor shortage while minimizing the chances of organized resistance. Moreover, Yucatecan peons were allowed only limited contact with the world outside the plantation. *Hacendados* discouraged fraternization among workers of different estates, which Yucatán's rudimentary road system made difficult in any case. An effort was made to seal the *campesino* off from potential allies in the urban areas. Whenever possible, city visitors and peddlers were kept off the haciendas—and peons were restricted to them.

This brutal plantation regime was combined with sophisticated use of the judiciary to redress the worst excesses. The result was a finely tuned system of coercion and co-optation, managed both by private landowners and by the state. Now if planter-supported *motines* were to blossom into social revolution, Yucatán's contending elites might lose everything—their properties, their social world, even their lives—in another "guerra de castas." That some planters would take such a chance and arm their peons demonstrates not only the deepening contradictions within the late Porfirian elite, but also their rising level of desperation.

Short-term economic conditions during the period must also be considered in any explanation of the volatile political climate that prevailed in the region. No doubt in part owing to manipulation of the price of fiber by International Harvester and Olegario Molina, the henequen market hit bottom in 1910–11. Commercial bankruptcies and foreclosures rocked the peninsula, in part because of the steep drop in fiber prices, in part because of the lingering effects of the severe economic crisis of 1907–8.[48] Meanwhile, in the countryside a severe locust plague ravaged the *campesinos'* *milpa* in 1910, destroying the food supply of the Maya villagers who had previously resisted falling into debt servitude on the henequen plantations.

48. Joseph and Wells 1982. We found extensive evidence of mortgage foreclosures, which were frequently attributed to setbacks dating back to the panic of 1907–8, in civil cases in the AGE, Ramo de Justicia, 1911–12.

Many now had little alternative but to move onto the estates, so dependent were they on local *hacendados* for subsistence. On these estates, human wretchedness proceeded apace, with the locust plague worsening the diet and increasing the incidence of pellagra to near-epidemic proportions.[49]

It is risky, however, to attribute the rural insurgency of the period to worsening economic conditions. More often than not, hunger and misery impede political mobilization rather than abet it. But tightening economic prospects plus widening political space did give some people who had room to maneuver in the *campo* both the incentive and the opportunity to join new political coalitions and even to lead revolts.[50] Independent villagers and plot holders, hacienda foremen, bandits, artisans, teachers, and ex-militia officers frequently became Yucatán's revolutionary *caciques* and the linkmen between the planter-led parties and local concentrations of *campesinos* in these revolts. And the combination of political space and a worsening economy put others, particularly peons on rural estates, in a position to be mobilized and armed by these planter-led factions—sometimes voluntarily, sometimes through coercion and deceit. Typically, *morenista* and *pinista* planters and middle-class intellectuals based in Mérida would plan a revolt (frequently timing their regional complot to coincide with a national-level conspiracy) and then, through an extended network of middlemen, mobilize sympathetic elements (and often coerce less-than-sympathetic ones) in rural towns, villages, and haciendas. Frequently these local tumults and riots spun out of control.[51]

Preliminary research in the criminal court records of the time provides some insight into the perceptions and motivations of the peons and *comuneros* who were mobilized in these *morenista* and *pinista* risings. Clearly

49. E.g., see AGE, Ramo de Justicia, "Diligencies en averiguación de la muerte de José María Eb, vecino que fue de la hacienda San José," 1912; "Diligencias con motivo del suicidio de Candelario Cauich, sirviente de la finca Chunkanán," 1913.

50. Even had there been no monopolistic collusion between IHC and the *molinista camarilla*, it is likely that the crash in fiber prices and the fall of Díaz would themselves have fueled a certain level of intra-elite strife in 1910–11.

51. E.g., see AGE, Ramo de Justicia, "Causa seguida a Jorge Rath y socios por el delito de rebelión," 1912; "Causa seguida a Juan Campos y socios por el delito de rebelión," 1912; "Causa seguida a Juan Jiménez y socios por el delito de provocación al delito de rebelión," 1913. Joseph and Wells 1985 provides a more detailed discussion of these early "seasons of upheaval."

their social agendas were different from those of the elites who recruited them. Isolated as most of them were on the henequen estates, Yucatecan *campesinos* had little awareness of the collusion between IHC and the *molinistas* who controlled production in its interest. Indeed, in the late *porfiriato* the world of the *campesino* had not been penetrated by North American influences. Even *béisbol*'s popularity did not yet extend much beyond the capital and port.[52] Yet the trial testimonies allow us to probe the bitter resentment that *campesinos* harbored toward planter hegemony, and to appreciate how elite-led mobilizations often gave the rural dispossessed an opportunity to strike at an immediate authority figure, typically a municipal or hacienda agent, a justice of the peace, or even a *jefe político*.[53]

Although it served the propagandistic needs of muckraking critics as well as the apologists of the Old Regime to portray the Maya *campesinado* as a mass of passive, inert peons,[54] in reality there was a surprisingly high incidence of resistance to the planters' brutal regime even before 1910. The Maya was no docile "sambo," meekly accepting his dependent status and extracting what meager morsels of benevolence the planter tossed in his direction. On the whole, workers rejected the weak paternalistic ethos of their masters, demonstrating their dissatisfaction in a variety of ways,

52. This observation is based on a careful reading of judicial testimonies and the regional press, as well as on a series of interviews with revolutionary-era participants and members of their families. E.g., interviews with Jesús Campos Esquivel, 26 December 1986 and 2 January 1987; and with Melchor Zozaya Ruz, 31 December 1986. Again, it should be kept in mind that North Americans did not own henequen estates in Yucatán and were not the identifiable presence that they were in the Mexican north. Contrast the very different picture of the North American economic and cultural presence that emerges in the other essays in this volume.

53. The classic case is AGE, Ramo de Justicia, "Causa seguida contra Pedro Crespo y socios por homicidio, rebelión y robo," 1911. Alan Knight correctly observes that "this violent, personalized attack had something of the quality of the slave revolts which . . . affected Cuba or the American south in the nineteenth century: responding to cruel treatment (rather than, say, to agrarian dispossession)" (Knight 1986a, 1:226). Yet he underestimates the level of organization that operated during some of these seasons of upheaval—particularly in the spring of 1911—as well as the important role that free *campesinos* and artisans often played in them.

54. Critics of the Old Regime like John Kenneth Turner (1910) put forth a rather static view of violent and unceasing oppression of the docile and faceless many by a greedy few. Planter apologists countered by painting labor conditions in aristocratically benign, almost consensual terms. For a critique of the contemporary polemic over the "labor question," see Wells 1984.

including running away, chronic alcoholism, and spontaneous though ultimately futile acts of local violence. During the *porfiriato,* such acts of hacienda violence were answered with excessive counterforce by the planter elite (Wells 1984; Joseph 1986:59–81). Nevertheless, particularly during the *morenista* and *pinista* revolts of 1911–12, local episodes of *campesino* violence proliferated to a point where the traditional oligarchical order faced a breakdown of its mechanisms of social control.[55]

It was ultimately for this reason that the intra-elite struggle to replace an entrenched regional oligarchy—a struggle that played itself out in several seasons of upheaval between 1910 and 1913—ended in failure. President Díaz' fall in mid-1911 temporarily interrupted the political rule of the *molinista camarilla* but never endangered its economic domination. In the resulting political vacuum, *morenistas* and *pinistas* vied for leadership, and rural violence reached dangerous new levels. General Victoriano Huerta's ouster of President Madero and the imposition of military rule in Yucatán early in 1913 institutionalized a political stalemate among the three contending elite factions, but it also allowed them an opportunity to reach an accommodation that would preserve the social peace.[56]

Thus, once again the process of rural revolt in Yucatán revealed a reciprocal or dialectical quality. Clearly, the seasons of upheaval that swept over the Yucatecan countryside reflected serious contradictions in the late Porfirian structures of power. The exclusive alliance that was established between foreign capital and a dominant faction of the regional elite, to the detriment of the vast majority of the population, engendered bitterness and frustration that, come the revolution, were expiated in a torrent of political activity by multiclass coalitions between 1910 and 1913. Yet the mass participation of subaltern groups in these cycles of rebellion began to infuse the struggle with an ideology of resistance to elite domination that became cause for concern among Yucatecan planters and U.S. corporate interests alike. In short order, excessive rural violence prompted local elites to reconcile their differences, a development heartily endorsed by IHC and

55. See Joseph and Wells 1985 and 1987. Cf. Hart's essay in the present volume, concerning the breakdown of order that accompanied attacks on large American-owned commercial estates in neighboring Campeche during the same period.

56. This entente of elites and its implications for *campesino* demobilization is discussed in Joseph and Wells forthcoming.

the other cordage interests, who meanwhile were calling upon their government to consider gunboat diplomacy should elite initiatives fail to guarantee an uninterrupted fiber supply.[57]

In mid-1914, when General Huerta was himself defeated at the national level by a revolutionary coalition of Constitutionalists, Yucatán's uneasy alliance of planter factions continued to resist the arrival of the Mexican Revolution. When bribes failed to keep the Constitutionalist revolution at arm's length, the old plantocracy defiantly mounted one last, futile, separatist rebellion in January 1915. The leaders and paymasters of the reaction were Olegario Molina, Avelino Montes, and the "divine caste." They were defeated in March by General Salvador Alvarado's 8,000-man army, which brought Yucatán a revolution from without.[58]

Because of a lack of significant mobilization, owing largely to the planter class's economic power and the preponderant political force they had regained prior to Alvarado's arrival in March 1915, Yucatán's revolution had to be imported from without and made from above. Interestingly, both Alvarado's bourgeois reform and subsequently Carrillo Puerto's idiosyncratic brand of socialism were inspired by U.S. models.[59] Although these *caudillos'* social projects were predicated upon different ideological constructs, drew upon different sets of economic and human resources, and proceeded at different historical conjunctures, both attempted to bring a viable social revolution to a dependent monocultural society that was structurally unprepared to participate in a process of revolutionary transition, even though it was in desperate need of revolutionary change.[60]

57. For the cordage interests' perceptions and response to *campesino* violence, see NARA, Record Group 59, Records of the Department of State Relating to the Internal Affairs of Mexico, 1910–29, Microfilm Copy 274, Washington, D.C., 1959, file 812.61325 for the years 1910–13. Even before 1900, IHC was directly financing or subsidizing experimentation in alternative hard fibers in the United States, other parts of the Americas, and the Philippines. Shortly after the turn of the century, the U.S. government joined International Harvester in these endeavors. See Navistar International Corporation (formerly International Harvester) Archives, doc. file 2395 ("Early Operations in Fiber and Twine"); Joseph and Wells 1983:91.

58. The Ortiz Argumedo revolt and the conquest of Yucatán by Alvarado's Constitutionalist army are detailed in Joseph 1982:prologue and chap. 4.

59. Carrillo Puerto's ideological influences have already been touched upon above; for Alvarado's, see Joseph 1982:chaps. 4–5, esp. pp. 99–111, 138–39.

60. This theme is developed in Joseph 1982:chap. 4; and Joseph 1986:105–9.

Conclusions

In both the historical episodes of Yucatecan rural revolt examined here, U.S. influences on the local agrarian society were mediated through regional elites. Unlike many other regional (mostly northern Mexican) cases examined in this volume, North American agents did not engage the *campesinado* directly, through investments in regional property. (Indeed, it has only been quite recently, in connection with the tourist boom on Mexico's Caribbean coast, that such foreign businessmen have sunk substantial direct investments in the peninsular economy.) In 1847, military intervention by the U.S. government served as the catalyst for yet another round of nineteenth-century elite feuding. As on two previous occasions, this latest episode of factional conflict expediently put arms in the hands of free Maya auxiliaries; but now, during the Mexican-American War, in the absence of even token national state power, space truly existed for peasant rebels to operate effectively and extend the lease on their traditional way of life.

Questions of causation are always thorny, and we cannot take the mere *correlation* of U.S. presence and rural revolt to imply *causation*. As we have seen, a determination of the rebellion's cause should give greatest weight to the interplay of internal structures, processes, and worldviews. Nevertheless, U.S. policy appears to have influenced the *timing* of what was probably the bloodiest, most successful peasant rebellion in Latin American history. Competing *meridano* and *campechano* elites had feuded for decades and undoubtedly would have fought again soon, but wartime exigencies prompted the U.S. government to goad on these bickering rivals, exacerbating existing grievances with new tensions and the specter of gunboat diplomacy. Once the feud heated up and the Maya villagers were armed, the continuing feebleness of the state and Yucatán's peripheral location served to prolong what rapidly became a genuine social revolution against commercial agricultural expansion. Before that revolution ran its course, it had destroyed the sugar industry on the southeastern frontier and in the process shaped possibilities for large-scale henequen production in the northwest.

Our examination of the rural insurgencies that followed in the wake of the *maderista* rebellion of 1910 suggests that U.S. economic influence, exercised privately through North American capital and market control, registered a more potent and extended impact on regional agrarian society than did isolated cases of official government pressure. Here the Yucatecan revolutionary experience supports the argument that Alan Knight has elaborated for Mexico as a whole.[61] International Harvester's corporate control of regional fiber production was mediated through an oligarchical *camarilla,* an arrangement that was (or at least was perceived by rival elites to be) ruinous to their own interests. Yet by forming rival parties and enlisting the aid of subaltern groups and intermediate strata in their rebellion against the *comprador* oligarchy, these lesser elites were not forging "nationalist" coalitions against an external threat. Rather, they sought a larger share of the spoils of the regional monocrop; most would gladly have substituted for Molina and Montes as International Harvester's collaborators.

Of course, subaltern groups had objectives of their own. Once again on the nation's far periphery and in the absence of a strong central state, peasant villagers (and many peons) began to turn elite feuds to their own advantage:[62] fleeing estates, lashing out at hated targets and, in certain noteworthy cases, building clientele that would later be consolidated into *cacicazgos* when the revolution gained a foothold in Yucatán (e.g., see Joseph and Wells 1987). It was this structural dichotomy—and corresponding ideological disjuncture—between popular and elite politics and mentalities, manifest in these *maderista*-era seasons of upheaval (as it had been during the Caste War), which ensured that the hegemony of Yucatán's foreign-tied monoculture did not go unchallenged. Indeed, in the years ahead, the planter class (and its foreign allies) would be forced to rethink and modify their political and economic strategies. Even prior to Alvarado's triumph in 1915, rural workers utilized the political instability of the post-Díaz years to secure some concessions from local authorities,

61. See Knight's essay in this volume. For treatment of the intermittent U.S. government pressures on Yucatán's revolutionary governments from 1915 to 1924, see Joseph 1982:chaps. 5, 8, and 9.

62. However, as we have seen, Yucatán's peripheral status, in combination with a stronger local state apparatus than had existed in 1847, also worked to impede the coherence of a *generalized* regional insurrection: Yucatán's "offside" location made communication and coordination with revolutionary movements in central Mexico exceedingly difficult, enabling regional authorities to isolate local flare-ups more effectively.

most notably a 1914 decree that abolished debt peonage.[63] Although the reformist decree was never implemented, representing an expedient measure that enabled the oligarchy to buy time, it provided an important precedent upon which later revolutionary governments, backed by substantial *campesino* support, would build.

63. Criminal court records in the AGE's Ramo de Justicia for 1913–15 similarly suggest a trend toward marginal concessions in the area of labor treatment on haciendas.

ANA MARÍA ALONSO

U.S. Military Intervention, Revolutionary

Mobilization, and Popular Ideology in

the Chihuahuan Sierra, 1916–1917

On 15 March 1916 the U.S. government sent 6,000 troops into Mexico on a "punitive expedition" whose ostensible purpose was to capture revolutionary leader Francisco Villa and destroy his forces. On March 9, Villa, with 500 of his men, had attacked the border town of Columbus, New Mexico, in response to what he perceived as an American threat to Mexican national sovereignty (Katz 1979b).[1] Indeed, beginning in 1915, Villa's ideology had become explicitly nationalist and anti-American (Katz 1979b, 1981:298–326; Knight 1986a, 2:342–54; Ulloa 1979:203–4).[2]

Eighty or ninety of the *villistas* who attacked Columbus, all seasoned revolutionaries, came from Namiquipa, a *municipio* located in the mountainous Guerrero district of Chihuahua, the "cradle" of the Mexican Revolution and the heartland of *villismo*. The American military forces made Namiquipa a prime objective, and by the end of March thousands of U.S. troops occupied the area. Colonel Frank Tompkins, an officer in Pershing's punitive expedition, described Namiquipa as "the most revolutionary town in all of Mexico," adding that in March there were two factions in the

The thirty-one-month period of ethnographic and archival research on which this essay is based was spent in collaboration with Daniel Nugent. The research was supported by grants from the Social Science Research Council, the Inter-American Foundation, and the Center for Latin American Studies of the University of Chicago.

1. In an account drawn from interviews with *villistas* who participated in the attack, the *namiquipense* historian Alberto Calzadíaz Barrera asserts that Villa chose March 9 because León Cárdenas Martínez, one of Villa's confidential agents, told Villa that 9 March 1916 was the sixty-ninth anniversary of the 1847 American attack on Veracruz (Calzadíaz B. 1977, 6:16).

2. In addition to the works cited in the text I have found numerous documents on this point in NARA, MR.

pueblo, "one of which threatened to fight if American troops entered" (Tompkins 1934:80).

Two months later, the local situation had changed radically. *Namiquipense* peasants were collaborating with the Americans, selling their labor and supplies to the troops and, more important, furnishing the invaders with military intelligence. Moreover, in response to a "suggestion" from General Pershing, the *namiquipenses* had formed a local militia which was to cooperate actively with the U.S. military in the destruction of local *villista* forces. Elsewhere in the once *villista* Guerrero district, initial hostility to U.S. military intervention was similarly transformed into active collaboration with American forces in the campaign against *villismo.* The erosion of Villa's popular base in the Guerrero district was such that in October 1916 Villa had to resort to coercion in order to recruit men from this onetime *villista* area.

What motivated the peasants in one of the most *villista* areas in Mexico to turn against their former leader and actively collaborate with foreign military forces in an anti-*villista* campaign? The course of events becomes even more puzzling when we consider that these peasants had supported Villa until the American intervention and had been exposed to Villa's anti-American, nationalist rhetoric. Did the bulk of Villa's supporters not share his anti-imperialist ideology?

This essay addresses these questions and assesses the impact of American military intervention on peasant revolutionary mobilization and ideology in the Chihuahuan sierra, especially in the *municipio* of Namiquipa,[3]

3. Namiquipa, established at the end of the seventeenth century as a Franciscan mission, was subsequently abandoned. It was refounded in 1778 as a military colony whose settlers received an extensive land grant from the colonial state in return for fighting the Apache Indians, whose continual raids impeded the socioeconomic development of the frontier until the Apache were decisively defeated in 1886. On the eve of the revolution, the municipality of Namiquipa had a population of about 4,000, distributed in two *pueblos*—Namiquipa and Cruces—as well as in outlying ranchos and haciendas. The majority of the population comprised a middle peasantry engaged in subsistence production on small plots cultivated with household labor. Unlike other sierra towns, Namiquipa had neither mining nor industry on any significant scale. A stratum of richer peasants, whose wealth depended more on cattle breeding than on agriculture and who had capital invested in petty commerce, formed a local elite. Both these groups identified themselves as descendants of the original colonists. Toward the end of the nineteenth century, a number of immigrants—petty-bourgeois entrepreneurs who invested in cattle, small-scale commerce, and eventually land—arrived in the mu-

where the peasantry had fought in the revolution from 1910 onward. The loss of support for *villismo* in Namiquipa provides one example of the effect of American intervention on rural revolt in Mexico. Moreover, the collaboration of *namiquipenses* and other Chihuahuan peasants with the American forces puts into question widely held notions concerning the centrality of nationalism and anti-imperialism in popular revolutionary mobilization and furnishes an opportunity to evaluate critically the place of nationalism in rural struggles at this time.[4]

One assumption operating in interpretations of this revolutionary conjuncture is that the *villista* resurgence in Chihuahua, which occurred in July 1916, can be attributed to a popular, nationalist mobilization against the U.S. presence in Mexico. However, as I will demonstrate, events in the Guerrero district suggest otherwise, indicating that we must seek different criteria to account for the *villista* resurgence.[5]

Clearly, the role of nationalism in popular mobilization and ideology

---

nicipality. These immigrants displaced the local elite and used their ties of clientship with the state oligarchy to gain control of local administration and resources, including the community's lands. This local class struggle was critical to the revolutionary mobilization of the middle peasantry. While some of the richer peasants also joined the revolutionary movement, most of them did not; their position in the local social structure was problematic since they had both benefited and lost from the domination of the petty-bourgeois immigrants.

4. *Contra* many investigators, Alan Knight (1985b:288–317) argues that nationalism and anti-imperialism were of little significance to popular mobilization and ideology in the Mexican Revolution of 1910–20 (see also Knight, above).

5. Although by the end of 1916 Villa was able to raise an army of several thousand men, many of them *carrancista* deserters, this was not owing to an upsurge of popular nationalism. To the contrary, popular rumors (based on the fact that Villa was receiving American ammunition from El Paso firms) that the United States was helping Villa against Carranza were gaining him recruits at the end of 1916 (MR, Record Group 393, I.S. [Intelligence Section] F 130, Ord, El Valle, to Campanole, Dublan, 26 December 1916). Villa seems to have recognized that the loss of U.S. support contributed to delegitimizing his movement, for by January 1917 he was announcing that, in light of the American withdrawal, the United States no longer considered him a "bandit," and that henceforth he would respect foreign interests (MR, Record Group 94, E 25 DF 2528244, Funston, Ft. Sam Houston, Texas, to Adjutant General, Washington, 31 January 1917). Villa's success in recruiting men after October 1916 can be attributed to three factors: (1) popular hatred and fear of the *carrancistas*, who abused the urban and rural populations in numerous ways; (2) the terrible social and economic conditions prevalent throughout the state of Chihuahua under the *carrancista* regime; (3) the fact that, at least by November 1916, Villa was paying his men in silver, and that for many the revolution had become a way of life.

must be problematized and situated theoretically in relation to a set of concepts amenable to concrete analysis. The next section of this essay identifies a variety of possible meanings of nationalism by discussing it in relation to the state and the peasantry, and in relation to several regionally and historically defined contexts in Mexico. A longer section follows, presenting an analysis of nationalism and the Revolution of 1910–20. There I examine the modalities of action and consciousness in a particular locale during that period, specifically the course of events in Namiquipa during the 1916–17 North American occupation of Chihuahua.

Peasant Nationalism and the Mexican State

NATIONALISM AND THE STATE

The "nation" may be defined as "an imagined political community . . . imagined as both inherently limited and sovereign" (Anderson 1983:15). As a universalistic style of imagining social ties, nationalism contrasts with such particularistic forms of configuring social relatedness as kinship and clientelism. For Anderson, the spread of literacy, as well as the regular movements or "pilgrimages" of social actors across a circumscribed territory, made possible that mode of apprehending the social world—marked by "simultaneity" and by a "deep, horizontal comradeship"—which is the nation (pp. 15–16, 29–31, 41–65).

Clearly there is a close relationship between nationalism and state formation. "The nation" is one of the key ideological forms through which the modern state constructs hegemony, forging a "collective will" through this image of political community. Hence, the production and reproduction of nationalism depends on the degree of state control over the sites and institutions of civil society through which ideological hegemony is constituted.

NATIONALISM AND THE PEASANTRY

The assertion that nationalism was central to popular revolutionary mobilization in Mexico is at odds with much social-scientific literature on the peasantry, literature that characterizes this class as "antinationalist" and "prepolitical." However, these essentialist characterizations of peasant consciousness should be dismissed on general theoretical grounds, and peasant participation in nationalist or antinationalist movements should be examined in concrete, sociohistorical terms.

We must consider several criteria when assessing the place of nationalism in peasant ideology. First, we must gauge the importance of forms of social reproduction organized by local or regional structures that articulate ways of imagining political community which are different from, and even opposed to, "the nation." Second, we must evaluate the character of attempts to incorporate the peasantry into the nation-state and the corresponding reaction of the peasantry to such efforts. Third, we must distinguish between antinationalism, on the one hand, and alternative "national" projects on the other. Peasant visions of how a national society should be organized may differ from those advanced by dominant groups and classes; but peasant resistance to elite forms of imagining a national political community should not be confused with antinationalism.[6] In other words, there may exist different and even conflicting modes of "imagining" the nation.

Finally, since the development of nationalism is a sociohistorical *process,* related to state formation and to the production and reproduction of ideological hegemony, instances of "contradictory consciousness" are possible. This concept of "contradictory consciousness" was formulated by Antonio Gramsci (1971:332), whose work suggests that popular consciousness may be *contradictory* to the extent that the ideology promulgated by the state and by dominant groups and classes may not be fully hegemonic and may be only partially internalized by subaltern groups and classes. It can coexist with other visions of society, grounded in popular everyday practice, whose reproduction is oriented by different meanings and values. Since different ideological horizons can be entertained simultaneously by social groups, nationalism and other antithetical modes of imagining political community can coexist—as facets of a "contradictory consciousness" that are selectively actualized in practice in response to concrete sociohistorical circumstances.

NATIONALISM IN MEXICO

Nationalism and the Mexican State. Robert Scott estimates that in 1910 nearly 90 percent of the Mexican population lacked a meaningful concept

6. I have benefited from the excellent discussion of this point in Mallon 1983.

of "the nation" (cited in F. C. Turner 1968:10). Although quantifying nationalism is a dubious exercise, the "statistic" nevertheless makes an interesting and valid point, suggesting that on the eve of the Revolution of 1910–20 nationalism was by no means fully hegemonic in Mexico. The Mexico of 1910 was "less a nation than . . . [it was] a mosaic of regions and communities, introverted and jealous, ethnically and physically fragmented," with weak nationalist sentiments (Knight 1986a, 1:2).

In the second half of the nineteenth century, under the Liberal and Porfirian regimes, the dynamic of modern nation-state formation had accelerated in Mexico, but this process, uneven and replete with contradictions, had not concluded by 1910. The bulk of the population was illiterate; communications were poor; ethnic, linguistic, and vertical differences mitigated against the formation of a nationalist "horizontal comradeship"; and the influence of the church worked against the secular, political imagining of community (F. C. Turner 1968:21; Knight 1986a, 1:14). Moreover, state centralization during the *porfiriato* assumed a particularistic, clientelist form. A national oligarchy subordinated parallel regional oligarchies (Knight 1986a, 1:21). Not only did the exclusion of popular groups and classes from national political life limit the development of a strong grassroots nationalism, it also led to an "ideological disjuncture"[7] between the state and the dominant classes, on the one hand, and the subaltern groups and classes on the other. Moreover, processes of nation-state formation were unable fully to transform and encompass variform, regional structures of social reproduction.

Nationalism on the Northern Frontier/Border. One such region was the northern frontier, characterized by distinctive socioeconomic structures and socio-ideological horizons (Carr 1973). Even today, northerners describe their region as "another country" while simultaneously affirming their identity as "Mexicans." The conflict between nationalism and regionalism evident in such statements suggests that the northern frontier was (and continues to be) characterized by a "contradictory consciousness" of political community.

As Eric Van Young (1986) points out, the concept of region deployed in

7. This concept is taken from Nugent 1987.

recent Mexican studies lacks analytical definition. He proceeds to define regionalism as "the self-conscious identification, cultural, political, and sentimental, that large groups of people develop over time with certain geographical spaces." The parallels to nationalism should be evident: regions and nations are both imagined as historically, socially, and territorially bounded communities. In both regionalism and nationalism, metonymy and metaphor configure a privileged relationship between "place" and social identity. I suggest that as regions become integrated into nation-states, they cease to be imagined as sovereign and are conceived instead as distinct sociocultural communities encompassed by the political community of the nation. In other words, through a hierarchical ordering of place and identity, "the nation" becomes the unmarked term that subsumes the meanings of the marked term, "the region."[8] Particularist identifications and loyalties become circumscribed by nationalist ones. But the long-term process of incorporation of regions, especially of frontiers/borders, into nations is fraught with conflict and contradiction and is often incomplete.

The issues of nationalism and anti-imperialism in the Mexican north require special treatment. Historically, the degree of integration of the frontier/border into the nation-state has been less than that of other regions of Mexico. Northern regionalism has its raison d'être in a "peculiar" sociohistorical experience, one shaped above all by a distinct mode of frontier conquest that resulted in the development of structures of social reproduction specific to the north.

Centuries of almost uninterrupted violent conflict between colonists and Apache Indians, persisting until 1886, overdetermined the structure and ideology of northern society. During the decades of violence between colonists and indigenes, the defense of a regional territory encouraged the development of a regional imagination of community. Moreover, especially after independence, the provincial rather than the central government played the key role in the organization and regulation of frontier warfare. The center's "abandonment" of the north to "the incursions of the savages" fostered a resentment of the national government among the northern colonists, particularly among subaltern groups and classes such as

8. "Marked" and "unmarked" are linguistic concepts. Unmarked terms (e.g., "man" and "nation") encompass and subsume the meanings of marked terms (e.g., "woman" and "region").

the peasants of Namiquipa, who bore the brunt of this warfare against the indigenes. In addition, the conditions of frontier warfare resulted in the emergence of a distinct ethnic identity in the north. An invented tradition of origins affirmed (and continues to stress) the "whiteness" of the *norteños* in contradistinction to the "brownness" of the *chilangos* (a contemptuous term used by northerners for Mexicans from the center and south). This contrast between the "whiteness" of the *norteños* and the "brownness" of the *chilangos,* constantly made in day-to-day life in Chihuahua, is but one index of a regional sense of identity and community whose particularism continually places a limit on the full development of the universalist comradeship of nationalism.[9]

Concurrently, the degree of U.S. penetration and influence has been strongest on the frontier/border, historically a space across which people "from both sides" have constantly moved. The perpetual "pilgrimages" from one side to the other have led to the "imagining" of this region as a distinct sociocultural zone that has more in common with the United States than with the rest of Mexico. This identification with "Americanness," yet another facet of a contradictory consciousness, is mobilized by northerners to articulate their resentment of the mode of incorporation of the frontier/border into the nation-state and to affirm their regional distinctiveness.[10] In addition, for *norteños,* "things American" have a charisma that "things Mexican" lack. *Hecho en México, mal hecho* ("Made in Mexico, Badly Made") is a popular saying in Chihuahua. *Norteños* prefer American commodities because they are signs of power, of status, and of "whiteness" (cf. Koreck, above).

These contradictory facets of the *norteño* consciousness of community are illustrated in the memoirs of Dr. E. Brondo Whitt, a petty-bourgeois *villista* from the Guerrero district. On the one hand, Brondo Whitt (1940:125) affirms that the revolutionary struggle forged a "horizontal comradeship" and a shared sense of "Mexicanness" among men from different regions of the Republic. On the other hand, he continually stresses the ethnic and cultural differences between the "white" men of the north

---

9. This argument is extensively documented and further developed in A. M. Alonso 1988b.

10. These observations are based on extensive archival and ethnographic research, including in-depth interviews with survivors of the revolutionary decade and their descendants.

and the "brown" men of the south (e.g., p. 34). Finally, he emphasizes that the northern revolutionaries are the least "Mexican" and the most "American" in their clothes and equipment (p. 25). Thus, in this revolutionary's ideological horizon, the identity of the *norteños* is simultaneously configured in relation to nationalism, regionalism, and "Americanness."

In conclusion, nationalism has not been fully hegemonic in the north, coexisting in contradiction with regionalism and with an ambiguous identification with "Americanness." Any one of these facets of a "contradictory consciousness" can be mobilized by social actors in a given set of historical circumstances. Thus, a priori generalizations about northern nationalism are difficult to make. When nationalism is affirmed, it is in response to concrete sociohistorical circumstances. In northern consciousness, nationalism does not fully predominate over other loyalties and forms of identification.

Nationalism and the Chihuahuan Peasantry. Prior to the end of the Apache Wars, the peasant-warriors of frontier military colonies such as Namiquipa enjoyed a relatively privileged class position and status.[11] By fighting the Apaches and advancing the state's project of territorial conquest and colonization, these militarized peasants gained access to personal prestige and social honor, as well as to state-conferred honors including land grants and tax exemptions. Moreover, these frontier peasant communities had enjoyed a great measure of local sovereignty.

Localism, the identification with and allegiance first and foremost to the *patria chica*, or "little motherland," was and remains central to peasant consciousness in Chihuahua. Like "the nation," *la patria chica* is a political community that is imagined as limited, sovereign, and horizontal; but localism differs radically from nationalism in its particularism. Although particularist forms of configuring community have sometimes been "explained" by evoking a concept of "primordial" ties and sentiments, such naturalizing and essentialist arguments can no more account for parochialism than they can for nationalism (see Geertz 1963). The complex concatenation of identity, community, and place needs to be examined in social and historical terms.

The localism of the Chihuahuan peasantry was a product of the particu-

11. The conclusions presented in this section are documented and developed in A. M. Alonso 1988b.

lar form that conquest and colonization assumed on the frontier. Peasant parochialism was encouraged by two aspects of the structuring of the frontier warfare. First in *pueblos* such as Namiquipa, the state had conferred rights to land on the community in return for the fulfillment of military obligations. Thus, peasants' rights to land became linked to the defense of their communities. Second, localism had been a key principle in the social organization of frontier violence. Peasants' primary obligation was the defense of their *patria chica.* Even when fighting outside their communities, members of subaltern groups and classes were organized by locality and placed under the immediate authority of "sons" of their *pueblos.* Thus, despite the state's attempt to weld the imagining of a national community to the defense of frontier territory, the form of "patriotism" that emerged during the Apache Wars was eminently regional and parochial. Among subaltern groups and classes, particularly the militarized peasantry, allegiance to and defense of the *patria chica* was foremost.

Beginning in the mid-nineteenth century, and especially after the end of the Apache Wars in the 1880s, the northern frontier became increasingly incorporated into the nation-state and the capitalist world market. But the national project of the Liberal and Porfirian states was antithetical to that of the frontier peasantry. Nation-state formation and capitalist development subjected the Chihuahuan peasantry to profound social dislocations: rights to land were violated, local democratic traditions were abrogated, and the sovereignty of the local community was threatened (cf. A. M. Alonso 1988b and 1986:11–17; Katz 1981:5–7; Wasserman 1980:15; Lloyd, above). Processes of state formation and capitalist development entailed the imposition of new forms of subjectivity/subjection[12] that denied peasants all social honor and conflicted with locally valued forms of social identity (A. M. Alonso 1988b).

Friedrich Katz calls this process of "transformation of the frontier into the border" the "greatest catastrophe in the history of the Mexican peasantry since the massive Indian mortality of the sixteenth and seventeenth centuries" (Katz 1988c:533). The peasant-warriors of the Chihuahuan si-

---

12. "Subjectivity/subjection" plays upon the doubleness of "subject," which as Michel Foucault points out means both "subject to someone else by control and dependence, and tied to his own identity by a conscience or self-knowledge" (Foucault 1982:212). I use this somewhat awkward coupling of terms in order to emphasize that power is inscribed in the very forms of social personhood.

erra did not accept this "catastrophe" passively. The social transformations that began to erode the relative political autonomy and independent economic base of many rural communities, and to undermine peasant control over the production and reproduction of social life, sparked a long-term process of rural rebellion that culminated in the Revolution of 1910–20 (A. M. Alonso n.d.:17–23; 1988b).

Localism was a critical factor in the mobilization of *serrano* peasants during this long-term process of rebellion (A. M. Alonso n.d.; Knight 1980; Almada 1938). That peasant identification with, and adherence to, the *patria chica* took precedence over nationalist loyalties is evinced in the alliance that the *serranos* established with the French invaders from 1865 to 1866. Resistance to the national project of the Liberal state led *serranos* from the Guerrero district to support the French invasion of Mexico. Pro-French *serranos* from Temósachic, Yepómera, Cruces, and elsewhere in the Guerrero district attacked the forces of Governor Manuel Ojinaga on 2 September 1865 and killed the governor himself (Solís 1936). Ironically, among the troops who defended Ciudad Chihuahua from the attack of Liberal patriots in 1866, there was not a single French soldier (Almada 1955:285). Instead, it was the *serrano* peasants of the Guerrero district, united in the Coalition of Pueblos and allied with the Conservatives, who fought in favor of the invaders and defended Ciudad Chihuahua against the Liberal patriots (Almada 1955:277–85). *Serrano* support for the invaders was such that, after the French were driven from the province, most of these peasant-warriors refused to sign the Certificate of Adhesion to the Chihuahuan Government which would have endowed them with amnesty.[13]

However, it would be misleading to characterize *serrano* peasant rebellion as simply "antinationalist." Late nineteenth- and early twentieth-century peasant petitions provide evidence of a nascent national consciousness.[14] *Serrano* peasant rebellion was, among other things, a reaction to the *specific* forms assumed by efforts to incorporate the local community

13. AMCG, Caja 8, exp. 100, April 1866, Colección de Actas de Adhesión al Supremo Gobierno del Estado de los Pueblos que se Habían Separado de la Obediencia de Su Legítimo Gobierno.

14. E.g., Manifesto, November 1893, Signed by Santana Pérez et al., AGN, Ramo Manuel González Ramírez, vol. 8, pp. 124–27; Petition from the Peasants of Namiquipa to Porfirio Díaz, 28 July 1908, ATN; Olea A. 1961.

into the nation-state during the second half of the nineteenth century, particularly after 1886. In other words, the *serranos* were struggling against particular national projects—those of the dominant classes. Moreover, although localist consciousness predominated in some conjunctures, an alternative peasant patriotism began to emerge in others, serving as a basis for supralocal and supraregional alliances.

But this patriotic consciousness which first appeared near the end of the nineteenth century was vague and ill-defined. Ironically, despite earlier peasant resistance to the Liberal regime, *serrano* patriotism was a vision of the Liberal national project, refracted through the prism of popular ideology and constructed by analogy to the imagining of the *patria chica* which commanded the Chihuahuan peasantry's primary allegiance.[15]

In conclusion, not only was the national vision of the Chihuahuan peasantry subordinated to localism and regionalism, but in the second half of the nineteenth century it also came into conflict with the national projects of Mexico's dominant groups and classes. Later, as we shall see, the peasantry's distinctive vision came into conflict with the nationalist project of the revolutionary leadership as well.

Nationalism and the Revolution of 1910–1920

THE TRANSFORMATION OF VILLA'S VISION OF THE NATION

Shaping the national project of the revolutionary *serrano* peasantry was a localist and regionalist vision. An idealized construction of the past—in which the peasant military colony of the frontier had a pivotal place and in which rights to land were legitimated by fighting—underwrote *serrano* visions of "the just society." Significantly, the reconstitution of the frontier military colony was central to the concept of agrarian reform held by the

15. The existence of a popular, peasant liberalism in Chihuahua prior to the Revolution of 1910–20 was crucial to mobilization, for it provided an alternative vision of how society *should* be constituted, making the revolution and the idea of a different, postrevolutionary social order *thinkable*. Moreover, peasant liberalism provided an ideological common ground with other social classes, facilitating interclass alliances and the participation of peasants in the broader, national revolutionary movement. The complex reasons why a popular liberalism developed among peasants who had earlier resisted the national project of the Liberal regime are discussed in A. M. Alonso 1988b.

revolutionary *serranos* of Temósachic and Namiquipa (A. M. Alonso n.d. and 1988b).[16]

The *serranos'* vision of a return to the frontier past profoundly affected Villa's own "dream" of postrevolutionary society, described to John Reed in 1914 (cf. Katz 1981:142–43). In Villa's words:

In all parts of the Republic we will establish military colonies composed of the veterans of the Revolution. The State will give them grants of agricultural lands and establish big industrial enterprises to give them work. Three days a week they will work. . . . And the other three days they will receive military instruction and go out and teach all the people how to fight. (J. Reed 1969:144–45)

This dream of a peasant republic based on popular self-defense represented a vindication of local and regional forms of social reproduction that had been undermined by processes of nation-state formation. Of primary concern were the local exigencies of the peasant community, rather than those of a national society (Córdova 1981:161–73). Paradoxically, the national project of both Villa and the *serranos* was highly *localist* and *regionalist*. Such a vision of postrevolutionary society could not achieve national hegemony because other social classes and groups, especially the bourgeoisie, had no place in this peasant utopia.

In 1913–14, Villa's attitude toward the American government and toward American enterprises in Mexico betrayed few signs of economic nationalism or anti-Americanism (Katz 1979a:38; Knight 1986a, 2:342). Yet by 1914, a concern with defending the *patria* from foreign aggression had begun to surface in Villa's thinking. As Villa explained to John Reed, the organization of revolutionary peasants and workers in military colonies would mean that "when the Patria is invaded, we will just have to telephone from the palace at Mexico City, and in half a day all the Mexican people will rise from their fields and factories, fully armed, equipped and organized to defend their children and their homes" (J. Reed 1969:145).

By 1915, anti-imperialism and economic nationalism had become central

16. For example, in 1912 and 1914, fifty revolutionaries from Temósachic petitioned the federal government for land to found an agrarian colony. The terms echo those of the colonial charters that established peasant military colonies and made community rights to corporate land grants, as well as household rights to particular plots, contingent upon the fulfillment of military obligations to the state. ATN, 1.232(06) E 716.

to Villa's dream. In February 1915, Villa told Duval West (a representative of the U.S. government) that the postrevolutionary government was to be guided by an economic-nationalist orientation, taking as its slogan "Mexico for the Mexicans" (Ulloa 1979). During the rest of this year, Villa's economic nationalism intensified and by the end of 1915 Villa was openly opposing American imperialism.

This ideological shift was not merely rhetorical; it was repeatedly instantiated in practice. For example, on 26 October 1915 Villa signed a contract with the inhabitants of Morelos, Sonora, committing himself to supply them with arms and ammunition to fight the North American Mormons "and to subdue by force the invasion of foreigners."[17] In effect, Morelos was to become a peasant military colony, much like those established on the Chihuahuan frontier by the colonial state. However, Mexico's enemies were no longer the Apache Indians but rather the Americans, those other "barbarians of the North."[18] The inhabitants of Morelos would "work the lands and distribute the products equally" while fighting to "throw off the yoke of the yankee." If they fulfilled their "promise" and prevented the Mormons from reestablishing themselves in the area, Villa was to send them cattle and funds to construct an irrigation system. But Villa's defeat at Agua Prieta a few weeks later, a defeat to which the Americans contributed by allowing *carrancista* reinforcements to pass through U.S. territory, prevented the fulfillment of this contract.

How do we account for this transformation of Villa's ideology? As Frederick C. Turner observes, the revolutionary struggle itself was a catalyst in the formation of Mexican national consciousness, speeding up internal migration and mitigating linguistic, ethnic, and social differences (F. C. Turner 1968:101). And Alan Knight asserts that national sentiments were the "offspring" rather than the "parents" of the revolution (Knight 1986a, 1:2). Revolutionary "pilgrimages" within the Republic fostered the development of a translocal, supraregional identity and sense of commu-

17. Signed by the inhabitants of Morelos, Sonora and Francisco Villa, 26 October 1915 (MR, Record Group 94, DF 2384662).

18. Villa characterized Americans as "our eternal enemies, the barbarians of the North" in an anti-imperialist manifesto, the text of a speech given in San Andrés, Chihuahua, in October 1916, thereby creating an analogy between the *serrano* military colonies' fight against the Apaches and the struggle he wished them to wage against the Americans. The San Andrés speech (also cited in Osorio, above) is discussed below in the present chapter.

nity. Moreover, popular leaders like Francisco Villa came into contact with middle-class ideologues who articulated a nationalist consciousness and began to internalize this mode of imagining community. Importantly, as Katz has demonstrated, during 1915 Villa became aware of plans, spearheaded by Leon Canova of the U.S. State Department, that would have transformed Mexico into an American protectorate had they been implemented (Katz 1979b). The surprising U.S. recognition of the Carranza government led Villa to the view that Carranza had indeed "sold the Mexican nation" to the United States. Thus, by the end of 1915 Villa had both personal and political grievances against the U.S. government and had developed an anti-imperialist nationalism that motivated his attack on Columbus, New Mexico, in March 1916 (Katz 1979b; cf. Osorio, above).

VILLISTA NATIONALISTS: TWO POPULAR LEADERS

To what extent did Villa's supporters share his new nationalist ideology? At least some popular *villista* leaders, particularly those who had close personal ties to Villa, internalized his nationalist vision. Pablo López provides a case in point. Prior to his execution by a *carrancista* firing squad in May 1916, López pointedly refused to grant interviews to North American newspapers. But since he considered the Irish a revolutionary and anti-imperialist people, he agreed to an interview with an Irish journalist. Speaking of the attack on Columbus, López said:

My master, Don Pancho Villa, was continually telling us that since the *gringos* had given him the double-cross he meant not only to get back at them, but to try and waken our country to the danger that was very close to it. Don Pancho was convinced that the *gringos* were too cowardly to fight us, or to try and win our country by force of arms. He said they would keep pitting one faction against another until we were all killed off, and our exhausted country would fall like a ripe pear into their eager hands. . . . Don Pancho also told us that Carranza was selling our northern states to the *gringos* to get money to keep himself in power. He said he wanted to make some attempt to get intervention from the *gringos* before they were ready, and while we still had time to become a united nation. . . . So we marched on Columbus—we invaded American soil.[19]

19. MR, Record Group 395, E 1210, Newspaper File, Associated Press, Interview with Pablo López, 25 May 1916.

López affirmed his anti-imperialism even in the last moments of his life, refusing to let any Americans witness his execution, facing death as his *"jefe,"* Pancho Villa, would have wished him to.

Another popular leader who clearly came to share Villa's anti-American nationalism was General Candelario Cervantes of Namiquipa. Born in 1884 into one of the middle-peasant families of Namiquipa, Cervantes, like Villa, adhered to a frontier code of honor. When the local Porfirian judge failed to prosecute a man who had attempted to rape Cervantes' sister, Cervantes did his best to avenge this affront to family honor by attempting to kill the offender.

After 1905, Namiquipa began to lose control of its extensive colonial land grant (see Lloyd, above). Unable to obtain a parcel to work, Cervantes was forced to sharecrop on the adjoining Hacienda de Santa Clara owned by the Müllers, a German American family connected by ties of patronage and clientship to the prerevolutionary Chihuahuan oligarchy. For Cervantes, having to sharecrop on this estate represented an affront to personal honor, particularly since the Müllers had tried to appropriate thousands of hectares of Namiquipa's land.

Cervantes' daughter remembers that her father's main motive in joining the revolution in 1910 was to secure the vindication of Namiquipa's land rights. Indeed, the Cervantes family had been very active in a local agrarian society formed in 1906 with the object of conducting a legal struggle to recover the community's lands. By 1912, Cervantes had attained the rank of captain and was recruiting men in the Guerrero district to fight the *orozquistas.* He received several promotions under Villa, whom he joined in 1913, and he was named general immediately before the Columbus raid.

Cervantes was a popular leader whose rise through the ranks depended on his ability to recruit and hold a local following. His authority was both traditional and charismatic. However, the tendency to "personal arbitrariness" (ever present in personalistic forms of authority) became progressively more marked in his leadership style as the revolution proceeded, and that tendency began to undermine popular belief in his legitimacy as a leader.

Like López, Cervantes adhered to Villa's anti-imperialism. Not surprisingly, López and Cervantes were Villa's most important officers in the

Columbus raid.[20] In late April and May 1916, Cervantes was trying to recruit men to fight the Americans in Namiquipa and to drive the invaders from Mexican soil. On 25 May 1916, while leading twenty to thirty *villista* veterans of Columbus in an attack on an American detachment in the municipality of Namiquipa, both Cervantes and his second-in-command, José Bencomo of Cruces, were killed.[21] Among the *namiquipenses* who identified Cervantes' body was his cousin, the revolutionary Teodosio Duarte Morales, who painfully recalled:

My cousin Candelario's body and face were black because they had lassoed and dragged him from their horses for over one and a half kilometers. . . . Moments after [his death], a cavalry squad had arrived and lassoed Candelario and José [Bencomo] by their feet, dragging them off. . . . An invading soldier of Mexican origin told me that when they dragged Candelario, he was still alive. This was the tragic end of one of the famous *Dorados* of Pancho Villa who, with José Bencomo, was loyal to Villa until his death, fighting for a cause they thought just. (Duarte M. n.d.:75–76; my translation)

Among the documents taken by the Americans from Cervantes' body was a proclamation with his signature. An American officer described the contents of this proclamation as "calling on all the Mexicans to support Cervantes and saying if they could not support him, at least they should not oppose him, and that he . . . would drive the Gringos out of Mexico."[22] This suggests that after both Villa and López were wounded, Cervantes

20. Cervantes had a personal affront to avenge. He had been Villa's representative in the munitions contract with Sam Rabel, a Columbus arms dealer. After accepting payment, Rabel refused to turn over the munitions, saying he did not conduct business with "bandits." During the attack on Columbus, Rabel's properties were destroyed and he escaped with his life only because he was out of town and could not be found by the *villistas;* on these points, see Calzadíaz B. 1977:15, 29–31.

21. MR, Record Group 395, Box 36, DF 5201, C.O., Cruces, to Pershing, Namiquipa, 27 May 1916. Also AHSRE, L-E 816, leg. 7, fols. 11–13; L-E 800 R, leg. 15(I), fol. 22.

22. Unfortunately I have not found the proclamation itself, only two references to it. The first (MR, Record Group 395, E 1187 DF 876-I, Walton, Cruces, to Chief of Staff, Namiquipa, 25 May 1916) says that the "proclamation" was addressed to "citizen chief Carranza army" and signed by Cervantes as *Colonel.* The second (USMHI, Richard McMaster Papers, Letter from Maj. Richard McMaster to Son, 28 May 1916) provides the description just quoted. Possibly Cervantes issued this petition during the Sonoran campaign; Villa sent a similar petition to the *carrancista* officers at Hermosillo, Sonora, on 22 November 1915 (Katz 1979b:32).

took up and attempted to lead the anti-imperialist struggle. Evidently, during his final campaign Cervantes had threatened the peasants of the municipality with death should they cooperate with the Americans in any way, forbidding them to sell their labor power to U.S. military forces.[23]

NATIONALISM VERSUS LOCALISM

Revolutionary pilgrimages had a contradictory impact on the *norteño* sense of community, producing a sense of solidarity with other "Mexicans" at the same time that they reinforced the *norteños'* sense of difference (e.g., Brondo W. 1940:passim). Thus, although men like López and Cervantes became anti-imperialists, other *villista* leaders and the bulk of Villa's followers did not internalize Villa's new ideology and nationalist vision. As a result, many did not support Villa's plans to invade the United States and to secure intervention. Villa's first attempt to attack the U.S. border at the end of January 1916 was aborted because about half his force deserted him en route.[24] As one *villista* from Namiquipa explained, "The reason for this large desertion from Villa's force . . . was due to the unwillingness of his men to go to war with the United States."[25] Villa had to resort to coercion in order to assemble troops for his next attempt. All *villistas* with previous service in the municipality of Namiquipa were ordered to join up or face being shot, along with their families, if they refused.[26] In addition, Villa

23. MR, Record Group 393, no. 1187, DF 5172, Report of Operations, 10th Cavalry, 10 May 1916. The preceding assessment of the changes in Cervantes' leadership style through six years of warfare was advanced by several older *namiquipenses* whom Daniel Nugent and I interviewed. See also Calzadíaz B. 1977.

24. MR, Record Group 393, Chief of Staff, Box 2-C, F 108, Statement of Maj. Juan B. Muñoz, *Villista* Taken Prisoner by the Americans, n.d. [1916]. Also see MR, Record Group 393, Chief of Staff, Box 2-F, American Intelligence Report, n.d. [1916], unsigned: "the mission as given out by Villa to his men at Los Tanques, January 19th, was unpopular with certain leaders of his command opposed to U.S. intervention, the object sought. These same leaders, however, would not have objected to fighting against Carranza on Mexican territory. These men, in other words, believed in fighting the Mexican troubles on Mexican soil with only Mexicans engaged."

25. MR, Record Group 393, Chief of Staff, Box 2-C, F 108, Statement of Maj. Juan B. Muñoz, n.d. [1916].

26. So said *villistas* who were taken prisoner by the Americans (MR, Record Group 393, E 1210). For example, Silvino Vargas of Cruces, Namiquipa, joined up only because

had to conceal from his men that the objective of the expedition was the American border town of Columbus.

When American military forces entered Chihuahua in March 1916, immediately after the Columbus attack, the initial reaction of the rural population was hostile and uncooperative.[27] However, the attitude changed from obstruction to collaboration during the course of the occupation. In a report written at the conclusion of the U.S. invasion of Chihuahua, the Intelligence Section of Pershing's punitive expedition noted that

in the advance of the American troops into Mexico the natives were found to be generally unfriendly. Information from them at the commencement of the operations . . . was not available. However, the Expedition gradually made a favorable impression upon the natives and within a short time . . . they assumed a more favorable attitude; while for the sake of appearances before the *de facto* [i.e., *carrancista*] forces they pretended aloofness, much valuable information was received from them, and upon our withdrawal, about four thousand of them accompanied the troops to the United States.[28]

A similar transformation in popular attitudes toward the American military presence was evident in the municipality of Namiquipa. By April, the *namiquipenses*, as well as other peasants throughout the Santa María Valley, were collaborating with the Americans, selling them supplies and, more important, providing military intelligence that aided U.S. forces in dispersing *villista* bands and capturing *villistas* who had gone to Columbus.[29]

Despite his status as a "son of the *pueblo*" and longtime revolutionary

his initial refusal had resulted in his father being taken in his place. Corporal Francisco Solís of Namiquipa agreed to go only after Candelario Cervantes ordered him whipped. These statements are consonant with the recollections of older *namiquipenses* Daniel Nugent and I interviewed.

27. E.g.: M R, Record Group 394, E 26 DF 2379210, Pershing, Namiquipa (via Ft. Sam Houston, Texas) to Adjutant General, Washington, 18 April 1916; Pershing's remarks here also refer to the urban population.

28. M R, Record Group 393, Chief of Staff, Box 2-G, F 110, Report of the Intelligence Section, Punitive Expedition, to the Commanding General, 5 February 1917. Note that this comment also gives a reason why a different interpretation of popular attitudes to the American intervention might appear in some *carrancista* sources: namely, the deliberate dissimulation of the "natives" in front of the *carrancistas*.

29. M R, Record Group 94, Box 8128, DF 4379210, Pershing, San Gerónimo, 7 April 1916.

leader, Candelario Cervantes' efforts in late April and early May to mobilize the peasants of his own municipality against the Americans met with failure. Even the few patently anti-American *villistas* in the municipality hesitated to join him because of the lack of popular support for an attack on U.S. troops. Captain Reidecel Aguirre, a *villista* nationalist who had deserted Cervantes' small force, responded to renewed attempts at recruitment with the following words:

If it's a matter of combatting the gringos, I'm ready when you call on me and when you need me but only if I see that we can strike a massive blow; otherwise, it's not in our interests, because as you know, *first and foremost, the pueblos won't help us and there's no one who will say I have the will to offer my services as a Mexican; no one; on the contrary, they are always trying to help the damned gringos and because of this one sees that it's not worth trying to do the people this good because one sees they will not even cover for us let alone help us.*[30]

The unwillingness of the *namiquipenses* to fight the Americans seems to have been echoed throughout the region. By the end of May, Pershing observed that the "natives are not generally arming to oppose us. Sentiment [is] rather general against war with [the] United States."[31]

Not only had Cervantes been unable to effect a popular mobilization against U.S. forces, but he was even less successful in preventing the peasants from cooperating with the Americans. On May 9, a Mexican guide reported to the Americans (who wished to hire local labor for road work) that "the citizens of Cruces [municipality of Namiquipa] held a meeting and decided they would work for Captain Graves . . . and that if Cervantes, who had forbidden them to do so [on pain of death], did not like it they would go against him." Remarkably, the people of Cruces defied Cervantes' orders and worked for the Americans, although at least some of them were evidently told by a U.S. soldier that the real objective of the punitive expedition was to annex the northern provinces, which Carranza had sold to the United States.[32]

---

30. MR, Record Group 393, Box 2-E, Reidecel Aguirre to Candelario Cervantes, n.d. [May 1916]; my translation, emphasis added. This letter was taken by the Americans from Cervantes' body.

31. MR, Record Group 395, E 1137, Pershing to Sample, 25 May 1916.

32. Rubén Osorio, interview with Concepción García Domínguez of Cruces. García Domínguez' remarks evince a contradictory consciousness. On one hand, he and others

The ideological disjuncture between Cervantes' nationalism and the localism of the *namiquipense* peasants forced him to rely more and more on coercion to secure obedience, thus putting in doubt the legitimacy of his authority. Loyalty turned into fear, and fear into defiance.[33]

In response to a "suggestion" from General Pershing, local peasant militias were established in Namiquipa and Cruces.[34] Formed on 23 May 1916, the Namiquipa "defensa social" had 155 members, a significant portion of the town's *jefes de familia*. Its ostensible purpose was "to sustain, by whatever means necessary, the reestablishment of peace and of respect for the lives and interests of the inhabitants" of the town.[35] A U.S. journalist put it somewhat differently: "The Namiquipa civil guard is organized for the purpose of cooperation with the Americans in ridding the country of bandits [i.e., *villistas*] and has rendered valuable assistance along the line of

---

continued to work for the Americans; on the other hand, on one occasion they refused to eat with the Americans. Interestingly, the reaction of the men of Cruces to the idea of U.S. annexation of the northern provinces was laughter, a common response to contradictions, ambivalences, and inversions. This reaction recalls the laughter that greets the joking suggestion, commonly made in Chihuahua today, that Mexico should settle its foreign debt by ceding the northern provinces to the United States.

33. Evidently, many *namiquipenses* were relieved when Cervantes was killed by the Americans. As Pershing reported to Sample on May 26: "[Cervantes'] death regarded by many people this vicinity as fortunate" (MR, Record Group 395, E 1137, Box 19, DF 876-I). Only twelve mourners, all women, attended Cervantes' funeral in Namiquipa; his body was barred from the church by the local priest, a Spaniard. The journalist George Clements reported on 29 May 1916 that at the funeral, "Attempts at rejoicing on the part of the citizens were quieted by a guard of civilians which maintained order" (MR, Record Group 395, E 1210, Newspaper File). These reports agree with oral history and tradition, in particular with the recollections of Cervantes' daughter.

34. MR, Record Group 94, E 26 DF 2379210, Pershing via Funston, Ft. Sam Houston, Texas, to War Dept., 29 May 1916. It has long been assumed that the *defensas sociales* were established in response to an "invitation" issued by the *carrancista* governor of Chihuahua, Ignacio Enríquez, on 10 January 1916. However, the first *defensa social* in the state was formed under American auspices at Namiquipa. The Cruces *defensa* was formed after Cervantes' death to "work [in] conjunction with us [i.e., U.S. forces]" carrying arms, tracking down and killing "bandits," or informing the Americans of their whereabouts (MR, Record Group 393, Box 2-E, Cruces, n.d. [May 1916], signed Roderick Dew). For a discussion of the *defensas* based on Mexican sources, see Rocha I. 1979.

35. MR, Record Group 393, Box 2-E, Acta de formación de la Defensa Social de Namiquipa, 23–24 May 1916; my translation. The anti-*villismo* of the *defensas* is evident in one of the clauses: "those who provide hospitality in their homes to people will be considered concealers and accessories and will be severely punished" (the "people," of course, are the *villistas*).

locating small bands and giving information which resulted in keeping the bandits on the move."[36] In addition to providing military intelligence, the Namiquipa militia arrested a number of local *villista* "Columbus raiders," nine of whom were subsequently taken as prisoners to the United States when the punitive expedition withdrew from Mexico.[37] Moreover, the *defensas* found and turned over a major *villista* arms cache to U.S. forces.[38] In short, the local militia assisted the Americans in achieving several of the main objectives of the punitive expedition: seizing *villista* arms caches, dispersing *villista* bands, and capturing *villistas* who had gone to Columbus.

Soon thereafter, *defensas sociales* were established throughout the Guerrero district and adjoining areas, in *pueblos* such as Bachiniva, Guerrero, Madera, Temósachic, Yepómera, Tejolocachic, Santo Tomás, Matachic, San Isidro, Tosanáchic, and Bocoyna.[39] Even after the end of June, when U.S. troops pulled out of the Guerrero district, the militias of the area continued to supply the Americans with military intelligence.[40]

If we examine the trajectory followed by *serrano* peasants in their dealings with the U.S. forces that occupied northwestern Chihuahua for nearly a year, it is evident that an initially weak nationalist response was soon replaced by active collaboration with the American project of destroying *villismo*. This pattern clearly points to the existence of a "contradictory consciousness" in which nationalism was subordinated to localism, par-

36. MR, Record Group 395, E 1210, Newspaper File, Article by George Clements, 29 May 1916. In the same vein, Pershing remarked that the militia was organized to work in conjunction with U.S. troops, providing guides and military intelligence (MR, Record Group 94, E 26 DF 2379210, Pershing to War Dept., 29 May 1916).

37. MR, Record Group 393, Box 2-E, Reed, Namiquipa, to Pershing, Dublan, 17 June 1916. Evidently the militia was reluctant to turn the prisoners over to the Americans. The militia commander was told that the Americans were taking the prisoners to prevent their falling into *carrancista* hands (MR, Record Group 395, E 1189, Box 57, Pershing, Dublan, to Hines, Namiquipa, 17 June 1916).

38. MR, Record Group 94, E 26 DF 2379210, Pershing to War Dept., 29 May 1916. The cache consisted of 400 rifles and 10 machine guns.

39. MR, Record Group 393, Box 2-C, Reed, Namiquipa, to Pershing, Dublan, 31 May 1916; Record Group 395, I.S. F 116–17, Ord, El Valle, to Campanole, Dublan, 11 December 1916. It is not clear whether the Americans played any direct role in the establishment of these other *defensas*. Cf. Rocha I. 1979; AMCG, Caja 78, exp. 671.

40. E.g.: MR, Record Group 393, Box 2-C, Biographical File, Jesús Pacheco, 6 December 1916; Record Group 393, Box 2-D, F 118, Ord, El Valle, to Campanole, Dublan, 14 December 1916; Record Group 395, I.S. F 173, Ord, El Valle, to Campanole, Dublan, 17 January 1917.

ticularly during the 1916–17 period. Peasant cooperation with U.S. forces suggests that localism became the predominant ideological horizon orienting social action at this time. Why?

After Villa's disastrous defeat at Celaya in April 1915, it became evident to his followers that the *villista* cause had been lost at a national level.[41] In January 1916, with the muted blessings of Villa, many *serranos* amnestied themselves to the *carrancistas*, returning to their *pueblos* to consolidate the gains of the revolution at the local level. Localism predominated over nationalism during this conjuncture: a war-weary and exhausted rural population turned to rebuilding what years of fighting had destroyed. At this time, *serrano* peasants were willing to support Villa so long as he advanced their localist projects. They were not willing to join him in a struggle against American imperialism, which had no significance within their particularist vision. Moreover, the coercion to which Villa and some of his leaders resorted in order to secure recruits and cooperation placed in question the legitimacy of their authority. Forced recruitment into the federal army had been one of the popular grievances on the eve of the revolution.

In contrast to 1914–15 when the *villista* government could tax businesses and expropriate the wealthy *latifundistas*, as *villismo* became a guerrilla movement in 1916 it was increasingly dependent on the *pueblos* of the sierra, the heartland of *villismo*, as a resource base. As a result of years of fighting, the local economy had deteriorated significantly. Villa's forces regularly commandeered the *pueblos'* livestock, horses, pasture, crops, and wood, in direct contradiction with the localist project of reconstruction. An ironic result was that it was precisely in some of those areas which had been most *villista* in the past that Villa began to lose popular support in 1916.

In this connection, it is instructive to quote Ramón Corral, a peasant born in San Andrés who was living in Namiquipa in 1986. A distant relative of Luz Corral, Villa's wife, Don Ramón told us that when Villa gave his nationalist, anti-imperialist speech in San Andrés, in October 1916, the people of this once emphatically *villista* town did not respond to Villa's call to arms. By this time, a *defensa social* had formed in San Andrés

---

41. MR, Record Group 395, E 1210, Statement of Prisoner Pedro López. The same apperception is also evident in oral testimonies collected in the field.

and the people were afraid of Villa. Corral added that Villa cried when he noticed this change in popular attitudes, and that he asked the people why they no longer wanted to follow him. I asked Corral the same question, and he said: "Ya Villa se estaba extra-limitando mucho; la gente no lo quería seguir" (Villa was overstepping the bounds of his authority; people no longer wanted to follow him).

THE INTERSECTION OF LOCALIST AND INTERVENTIONIST PROJECTS

For *serrano* communities, there were distinct short-term advantages in cooperating with the Americans, and the latter were able to exploit those felt advantages for their own ends. Paradoxically, the interventionist project of the U.S. government and the localist project of the *serrano* peasantry intersected: the Americans wanted to wipe out *villismo,* and the *serranos* wished to prevent all outsiders, whether *villistas* or *carrancistas,* from interfering with local reconstruction. The very label "pacíficos" which was assumed by the peasants at this time, as well as the ideology of the *defensas sociales,* makes explicit that the local desire for "peace" predominated over all other considerations. Because the Americans' project advanced local efforts at reconstruction, the *serrano* peasantry was willing to ally itself with foreign military forces. An American journalist reported that when the inhabitants of the Namiquipa Valley learned that *carrancista* columns were planning to occupy the area should the Americans withdraw, they protested:

They say the Americans are giving much better *protection* than can possibly be had from the Carrancistas at no expense to the inhabitants, while the Carrancistas, so far from buying from them for cash the supplies needed, will ask that they be furnished by the people of the towns. "Instead of spending good gold money for supplies, as the Americans do, the Carrancistas will compel us to feed them free of cost to them, or oblige us to take Carranza paper money" is the manner in which one native expressed himself, and he spoke for nearly every Mexican in the neighborhood.[42]

42. MR, Record Group 395, E 1210, Newspaper File, George Clements, 29 May 1916; emphasis added. On the same point, one month later, see MR, Record Group 94, DF 2424492, Funston, Ft. Sam Houston, Texas, to Adjutant General, Washington, 1 July 1916.

Not only did the Americans provide "protection" from the *villistas* and the *carrancistas,* then, but they also paid in gold for supplies, labor, and services. Local attitudes to the Americans were so positive that by the end of May, Pershing asserted that "the natives" would favor an indefinite occupation of the area by American forces.[43]

During their October 1916 occupation of the Guerrero district, *villista* forces stripped the countryside of crops, livestock, and horses and took revenge against a number of locals who had betrayed the *villista* cause. Nearly 1,000 men were forced into service in the *villista* ranks after being informed that Villa's purpose was to fight the U.S. troops in Mexico.[44] As a result, popular attitudes throughout the area decidedly came to favor "[re]occupation by American troops for protection against bandits."[45] The evidence could not be clearer: cooperation with the Americans was subjectively taken to be in the localist interest of peasant communities.

In addition, the Americans were able to exploit local factionalism. A preliminary analysis of the social composition of the militia (*defensa social*) in Namiquipa indicates that it included members of groups that had suffered reversals because of transformations effected at the local level by the revolution.[46] These groups included richer peasants—sympathetic to *villismo* at its apogee, perhaps only out of opportunism—who, as a result of

43. M R, Record Group 94, E 26 DF 2379210, Pershing to War Dept., 29 May 1916.

44. M R, Record Group 395, E 1201 F 5270, Pershing, Dublan, to Commanding General, Southern Dept., Ft. Sam Houston, Texas, 2 November 1916; Record Group 395, E 1187, Box 36, DF 5242, Allaire, El Valle, to Reed, Dublan, 15 October 1916; Record Group 395, E 1187, Box 19, DF 876, Ord, El Valle, to Campanole, Dublan, 24 October 1916; Record Group 393, Box 2-C, I.S. memos 18 and 30 October 1916; Record Group 393, Box 2-D, I.S. memo, 9 November 1916. Also interview with José Rascón Iguado, Cd. Chihuahua, 1985.

45. M R, Record Group 94, DF 2457961, Pershing via Funston, Ft. Sam Houston, Texas, to Adjutant General, Washington, 9 November 1916; my interpolation. Moreover, the Guerrero *serranos* who had been pressed into service soon began to desert in large numbers, returning to their homes in the ensuing weeks; deserters also included men from the Galeana district, which was still occupied by U.S. troops. M R, Record Group 393, Box 2-C, Biographical File, Jesús Almeida (28 December 1916) and José Mendoza (26 December 1916).

46. However, the social composition of the *defensas* was heterogeneous. Obviously in 1916 it contained very few *villistas:* since the majority of *villistas* had gone to Columbus, they were forced to remain under arms in small bands in the mountains, to maintain a "low profile" at home for fear of being captured by U.S. forces or, paradoxically, *to take refuge in the United States.* After the American withdrawal, former *villistas* did join the *defensas* in Namiquipa and made up about 25 percent of the membership.

the local agrarian reform measures initiated by middle peasants between 1911 and 1915, had lost control of plots of municipal land purchased before 1910.[47] Also represented were immigrants who had been denied rights to community lands since they were not descendants of the original colonists. By establishing a clientelist alliance with the Americans, members of these groups were able to advance their own local interests. Empowered initially by the Americans and later by the *carrancista* government of Chihuahua, this faction was eventually successful in its bid for power, consolidating its local hegemony over the ensuing decade.[48]

Finally, the American construction of *villismo* as "banditry" and the American rationale for the *defensas sociales* had an impact on local ideology, further delegitimating *villismo* while giving legitimacy to *serrano* peasant collaboration with a foreign army. The intersection of localist projects with the interventionist project of the United States formed the basis for this inflection of local ideology by the American vision. The key to the U.S.-constructed rationale for the militias lies in the appellation "home guard," used to refer to the *defensas*. The militias came to be construed, both by Americans and by "natives," as forces of order and local reconstruction, whose object was to protect the lives, interests, and honor of the members of the *patria chica* against the "vandalic hordes" of Pancho Villa. This interpretation played upon a localist consciousness as well as upon a frontier history, drawing an implicit analogy between the decades of *serrano* struggle against the Apache Indians and the fight against *villismo*.

One local militia member whom Daniel Nugent and I interviewed likened Villa explicitly to an Apache. References to Villa's "vandalic hordes" or to Villa as a "barbarian" or a "bandit" are common in contemporary documents as well as in present-day local discourse. Thus, the betrayal of *villismo* and the cooperation with foreign military forces were interpreted and idealized as a heroic struggle against forces of disorder bent on destroying the *patria chica*, and as a continuation of the "golden age" of the frontier past in which brave men, the vanguard of civilization, had defended home and family from the incursions of "barbarians."[49] This

47. This observation is based on numerous documents from the AMN and the AMCG, as well as on information obtained from oral histories. For a discussion of locally initiated efforts at agrarian reform during the revolution, see A. M. Alonso n.d.

48. Documents from AMN and oral histories.

49. There is a certain irony to this characterization of Villa as Apache/barbarian after

transposition of the *serranos'* past as military colonists into the present of 1916–17 is especially ironic when we recall that they were to have been the main protagonists in the realization of "Villa's dream," the instantiation of the *serranos'* frontier utopia.[50]

Conclusions

The case of *serrano* peasant collaboration with the U.S. military forces occupying portions of northwestern Chihuahua from March 1916 to February 1917 indicates a need to problematize and critically investigate the question of nationalism in the revolution, especially at the popular level. Because nationalism is routinely naturalized, scholars forget that it is a relatively recent social and ideological phenomenon, part of a long-term process of modern state formation (but see Corrigan and Sayer 1985; Corrigan, Ramsay, and Sayer 1980). Investigators have been too willing to attribute a nationalist orientation to social groups about whom very little research has been done, especially as regards ideology. Nationalism cannot be assumed. It must be demonstrated. Moreover, such a demonstration must be based on an analysis of ideology. Too often scholars have concluded that the diverse forms of American intervention lead *mechanically* to nationalism and anti-imperialism. The collaboration of Chihuahuan *serranos* with the U.S. military should suffice to demonstrate that this is by no means always the case. And their earlier collaboration with the French imperialists should suffice to show that foreign invasions do not automatically "trigger" a nationalist response.

Recent studies of the revolution demonstrate that popular mobilization was linked above all to local and regional conditions. Although these conditions reflected the impact of macro-level processes and developments, they were also a product of (*a*) variform local and regional structures of social reproduction and (*b*) the contingencies of distinct histories.

1916 in Namiquipa. See note 18 above, where Villa charges "barbarism" in his description of the North Americans.

50. My sources for this paragraph include numerous documents from the AMN and ADN, as well as oral histories and traditions. Among the American sources see MR, Record Group 393, Box 2-D, F 118, Reed, n.d., and Acta de formación de la Defensa Social, 24 May 1916; Record Group 393, Box 2-E, Francisco Antillón, Head of the Defensa Social, Namiquipa, to the Governor of the State of Chihuahua, 7 October 1916.

Moreover, these conditions were understood and rendered significant only through a highly localist and regionalist consciousness, one that was not fully subordinated to the national imagination of community. Although the period of armed struggle was a catalyst in the development of nationalist consciousness, this ideological horizon is largely a product of the hegemonic project of postrevolutionary Mexican state formation.

Historians have assumed that the Pershing punitive expedition was a failure, and on a number of levels that is an accurate description. The expedition failed in its principal stated objective of capturing Francisco Villa and destroying his movement. Despite the considerable number of U.S. troops that participated—more than 10,000—the U.S. Army was reluctant to engage any organized Mexican forces in battle. Most of the "accomplishments" of the *punitiva* (e.g., the disarming of *villista* soldiers, the seizing of *villistas* for trial in the United States, and the gathering of intelligence) relied on techniques such as intimidation, betrayal, and bribery. The U.S. Army immediately withdrew from southern Chihuahua after American troops were fired upon as they left the city of Parral in April 1916.[51] Furthermore, after an encounter with *carrancista* troops at Carrizal in June 1916, the bulk of the U.S. troops in Chihuahua retired to Dublan (a Mormon colony near Casas Grandes) for the duration of the occupation.

Yet American military intervention did have critical consequences for popular mobilization and ideology in the *villista* "heartland," the sierra of Chihuahua. First, it helped destroy the Villa movement there, dispersing local *villista* bands, killing key leaders such as Candelario Cervantes, and occupying former *villista* strongholds, including Namiquipa. By mobilizing former *villista* sympathizers in anti-*villista* militias, American inter-

---

51. Anti-American "nationalism" may well have played a more significant role in urban areas of Chihuahua, on the part of the working classes and the middle classes alike. It is worth recalling that Parral was home to the Herrera family, popular revolutionary leaders and for a long time nationalist anti-imperialists. However, Elisa Grienssen, the twelve-year-old girl who led the crowd that drove the American troops out of Parral, states that the municipal president of Parral, José de la Luz Herrera, mocked her when she reproached him for his complete inactivity in the face of the American presence (Barrón del Avellano 1971:15–17). Curiously enough, Grienssen affirms that *the crowd which drove the American troops out of Parral was largely composed of women and schoolchildren.*

vention contributed to the destruction of Villa's bases of support in the *pueblos,* bases that were particularly critical during this, the guerrilla phase of *villismo.* After the American intervention, the *defensas sociales* began to cooperate with the *carrancista* government and would later play an important role in the "pacification" of the state of Chihuahua.[52]

Second, the American intervention empowered certain factions within peasant communities at the expense of others. In Namiquipa, richer peasants and petty-bourgeois immigrants were able to use the Americans' support to advance their own local interests. Eventually these groups were

52. According to Francisco Murguía, support for Villa in the Guerrero district was strong in December 1916 (ADN, Murguía to Obregón, 11 December 1916). However, in a letter dated 16 December 1916 (also in the ADN) he mentions that in the Guerrero district, "we could organize elements willing to cooperate with us." The need to send troops to the Guerrero district is one of the reasons Murguía gives for his unwillingness to send reinforcements to Torreón to fight Villa (ADN, 25 December 1916). Murguía's assertions are puzzling, because two months earlier Villa had to resort to force to recruit men in the same area, according to American *and* Mexican archival sources (e.g., ADN, Treviño to Obregón, 28 May 1916) as well as oral histories. In addition, American sources present a rather different picture of events in the Guerrero district in December, providing considerable information on the mobilization of the *defensas sociales* of a number of sierra towns against Villa at this time. This assessment was based on intelligence obtained from a number of persons, including militia members and other "natives." Lastly, an article published in a Chihuahuan newspaper on 19 January 1917 makes reference to a manifesto to be issued by Murguía to the inhabitants of the sierra "who by force or voluntarily have joined Villa" and who are "now deserting" and fear returning to their homes, offering to take no reprisals against those willing to "reform"; the article mentions that "a great number" of men from the sierra have joined the Constitutionalist (i.e., *carrancista*) army (MR, Record Group 393, Box 2-E F 392). This manifesto contradicts Murguía's earlier claims regarding the degree of popular support for Villa in the Guerrero district. The conclusions I draw from a comparison of these different accounts and from oral histories are that (1) by December 1916, Villa's popular base in the Guerrero district had been seriously undermined and local militias were fighting against him, both on their own and in conjunction with the *carrancistas;* (2) it is possible that Villa did win some recruits in those sierra towns that had suffered *carrancista* abuses; (3) if Villa did get some *volunteers* from the sierra, this was not by dint of nationalism, especially since the Americans had already pulled out of the Guerrero district, but because of popular disgust with deteriorating conditions in the region and with the corruption of the *carrancistas;* and (4) Murguía greatly exaggerated the degree of popular support for Villa in the Guerrero district at this time, perhaps because he was either trying to discredit Treviño (Katz, personal communication) or did not want to send troops to Torreón or, alternatively because he had some other reason for sending troops into the Guerrero district.

able to construct a new *caciquismo* at the local level, with multiple consequences for "democracy" within the *pueblo* as well as for agrarian reform. Petty-bourgeois immigrants were able to secure rights to land, and richer peasants connected to the *defensas* were able to acquire more land. Moreover, since the groups in the *defensas sociales* became clients of the post-revolutionary state, they were able to determine the form that agrarian reform would take at the local level. Significantly, it was the head of the *defensas sociales* who signed the *acta* making Namiquipa an *ejido* in 1926. Led by two former *villistas,* the majority of Namiquipa's peasants had opposed the formation of the *ejido,* since it was antithetical to their vision of land reform (cf. Nugent 1989; Nugent and Alonso 1994). In this sense, the American intervention is one of many factors that had as their outcome the marginalization of *villista* peasant aspirations at the local level.

Third, the American construction of *villismo* as "banditry" contributed to the delegitimization of the *villista* movement. Moreover, the American rationale for the *defensas sociales* inflected the ideology of the militias. Paradoxically, the *carrancista* government's perception of these militias and of *villismo* paralleled the American vision (and echoed the representation of *villismo* advanced earlier by the counterrevolutionary classes of Chihuahua). In *serrano* towns, this interpretation of the role of the *defensas*—i.e., as the heroic vanguard of the struggle against *villista* "barbarism"—predominated; and it continues to be articulated in popular social memory. Finally, although the effects of U.S. military intervention on the *carrancista* government of Mexico are complex and contradictory, at least in the towns of the Chihuahuan sierra, the final result was an alliance between the Chihuahuan government and the *serranos* that contributed to the demise of *villismo.*

More generally, what *serrano* collaboration with American military forces demonstrates is that the interrelations between rural revolt, the Mexican state, and forms of U.S. intervention cannot be understood from a macro-level perspective alone. Ultimately, what determined the trajectory of resistance in the Chihuahuan sierra was the intersection of the American interventionist project with the localist projects of *serrano* peasants at a specific historical conjuncture. Although rural revolt is critically conditioned by international power relations, the effects of U.S. intervention are mediated by local ideology, social relations, and historical contingencies.

A Note on Sources

Although the interpretation advanced in this chapter is based on research in more than two dozen Mexican and American archives, I have listed only those which contain documents I have actually cited. In this chapter, I have made extensive use of documents from the U.S. National Archives for two reasons: (1) because of the disruption of administrative routines by the revolution, and the destruction of archives by *villista* forces, Mexican local- and district-level archives contain little detailed information on the years 1916–17; (2) the records of Pershing's punitive expedition are a valuable but largely ignored source; they are particularly rich in local detail, since the Americans were able to gather "intelligence" from "natives" until the U.S. military's departure from Mexico. I have carefully cross-checked the information obtained from the American archives with that gleaned from Mexican archives and from oral histories.

I am indebted to Friedrich Katz for making available to me the notes he took from documents contained in the ADN. I am also grateful that Marta Rocha Islas shared with me some of her notes from the ADN specifically concerned with Namiquipa.

Lastly, the interpretation advanced here is based not only on archival research, but also on the two years I spent in Namiquipa between 1983 and 1985, conducting ethnographic research and collecting oral histories and traditions. I have resisted using more oral history to support my argument, out of fear that this might be prejudicial to the *namiquipenses*. Survivors of the revolutionary decade have confirmed that many of the *namiquipenses* who went on the Columbus raid were pressed into service, that the *namiquipenses* collaborated with the Americans, and that they were unwilling to obey Cervantes' orders to fight U.S. forces. The Americans are recalled with no hostility and are remembered chiefly as a source of much-needed revenue for the community, since they paid for local labor and merchandise in gold.

Remarkably, one *villista* woman I interviewed, whose father was among the *villista* prisoners taken to the United States by the Pershing punitive expedition, expressed no resentment of the Americans, even though we questioned her repeatedly on this point. Her testimony was not influenced by our nationality since she believed us to be Mexicans. For her, the Americans were outsiders who were not a party to *local* disputes and, thus, could not be the object of hostility or resentment. Her anger was largely directed against the local man who had informed the U.S. troops that her father had been on the Columbus raid. From her point of view, the Americans were taking her father prisoner in retaliation for his participation in the raid on Columbus and this was intelligible to her even if she lamented the consequences it had for her family. In response to my insistent attempts to elicit some spark of anti-Americanism, she pointed out that if she and her family had in fact felt any hostility, they could easily have killed the U.S. soldiers who came to arrest her father; that they did not, she affirmed, was a sign that no such resentment was felt. In addition, although she was critical of *namiquipense* collaboration with the Americans, this was not because she judged it "unpatriotic," but because she thought it was stupid. As a personal betrayal of Villa (*not of Mexico*), she said, that collaboration was responsible for Villa's retaliatory raid on the *pueblo* of Namiquipa in April 1917.

FRIEDRICH KATZ

From Alliance to Dependency:

The Formation and Deformation of an Alliance

between Francisco Villa and the United States

No Mexican revolutionary between 1910 and 1920 earned as much praise from the United States, both from members of the Wilson administration and from American businessmen, as Pancho Villa; and no other major revolutionary leader came as close as did Villa to a real alliance with the United States. In a conversation with a French military attaché in Washington, Woodrow Wilson stated: "Villa today represents the only instrument of civilization in Mexico. His firm authority allows him to create order, and to educate the turbulent mass of peons so prone to pillage."[1] John Lind, Woodrow Wilson's special representative in Mexico, clearly had Villa in mind when he wrote to the president:

We must be the pillar of cloud by day and the pillar of fire by night and compel decent administration. From this necessity there is no escape, unless revolution and anarchy are to continue to be the order of the day in Mexico. Let this house-cleaning be done by home talent. It will be a little rough, and we must see to it that the walls are left intact, but I should not worry if some of the verandas and french windows were demolished. General Villa, for instance, would do the job satisfactorily. (Quoted in Stephenson 1935:246)

American attitudes toward Villa had not always been this favorable. In 1911, after the capture of Ciudad Juárez by Mexican revolutionary troops led by Francisco Madero, the *New York Times* wrote: "As for Colonel Villa, he is one of the dangerous weapons that the leaders of revolutions so often consider themselves forced to use, tolerating their faults in the day of need,

---

1. AMGVF, no. 7 of 1,716 reports, French Military Attaché in the United States Bertrand to Deuxième Bureau, 30 December 1914.

and doing what they can after that day has passed to minimize the consequences of having followers hard to control."[2]

In 1912 the American consul in Torreón, George Carothers, called Villa a "bandit,"[3] and U.S. Ambassador to Mexico Henry Lane Wilson was instrumental in having Villa arrested by the *maderista* authorities in that year.[4] The first favorable change in the American attitude toward Villa occurred in October 1913. What deeply impressed American representatives was Villa's behavior after the capture of Torreón.

In October 1913, Villa led an army mainly composed of rebels from the Laguna area and from Durango—his own Chihuahuan troops were in the minority—in the capture of the large railway center of Torreón. A few weeks before, these men, under the leadership of Tomás Urbina, Calixto Contreras, and a series of other revolutionary leaders from the state of Durango, had captured the capital city of Durango and immediately followed up their victory with an orgy of plunder. Pastor Rouaix, one of the intellectual leaders of the revolution in the state of Durango, vividly described the events that followed the revolutionaries' occupation of the capital city of the state:

The victorious army of about eight thousand men entered the city without order, without leaders and like an avalanche that descends from the mountains, fused their forces with those of the lower classes, full of desire for vengeance, destruction and plunder, and began to assault stores, carrying out shameful acts of plunder while other groups, animated by the innate suspicions characteristic of peasants, were shooting at fictitious enemies and there was no end to constant dynamite explosions and rifle fire. (Quoted in Cruz 1980:211)

Yet only a few weeks later—after Villa assumed control of these same troops who had formed the core of the army that captured Torreón—a very different image emerged in American eyes. Consul Hamm, who had also witnessed the pillage of Durango, wrote:

At 11:00 I went in a carriage to the city of Torreón on a tour of inspection. Splendid order prevailed in the city at that time. There were guards placed at all the stores that had been sacked or partially sacked, and the order was out to shoot anyone

2. *New York Times*, 19 May 1911.
3. NARA, SD, 312.115.T541-16, George Carothers to State Dept., 5 May 1912.
4. NARA, SD, 812.00-4169, Montgomery Schuyler to State Dept., 5 June 1912.

who attempted to steal anything. I consider that 500,000 pesos will cover the actual loss from sacking. This is less than five per cent of what was expected by the people of Torreón in the event of the capture of the city, and everyone expressed great admiration for General Villa in being able to maintain such order.[5]

It was this idea of Villa as the one strongman capable of maintaining order in Mexico that led both the Wilson administration and American businessmen to consider him not only as an element of order but as the leader of an American-style revolution in Mexico. This attitude forged closer and more cordial relations between Villa and the administration in Washington, as well as between Villa and American businessmen, day to day. It is easier to assess the reasons for this mutual cordiality, however, than to spell out how it functioned and discover its concrete manifestations.

Bases for an Alliance

An analysis of U.S.–Villa relations is especially difficult because, unlike the Carranza movement, the Villa movement in 1913–14 was not a real government. Carranza had a secretary of foreign affairs, a secretary of finance, and a host of other officials. He employed a number of personalities who were primarily responsible for relations with the United States, such as Isidro Fabela or Luis Cabrera. By contrast, the Villa administration was for a long time a very loose affair. For many months Villa considered the Carranza administration as the legal government of Mexico. There was no one in the leadership of the Villa movement who functioned as his secretary of foreign relations, although Villa maintained in the United States a series of semiofficial representatives whose real power and influence is still unclear. When the government of the revolutionary convention was established at the end of 1914 with all the trappings of a real government, Villa officially recognized its authority but in practice did not let it influence his actions. It is thus difficult to determine through what channels and in what way relations between Villa and the United States were shaped. These difficulties were compounded by the fact that Villa, unlike other revolutionaries, left practically no archives. Another, even more complex problem is to assess what both the Wilson administration

5. NARA, SD, 812.00-9658, Carothers to State Dept., 15 October 1913.

and U.S. business interests wanted from Villa, what both achieved, and how much of that they owed to Villa's pro-American policies.

Woodrow Wilson hoped the Mexican Revolution would lead to a U.S.-style democracy, with free elections and the maintenance of the free-enterprise system. While Wilson advocated some sort of agrarian reform in Mexico, he also stated clearly that foreign interests should be respected and that reforms should not take place at their expense. He repeatedly demanded that the revolutionaries guarantee all properties belonging to Americans (R. F. Smith 1972:31–32).

The latter demand was also voiced by the large American companies in Mexico, although for them the term "protection" had very broad connotations. They demanded the type of protection that they had enjoyed from Porfirio Díaz. This meant protection from confiscation by the state; protection from high taxes (or what U.S. business interests called high taxes, which by present standards would be extremely low); protection from "bandits," which also meant protection from insurgents, peasants, revolutionaries, and strikers (the term "bandits" as American companies saw it was very broad); protection from subordinates of Villa and from his bureaucrats; protection from unions and anti-U.S. agitation; and, finally, in addition to the maintenance of the rights they already had, protection of the many properties they were acquiring as a result of the revolution when many Mexican landowners decided that it would be better to sell to Americans, even at cut-rate prices, than to risk confiscation by the *villistas* (Katz 1981:158–67). On the whole, Villa granted these demands. There were no expropriations of American property. He effectively protected foreign business interests from real bandits and at times from revolutionaries labeled as bandits by foreign enterprises.

To some extent these policies of Villa's were no different from those of other revolutionary leaders in the north who, like Villa, tried to gain the goodwill of the Wilson administration, which above all meant access to American arms. Nevertheless, in three ways Villa's policy toward American interests went beyond those of other revolutionary leaders, especially Carranza and Obregón. The taxes Villa levied on Americans were lower. He expelled iww organizers from Mexico, and he did not allow any nationalistic anti-American rhetoric either in speeches by his officials or in his newspaper, *Vida Nueva*. In addition, one finds in the messages that Villa sent to Woodrow Wilson professions of deep loyalty that one does not find elsewhere. Unlike Carranza, Villa never protested against the American occupation of Veracruz in 1914.

Villa's extremely favorable attitude toward the United States was partly the result of practical need: Villa's División del Norte had turned into a regular army, and a large part of its supplies—most of its arms and, above all, most of its ammunition—came from the United States.

There was yet another way in which Villa relied on the United States. He printed increasing amounts of paper money whose value was boosted by the fact that American companies bought large amounts of it at a discount. They hoped that once Villa succeeded in dominating all of Mexico, its value would rise. In addition, the American companies needed Villa's currency in order to pay their taxes and their employees in the territories controlled by the División del Norte.

Villa's favorable attitude toward the United States was also influenced by the fact that, unlike many other revolutionaries, he had never belonged to one of the two parties formed with strong nationalistic and anti-American leanings prior to the 1910 revolution: the Partido Liberal Mexicano, headed by the Flores Magón brothers; and the Democratic Party, which promoted the vice-presidential candidacy of Bernardo Reyes.

Paradoxically, one of the main reasons for Villa's favorable attitude toward the United States was his social radicalism. In this regard he was very different from Venustiano Carranza. Carranza wanted to crush the Huerta regime and to dissolve the federal army, but he also wanted to maintain as far as possible the existing social structure, above all the hacienda system; this was precisely the system that Villa wanted to change. After the outbreak of the second phase of the Mexican Revolution in 1913, both Villa and Carranza were faced with a basic and immediate problem: how to finance the revolution. There were in fact only two possible sources of finance: either the foreign interests or the domestic oligarchy. Villa's main source of income was the expropriated holdings of the large Mexican owners, especially in Chihuahua, while Carranza attempted to force foreigners, through an increase in taxes, to defray a large part of the costs of revolution. These very different approaches, Villa's social radicalism and Carranza's social conservatism, thus had paradoxical consequences for their attitudes toward the large American companies.

Playing a significant role in shaping Villa's alliance with the United States were a few intermediaries, above all the United States' special representative to Villa, George Carothers, and the U.S. chief of staff and head of the Southern Command of the American army, Hugh Scott. Villa implicitly trusted George Carothers,[6] a former liquor salesman and U.S. consul in Torreón, not because he was honest but because he was corrupt. Villa paid him and made lucrative business dealings available to him. Carothers in return wrote extremely favorable reports on Villa to the State Department and to Secretary of State William Jennings Bryan, with whom he had a personal relationship. He was thus able to influence the U.S. government's perception of Villa.

The other important intermediary between the United States and Villa was of a very different caliber. If Carothers was a Mr. Hyde, General Hugh Scott (on whom see Clendenen 1961:121) was a Dr. Jekyll. His image of Villa and his relations with him were determined by very different paradigms. Scott had a long fighting experience, first on the American frontier and then in the Philippines. He had been very successful in aligning himself with Indian groups and Indian chieftains against rival Indian tribes. Scott's experiences with North American Indians greatly influenced the way he dealt with a Filipino insurrection against U.S. occupation forces. In the last years of the nineteenth century and at the beginning of the twentieth, Scott served as governor of a Filipino province populated by Moros, a group of Moslems with a long fighting tradition. Scott succeeded in pacifying the Moros by aligning himself with the sultan of Moro and by working through him to control the Moro region. In many respects Scott seems to have considered Villa as another man in the mold of the Comanche and Apache leaders, another man like the Moro sultan—men with whom he had dealt before. The hopes that Scott pinned on Villa are perhaps best expressed in a letter he wrote to his wife:

I have been struggling for fame ever since coming into the service, nearly forty years ago and have at last arrived at the result, that my title to consideration in Washington is that of being a friend of Villa's. That is my distinction. They all thought me crazy when I came up from the border a Villista last April but the Spanish and English ambassadors have now come around to my way of thinking and have so informed their governments. Villa himself seems to have taken a romantic regard to me and sends me messages here and there.[7]

6. See Hill 1974:196–97, 227.
7. LC, Hugh Lennox Scott Papers, Letter from Scott to His Wife, 26 September 1914.

Scott even considered joining Villa for a year in order to influence his policies.

Apart from their close relations with Villa, the only thing that Carothers and Scott had in common was their conservative social leanings. It is significant that the men who represented Villa in negotiations with the United States were equally conservative. One of them was Felix Sommerfeld, a German who had headed Madero's secret service in the United States and thus enjoyed Villa's confidence. Sommerfeld professed to be a revolutionary but was, as the U.S. consul in Chihuahua who knew him well stated, a deeply convinced conservative who believed only in absolute monarchy (see Katz 1981:333–37). He was anything but loyal to Villa, for he secretly also represented the German secret service and Sherburne Hopkins, the lawyer for the Waters-Pierce Oil Company in the United States. Like Carothers, Sommerfeld was corrupt and managed to become a rich man while representing Villa. The same was true of another Villa representative in the United States, Lázaro de la Garza, an arms buyer for Villa, who at a decisive moment in the history of the División del Norte betrayed Villa by selling arms destined for him to the French, who needed them to fight the Germans in World War I.[8] Unlike Villa's other representatives in dealings with the United States, Felipe Angeles, one of Villa's closest political and military advisers, was an honest man (but also a conservative).[9] He did not believe in immediate radical reform and felt that only a close relationship with the United States could guarantee the future of the Mexican Revolution. The radical intellectuals who joined Villa and who played a prominent role in his movement, such as Federico González Garza and Silvestre Terrazas, had no input into Villa's dealings with the United States. Thus they were unable to counterbalance the influence of either the American or the *villista* conservatives.

Villa's increasing links to the Wilson administration and to American businessmen repelled most American radical intellectuals, who refused to establish any links to the Villa movement and thus could not constitute a counterbalance to Villa's conservative advisers.[10] The only significant ex-

8. BLAC, Lázaro de la Garza Papers.

9. For very contradictory assessments of Angeles, see Cervantes 1964; Jackson 1976; Mena B. 1956; Krauze 1987; and Matute 1982.

10. Lincoln Steffens, who sided with Carranza, is but one example of many. See Clendenen 1961:200–201.

ception to this rule was John Reed, who greatly admired Villa and did much to improve his image in the United States. Reed, nevertheless, was not an intermediary or an adviser, but a journalist. In addition, he returned to the United States before Villa broke with Carranza and became a full-fledged national leader of Mexico.

It would nevertheless be a mistake to attribute Villa's openness to U.S. influence merely to his personal attitudes and to those of his conservative supporters. His links to the United States were never kept secret. They were public, and there was no large opposition to them within his movement. This receptivity obviously reflected the fact that the mass of the peasants who followed him were not anti-American. The most profound opposition to the United States was to be found above all in the ranks of the *magonistas,* many of whom were miners and industrial workers who joined Orozco and constituted Villa's fiercest enemies. This would tend to confirm Ana Alonso's hypothesis that northern Mexican peasants were far less anti-American than the inhabitants of Mexico's cities (see Alonso, above).

Villa's positive attitude toward the United States was not based exclusively on practical need. It was also the result of what could best be called Villa's code of honor. Villa's relationship with both President Madero and Governor Abrahám González hinged on what Villa considered a reciprocal loyalty. He supported them against their enemies, and he expected similar support from them against his own enemies. Villa's attitude toward Woodrow Wilson, then, was not based solely on opportunism but also on the conviction that in Wilson he had found another man who would reciprocate the loyalty Villa showed him. Villa never met Wilson, but it is quite probable that General Hugh Scott became a kind of personification of Wilson for Villa.

The Alliance Weakens

By mid-1914—following a brief cooling of relations with the United States after Villa killed the British landowner William Benton, provoking virulent anti-Villa feelings in Great Britain and to a certain degree in the United States—Villa's relations with the United States again reached a high point. After the U.S. invasion of Veracruz, Carranza had sent a sharp letter of protest to the U.S. government, while Villa clearly stated that he would never wage war against the Americans.

It has been generally assumed that the excellent relationship between Villa and both the Wilson administration and U.S. business continued well into 1915. The United States, it was assumed, not only expected but hoped for a *villista* victory. It was only after Villa's major defeats in early 1915 that the Wilson administration was forced to carry out a reappraisal of its policy toward the Mexican revolutionaries and finally to recognize Carranza. In fact, events evolved in a very different way. By the end of 1914, even before Villa's crushing defeat at Celaya, his relationship with the Wilson administration and with U.S. businessmen was already deteriorating rapidly.

That deterioration was caused first of all by Villa's inability by 1914 to maintain his earlier policy of not imposing high taxes on the Americans. His own resources, especially the cattle from Chihuahua and the cotton of the Laguna, were rapidly being exhausted. He did not have access to the oil fields, which Carranza controlled. Within the territories Villa did control, the only fresh sources of income were the estates and mines belonging to Americans. Villa now began to impose new taxes on American-controlled haciendas and to put pressure on U.S. mine owners who had stopped production because of the uncertainty the revolution had brought. Villa threatened these mine owners with confiscation unless they resumed work, and those threats provoked tensions with the United States (Clendenen 1961:183–86). The new pressures that Villa put on Americans led to increased protests by U.S. officials against his policies. When such protests occurred, Villa made some conciliatory noises and even acceded to one or another American demand. Nevertheless, even if he had wanted to, he could never have resumed his generous policy toward Americans. In addition to the drastic decrease in the resources he controlled, World War I, which had broken out in July 1914, profoundly transformed the market for American arms and ammunition in the world. Pancho Villa and Mexican revolutionaries in general had to compete for the purchase of American arms with France, Russia, and Britain, all of whom were inundating the United States with orders. As a result, there was a tremendous increase in the price of arms precisely at a time when Villa was least able to pay for them. Villa thus had no choice but to increase economic pressure on the Americans; he could only hope that once he achieved final victory, the Wilson administration would have no choice but to recognize his faction as the one that would rule Mexico.

The increasingly tense relationship between Villa and the United States was by no means owing to these economic conflicts alone. Villa deeply resented the fact that the Wilson administration, after evacuating the port of Veracruz, had turned it over not to his faction but to the *carrancistas,* thus giving them a new lease on life. Carranza gained access to huge amounts of arms that were stored in the port, as well as to the customs revenues that Veracruz generated (Hart 1987:299–301).

Finally, by late 1914 and early 1915 the maneuvers of a series of American plotters convinced Villa that the relationship the Americans envisaged with him was not one of equality but one of subordination. A series of agents directed by the head of the Mexican desk in the State Department, Leon Canova, offered recognition to Villa in return for wide-ranging concessions by his faction to the United States. The most important concessions Canova demanded were that the British-owned Tehuantepec railway linking Mexico's Atlantic and Pacific coasts be turned over to American interests, that Villa agree to having American troops stationed along Mexico's railway lines, that the United States be granted a naval base in Baja, California, and that all appointments to three important positions in the Mexican cabinet (including the ministries of Foreign Affairs and of the Interior) be approved beforehand by the U.S. administration (see Katz 1978b).

Canova had made these demands without the assent of either Woodrow Wilson or Secretary of State William Jennings Bryan, but Villa could not know this and assumed the proposals came directly from the White House. Villa did not accede to them and became increasingly resentful of the United States. This resentment was clearly expressed in a conversation he had with Duval West, Wilson's special envoy, who traveled to Mexico at the request of the U.S. president to assess the situation and to make policy recommendations. Villa now expressed a nationalism he had never shown before. In a conversation with West, Villa stated that Mexican industry should be primarily developed by Mexican capital. "I received the impression," West reported to President Wilson, "that he held to the popular demand, Mexico for the Mexicans, and that he saw an open door for foreign investments as a danger for the country."[11]

Less than one year later Villa would express his resentment at American policies in a much more direct way. In March 1916 Villa attacked the town of Columbus, New Mexico, on the basis of his firm conviction that the October 1915 recognition of the Carranza government by the United States was primarily a reward to Carranza for agreeing to Canova's demands (Katz 1978b).

U.S. Intervention and *Villista* Social Policy

This brief survey of the relations between the United States and Villa shows that this relationship was much more complex than has generally been assumed. It is by no means clear, as has been so frequently assumed, that the *villista* faction remained the United States' favorite until Villa was defeated in the field. But two basic questions related to the subject of this volume remain unanswered: (1) Did the United States play a decisive role in bringing about Villa's defeat? and (2) Would victory for Villa have meant that his faction would have carried out a very different kind of social policy in Mexico?

At first glance, question (1) seems easy to answer. While the United States did turn over Veracruz with its great resources to Carranza and did allow the latter's troops to cross into the United States and thus to inflict a decisive defeat on Villa's Division of the North at the battle of Agua Prieta, Villa's decisive military defeats in early 1915 were above all owing to Obregón's superior strategy.

Nevertheless, Villa's most intelligent and perspicacious intellectual supporter, Federico González Garza, was convinced that Villa's military defeats would not have been decisive had he followed a different social policy and carried out a radical agrarian reform while he had the power to do so. In a letter to his brother, written in 1915, González Garza wrote:

Since Huerta was ousted, we have to agree, that from a practical point of view, if we had known how to conduct an orderly confiscation subject to strict rules, and if we

11. NARA, SD, 812.00-14622, Report by Duval West to the Secretary of State, undated.

had had a distribution of land guided by an intelligent plan and without violence, we would by now have created new interests which would have helped to sustain the new regime.

This is how the constitutional assembly proceeded during the first period of the French Revolution, seizing the land of the nobles and immediately redistributing it, and this constituted the basis for the resistance of the Republican Regime. Despite all the horrors that accompanied the convention, neither the directory nor the succeeding consulate dared to undo the work of the First Assembly; they did not dare to decree the restitution of the confiscated estates. Napoleon, himself converted a while later to a monarch, understood that in order to secure his power he could not meddle with the Republican's work, but on the contrary he had to ratify, confirm, and incorporate into laws the institutions that had been created and implemented during the violent period of the revolution. If we want to create a solid structure, we must not forget the lessons of history.[12]

This assessment raises two fundamental issues: Is there any reason to assume that the *villista* faction was any more radical in agrarian terms than the *carrancistas?* Even if this were the case, is there any reason to assume that it was U.S. policy that was responsible for the fact that the *villistas* carried out no agrarian reform?

Alan Knight does not see any fundamental difference in either the social composition or the social policies of the two movements. The only difference he finds between them is in the attitude of their leaders toward national policies. While the *carrancistas* had a coherent national policy, the *villista* leaders were essentially parochial and regional-minded. "It is therefore hard to sustain even at the nuclear level that Villismo and Carrancismo differed according to some fundamental class distinction. The differences were more subtle and only secondarily if at all related to class" (Knight 1986a, 2:270). Knight also feels that,

given the nature of northern rural society, the classic village hacienda conflict did not dominate the policy of revolutionary regimes and it was more easily swamped by other concerns. . . . It was also the case that northern agrarian disputes frequently pitted villagers against caciques rather than hacendados and often formed part of a more general popular rejection of oppressive centralized government. (2:121)

12. Papers of Roque González Garza, Mexico City, Federico González Garza to Roque González Garza, September 1915, quoted in Katz 1981:286–87.

Knight feels that this problem was solved once the *caciques* were ejected from their villages, after which "popular pressure for radical reform waned."

I disagree with both of these views, but it must be said that at first glance many of the traditional arguments that have been espoused to explain why the *villistas* were more radical in social terms than their enemies are not very convincing and, in fact, have bolstered Alan Knight's point of view. It has been argued that Villa, who came from a family of hacienda peons, was far more sympathetic to the demands of Mexico's poor peasants than Carranza, the *hacendado*. Apart from the fact that any assessment of a social movement based solely on the social origins of its leader can only be extremely superficial, Villa had in fact been not only a peon but also a bandit, a small trader and, later, a well-to-do merchant. He had never participated in any of the frequent peasant movements that had taken place in Chihuahua prior to the Revolution of 1910. Thus, applying any simple label to Villa would be extremely difficult.

A second argument made to show that *villismo* was a radical agrarian movement is based on John Reed's book *Insurgent Mexico*, where he stated that Villa had divided the lands of the large haciendas among Chihuahua's peasants (J. Reed 1969:130). If this were indeed the case, Villa's *agrarismo* would be so evident that this whole discussion would be superfluous. Reed, however, mistook intention for reality. While some municipal lands were either distributed or redistributed, the large haciendas remained under government control during the whole of *villista* rule.

A third argument that has been brought to bear on this question is that Villa's alliance with Zapata and his recognition of the validity of the Plan de Ayala showed that he was far more of an *agrarista* than Carranza. This argument, in my opinion, has only limited validity. While Villa did in fact recognize the Plan de Ayala, it was never implemented in the north and did not constitute the basis of Villa's agrarian plans. As far as the alliance with Zapata was concerned, alliances during the Mexican Revolution were by no means exclusively ideological. Villa aligned himself with the governor of Sonora, José María Maytorena, who was not only more conservative than Villa but in many respects even more conservative than Carranza. Zapata, despite his radical agrarianism, was ready in later years to make an alliance with Félix Díaz, the leader of the most conservative faction in Mexico at the time, who had only one thing in common with Zapata: his opposition to Carranza. Nevertheless, the argument that Villa's alliance with Zapata did indicate some commonality of purpose cannot be entirely dismissed. Before entering into an alliance with Villa, Zapata sent one of his closest and most intelligent advisers, Gildardo Magaña, to Chihuahua to examine Villa's social policies. Magaña returned to Morelos firmly convinced that Villa was an agrarian revolutionary (Magaña 1985, vol. 3:chap. 15).

The most important point that one can make for a fundamental difference with respect to agrarian problems between *villismo* and *carrancismo* lies in the profound differences in their respective core constituencies. While Alan Knight tends to see the northern peasants as in the main a homogeneous group of *serranos* (i.e., peasants whose main conflict was with local *caciques* and above all with the government), I see fundamental differences between the situation in the countryside in the respective core regions. In Sonora, one of the two core regions of the *carrancista* movement, there had been very little land expropriation (with the very important exception of the Yaqui Indians), as Héctor Aguilar Camín has convincingly shown (1977:431–35). To judge from the very few complaints from Coahuila's peasants that I have seen (with the exception of the Laguna region, which was controlled by Villa), the same seems to hold true for Carranza's own state.

By contrast, for reasons that go beyond the scope of this essay, the bulk of the former military colonies, Indian villages, and settler communities that had been strongly affected by expropriations were concentrated in Villa's own bailiwick of Chihuahua and Durango. While there is no doubt that *caciques* did play an important role in these expropriations, so did the *hacendados*. Frequently villages were attacked on both flanks. The lands of Namiquipa, a former military colony and one of the bulwarks of *villismo* in the years 1913–15, were under attack both by *caciques* and outside settlers and by one of the wealthiest *hacendado* families in Chihuahua, the Müller family (see A. M. Alonso 1988b; Nugent 1993). While the peasants in Cuchillo Parado, home of the *villista* peasant leader Toribio Ortega, were above all victims of a local *cacique* (see Koreck, above), those of the neighboring villages of San Carlos and San Antonio, an important part of Ortega's constituency, suffered from expropriations by Enrique Creel, owner of the large adjoining hacienda of "Los Orientales."[13] The men

13. ATN, Queja de los vecinos de San Carlos y San Antonio, distrito de Ojinaga.

who formed the core of Calixto Contreras' army were the Ocuila Indians whose lands had been taken by the hacienda of Sombretillo, or the inhabitants of Peñón Blanco who had been feuding for years with the neighboring hacienda of "Santa Catalina."[14] Even in those cases where villages had not been directly expropriated by haciendas, they were strongly affected by the closing of the open range by the *hacendados* and the loss of traditional grazing rights and access to wood and other resources on public lands. Independently of Villa's or Carranza's personal ideology, the pressure of Villa's supporters for land reform was thus far greater than that of Carranza's backers in northern Mexico.

This discrepancy was clearly reflected in the leadership of the two movements. While there were leaders among *carrancistas* as well as among *villistas* in northern Mexico who had been identified with radical opposition to Porfirio Díaz during the latter's dictatorship, the kind of opposition they represented was very different. Pablo González and Manuel Diéguez, the two most outstanding former opponents of Porfirio Díaz in the *carrancista* ranks, were both identified with the Liberal Party and with working-class opposition to Díaz. The *villista* leaders who had opposed the Díaz regime long before the revolution broke out, such as Toribio Ortega, Calixto Contreras, Porfirio Talamantes, and Severiano Ceniceros, all had been peasant leaders who fought against the expropriation of their village lands.

There is little doubt that Villa was very conscious of the need to satisfy the demands of his important and radical peasant constituency. He had, after all, witnessed the disastrous result that a lack of recognition of peasant demands had had for the revolutionary *maderista* governor of Chihuahua, Abrahám González. Great numbers of disillusioned peasants had joined the Orozco rebellion. Apart from Villa's ideology, it is both the nature of his constituency and the composition of his leadership that explain the very different attitudes toward the *hacendados* and the agrarian problem that Villa assumed in the territories he controlled—attitudes that were fundamentally different from those of Carranza. While both factions confiscated the estates of hostile or presumably hostile *hacendados* in order to finance the revolution (Carranza strongly opposed such expropriations but could not prevent them), only Villa linked this expropriation to agrar-

14. AMR, Gómez Palacio to Barbarita, 30 July 1911.

ian reform. Only Villa had promised his soldiers that they would obtain land after the victory of the revolution. From the experiences of Abrahám González in 1912, Villa knew that breaking such a promise could entail grave consequences for him.

Another manifestation of the profound differences between the respective constituencies of the two leaders and the nature of their leadership was that while Carranza wished to return the expropriated estates to their former owners, and did so without encountering significant opposition, Villa adamantly rejected such a policy. In fact, one of Villa's main intellectual advisers, Silvestre Terrazas, who was in charge of administering the confiscated estates, considered that the issue of their disposition was one of the main reasons for the break between Villa and Carranza:

> One of the leaders wants to act very radically, confiscating the properties of the enemy and expelling the corrupt elements; the other disapproves of this conduct, proposes the return of some of the confiscated properties and allows himself to be influenced by an infinite number of enemies, who day after day estrange him from the aims, principles, and goals of the revolution.[15]

If the social basis of *villismo* was so different from that of *carrancismo*, why did it not express itself in the shape of a massive *villista* land reform? I believe that in this respect the influence of the United States on Villa's policies was decisive. Villa's strategic location on the border of the United States—and the fact that the Wilson administration permitted Villa to buy arms in the United States and to sell his goods there—made it possible for Villa, unlike popular peasant leaders in southern and central Mexico, to transform his army rapidly from a guerrilla force into a regular army. The maintenance of such a regular army imposed its own social and economic imperatives. The large estates constituted Villa's main source of goods and money to pay for the arms, ammunition, uniforms, and other supplies he bought north of the border. Had he divided up the land, many peasants would have reverted to subsistence agriculture or would have marketed their own crops instead of producing the income Villa so urgently needed. In addition, any immediate land reform could easily have led to mass desertions from Villa's División del Norte. As one of Villa's representatives at the revolutionary convention put it, "Let us suppose that the land would

15. STC, Silvestre Terrazas to Luis Caballero, 2 July 1914.

be divided immediately. Fine; but those peasants who are to get land are in the process of fighting in the army at this moment. They will face the choice of either leaving the army or, if they do not, they will not receive any land and this would be notoriously unfair and inequitable."[16]

Not only would it have been counterproductive for Villa to carry out an immediate land reform, he had other means of gaining and maintaining the loyalty of his soldiers. The large resources at his disposal, as well as American support of his currency, gave him the possibility of paying his men in money instead of in land. In those regions of Mexico that had no border with the United States, popular leaders whose social base was largely of peasant origin had no similar possibility of transforming their guerrilla forces into regular armies. They had no cash to pay their troops, and the only way they could maintain the loyalty of the peasants who were fighting for them was by giving them land. This was the case not only for Zapata in Morelos but also for the Arenas brothers in Tlaxcala and the Cedillo brothers in San Luis Potosí, all of whom made substantial land grants to their backers.

It is also possible (though I have not found direct proof for this) that Villa feared massive land reform might antagonize the United States and thus prevent his acquisition of the arms and supplies that were so vital to his movement. While Woodrow Wilson repeatedly insisted that some kind of land reform would have to be effected in Mexico, his representatives who dealt with Villa—above all Wilson's special representative, George Carothers, and the head of the Mexican desk at the State Department, Leon Canova—were far more conservative than Wilson and had close links to many of Mexico's landowners. It is probable they communicated to Villa their view that an immediate land reform would arouse opposition north of the border.

As a result of Villa's failure to carry out an agrarian reform, most of Mexico's peasants refused to fight for him after he was defeated. Their attitude sharply contrasted with that of the peasantry of Morelos and San Luis Potosí, who continued to wage guerrilla warfare in order to defend the land that they had been given.

16. Intervention of Niento at the Meeting of the Revolutionary Convention, 4 February 1915, *Crónicas y debates de las sesiones de la Soberana Convención Revolucionaria* (Mexico, 1965), 2:258–59.

Conclusions

The specific characteristics of the complex relationship between the United States and Villa are illuminated by considering the more general problem of how U.S. policy throughout the revolutionary years from 1910 to 1920 affected the outcome of the revolution. Was American policy the determining factor that led to Madero's victory, to the success of Huerta's coup, and later to the fall of Huerta and the victory of Carranza? There is little doubt that American policy contributed to these outcomes. What is debatable is how decisive U.S. policy was in these events.

It can be argued that if American authorities had treated Madero in the same way they treated the Flores Magón brothers, who were arrested because they tried to foment revolution from American soil, the Mexican Revolution might have taken another turn. I tend, however, to agree with Alan Knight that domestic factors played a decisive role in the Madero victory. That would still be so even if the hypothesis that American oil companies gave money to Madero proved to be true.

The role of the United States was much more important in Huerta's fall. The United States allowed the revolutionaries to buy arms across the border, prevented Huerta from gaining financial help in Europe and in the United States, and finally occupied Veracruz to prevent the arrival of arms shipments to the Huerta regime. Nevertheless, no categorical statement can be made as to whether domestic or foreign factors were most decisive in this second phase of the Mexican Revolution. Even if a definite answer to this question could be given, I do not think it is of decisive relevance to the problem of determining the importance of U.S. policy with respect to the peasantry in the Mexican Revolution.

What is decisive is that U.S. policy in Mexico between 1910 and 1920, independently to a large degree from the wishes of the Wilson administration, contributed decisively to the destruction of the existing Mexican state. The administration's at least limited tolerance of the Madero movement and its alliance with revolutionaries from the end of 1913 until mid-1914, contributed in a decisive way to destroying the most essential elements of the old Porfirian state: its army, its police, and to a large extent its bureaucracy. By preventing Carranza from acquiring arms or obtaining loans and financial help, the Wilson administration played a decisive role in preventing the Carranza government from reconstituting a powerful

Mexican state. For the Mexican peasantry, the weakening (and at times the disintegration) of the state had profound consequences. It gave peasant movements a degree of freedom they had not enjoyed before. It forced the new rulers of Mexico, who after 1920 emerged from the revolution, to make important concessions to the peasantry in order to be able to reconstitute and reform the Mexican state. These measures ranged all the way from recognizing land reforms carried out by radical leaders during the armed phase of the revolution (i.e., official recognition of the reforms that had taken place in Morelos, San Luis Potosí, and Tlaxcala) to carrying out agrarian reforms in other parts of Mexico. It meant creating armed peasant militias in order to counteract rebellious military chieftains.

Another decisive way in which U.S. policy affected the Mexican peasantry, discussed in this essay, was by making one of the most potentially radical and powerful revolutionary movements, the *villista* movement, dependent upon the United States both for arms and for the support of Villa's currency. This, in my opinion, was the decisive reason why the *villista* faction did not seize the one chance that history had given it to completely transform the Mexican countryside.

Independent of the policies of the U.S. government, the mere existence of a long border between Mexico and the United States played a decisive role in the Mexican Revolution. The border was extremely difficult to control either by American or by Mexican authorities. This was owing not only to its great length but also to the fact that a large part of the border population on the U.S. side consisted of Mexican Americans, many of whom had strong sympathies for the revolutionaries. As a result, northern Mexican revolutionaries acquired arms in the United States, found sanctuary there, and frequently obtained financial help from north of the border. One of the most important consequences was that northern Mexican revolutionaries had easier access to arms than revolutionaries anywhere else in Mexico, or for that matter anywhere else in Latin America. This geographical situation also played a key role in making the northern revolutionaries the arbiters of Mexico's destiny. For many years this fact would profoundly influence Mexico's agrarian policies and consequently the nature of Mexico's peasantry.

IV *Resistance and*

Persistence

ADOLFO GILLY

Chiapas and the Rebellion of the Enchanted World

1. Rebellion as Culture

For Marx, revolutions are the locomotives of history. But maybe things are different. Maybe revolutions are really the form through which humanity, which travels in that train, throws the emergency brake. WALTER BENJAMIN

I

The preceding fragment from Benjamin could serve as a concise summary of the long history of rural rebellions in Mexico. A typical example is the *zapatista* revolution of 1911, described in John Womack's now classic turn of phrase as a matter of "country people who did not want to move and therefore got into a revolution" (Womack 1969:ix). In the most general sense, these rebellions appear as movements defending a traditional society and its communal links with the land against the irruption of modernity—a modernity fleshed out on one side in the world of mercantile exchanges, where money functions as the mediator and vehicle for all human relations, and on the other side in the modern national state with its juridical order guaranteeing the universality of those exchanges.

Two chapters in this book illustrate this resistance in the northern and southern extremes of Mexican territory and its cultural substrata. In Chihuahua, at the very height of the "Porfirian Peace," where the revolution was gestating and where it would break out five years later, even if no one knew that at the time, Governor Enrique C. Creel pushed through the Municipal Land Law of 1905. As Jane-Dale Lloyd writes in her chapter:

On 25 February 1905 . . . Creel decreed the law for the survey, expropriation, and sale of municipal land which set the *pueblos'* boundaries and specified that all municipal land in the state was to be subdivided and sold to those who could afford to purchase it. . . . As the governor pointed out in his 1905 annual address, this law represented the final attempt by the oligarchy of Chihuahua to modernize the structure of land tenure in the state. . . . Its implementation would affect what was left of the colonial *ejidos,* as well as municipal land, and would convert what remained of the *fundos legales* into merchandise to be placed on the market, promoting land speculation in those areas of the state where livestock and agricultural production were most developed.[1]

According to Lloyd, there is a direct correlation between the application of this law and the subsequent emergence of *magonismo* in the region. More notable is that, notwithstanding the quite evident conviction on the part of the ruling class that this legal reform would not generate a social response, exactly the opposite occurred. Almost all of the local popular activists who opposed the 1905 law subsequently figured as leaders of the local and national revolutionary movement after 1910 (see Lloyd, above).

In 1847 the Mayan rebellion known as the War of the Castes broke out in Yucatán. In this rebellion, Gilbert Joseph detects the *modern* theme of the equality of all people—whatever their race—before the law, alongside the *ancient* theme of the forests being common property that could not be put on the market. "A dominant theme found in the communications of the Indian leaders is that laws should apply to all peoples, whatever their ethnic background. The burden of taxation should be borne by all racial categories, land should be available to everyone (and 'the forest should not be purchasable'), and no ethnic group should have the right to abuse another with impunity" (see Joseph above).

In both these cases, as distant physically as they are culturally, the modern world with its connected forms of the market and the state alter and threaten the life and the equilibrium of the agrarian community. The agrarian community for its part resists, defending the image it has of its own being, its identity, and it seeks protection and legitimacy for its actions in "the universal peasant vision of a society free from the predations of outsiders" (Coatsworth 1988:21–62). This, then, is its ultimate moral law.

Such agrarian rebellions or uprisings reveal in their multiple forms common bases often overlooked by the rebels themselves: resistance to the conversion of land into a commodity; refusal to surrender those aspects of

1. See also Nugent 1993:68–71. With this law, Nugent writes, "capitalists proceeded to do to independent agrarian communities what the Apaches had failed to do: destroy the pueblos and steal the land" (p. 68).

daily life that are the cultural and historical substrata of direct relations between members of the community to a world of mercantile exchanges; and opposition to the external world interfering in the order of those interrelationships conceived as they are as part of the natural order.[2] If the land is successfully converted into a commodity, people—along with their community; inseparable as they are from its territory—wind up having sold their body and lost their soul. In other words, *the law of the land* is opposed to and resists *the law of money,* even though as time passes the latter permeates all exchanges and relationships.[3]

Eric Van Young has explained this phenomenon, writing about colonial Mexico in terms that still resonate with significant aspects of modern Mexico:

> The strong probability that until very recent times access to means of subsistence, to affective ties, and to spiritual goods, fell for most people to their pueblo of origin and residence, contributed to a profound identification between "I" and "We." On the other hand, during the colonial period and after, the porous though still intact existence of *la república de indios* in many parts of Mexico indicated that ethnic and economic conflict with the surrounding society tended to devolve to a particularly explosive combination, since the focus of economic identity—the poblado—considerably overlay the focus of cultural identity—also el poblado. The contentious discourse and practices of resistance—in legal disputes, local agitations, or large scale insurrections—indicated the primordial value for the rural population of the defense of community, whether or not an "economic dimension" (a conflict over land, say) were evident in each given instance. (Van Young 1994)

Hence, rebellions present themselves as secular and successive collective acts, material and symbolic, at times very diverse in the immediate motivations apparent to their participants,[4] but whose ultimate content could be

2. This would be the substance of a "moral economy" (in E. P. Thompson's classic formulation) motivating the decision of the peasantry to rebel: "An outrage to these moral assumptions, quite as much as actual deprivation, was the usual occasion for direct action" (E. P. Thompson 1971:76–136; see also Scott 1976, 1985, 1990). The same basic argument appears already in Moore 1969 [1966] and Wolf 1969.

3. In *Capital,* vol. 1, Marx notes this opposition between the two norms or laws at the level of forms of power: "The opposition that exists between the power of agrarian property based on personal relations of domination and dependence and the impersonal power of money is clearly expressed in the two French sayings: '*Nulle terre sans seigneur,*' '*L'argent n'a pas de maitre.*'" (cited in Dumont 1977:215).

4. See, e.g., Taylor 1979; Tutino 1986, esp. 33; or Di Tella 1973.

found in *the will of these communities to persist*. The participants resist and
rise up in order to persist, because they can persist only by resisting the
movement of a world that dissolves and negates their Being. The inherited
common substratum of this Being in Mexico is the land and a more ample
sense of territory, *a* territory, that territory with which the peasant community identifies (cf. e.g., Tutino 1986:274; Bonfil 1980:240–41; Bonfil 1991;
Magagna 1991).

Guillermo Bonfil defined it in the following terms:

> In the Mesoamerican communities there was an overweening preoccupation with
> chronology, but a sense of space as a dynamic element of history was also present.
> The drawing together of temporal sense with a concrete space would be related, on
> the one hand, with the memory of an ethnic territory historically attached to each
> village, the recovery of which figured in all the Indian revindications; and, on the
> other hand, with the idea of people as part of nature and not as its very enemy. The
> cosmic sense of the Indian vision of humankind (every person is a moment of
> living and total synthesis of the history of the cosmos and of all people who
> preceded and would follow, hence of all future peoples) would provide the basis for
> this conception and would be the very foundation of the civilizing project, in which
> harmony with the natural world would supplant its exploitation by people. (Bonfil
> 1980:240–41)

Nevertheless, the external world does exist, and does interfere in this life
and this territory. Not only was the modern world born in the medieval
clothing of conquest and colonial institutions—including the still un-
equaled genocide of the sixteenth century in Mesoamerica—but in the
wake of that unparalleled depopulation of the conquered territory, the
colonial regime could coexist in a sort of tributary symbiosis with the persistence of indigenous agrarian communities.[5] But, above all, it was the

5. On the initial judicial regime established in New Spain and the discussions about *la
república de indios*, see Borah 1983:25–78. On page 26 Borah lists his native population
estimates for the Audiencia de México and parts of the Audiencia de Guadalajara, or
Nueva Galicia, as follows: 1518, 25.2 million; 1532, 16.8 million; 1548, 6.3 million; 1568, 2.5
million; 1585, 1.9 million; 1595, 1.375 million; 1605, 1.075 million; and, finally, for 1622, a
century after the fall of Tenochtitlán, 750,000 inhabitants. Starting in the second half of
the seventeenth century the native population starts to steadily, if slowly, increase. In
1570, meanwhile, there were 57,000 "Spaniards" (actually Europeans of diverse origin
and *mestizos* embracing Hispanic culture); in 1646, 114,000; by 1793, 780,000. Borah

world of the new modernity that irrupted with the Bourbon reforms and encouraged a pattern of resistance and agrarian rebellion in which were inscribed, a century apart from each other, the two great agrarian wars in Mexico: the Revolution of Independence and the Mexican Revolution (Tutino 1986; Gilly 1989:intro.; Van Young 1993:31–61).

This pattern of resistance in Mexico had peculiar forms that marked the society, history, and culture of the country well beyond strictly rural regions. John Coatsworth sharpened the point:

Patterns of resistance and rebellion now associated with uniquely rural settings were common in mining towns and administrative centers throughout the Spanish empire, and continued long after independence. The separation of town and country, a central feature of modern society, did not take definitive shape until late in the nineteenth century in most of Latin America. Patterns of urban revolt—like food riots, miner's protests, and tax revolts—all retained their ties (direct or indirect) to traditions of rural rebellion until well into the twentieth century. Excluding these conflicts forces the historian to omit treatment of important continuities in the development of social movements in premodern societies. (Coatsworth 1988:24)

The frequency and spread of this type of rural resistance in the constitution of the relations of Mexican agrarian society with power—whether central or local—has no parallel in Latin America (Coatsworth 1988; Katz 1988b). It is manifest equally in the Yaqui rebellions of the nineteenth and twentieth centuries, in the resistance of the military-settlement colonists in Chihuahua, in the unending history of *motines* and rebellions in the center and south of the Republic, and in the Maya rebellions during the eighteenth and nineteenth centuries in the extreme southeast of the country and in the province of Chiapas.

The agrarian community, with its hierarchies, its beliefs, its values, and its networks of internal relations, is the subject and author of rebellion. This has been proven empirically in rebellion after rebellion in Mexican history, from the "Tzeltal Republic" of 1712 (Gosner 1992; Bricker 1981:55–69; Wasserstrom 1983:78–86; Klein 1966) and the rebellion of 1869 in

---

notes, "Hence there were two significant communities living in the same territory, and the need to regulate their relations was made all the more urgent as the Spanish population increased" (1983:27).

Chiapas (Rus 1983), through the revolution of Emiliano Zapata between 1911 and 1920 (Womack 1969), to the indigenous *neozapatista* rebellion in Chiapas from 1994 forward (EZLN 1994, 1995).[6]

But this phenomenon is always assimilated only with difficulty by the dominant regime, which interminably searches for outside agitators to explain rebellions by the dominated, who are presumed to have neither thoughts of their own nor a capacity to take the initiative. This negation is a psychological need that legitimates domination, even as it is one of its weaknesses at the hour of revolt.[7]

Ranajit Guha explains the political character, painstakingly elaborated within the community, that can be found in each peasant rebellion in the history of India:

There was no way for the peasant to launch into such a project in a fit of absent-mindedness. For this relationship was so fortified by the power of those who had the most to benefit from it and their determination, backed by the resources of a ruling culture, to punish the least infringement, that he risked all by trying to subvert or destroy it by rebellion. This risk involved not merely the loss of his land and chattels but also that of his moral standing derived from an unquestioning subordination to his superiors, which tradition had made into his dharma. No wonder, therefore, that the preparation of an uprising was almost invariably marked by much temporization and weighing of pros and cons on the part of its protagonists. In many instances they tried at first to obtain justice from the authorities by deputation (e.g., Titu's bidroha, 1831), petition (e.g. Khandesh riots, 1852), and peaceful demonstration (e.g. Indigo rebellion, 1860) and took arms only as a last resort when all other means had failed. Again, an *émeute* was preceded in most cases by consultation among the peasants in various forms, depending on the organization of the local society where it originated. There were meetings of clan elders and caste panchayats, neighborhood conventions, larger mass gatherings, and so on. These consultative processes were often fairly protracted and could take weeks or even months to build up the necessary consensus at various levels until most of an entire community was mobilized for action by the systematic use of primordial networks and many different means of verbal and non-verbal communication. There was nothing spontaneous about all this in the sense of being

---

6. For an exhaustive study of Chiapan rebellions up to the 1980s, see García de León 1985.

7. Such is the point of view assumed by Carlos Tello Díaz (1995).

unthinking and wanting in deliberation. The peasant obviously knew what he was doing when he rose in revolt. (Guha 1983a:9)

This cultural, political, and historical reality explains the density and the multiple meanings borne by the demand for *autonomy* advanced by agrarian communities, whatever their specific juridical form. To limit oneself in the discussion of each case to the juridical form provided by the framework of the nation-state, without taking into account this imaginary and its historical construction, is to ignore the essence of the question, the meaning of what is being fought over and, above all, as the old saying has it, the roots and reasons of the demands in the minds of the subjects and protagonists of rural revolt.

II

As is well known, the Mexican revolution was a kind of condensation of this long history in the course of which relations of power and governance were mediated not only by property, economy, and civil and criminal law, but also by revolt and by the weapons available to those charged with enforcing the law in the countryside and elsewhere. For the rulers, the use of violence is always present as a possible and conceivable option.

Peasant violence, meanwhile, if most of the time only potential, winds up being just one more element in the disputes and conflicts among the ruling elites. Repeatedly, from Hidalgo's rebellion (Tutino 1986:chap. 3) through the Mexican Revolution—including the intervening period of the Caste Wars in Yucatán (Joseph, above)—elites could not resist the temptation to rely on armed peasants (Katz, cited in Joseph and Nugent 1994a:3–4). Time and again the unwanted result was that processes of rebellion were unleashed that contending elite factions were unable to control (see de Vos 1995b).

Giving in to such a temptation is not, in my judgment, the result of a defect in understanding on the part of those elites with respect to the implicit danger of their attitudes. Rather, it originates, on the one hand, in the lasting presence or latency of agrarian conflict in the formation of the Mexican polity and the relationship between those who command and those who obey and, on the other hand, in the persistence of relationships of personal dependency—rooted in the countryside—between those who command and those who obey, in the "personalization" of rule in the form of *caciquismo*, clientelism, and kinship.

The consolidation of the idea of the nation as opposed not only to the foreign, or the alien, but also to local agrarian particularities, is a slow process. Equally slow is the consolidation of a unified national consciousness among elites.[8] And in reality, when that consolidation was achieved in the long process culminating in the Mexican revolution, the peasants figured in the Constitution of 1917 (Article 27) with *status* and specific rights as peasants, not abstractly as citizens; a *status* that includes their expectation of protection by the state in exchange for their obedience to the rulers of state (A. Bartra 1985). In this way, rural rebellion ended up establishing itself, over the long run, as one of the *modes of conformation and existence* of the Mexican state community; in other words, as one of the elements with a potential for constituting the very relationship between rulers and ruled, between those who govern and those who are governed (Roux 1996).

For this reason, albeit to general surprise at the time, Francisco I. Madero's call to arms, his appeal to Mexico's citizens to reestablish a legitimate electoral democracy—travestied by the regime of Porfirio Díaz—wound up taking the unexpected form of a peasant war that not only destroyed the previously existing state but changed the very form of the state in Mexico. And for the same reason, when peasants who voted for Cuauhtémoc Cárdenas in 1988 felt that the electoral results had been, or would be, fraudulently altered by the government, they turned to the ancient image of armed rebellion in order to make known the depth of their determination. Letters sent to the opposition candidate from the countryside are significant:

"We want you to assume the presidency for good or bad, it mattering not to us that we must do as our predecessors, who spilt blood to secure freedom" (letter from Michoacán). "We are with you *en las buenas y en las malas*, you're not alone nor will you be, we'll put you in the presidential chair with machine guns in our hands if the PRI wants it that way, but the PRI should accept its defeat peacefully" (letter from Guerrero). "We are with you in defense of the vote, and if it becomes necessary to take up arms, all Mexicans are ready" (letter from Veracruz). "I am determined to

8. "As a universalistic style of imagining social ties, nationalism contrasts with such particularistic forms of configuring social relatedness as kinship and clientelism" (Alonso, above).

take up arms when you, Ingeniero Cárdenas, so decide. My family is very poor, and is willing to struggle for you" (letter from a Michoacán schoolteacher). "All the *ejidos* mentioned above are ready, if it is necessary, to take up arms" (letter from Campeche). "We're ready for whatever happens, even the necessity to take up arms; because in this region arms are a delight, and we are prudent people, not stupid like the thieving *priistas* consider us" (letter from Puebla). (Gilly 1989:54–56)

"Take up arms." Coming as it did from every peasant region of the country, this was not a rhetorical expression but one of the early signs that in the consciousness of the peasantry, the legal regime of obedience to orders had entered a crisis. Peasants had responded with images from ancient experience.

In a photograph endlessly reproduced by successive governments, one sees a peasant turning over the gun he used during the revolution to President Cárdenas, at the very moment in 1936 when Cárdenas set in motion the distribution of land in the Comarca Lagunera. If that pact originating in the armed revolution has now been broken, even if only symbolically, the right to take up arms is once again ours.

III

Coming directly out of the revolution of 1910–20, this regime of power was codified in several key articles of the Constitution of 1917, especially in Article 27, the fulcrum on which the Mexican state community balanced. Article 27 mandates that the soil and subsoil rights of Mexico belong to the nation, which has the right to establish forms of individual property. Petroleum belongs to the nation. Land expropriated from communities will be restituted. Just as the nation has rights to its petroleum, so the peasants have rights to land. This, in a nutshell, was the content of Article 27. And every agrarian conflict since the Mexican revolution was played out against that content, its diverse interpretation, and the legal dispositions it generated.

In other words, Article 27 included peasants' struggle for land among the constitutive norms of the relationship between the state and its subjects, affording, as already stated, a particular status to peasants, who are differentiated from other citizens (and affording another status to wage workers, in Article 123). On the one hand, Article 27 absorbed agrarian revolt into the law; on the other, in subsequent debates over the content and scope of the legal text, it reintroduced the methods and forms of rebellion. The persistence and occurrence to this day of land invasions, whether rural or urban, as a preferred method to secure rights or tenancy or property, is one of the sequels to that act of absorption.

During the 1920s and the first half of the 1930s, diverse forms of armed mobilization for the land never ceased: the war between *agraristas* and *cristeros*, the *tejedista* "guerrillas" in Veracruz, the armed peasants of Saturnino Cedillo in San Luis Potosí, armed disputes between neighboring villages, invasions of haciendas and other properties, *gavillas* all over the place. Alan Knight describes the situation thus:

> Whether Catholic or agrarista, the peasants of 1930s Mexico all lived in a post-revolutionary society; the neap tide of popular insurgency had ebbed, but the waters remained agitated. Society witnessed sustained popular mobilization, rival propaganda, competitive (albeit dirty) politics, and endemic local violence. In such a Hobbesian world there was (*pace* some historians) still no Leviathan, no securely dominant elite, and no thoroughly dominated peasantry. The days of mass guerrilla were gone, but, inverting Clausewitz, we may say that the (agrarian) politics of the 1930s were in many ways the continuation of the guerrilla war by other means. (Knight 1994:52)

All the same, these actions were not proposals to change the regime, but rather to negotiate relations between the elite in power and those governed by it, between the architects of the agrarian redistributions and the peasantry. The government of Lázaro Cárdenas and his profound agrarian reform were the national, juridical, and political culmination of a prolonged violent, regional, and dispersed "negotiation" in which *caudillos, caciques,* and peasants were confused and bound up with one another.[9]

With the redistribution of land, what had until the late 1930s been no more than a promise included in Article 27 became in many respects a reality, a reality institutionalized in the implementation of the terms of Article 27 during the years that followed. That sector of the ruling elite which pushed forward the demand for land, making itself the mouthpiece for and executor of reform, came out on top, affirming its power and unify-

---

9. This theme is demonstrated in the rich and considerable literature comprising regional studies. Besides the essays in this volume, see, among many others, those in Brading 1980; and Benjamin and Wasserman 1990.

ing the force, legitimacy, and internal control necessary for the national—not peasant—confrontation with England and the United States over Mexico's petroleum: the other part of Article 27.

The expropriation of the foreign oil companies, the restoration of subsoil rights to the eminent domain of the nation, and the termination of extraterritoriality for oil concessions: these actions secured unprecedented national support and completed an image of Mexican national territory. The expropriation of the oil companies presented itself as "el desquite," the retaliation for territory lost to the United States in the war of 1847 (Gilly 1994:253–65). Resulting from prolonged confrontation, the nationalization of oil and the (partial) redistribution of land came to be, rather like the living myth of the Mexican revolution, essential components of the form in which the national community imagined itself and of the ideology comprising Mexican nationalism (Anderson 1983; Castoriadis 1987).

IV

A mode of governance emerges out of the routinized practice of such confrontations alongside the elite's construction of a particular imaginary, an imaginary sustained through practical experiences lived by all. In this mode of governance, the action by which the elite constructs its hegemony, affirms its legitimacy, and consolidates its right to rule (and to accumulate capital) is decisive. No less decisive, though, are the Mexican traditions of the negotiation of rule, with the always-present mediating figure of the *cacique* appearing in its rural and urban transfigurations.

Mediation and negotiation of rule are constituent elements of the form of domination—which is to say, of the specific conformation of the Mexican state community.[10] One of its roots is the long-standing nature of relations of personal dependence, a theme I have discussed elsewhere (Gilly 1985). *Dura lex sed lex* (The law is hard, but it is the law) is not an aphorism appropriate to Mexican politics. Rather than fix norms valid for

10. The "state" is here defined as that community in which rulers and ruled, dominators and dominated, ruling and subaltern classes, or any other equivalent designation are included and recognized. I define it, then, as a *social relation* recognized and accepted by all, and governed by (written and unwritten) political norms for the exercise, conservation, and reproduction of power and by (written and unwritten) norms regulating the interchanges and the social and economic relations between the elements of the community. This I call the "state community."

every case, the law in Mexico determines a framework in which negotiation occurs on a case-by-case basis. As Benito Juárez, the founding father of the modern state in Mexico put it, "A los amigos, justicia y gracia; a los enemigos, la ley a secas."[11]

Viewed from without, this anomalous juridical trajectory seems confused and threatening, a dark world where anything can happen without anything appearing to have occurred. Thus did two lucid, if somewhat disconcerted, English writers register the point in 1939 in their similar book titles: Evelyn Waugh's *Robbery under Law* (his chronicle of travels in Mexico) and Graham Greene's *The Lawless Roads*. This is the shadowy space where the refined instinct of the negotiator and mediator moves, where the *cacique*—that inescapable figure of a simultaneously formalist and ambiguous juridical sense, whatever the name he bears—lives. His purest function consists in knowing how to keep the lid on an always potentially explosive situation, when to turn up the heat, and when to back off. The *cacique* is the leader and orchestrator of the shadows and its people; those on top and those on the bottom, insiders and outsiders, all confide in him.

Discussing the case of the Indians of Chiapas, Jan de Vos defines the place of negotiation among the various practices of resistance in the Mexican world:

They have deployed three fundamental strategies over the course of four and a half centuries of colonial and neocolonial domination: open resistance, veiled resistance, and negotiated resistance.

The first form of resistance consisted above all in armed uprisings during periods of particularly acute oppression, but it also included movements of territorial retreat conducted by various groups or individuals toward unpopulated regions beyond governmental control.

The second form refers to the complex of everyday practices, permitted to a certain extent by civil and ecclesiastical authorities because considered inoffensive or impossible to eradicate. Among these should also be mentioned those practices that simply went unnoticed, not least of all because those who engaged in them conducted them in secret, in the intimacy of the household or the isolation of the bush.

Finally, the third category is constituted by that intermediate space where the

---

11. Or, as Francisco Villa, destroyer of the Mexican state put it, "Por los buenos, bueno; y por los malos, peor"—Ed.

Indians—and among them, above all, the *caciques* and other *principales* of the communities—made major or minor concessions to their rulers to the end of safeguarding or securing privileges, not without running the risk of losing their autonomy, either partially or totally. (de Vos 1995b:239–40)[12]

The hegemony, legitimacy, and right of the rulers are not constituted in a vacuum. Such authority is constructed and defined by taking into account as a given fact the active or passive resistance of the ruled, not their inert subordination. Thus, the established rule in Mexico is *the permanent negotiation of authority*, case by case and space by space, within frameworks recognized by all.[13] Since the colonial period, the impossible and invariably disadvantageous (for the peasants) arguments before the courts have been one of the historic spaces for these disputes. It is natural that peasants and Indians have more recently been sensitive to the enlargement of that space by Article 27 of the Constitution and by subsequent legislation.[14]

The revolutionary elites of 1917 had brought together in Article 27 three ideas—land, oil, and nation—that were not necessarily united in the imagination of those who had participated in the revolution: the peasants, the urban artisans and workers, the emergent middle class, the officers of

12. Compare this typology of strategies of resistance with the methodological proposal of James C. Scott (1990).

13. This is an underlying idea of the essays published in Joseph and Nugent 1994a. Those essays originated from a discussion of James C. Scott's proposals regarding everyday forms of peasant resistance (1985) and Philip Corrigan and Derek Sayer's study of English state formation as cultural revolution (1985). In his contribution to the Joseph and Nugent volume, Alan Knight (1994:54) writes: "The revolution—itself the result of a failed (Porfirian) hegemony—gave birth to a state that struggled to assert its authority in the face of powerful enemies possessed of their own counterclaims to authority. The common people of Mexico were both victims and participants in this secular struggle. And the outcome was, at least in part, a new hegemony, more durable than that of the past: A Mexican Great Arch, the work not only of elite architects but also of the calloused hands of common peons."

14. Woodrow Borah signals the enormous consequences generated by the introduction of a juridical order in the Spanish legal principles pertaining to rights of appeal and protection: "Within the Indian community, litigation before Spanish courts and petitions for administrative review and protection became the principal means of carrying on the long series of disputes unleashed by the Conquest over land, status, and virtually all other relationships. The conquerors were amazed that subjects so meek showed such ferocity and tenacity in litigation." Borah then reproduces an extraordinary mid-sixteenth-century description by the *juez de Audiencia* Alonso de Zorita regarding "pleitismo indígena" (Indian litigation) (Borah 1983:40ff.).

the revolutionary armies. For the twentieth century, the unique feature of the *cardenista* period consisted in these ideas being converted into a reality for the country, for Mexico, appearing as an achievement and realization with the participation of everyone in society. In other words, to return to a theme I have touched on elsewhere (Gilly 1994), these ideas were *materialized* in the everyday life of a national community, their contents converted into a founding pact between governors and governed.

Thus was constituted—in history, not just in legal texts—the "framework recognized by all," within which the relation of command/obedience that came out of the revolution would henceforth be exercised. That relation consolidated itself as the secular cultural construction of a state community with inherited traditions of ancient agrarian resistance—traditions that were extended into a society, for the most part urban, that hadn't stopped changing with the times. Secular peasant resistance molded political culture from below and, in many respects, conditioned the character and mode of governance by the elite, including some aspects of the elite's relations among themselves, which were also and at the same time partly an inheritance from their own *caudillo* and *cacique* traditions.

The political culture specific to the Partido Revolucionario Institucional—which is to say, the Mexican state after 1920—is a fine distillation of this process. Its two faces, as is apt for all good mediators, look one toward the past and the other toward the future, one down and the other upward, and each of them covers all the other angles as well. When this adjustable equilibrium is upset, mediation ends.

If that's the way it is, it is difficult to see the peasants as the losers of the Mexican revolution. A revolution is not a war between nations; rather, it is a violent transformation of the relations of power within a specific nation or society. In that transformation, the ancien régime that disappears from the scene is vanquished. But in the alliance of the winners, if indeed there are some who obtain power and others who do not (and, it goes without saying, some who are able to enrich themselves and others who cannot), the rules for the exercise and reproduction of power—the command/ obedience relation between rulers and ruled—establish themselves according to norms whereby those who fail to obtain power are far from seeing themselves as defeated, however far they also are from considering themselves winners.

In the Mexican revolution, peasants (whether armed or "pacíficos") and the towns and villages they came from acquired the idea of nation through the lived experience of ten years of conflict. Indeed, once the Old Regime was destroyed, nothing less than the very definition of a nation became the task at hand. Today that definition includes, in collective memory, not only the ideas and actions of Constitutionalism and its various currents, but also those of the Division of the North and the Liberation Army of the South. Notwithstanding that the latter forces did not participate in the Constitutional Congress of 1917, the constitutional definitions that came out of that congress would not have been the same without them.

Above all, however, without the peasant war, the imaginary according to which the Mexican community made itself as a result of ten revolutionary years (and those that followed) would not have been the same. The Paris Commune was defeated and razed by the victors. Nevertheless, its echoes and myth marked the history of subaltern classes in France and elsewhere, even reaching the *zapatista* revolution of 1911. The peasant commune of Morelos was unable to win and carry on, but those who assumed power with Alvaro Obregón had to enter into a pact with it. And thus, finally, as with every peasants' revolution, the winners can bring it to an end only by entering into a pact with the losers to affirm their own power.

The ruling elite was left tied to this pact. Only in the 1930s, when it was able to define the terms of its relationship with the subaltern classes—peasants, urban and industrial workers—could it get around to fixing its relationship with external powers and with the true frontiers of its nation and state via the expropriation of the oil companies. In the latter task it enjoyed the support of the supposed "losers," who saw themselves as "winners" by dint of their stubborn struggle to secure agrarian redistribution and other social victories (Gilly 1994).

Hence it does not seem to be wise to see the forms of resistance *legitimated within the constitutive pact of this community* as a simple rejection of the modernization of Mexican social relations, from relations of personal dependence to relations of mercantile exchange. In social practice, forms of resistance present themselves, instead, as forms of conceiving and conditioning modernization from below and, once again, of negotiating the terms and not being excluded. One could say that the strategic proposition is to preserve rather than destroy it, the national state community, as it is imagined from below, against those who would want to take it down an unknown road (see Knight 1990a).

In other words, any attempt to transform political culture—that is, the forms in which power is exercised—and economic relations which ignores the historical construction of the Mexican state community, putting it to the side as an obstacle or relic of the past, runs the risk of throwing that community into a crisis and tripping over itself.

At the end of 1991, a new leading elite—now linked to the expansion of finance capital and to the processes of economic globalization in which Mexico had inserted itself—modified Article 27 of the Constitution. With that act it closed off the possibility of any future agrarian redistributions; it legalized the privatization of ejidal and communal lands, which henceforth could be sold, purchased, or used to guarantee loans, and facilitated the purchase of blocks of land by private investment companies. Beyond that, the new legislation permitted the *caciques* to strengthen their alliances with private companies and move ahead with the purchase of land from their poorest neighbors, with the consequent deepening of divisions within rural communities (Harvey 1994, 1995b; García de León 1995). On the other hand, the modification of Article 27 is commensurate with, and provides a juridical basis for, an eventual privatization of petroleum wealth.

That the governing elite believed, given the diminished weight of peasants demographically and in the national economy, that it could get away with this maneuver without any ill effect meant that a crack had appeared in the already battered Arch of the Alliance between state and peasantry. Step by step they committed exactly the same error of failing to appreciate the consequences of their policy as had their modernizing ancestor, Chihuahua Governor Enrique Creel, almost a century earlier. And it would not be long in generating similar results.

Moreover, the modification of Article 27 was a major step toward the juridical homologation of Mexico and the United States, having been designed to take effect together with the North American Free-Trade Agreement on 1 January 1994. The Salinas government had satisfied the long-standing demand of the United States—repeated since the sanctions imposed by the Constitution of 1917—to modify or abrogate those terms of Article 27 referring to soil and subsoil rights as the public property of the Mexican nation (L. Meyer 1972; Gilly 1994).

Then, unexpectedly on New Year's Day 1994, at the very hour when the financial elite celebrated Mexico's entry into the First World with the

NAFTA, an Indian rebellion seized the plazas of four cities and three towns in the state of Chiapas, including San Cristóbal, the old Ciudad Real of the colonizers and landlords, occupied on that day by thousands of Indians, some armed, others unarmed. On January 2, the Zapatista Army of National Liberation declared war against the "federal army," requested that the legislative and judicial powers "depose" the "illegitimate government" of Carlos Salinas de Gortari, and ordered its troops to "advance to the capital of the country." To this apparently immoderate and overstated, if hardly unprecedented,[15] gesture—understandable only in the same symbolic dimension as the act of seizing San Cristóbal—the EZLN declaration added as well eleven "basic demands": namely, *"work, land, housing, food, health, education, independence, freedom, democracy, justice, and peace"* (EZLN 1994:33–35; STF 1995:52–54).

Peasants, once again, had come to object.[16]

2. The Last Glow of the Mexican Revolution

I

Since the time of Don Porfirio, the liberal Mexican state has claimed a pre-Hispanic Indian ancestry for itself while denying the rights common to all citizens to those Indians actually living in Mexican territory. This was in the tradition of nineteenth-century liberalism in Mexico, where since the Constitution of 1824 the Indian majority had been unevenly assimilated to the category "citizens"; only as individuals did they enjoy the supposed "legal equality" that is the recognized right of every citizen (Reyna A. 1993). And there they sort of remained. The law rendered them as invisible as Garabombo, Manuel Scorza's fictional Peruvian Indian.

Guillermo Bonfil provides an ironic description of the cultural divestment which that entailed:

15. The symbolism and audacity of that gesture have been recurrent for many generations in Mexico. John Tutino reminds us that "at least since the rise of the imperial city of Teotihuacan, over a thousand years before the Spanish conquest, every regime that has ruled Mexico has ruled from these central valleys" (Tutino 1986:139). There was decided the fortune of the Hidalgo rebellion. There, too, the destinies of Villa and Zapata (1914–15), Obregón and the Sonoran dynasty (1920), were played out.

16. This phrase is taken from the title of Arturo Warman's study of the Morelos peasantry and the national state (Warman 1976).

The Indian past is converted into a common past to which all enjoy rights. Even more, the past expropriated from the Indian is transformed into the fundamental reason for the independence of Latin American countries, just as later it would be used to symbolize the yearnings of the Mexican revolution of 1910. Ideologically, a separation between the precolonial past and living Indians is invariably realized. The builders of Teotihuacán and Chichén Itzá become illustrious ancestors of the non-Indians, and the Indians once again are left on the margins of history. It even gets to the point of the paradoxical relation between nationalism and *indigenismo* in which all Mexicans are descendants of Cuauhtémoc except for the Indians, who must "integrate" themselves (which is to say, stop being Indians) in order to also be legitimate children of Cuauhtémoc. (Bonfil 1980:232–33)[17]

Neither were Indians as such included in the constitutional pact of 1917. Instead they appeared in that modifying successor of liberal pedigree under the general rubric of "peasants" and "communities" with rights to land. The national project of the new Mexican state, expressed in the official ideology of *indigenismo,* involved the assimilation and absorption of the indigenous in the Mexican, and the "citizenization" of Indians through public education, state protection, and economic development.

As is well known, the province of Chiapas was left at the margin of the Mexican revolution, not even experiencing a "revolution from without," as did Yucatán (Joseph 1982). The Obregón government entered into a deal with the local landlord oligarchy, lending its political support to the maintenance of the oligarchy's domination of peasant and Indian *pueblos.* For the Chiapan oligarchy, this deal was one more step in its history of "modernization" from above without the slightest change in social relations. Railroads, highways, investment, state administration—all were laid over obscure and violent servile relations maintained by force and by ignorance about the residents of the Chiapan countryside, negated not only in their condition as Mexican citizens but even in their condition as human beings (see, e.g., García de León 1985; Benjamin 1989). Chiapan reality continued to be immutably faithful to what was described by Rosario Castellanos in *Ciudad Real* or in *Oficio de tinieblas.*

17. See also Van Young: "The multivocality of the concept 'Indian' is turned at one and the same time to nation- or state-building, to the invention of tradition, and to the construction of an imagined community, while it is also employed to squash resistance to the state project and destroy a real community" (1994:356).

In a kind of suspended time, this reality reproduced colonial-period sociocultural relations of command/obedience within Chiapas even while its external appearance vis-à-vis the political system was that of the Republic. The situation of Indians during the liberal regime of Porfirio Díaz was not very different, as Eric Van Young described when referring to the doctrine of the "just war" against the Yaquis of Sonora occurring simultaneously with the installation of the monument to Cuauhtémoc on the Paseo de la Reforma:

None of this was new, of course, but stretched far back into colonial times, offering yet another in a series of continuities in Mexican cultural history. In the colonial period, Indians for the most part were viewed by those in authority not only as children of diminished intellectual capacity but also as ignorant, lazy, drunken, vicious sodomites naturally prone to suggestion, extreme violence, and religious backsliding. Nor did this complex of attitudes towards indigenous people have much to do with Enlightenment thought, with its mania for classification, though the Enlightenment may have laid an ideological patina over the basic conceptual arsenal. It goes back much further in the history of European-native encounter, finding its roots not only in the radical otherness of American native cultures in the eyes of the Europeans but also in the daily praxis of exploitation and asymmetrical power relations. Indeed, I am tempted to remark that the expropriation seems ontologically prior to the ethnic elements. (Van Young 1994:356)

It was against the crucial blindness of this "complex of attitudes" that the indigenous *zapatista* rebellion rose up in 1994. In declarations, gestures, spatial movements, clothing, attitudes, in a vast symbolic language directed to the rest but above all to their following, they made that point; and, if it were required, the rebels would not tire of repeating it. It was summarized in one word, *dignity*. Before proceeding further, let us try to see why.

After the revolution, exploitation and its corresponding forms of domination changed much less in Chiapas than the political and economic forms in which they were enveloped. But at least three processes occurred. First, Mexico was changing in its laws, its relations of power, and its modes of negotiating rule. Second, notwithstanding their outright rejection, Indian communities preserved their forms of internal relations—their offices, beliefs, myths, histories and, above all, their languages, their entire cultural universe—and put into place a determined constellation of forces and forms for their protected and continued use. Finally, between those two processes, a slow and unavoidable osmosis—however invisible and negated—took place, since Chiapas is in Mexico and not somewhere else.

In other words, the absence of the Mexican revolution, a "modernization" without social change, and the oft signaled "freezing" of the communities were real but not absolute. And if finally modernity burst onto the scene even more violently in the Indian rebellion of 1994, it was above all with that first demand, the strangest because the most universal and the most abstract: *dignity*.

This demand is invariably disconcerting and irritating to those who unlawfully retain power. They haven't a clue how to place it or understand it, never mind respond to it. How can one satisfy a demand if one understands neither what it is nor what the other means to say by it? Faithful to the dominant regime's system of beliefs, they essentially keep seeing Indians as they were seen in the time of Don Porfirio. Sometimes, not even people expressing solidarity with the rebels thoroughly embrace the demand of the latter, because their own experience is limited to an Enlightenment idea of the dignity of the individual (another idea not respected by the regime).

This other sense of dignity includes the dignity of the individual, but it also embraces a more ancient and more complex universe, opaque to the rational gaze of the Enlightenment but conserved alive and whole in the occult history and collective life of the communities, in their histories, myths, beliefs, and desires. It is this lived and inherited dimension, the communitarian idea of what it is to be human—which is to say, dignity as definitive of and inherent to the human condition—that nurtures the ultimate base of the moral economy of this and other rebellions of the oppressed: "perhaps an ancient fury / nameless generations / crying out for vengeance" as the song of Francesco Guccini says (Gilly 1980).

The Indian idea of community (territory, language, and history) is rooted "in the sacred order (of religious beliefs, symbols and practices) where dominion over a locality is anchored (the political structure and history of the place) and where its time (from 'immemorial times' to the historical present) is calculated" (Van Young 1995:164). This order is not egalitarian but hierarchical, as are the internal relations specific to the agrarian community that guarantee its subsistence and reproduction (Dumont 1980 [1966], 1985).[18] Respect for human beings is rooted in respect for this order, which defines the traditional norms of reciprocity, rights, and responsibilities within the community. Both the sense of dignity and those acts which negate it—humiliation, insult, affront—are lived in the same manner but have formed themselves in different worlds. It could be that the slogan of the Industrial Workers of the World at the start of the twentieth century explains this lived character better: "An injury to one is an injury to all."

It is in this feeling of injustice, of moral outrage demanding reparation from the heavens, that the roots of the rebellion of poor folk, whether urban or rural, are combined and nurtured. Barrington Moore recalls for us that

for this to happen, people must perceive their situation as the consequence of *human injustice: a situation that they need not, cannot, and ought not endure.* By itself of course such a perception, be it a novel awakening or the content of hallowed tradition, is no guarantee of political and social change to come. But without some very considerable upsurge of moral anger such changes do not occur. (Moore 1978:459; emphasis added)

In moments such as these, injustice is lived as the negation of dignity (whether individual or collective), as a threat to the essence of the human condition as each community or human being conceives or imagines it. And only then does the decision to risk everything, in rebellion against a "situation that they need not, cannot, and ought not endure," ripen in the consciousness.

It is always good to recall that the slogan of Emiliano Zapata and his Liberation Army of the South was not, as many have said, "Tierra y Libertad," but rather a slogan that came out of the history of the agrarian *pueblos* and their relation to power: "Reforma, Libertad, Justicia y Ley." It

18. See also Magagna 1991, which maintains that before class, community is the key to collective action in rural societies, even as the lines of conflict and cooperation are determined by whoever has the power to define the rights and responsibilities of the members of the community (p. ix). At the same time, rules of hierarchy and inequality based not in property but on status, gender, age, and office both exist and are necessary for the life of the community; these are compensated for by obligations of reciprocity. The community defends those rules and equilibriums as inherent aspects of their very existence and reproduction against external intervention (pp. 12–19).

was upon these ideas that the *zapatistas* constructed their government and legislation in the *pueblos* of Morelos.

Justice is the word on which all the others depend. The lived context— the *material*, if you will, of insult, reparation, and reestablishment of justice—appears to escape the notice of those who want to explain the logic of rebellion above all in terms of individual interest and the commercial reasoning of the modern world. They cannot comprehend that interest and reason in a world of collective solidarities are articulated differently, nor see the community as an intelligent and thoughtful whole, a totality; even less can they see religion—that millenarian incarnation of equilibriums and reasons to Be of the agrarian *pueblos*—as an instrument of legitimation of reason and interests.[19] Perhaps it will be to the sacred order, an order whose ultimate essence is to be found in notions of justice and injustice, that one must go to search for the point where finally that communitarian dignity and its secular, individual, and Enlightenment version are fused: a place crisscrossed by the secret passageway of coming and going between the enchanted world and the modern word.

There are few better ways to define the undefinable than simply to indicate it with a gesture. To know which "dignity" we are talking about, I can think of nothing better than to turn to Herman Melville:

Men may seem detestable as joint stock companies and nations; knaves, fools, and murders there may be; men may have mean and meagre faces; but man, in the ideal, is so noble and so sparkling, such a grand and glowing creature, that over all ignominious blemish in him all his fellows should run to throw their costliest robes. That immaculate manliness we feel within ourselves, so far within us, that it remains intact though all the outer character seems gone; bleeds with keenest anguish at the undraped spectacle of a valor-ruined man. Nor can piety itself, at such a shameful sight, completely stifle her upbraidings against the permitting stars. But this august dignity I treat of, is not the dignity of kings and robes, but that abounding dignity which has no robed investiture. Thou shalt see it shining in the arm that wields a pick or drives a spike; that democratic dignity which, on all hands, radiates without end from God; Himself! The great God absolute! The centre and circumference of all democracy! His omnipresence, our divine equality! (*Moby Dick,* chap. 26)

19. For an example of the trap that modern reason and the logic of the market sets for itself, see Lichbach 1994 and note 32 below.

In light of the concept of dignity being diversely defined, imagined, or perceived in distinct quarters, it would be a curious but significant development were the rebels to wind up negotiating with those in power. I suggest this in advance here, because it anticipates and explains part of what follows.

II

Jan Rus writes that for Mayan peasants of highland Chiapas the word "revolution" is unrelated to the revolution of 1910. For them, that was little more than a civil war between two dominant factions—one local the other central—for control of the region; peasants were excluded and mistreated equally by both factions (Rus 1994). For the Indians, the true revolution occurred during the time of President Cárdenas in the second half of the 1930s, when a partial agrarian reform, unions, and the abolition of debt peonage finally reached Chiapas.

The years between 1936 and the early 1940s are sometimes called the time of "the revolution of the Indians" (Rus 1994). This revolution was neither peaceful nor only made from above, because nothing ever changes that way. Some figures such as Erasto Urbina, a modest functionary of the *cardenista* government, were later local legends, leading groups of armed men who assured that a redistribution of lands and the application of legal dispositions were achieved *manu militari* (Wasserstrom 1983:162–69; Rus 1994:272–80). Maya Indians were finally included in the revolution: but really only as peasants and *ejidatarios,* less (or not at all) as Indians. The price of this limited inclusion was the subordination of the communities and settlements to the tutelage of the state, which is to say to a constitutive interchange with the Mexican state community; guardianship in exchange for protection.

The state successfully incorporated communities that had their own ancestral, corporatist traditions of social organization and politics, interlaced with community beliefs and religious offices. Out of this hybridization surged an unforeseen imbrication, different from that according to which the very same state had integrated other urban or peasant sectors. Jan Rus describes the result:

With the passage of time, it turned out that they managed to co-opt not only the native leaders who were their direct collaborators but also, ironically, the very community structures previously identified with resistance to outside intervention and exploitation: independent self-government, strictly enforced community solidarity, and religious legitimation of political power. As a result, by the mid-1950s, what anthropologists were just beginning to describe as "closed corporate communities" had in fact become "institutionalized revolutionary communities" harnessed to the state. (Rus 1994:267)

This incorporation, in turn, produced another result already known throughout Mexico: it converted the state into the peasants' primary interlocutor, to whom all their demands, expectations, and requests would henceforth be directed. In other words, it was no longer landlords but the state and federal governments that were left as the *true counterpart to the peasantry*. The strength of this corporatist paternalism of the state, however, which could convert the peasantry into its "favored children"—its *hijos predilectos*, to borrow a phrase from Arturo Warman—also turned out to be its weakness; for it was unable to rid itself of the stubborn and discomforting presence of the peasantry. In the years that followed, Indian communities in Chiapas, like *ejidos* and *pueblos* in other parts of Mexico, discovered not only the persons through whom to negotiate their relations with the national and local governments but, at the same time, a way in which to maintain their own customs and internal relations that would conserve rules of domination internal to the communities and at the same time be functional vis-à-vis the ruling state.

The key figure in this relationship was, of course, the local community leader, with one foot in the community and its "traditions" and the other in the PRI's system of negotiation and co-optation. His power as *principal* derived from the confidence the community conceded him as one of their own, capable of mediating with the outside world. This functionary, at the same time, accumulated income and privileges for himself and his family not always visible to the community, deriving as they did from the integrating and co-opting logic of the Mexican system of domination. The more he compromised himself with the state, the more he invoked his own "Indianness" and the defense of "Indian culture" (Rus 1994:293–300).

At the nexus between the peasant community cultures and their domination by the national state there appeared, as throughout Mexico, the well-known and irreplaceable figure of the *cacique*. In the case of Chiapas, though, the system of negotiation and mediation within which the *caciques* and "power brokers" operated assumed particular characteristics. First of all, the state's domination of the Indians remained based on the isolation and enclosure of the Indian communities, set apart from the national community by language and by the racism of the Chiapan ruling oligarchy (Gall n.d.:6; see also the "fictions" of Rosario Castellanos). The Mexican Constitution, which explicitly included peasants, did not cover Indians; they were excluded from the national community (see Knight 1990b).

Second, the modernization of the elite and the extension of investment and capitalist relations in Chiapas during the period of economic expansion between the Second World War and the late 1960s did not modernize the exploitation of Indian communities. The appropriation of their lands and the products of their labor, feudal subjugation and servile labor relations, and institutionalized repression remained as the methods for dealing with Indians.

Third, the specific form of the communities' subordinated absorption into corporatist relations "froze" those communities' internal social relations, thereby preserving them little modified and in community hands. This conservation, functional to the mode of domination and a "modernization" without social change, at the same time left the Indians in control of the beliefs, values, and hierarchies of their own world: a world apart, subordinated to, but neither modified by nor absorbed into, the political culture of the ruling regime.

For the Chiapan elite, the apparently closed character of rural communities was an inevitable result of the "backwardness," "ignorance," and "inferiority" of the Indians. In due time, as happened in so many other places, this secret world, invisible to the dominators, changed from a place of silent subordination to, first, a place of equally silent resistance and, later, to one of secret subversion accessible only to those belonging to that world. But, it turns out, there were tens of thousands who belonged to that world.

At the end of the 1970s, coincident in time with the national political crisis revealed in the student movement of 1968, a new period of struggle—this time against the *caciques*—started in the Indian communities, particularly among the Chamulas. Once again the response was repression, the expulsion of dissidents from the communities as "enemies of tradition," and finally the flight of thousands of exiles to found dozens of new colonies in San Cristóbal and in the Selva Lacandona during the 1980s (Rus 1994:299–300).

Also in the 1970s, a crisis was emerging within the Confederación Nacional Campesina (CNC), the national pinnacle of mediation between peasants and the state. Because the CNC was no longer able to fulfill its functions—since official resources earlier destined for the peasantry were drying up and/or being redirected toward private, commercial agriculture—this crisis was exacerbated (Harvey 1990). In response to this process in Chiapas (and other states), new independent organizations of *ejidatarios* and peasants formed, launching a struggle not only for land but also for credit, access to services, improved conditions for selling their products, etc.

The crisis of the old *caciques* and power brokers coincided with the appearance of new local leaders, shaped by the new forms of organization and interlocution with the state and its credit and commerce agencies (e.g., the Instituto Mexicano del Café, established in 1973), as well as through the direct presence of *ejidos* and unions of *ejidos* in the market, even as exporters of commercial crops. These leaders learned to take advantage of differences between national and state government policies and to move effectively within the dense tangle of state plans for selective credit, which had been designed in the first place to benefit above all private producers.

The deterioration of the old corporatism and the redirection of federal agencies toward a commercial economy and away from subsidies for the cultivation of maize and coffee were dissipating the old system of state protectionism, substituting for it a more commercial relationship with federal agencies. But this purported "modernization" occurred without any substantial change in the corporatist political structures upon which were based the domination and reproduction of the national and local political regime. On the contrary, under cover of and through traditional channels of the regime, a new alliance was developing between vigorous national finance capital and the old Chiapan ruling oligarchy, the two parties linked by their investments and interests in cattle, coffee, precious hardwoods, and construction.[20] Also during the 1970s, large oil reserves—one of the major inducements for the privatization of industry—were detected in Chiapas.

20. García de León (1994:26) mentions "modern interests of all kinds, especially a new group of agroindustrial impresarios linked to bank frauds, concessions to construction companies, banana production, and money laundering for drug traffickers of the new 'Southeastern Cartel' which embraced Veracruz, Tabasco, Chiapas, Campeche, and Yucatán."

Starting with the government of Carlos Salinas de Gortari, the "modernizing" governing group sought new sustenance and support from this type of regional and international alliance, utterly distinct from the old corporatist apparatus. Privatization of public companies, foreign investment, and entering into the NAFTA would complete the consolidation of a new leading elite in Mexico. This elite nevertheless preserved the old mechanisms of corporate political control and the federal government's monopoly of power through a single party, the PRI, whose dominance had been an unwritten law since 1929. The combination of economic liberalization without political democratization would turn out to be explosive.

Meanwhile, popular movements fighting for land in Chiapas were losing any chance of success thanks to the legal consolidation of the properties of landlords, especially cattle ranchers. The government of Miguel de la Madrid (1982–88) issued 2,932 "certificados de inafectabilidad de propiedades agrícolas" (75 percent of the total number of such certificates issued since 1934) and 4,714 certificates for cattle properties (90 percent of the total for the same period. The effective conclusion of land redistribution antedated by almost a decade its legal conclusion with the reform of Article 27 of the Constitution at the end of 1991.

At the same time, the government developed policies for the cooptation of local leaders and the insertion of new experts and "influential" brokers through its credit and marketing agencies. Some of these leaders, experts, and brokers came out of old leftist organizations from the 1970s, convinced that they were actually realizing the Maoist slogan "Serve the People" in the context of the era of the market. (Some of them, along the way, "served themselves" in that ubiquitous recycling of knowledges and sources of income.) Corporatism continued to demonstrate a surprising capacity for mutation as a way of guaranteeing its reproduction in a period of change while perpetuating itself as the unsubstitutable mechanism of the political regime.

But that mechanism could not erase the parallel innovations in popular organizational forms and the presence of new and active local peasant leaders. Chiapan peasants and Indians were involved in multiple forms of mobilization: marches to cities in the state and to Mexico City, vigils in urban plazas and outside public buildings, hunger strikes, demonstrations. A new and diverse panorama was "modernizing" social movement from below, in practice, and revitalizing its forms and autonomous decisionmaking.

The crucial point at which these movements converged and from which much of what followed took off appears to have been the First Indian Congress of Chiapas in October 1974, with representations of Tzotziles, Tzeltales, Tojolobales, and Choles. Also participating were catechists and deacons from the diocese of San Cristóbal, who brought to the Indians the influence of the church, and brought to the church the force of attraction of the demands, suffering, and exigencies of Indian religiosity. The state government initially supported the congress, but withdrew that support in the face of its radical demands and denunciations, later refusing to recognize it (García de León 1994:22).

Unforeseen and unplanned by anyone, a secret plot at the margins of a worn-out corporatism was constituting itself equally in ideas and modes of belief as well as in practices such as simply being together; discussing, organizing, making decisions. This plot was opaque and resisted penetration by the regime's mechanisms of domination, even as it was in friction and permanent engagement with those mechanisms. Although the word "autonomy" was not used, an effective autonomy from the state was forming itself within that hidden world—even less perceptibly because, from without, that world had to maintain relations and exchanges with its privileged interlocutor, the power establishment.

These factors contributed to the circumstance that the state's relations with the new peasant organizations were not determined in the first place by concessions (which in any event were exhausted) but above all by repression and growing official violence to contain popular mobilizations and prevent independent organization. The repression involved direct action by state police, the federal army, and the private armies (*guardias blancas*) of the ranchers and landlords, alongside the method of encouraging rivalries over lands and boundaries within different *ejidos* and communities or exacerbating internal conflict over religious questions or prestigious offices at the heart of the communities. Thus: "Since 1974 Chiapas is a region aflame and dislocated, even if during twenty years this little war has been silent and silenced. . . . This cycle was initiated in March of 1974, when 40 soldiers from the 46th Battalion torched the 29 hovels in the shantytown of San Francisco in Altamirano" (García de León 1994:21). During the years and governments—whether federal or state—that followed, repression never let up: 120 evictions in La Frailesca in 1976 (20 people wounded, 250 jailed); rebellion in Venustiano Carranza in 1976 (2 peasants and 7 soldiers dead, many wounded, 6 women raped, 13 *comuneros* jailed); in May 1977, detentions and torture of peasants in San Quintín in the Selva Lacandona by landowner-hired policemen, who later were ambushed and executed by the peasants; in July 1977, reprisals by the army far from San Quintín against 16 *ejidos* in Simojovel and Huitiupán, with children smothered in the attempt to escape and 2 Indian leaders thrown out of an army helicopter; in April 1978, the military eviction of Nuevo Monte Líbano, in the Selva Lacandona (years later the source of one of the first nuclei of the EZLN), with 150 dwellings burned to the ground, 2 Tzeltales killed, and 6 tortured; in 1980, bloody evictions in Soconusco and, in May and June, peasant land invasions of 68 fincas in Sitalá, Tila, Tumbalá, Yajalón, Bachajón, and Chilón.

The military offensive peaked in July 1980. Under the command of General Absalón Castellanos, who would be governor of the state between 1982 and 1988, the army attacked the Tzeltal settlement of Wololchán, in Sibacá. Twelve Indians were killed and their bodies were burned. Wololchán disappeared, erased from the map; its residents fled to other settlements or to the forest. Antonio García de León published the following story, told by an Indian who witnessed the killing:

And they used an apparatus unknown to me, a machine gun. A bomb goes off and explodes, and bullets are flying all over the houses. It's a terrifying thing, and that's how it went. We all said get out of here 'cos we weren't returning the fire. Some *compañeros* were left dead, a woman was left lying there. Many were wounded, even babies. Poor children and poor women: they came out of their houses like pigs, covered in mud . . . we were treated like vile dogs, and the landlords were right there. The agreement was clear, money gets what it needs, it was money that made the soldiers come to Wololchán. (García de León 1994:24)

"Money gets what it needs" says the Tzeltal, money "made the soldiers come." His reasoning is unequivocal: the law of the land is life, the law of money is death.

Between 1982 and 1987, according to Amnesty International, 814 peasants were assassinated in Mexico, most of them members of independent organizations. Seventy-five percent of those assassinations took place in states with a high Indian population—Chiapas, Oaxaca, Guerrero, Puebla,

Michoacán, and Veracruz—and high levels of agrarian conflict (Harvey 1990:192). The bulk of these crimes figure as part of a scheme of repression in which assassination or jail is used to selectively eliminate the most outstanding leaders of those organizations (for the period 1950–80, see Benjamin 1989:223–43). By the end of 1987, the picture in Chiapas could be summarized in five points: ranchers and landowners are better protected by the law and the government; official corporatism is in crisis; the independent opposition is growing; an Indian, not just a peasant, identity is a visible feature of that opposition; ceaseless repression is accompanied by a modernizing and paternalist language, what Thomas Benjamin has called "bloody populism."

For the majority of the 1 million Indians of Chiapas, the basis of their economy and their culture is access to land and the cultivation of maize and coffee. In 1990, 67 percent of the maize grown in *ejidos* and agrarian communities was destined for the market, and only 33 percent was used for subsistence. Of the 1,714 *ejidos* and agrarian communities extant in 1988, maize was the primary crop in 1,264 of them, coffee in 349. While these *ejidos* and agrarian communities comprised 41.4 percent of the workable land in Chiapas, 95.9 percent of those lands were rain-fed fields utterly lacking in capital investment and agroindustrial equipment (Harvey 1995b:211–37).

The withdrawal of INMECAFE from the market in 1989, the drastic contraction of credit from the state, the increased costs of production resulting from the overvaluation of the peso, and the 50 percent collapse of coffee prices on the international market provoked a disaster for the small-scale Chiapan coffee producers. Thousands abandoned coffee cultivation between 1989 and 1993.

A similar combination presented itself to the 2.5 million maize producers in Mexico (where 80 percent of *ejidatarios* cultivate maize) and, of course, to the 74 percent of *ejidos* and agrarian communities in Chiapas where maize is the principal crop. The World Bank's demand for the elimination of price supports combined with the threat of Mexico's impending entrance into the NAFTA to create an anxious situation. As is well known, the average yield of maize in Mexico is 1.7 tons per hectare, while in the United States it is 6.9 tons. The prospect of an end to price supports and the obligation to compete on the international market was a death sentence for maize cultivators in Chiapas.

III

Two events whose importance for Chiapas was not immediately evident to many occurred in 1988 and 1989.

In 1988 an opposition candidate, Cuauhtémoc Cárdenas, the son of General Lázaro Cárdenas, won the elections for the presidency of Mexico. The perception and conviction that that was the real result were generalized from the start throughout Mexico (Gilly 1989). In an outrageous act of electoral fraud, even in the recount, Cárdenas' victory was overturned to the benefit of Carlos Salinas de Gortari. That stain of illegitimacy on Salinas' presidency would never be erased and in the end was immensely destructive. Although the rulers didn't suspect it at the time, that stain would prove to be fatal to a state community so thoroughly constituted in history as is the Mexican one. At that point, the social pact had been broken. One of the evident political manifestations of the rupture was a subsequent increase in voter abstention and a general lack of interest in elections. Those who once were hopeful had, in the next moment, given up hope.

In 1989, Patrocinio González Garrido, outstanding exemplar of one of the ancestral lineages of the "familia chiapaneca" (his father, Salomón González Blanco, had been governor ten years earlier), was designated governor of Chiapas. Immediately he struck a deal that resulted in a fusion of the local oligarchy and the giant national financial interests that were linked to the Salinas government. The new governor continued the repressive policies of his predecessors and complemented them with the exertion of growing pressure on the diocese of San Cristóbal and its bishop Samuel Ruiz (Harvey 1995b:225–31). It is well known that in private meetings Patrocinio González would boast about having at his disposal his own private FBI. If asked what that stood for, he responded: "The state police: la Fuerza Bruta Indígena."

As the neoliberal turn of the federal government was accentuated, Secretary of the Interior Fernando Gutiérrez Barrios was removed from office in January 1992. A key figure in national security affairs for thirty years, Gutiérrez apparently was opposed to the modification of Constitutional Article 130 with respect to relations between the Catholic church and the Mexican state, and he was reluctant to go along with the wholesale aban-

donment of the postrevolutionary model of that state. His replacement
was laden with meaning for Mexico's destiny: Gutiérrez' successor was
none other than Governor Patrocinio González Garrido.

This change had at least three long-term implications, not apparent to
many at the time. First, besides weakening even further the nationalist
sector's links to the state apparatus, the government was left (*a*) without
Gutiérrez' critical personal knowledge in matters of internal security and
(*b*) without his ability and experience with respect to combining repression
with negotiation. Second, it strengthened the alliance of the federal government with the Chiapan oligarchy, whose most distinguished political
figure would assume the important post of secretary of the interior, responsible both for gearing up the machinery to win the presidential election of 1994 and for looking after internal affairs in Mexico during the
short period leading up to the implementation of the NAFTA on 1 January
1994. Third, and possibly unappreciated by everyone except for Chiapan
Indians and the movements in which they participated, Gutiérrez' replacement by González Garrido removed from Chiapas a key and well-
placed figure involved in the containment, destruction, infiltration, and
repression of the popular movements. Only the self-deception of suppos-
ing that their own backs were well covered could explain how the government made such a move as this.

Yet another event, though invisible to everyone except for the few participating, also occurred in 1988 and 1989. Formally established in November 1983, the Zapatista Army of National Liberation had about a hundred
members five years later and was totally unknown elsewhere in the country. After the electoral fraud of 1988, repeated in the 1989 state elections in
Michoacán, the EZLN's membership grew over the course of the next year
to some thirteen hundred people.[21] In retrospect, it is difficult not to see

21. Interview with Subcomandante Marcos, La Garrucha, Chiapas, 9 May 1994. In an
interview on 24 October 1994, Marcos gives more exact figures: "We *zapatistas* went
from being hundreds to thousands in a short time: I'm talking about one year, 1988–1989.
We went from being 80 combatants to 1,300 in less than a year" (Subcomandante
Marcos 1995b). By way of contrast, though, Marcos and his comrades did not at that
time detect any correlation between the theft of the elections in 1988 and their own
growth: "We didn't attach any value to the phenomenon of *cardenista* civil insurgence
and we saw it as a normal phenomenon. Only years later did we figure out how big it had
been and what an impact it had had in people's consciousness" (interview with Yvon
Le Bot, September 1996, unpublished).

the correlation between this unexpected expansion of EZLN ranks, the electoral fraud of 1988, the sharp expressions in the letters to Cuauhtémoc Cárdenas, and the armed seizures of town halls in Michoacán in 1989 to protest the latest fraud. They were indications of a change in the spirit and expectations of important sectors of the population.[22]

In these circumstances an important breaking point was registered in the development of nonclandestine peasant and Indian organization in Chiapas. Toward the end of 1989 the Alianza Campesina Independiente Emiliano Zapata (ACIEZ) was formed in Altamirano, Ocosingo, San Cristóbal, Sabanilla, and Salto de Agua. At the start of 1992 the name was changed to ANCIEZ by the addition of the word "Nacional" and the announcement of affiliates in six states of the Republic. In Chiapas it had extended its bases among the Tzotzil, Tzeltal, and Chol communities of El Bosque, Larrainzar, Chenalhó, Chanal, Huixtán, Oxchuc, Tila, and Tumbalá (Harvey 1995b:231).

At the end of December 1991, the state police dispersed a gathering of Indians in Palenque with the usual violence—clubbings, detentions, torture. These Indians were protesting against the corruption of their municipal presidents, demanding the construction of public works and distribution of land as promised, and expressing their opposition to the reforms to Article 27 of the Constitution. The state government invoked the 1989 reform to the Chiapas Penal Code as the legal basis for the police action. Articles 129 and 135 of the new Penal Code stated that participation in unarmed collective protests constituted a threat to public order punishable by two to four years in prison.

On 7 March 1992, the Xi'Nich ("ant," in Chol) march left Palenque for Mexico City. The 400 Indian participants arrived in the capital six weeks later, after securing the support of communities in Tabasco, Veracruz, Puebla, and Mexico State along the route they traveled. The Indian question and the repression in Chiapas finally made it into the national press. The federal government promised solutions, but failed to make good on any of its promises (Harvey 1995b:230).

On 12 October 1992, to commemorate five hundred years of Indian resistance in America, thousands of Indians coming from all the towns in

22. In my interview on 9 May 1994 (see note 21 above), Marcos commented after looking at the letters sent to Cárdenas in 1988: "They're the same as the letters now being sent to me." The displacement or bifurcation of expectations was evident.

the surrounding region—some witnesses say as many as 10,000—occupied the city of San Cristóbal in an orderly demonstration. The demonstrators roped the statue of the conquistador Diego de Mazariegos, founder of the Ciudad Real, and tore it down. As would later be seen in the taking of San Cristóbal on 1 January 1994, this was a kind of trial run. The thousands of Indians who later joined the ranks of the EZLN *guerrilleros* were, in large part, the very same group that had demonstrated on the quincentennial 12th of October. At the start of 1993, the ANCIEZ went underground.

In May 1993 there was an armed confrontation with the federal army at an EZLN training camp in the *pueblo* of Corralchén. Although the national press published the news, the government said it was unimportant and denied that there was any guerrilla activity. An image of prosperity and internal peace had to be maintained in order not to awaken worries in the United States and Canada or upset the still-awaited entrance into the NAFTA on 1 January 1994. It is logical to suppose that the governments of those countries were informed of the military battle through their embassies but collaborated in maintaining silence.[23]

The interested parties couldn't have done a better job if they had agreed in advance to guard the secret of what became the grand spectacle of the next New Year's Eve.

IV

On 12 October 1992 the fundamental elements of conflict that would be inaugurated on 1 January 1994 were already in place. The only thing lacking was a decision to launch a full-scale insurrection. That was the subject of discussion in the communities during the course of 1993, a discussion conducted according to forms and methods similar to those which Ranajit Guha describes for rebellions of agrarian communities in India.

Those elements were eight in number. First, there was the *affirmation in*

23. EDITOR'S NOTE: Dolia Estévez (1994:47) writes: "If the CIA was surprised at the New Year's Day insurrection, it was not from lack of warning signs. The first Mexican press reports on guerilla training camps in Chiapas appeared in May 1993, around the time Cardinal Juan Jesús Posadas was killed by drug traffickers in Guadalajara, Mexico. . . . All the major Mexican dailies and various European media carried the news [of Mexican army operations in Chiapas in late May, after it lost two soldiers in a shootout in the Chiapas jungle], but reporting in the U.S. was virtually non-existent."

practice and experience of an indigenous identity to organize the community and define its relations with the state and federal governments. This identity was a positive response to the exclusion of Indians, as such, from assuming their identity and rights as Mexican citizens. When going into combat, the first thing one needs to know is *who we are* in order to know who is the other.

The art of domination at the center of the corporatist pact in Mexico consisted always in erasing or dissolving this clear and coherent line of difference. Yet Indians, having been excluded from that pact, were moved to affirm their own identity in order to gain the power to subsist, resist, and persist. The dividing line was crossed from the other side.

When rebellions occur, one of the first preoccupations of the rebels is to affirm that identity:

The commanders and troops of the EZLN are mostly indigenous people of Chiapas. . . . We are thousands of indigenous people up in arms, and behind us are tens of thousands of people in our families. . . . Currently, the political leadership of our struggle is completely indigenous. One hundred percent of the members of the indigenous revolutionary clandestine committees in the combat zone belong to the Tzotzil, Tzeltal, Chol, Tojolabal, and other ethnic groups. It is true that not all the indigenous people of Chiapas are with us. . . . Nevertheless we are already thousands of people, and that must be taken into account. We use ski masks and other methods of hiding our faces as an elementary security precaution and as a vaccine against *caudillismo.* (EZLN 1994:74; STF 1995:57)

The second element was the *persistence of the ancient community,* its bonds and its beliefs. The "revolutionary institutional community," as Jan Rus calls it, was a method by which the corporatist state absorbed and put at its disposal the internal relations characteristic of the indigenous community. Nevertheless, controlling the indigenous community while at the same time excluding it does not dissolve its internal relations into those of the corporatist republic; it preserves them and, at base, ignores their otherness in the face of that republic.

When the period of independent organization began, these relations were an instrument of *autonomy* because they were *other* than those of the dominant and exclusive Mexican state community. This is an important factor that can help explain the paradox of a "mass conspiracy": tens of thousands of Indians who were able to secretly prepare the rebellion and conceal their intentions until the very moment at which they struck.

That said, I should reiterate the necessary methodological precaution of neither (*a*) falling into the trap of idealizing those internal relations specific to the agrarian world—which are by nature closed and hierarchical— as a new, universal model of "democracy" nor (*b*) being deceived by the old mirages of agrarian romanticism or Russian populism that have returned to dazzle ill-prepared commentators and recent observers.

The third element was *accumulation of collective experience* and the *formation of the indigenous communities' own leaders* over the course of at least twenty years of organization and mobilization of all kinds. Many such leaders were assassinated during those two decades. Those who survived were tempered through experience in the diverse arts and methods of organization and secured an indisputable authority among their people. In an interview in October 1994, Subcomandante Marcos discussed the EZLN's first guerrilla group (formed in 1984) and referred to these leaders, whose existence is evident through the simple recounting of the successive movements, in the following terms:

the comrades of the first group—the first Indian group, not the *mestizos*—were people with a high-level understanding of politics, very experienced in mass movements. They knew all about the political parties' disputes because they had been in all the political parties of the left. They knew well the insides of a good number of prisons in the country and in the state, torture and all that stuff. (Subcomandante Marcos 1995a:132)[24]

In Yvon Le Bot's interview in September 1996, Marcos would reiterate that the Indian movement in which he would become a part of the nucleus had two vertices: one, the Indians in the communities; the other, a group of local leaders ("a few, not even a dozen") who were

the organic intellectuals of those Indians, political activists of great organizational capacity, with very rich experience in political struggle, who were in practically all the political organizations of the left and knew all the prisons of the country. They

24. In the same interview, Marcos says that in 1984 there were six *neozapatistas* (three *mestizos* and three Indians), and that in 1986 there were twelve (eleven Indians and one *mestizo*) and then two more *mestizos* joined.

had figured that to address the problems of the land, living conditions, and political rights the only way out was violence.

Their existence and their presence constituted a political patrimony created and treasured by the Indian communities. They knew how to organize, how to mobilize, and also how to negotiate on the side of the communities, and had gained the confidence of the communities as a result of their actions. Their trajectory and formation provided a different, even opposed, group to the *caciques* and brokers of an earlier time, those formed in the integrating practices of the "revolutionary institutional community." Since the First Indian Congress in 1974, at least twenty years of indigenous movements had led to this group, which provided its own leading elite, linked to others who did not participate in the guerrilla movement but lived, as always, the quotidian life of the indigenous settlements.

Fourth element in our list is *relations with the Catholic church.* This process, which some have wanted to see as a conspiracy, turns out to be a natural product of the beliefs and spiritual necessities of the Indian population, one part of which expresses itself in the terms, symbols, and beliefs of the church.[25]

Anthropologists and historians have described and studied how Indians appropriated the religion of the conquistadors and dominators to their own ends, translating that religion into the symbols and language of their own ancestral beliefs. That religion was integrally absorbed by the conquered populations in such a manner that it effectively functioned over the long term as an ideology of domination and subordination. But when the time for *in*subordination arrives, the same ideology may take on another constellation of values also implied in it (if not, it would not have served to subordinate), giving rise to the Soldiers of the Virgen, the Talking Crosses, the Santa de Cabora, the catechists and deacons of the diocese of San Cristóbal, and even to Tatic Samuel as a key figure in the hour of mediation with the existing powers.

As General Plutarco Elías Calles knew well—having learned it from the *cristeros*—when the totalizing and protective ideology of a corporatist State

---

25. On 6 January 1994 the EZLN declared that it "does not have any connection to authorities of the Catholic church, nor to those of any other creed. . . . Those who fight in our ranks are primarily Catholic, but we are also people of other beliefs and religions" (EZLN 1994:74; STF 1995:57).

in Mexican territory begins to lose ground in people's consciousness, another protective, totalizing, and multisecular ideology borne by an institution different from the state (viz., the church) moves in to fill the void, as
much to conserve order as to encourage rebellion.

The fifth element was the appearance in the Selva Lacandona of a small
surviving nucleus of urban guerrillas who were by and large exterminated in
Mexico during the 1970s, namely individuals from the Ejército de Liberación Nacional (ELN), to which were added in 1983 younger people who
had not shared in the experience of the 1970s (among these, the present-
day Subcomandante Marcos). This nucleus was part of the founding basis
of the EZLN in November 1983.

The ideas of this group, ideas that time and experience would modify,
came from the ideology of Marxism-Leninism, the influence of *gueva-
rismo,* and the absorption of a complex of social and socialist ideas rooted
in Mexican history and the study of some of its texts, as would later
become evident in the names and symbols selected every step of the way by
the EZLN (*zapatismo;* the Convention of Aguascalientes; the state party; a
repudiation of dominant politics, expressed in terms closer to *magonismo*
and anarcho-syndicalism than to any other earlier currents; black and red
insignia; and the Mexican flag).

Marcos at least also brought his earlier formation in the academy, a
philosophical and historical education that would later appear with clarity
in his writings. That this nucleus was a fundamental element in the initial
logistics of what subsequently became an insurrectionary movement of
Indians is also obvious.[26]

The sixth element was the *gradual integration* of the nucleus from the
cities into the womb of the communities in a sincere process of adoption by
the latter. This process and its difficulties—a veritable *initiation* in the
classic sense of the word, with all its tests and phases—produced, as is
natural, a selection within the group and an assimilation and transforma-

26. In his September 1996 interview with Yvon Le Bot, Marcos says that until 1985 the
EZLN was a politico-military organization, "similar to the guerrilla organizations in
Central and South America," with ten to twenty militants and in which the ideas of
socialism, dictatorship of the proletariat, guerrilla *foco,* and prolonged people's war con-
verged. In their subsequent preparations for the war, he says, they were distancing
themselves from the "socialist camp" and finding out that "all the others" (especially the
Central American movements) were opposed to any group starting a guerrilla war in
Mexico, long considered a "strategic rear guard" for those organizations.

tion of its initial ideas under the influence of Indian thought and the experience of a life lived within its womb.[27]

The steps and stages of this always necessary ritual for the formation of a community of fighters are also identifiable, although this is not the place to go into them at length. In some of his letters and interviews Marcos has alluded to this process:

They . . . taught me how to walk, which is done in a certain manner, as they say. To walk in the highlands, to learn how to live there, to identify animals, to hunt them, to dress them, which is to say, to prepare them for the kitchen, is done in a certain way. . . . And to make myself part of the highlands. . . . I think that once I had learned that, I was accepted in the guerrilla group. Not when I was a teacher, when I came to give classes, but when I made myself part of them. This is the first stage, and a very difficult stage, very lonely. . . . For them, too, it was hard because they were away from their community. (Subcomandante Marcos 1995b)

Here Marcos restates, in Mexican terms, the earlier experience of peasant organizers who had come from the cities, in Vietnam or China, in Bolivia, Peru, or Guatemala. Two processes of obstinance are united: one centuries long, the obstinance of communities determined to persist; the other short, a decade long maybe, the obstinance of a few refugees from the 1970s. If you want to acquaint yourself with a fable of a similar encounter in sixteenth-century Japan, just watch Akira Kurosawa's *The Seven Samurai.*

At the other extreme, we have the seventh element: a *politico-financial integration* of the Chiapan oligarchy and what Antonio García de León calls the "Southeastern Cartel," on the one hand, and large financial and economic interests related to the policies of the government of Carlos Salinas, on the other. The symbol and token of this assumption of the "Chiapan family" into the heavenly heights of power is the exalted political position conceded to Patrocinio González Garrido in 1992.

Finally, in 1992 and 1993 two juridico-political decisions completed the framework of elements. On one side was the already mentioned reform of Article 27; on the other was the Mexican and U.S. congressional approval

---

27. "Our square conception of the world and of revolution was left pretty well beat up in the confrontation with Chiapan Indian reality. Out of the blows came something new (which is not necessarily to say 'good'), what today is known as *neozapatismo*" (Subcomandante Marcos 1995:22).

in 1993 of the NAFTA, which would go into effect on 1 January 1994.[28] The first decision deprived the peasants, among other things, of any basis of hope for securing legal access to land and opened the way for *ejidos* and communities to lose what land they had through sales or to cover debts. The second introduced the products of peasant labor, no longer protected by official support, into a market where the costs of production made it impossible for them to compete. In other words, as their land *entered* the market, they and the products of their labor were *expelled* from it.

In a single movement, the market threatened to carry off land and life. The rebellion invoked both of those reasons among its motives.[29]

V

The manner in which the indigenous communities made the decision to rebel merits its own section. Here the testimony is from Subcomandante Marcos. Between 1990 and 1992, he says, the *zapatista* army "made itself bigger, made itself more Indian, and definitively contaminated itself with communitarian forms, including indigenous cultural forms. The civilian population, the civilian authorities, in this case *zapatistas*, had total control of the territory. They are part of our organization, but they are civilians" (Subcomandante Marcos 1995b:140).

At the start of 1992 the state government's repression continued; the

28. There is a never-clarified disparity between the names for this document in English (NAFTA) and Spanish (TLC): North American Free-Trade Agreement or Tratado de Libre Comercio. "Tratado" (treaty) has a stronger connotation than "agreement" (*acuerdo*), and in diplomatic language the two words designate different things. What for the Anglophone world is merely an *agreement* is known as a *treaty* south of the border. It is difficult to imagine the political reasons why it was approved in the United States and Canada with the *weak* connotation and in Mexico with the *strong* connotation. Apparently no one was bothered by the disparity, and no one asked that the wording be coherent.

29. In its first sheet of demands, presented on 3 March 1994 at the dialogue with the government in the cathedral of San Cristóbal, the EZLN asked in point 7 for the "revision of the TLC signed with Canada and the United States, 'cause in its present form it does not consider the Indian populations and sentences them to death for not having qualifications to work"; point 8 says that the reform of Article 27 ought to be annulled, and "the right to land ought to return to our Magna Carta." Neil Harvey notes: "The rebellion of Chiapas revealed that the initial struggles for land and autonomy were still alive, but it also demonstrated the resistance to reforms that would toss the peasants out of the market and off of their land" (1995b:213).

modification of Article 27 was a watershed for the peasants. The *zapatista* civilians in the towns and villages started to let the military leaders of the EZLN know that "the people want to fight." The military leaders advised that the international situation—including in Central America—was not favorable to any attempt at revolution. To that, Marcos continues, the *zapatista* civilians responded with remarks like:

"I don't know, we don't want to know what's happening in the rest of the world, we are dying and you gotta ask the people. Don't you all say that you must do what the people say?" "Well . . . yes." "Well then, let's go and ask them."

And they sent me [Marcos] to ask around in the towns.

Yeah, I went to most of the *pueblos* to explain things. I told them, "Here is the situation like this: it's a situation of misery and all that; this is the national situation, and that's the international situation. Everything is lined up against us. What are we gonna do?"

They kept on discussing for days, for many days, until they took a vote and drew up the results that said: "So and so many children, so and so many men, so and so many women, so and so many say yes to war, and so and so many still say no." And the result, by several tens of thousands, was that the war would have to start, in October of 1992, with the quincentenary. (Subcomandante Marcos 1995b:140–41)

That 12th of October in 1992, according to Marcos, they went to the demonstration to issue "the last call for peaceful, civil struggle." After that, there were more meetings in the settlements, and in a recount done in November 1992 the decision to launch a rebellion was ratified.

In January 1993 the Clandestine Revolutionary Indigenous Committee (CCRI) was formed "to formalize the real power they had in the communities and the no less real subordination of the EZLN to the CCRI." The CCRI, whose members had the title of Comandante, then decided "It's time" and, according to Marcos, put him in charge of military command. Preparations went on throughout 1993 (Subcomandante Marcos 1995b:141).

This reconstruction of the sequence of events prior to the rebellion is based above all on the version given by Subcomandante Marcos and the *zapatistas*. We have to hope for or search out other sources, particularly the memories of the Indian participants, in order to corroborate it. Nevertheless the *zapatista* version, in my judgment, has the ring of truth.

First of all, the sequence of the decisions has not been disputed by opposed official versions, or by any others for that matter. Second, the form of the decisionmaking process corresponds, in effect, to the modes developed in agrarian communities when facing similar circumstances, as is corroborated by history, anthropology, and the accounts and life stories of those who at one time or another have taken part in the concrete organization of rebellions by subaltern communities, especially of miners and peasants. One of the finest studies of these processes of collective reflection may be found in Leon Trotsky's history of the Russian Revolution.

Third, the declarations by Marcos made at different times, taken comparatively, permit one to deduce this probable accuracy. In his account, Marcos says (1) that the communities had been inclined toward rebellion since 1992, under pressure of their own situation and perhaps also by the long wait; and (2) that the leaders resisted rebellion, preoccupied by an international situation that they saw as unfavorable while the communities were indifferent to it. This divergence between the communities and the leaders of the EZLN could have been invented or exaggerated by Marcos in order to underscore the popular or democratic character of decisionmaking in a movement "from below" or in order to counterbalance official accusations that the rebellion was the simple product of outside agitators "deceiving" or "manipulating" "the masses." Nevertheless, another declaration by Marcos, in a different context, serves to confirm the difference of perception between leaders and the communities with respect to the conditions for insurrection.

In his interview with Yvon Le Bot in September 1996, Marcos says that in 1988 the leaders of the EZLN failed to evaluate "the civil insurgency of *cardenismo*" and that only many years later did they realize its magnitude and "what an impact it had had in people's consciousness." Meanwhile, between 1988 and 1989, their membership increased from fewer than 100 to 1,300. As seen earlier, this growth in the EZLN ranks at that time, along with the subsequent disenchantment with elections in the face of fraud and the repression directed against democratic movements, could be considered symptomatic of how the "impact in people's consciousness" that went unnoticed by the leadership of the EZLN translated into practice.

There existed in that moment an unexplained difference of perception between the communities and the leaders regarding the new eruption of *cardenismo*. The communities lived and breathed *cardenismo* and registered it as part of their experience, in their familial and social contacts, in their everyday lives, in the specific forms of their imaginary, even if they did not translate it perhaps into the words of politics. The leaders, as a natural result of the mode of thinking necessary for their own struggle, perceived *cardenismo* as a new but predictable failure of "the electoral route," their perception being confirmed by their vocation: after electoral *cardenismo,* insurrectional *zapatismo* would follow. In any case, the reinforcement of EZLN ranks between 1988 and 1989 would tend to confirm that analysis.

Here two different (not necessarily contrary) ways of perceiving the crisis of the State intersect: that of the experience of the communities (and of the population in general) and that of the leaders and organizers of the revolutionary left. The communities perceive in *cardenismo* above all else insurgency, a rupture with the regime from below; they tend not to share the electoral and institutional preoccupations of the political leaders. Those Indians were in tune with the manner and mental universe of those who wrote letters to Cárdenas threatening to take up arms in 1988 and who in effect took up arms in Michoacán one year later. The leftist leaders see above all the limits of the *cardenista* movement: its encompassment within a legal and electoral framework makes it difficult to fathom the depth of the fissure opened from below in the national state community as it had constituted and consolidated itself since the 1940s.

The channels through which communities, on one side, and the leadership of the EZLN (or for that matter any other left-wing organization), on the other, get their perceptions of the surrounding society are not the same; nor are the filters and the codes according to which they are interpreted. This difference, invisible to all in "normal" times when the capital decision—insurrection—is not in play, comes to light at the moment of making that decision. For that reason, while some see in the "disappearance of the Soviet Union" a negative factor, others who are distant from that interpretation of an upheaval, regarding which they are not concerned, measure by other methods—against the arc of their own lives— the maturation of conditions for rebellion. It is here that the memory of the old-timers, as an indivisible part of collective thought, occupies the place that, in a political framework, would be given over to doctrinal or theoretical considerations. But when all is said and done, isn't theory a generalization of experience and, as such, of memory? And isn't an ancient memory therefore more reliable than a theory under pressure?

That having been said, it ought to be noted that, until the decision was made to start the armed rebellion, for the EZLN leadership it was not only logical but also, in a sense, necessary within its own legitimate categorical universe, to maintain its particular vision of *cardenismo* as a way to preserve and affirm the convictions and organizing forms that would prepare the EZLN to head the rebellion. And when that moment got closer, *la consulta*, "consulting the civilian following"—which does not exist in other types of organizations—appears to have been the effective instrument for correcting or equilibrating their perceptions and putting them in tune with different visions.

Only firsthand investigation with the protagonists and participants in the movement could give an extensive and precise account of these processes. That work remains to be done.

VI

On 1 January 1994, the rebellion was launched. The first response was an offensive by the federal army against the insurgents and the indigenous settlements in the rebel zone. Many people were killed, wounded, or disappeared. On January 10, Patrocinio González Garrido was removed from the Ministry of the Interior and the government named Manuel Camacho Solís as "Commissioner of Peace" vis-à-vis the Chiapan conflict. On January 11, feeling the pressure of massive popular demonstrations—especially in Mexico City—carried out under the slogan "Stop the Massacre," the government ordered a cease-fire. The army halted its advance and established a cordon around the *zapatista* zone; the EZLN was left in control of a portion of Chiapas. Toward the middle of February, a Dialogue for Peace and Reconciliation, with Bishop Samuel Ruiz of the diocese of San Cristóbal acting as mediator, was initiated between representatives of the federal government and representatives of the EZLN in the cathedral of San Cristóbal.

Significantly, the national government accepted what no other government would have tolerated: it entered into public negotiations with the leaders of an armed force who appeared with their faces covered by ski masks. No matter that the government had little doubt about their identities: weapons and ski masks, the symbol is what counts. Negotiating flexibility is one of the survival techniques of the Mexican State, alongside its repressive capacity.

At the opening of the dialogue on March 1, a list of demands was presented in the name of "the indigenous peoples of the state of Chiapas, risen up in arms." First the reasons underlying their rebelliousness are set forth. Written in the style of an ancient memorial of affronts, the document explains:

The reasons and causes of our armed movement are the following, problems to which the government has never offered any real solution:

(1) The hunger, misery, and marginalization that we have always suffered.

(2) The total lack of land on which to work in order to survive.

(3) The repression, eviction, imprisonment, torture, and murder with which the government responds to our fair demands.

(4) The unbearable injustices and violations of our human rights as indigenous people and impoverished peasants.

(5) The brutal exploitation we suffer in the sale of our products, in the work day, and in the purchase of basic necessities.

(6) The lack of all basic services for the great majority of the indigenous population.

(7) More than sixty years of lies, deceptions, promises, and imposed governments. The lack of freedom and democracy in deciding our destinies.

(8) The constitutional laws have not been obeyed by those who govern the country; on the other hand, we the indigenous people and peasants are made to pay for the smallest error. They heap upon us the weight of a law we did not make, and which those who did make are the first to violate. (EZLN 1994:178–85; STF 1995:156)

Then the document sets forth thirty-four demands, among them the following: truly free and democratic national elections; the resignation of President Carlos Salinas de Gortari; recognition of the EZLN as a belligerent force; political, economic, and cultural autonomy for Indian municipalities and communities; new elections in Chiapas; revision of the NAFTA/TLC; annulment of Salinas' revision of Article 27; hospitals and doctors in rural municipalities; the right to true information and "an indigenous radio station . . . directed by indigenous people and run by indigenous people"; housing, electricity, potable water, roads, sewer systems, telephones, transportation; free education from preschool up to university; official recognition of the languages of all ethnicities; respect for the rights and dignity of indigenous peoples, recognizing their cultures and traditions and agreeing that they may administer justice in their own communities according to their own customs and traditions; decent jobs; a fair price for products from the countryside and the cancellation of all debts; cooperative stores with fair prices; freedom for political prisoners; removal of the federal army and all police forces; indemnification for the damages produced in the days of war; revocation of the Chiapas Penal Code, which "doesn't permit us to organize in any way other than with arms, since any legal and peaceful struggle is punished and repressed"; the return of displaced peoples to the communities from which they were expelled by the *caciques;* and one special point with twelve specific demands from the "indigenous peasant women," including childbirth clinics, day-care centers, food for children, collective kitchens and dining halls, technical assistance for family farms, craft workshops, schools for women, and transportation (EZLN 1994:180–84; STF 1995:156–62).

Almost three years later, Comandante David would greet an international Peace Council delegation, guided by Bishop Ruiz to the hamlet of Oventic ("dignified heart of the *zapatista* Indians," David says). In his explanation of the uprising, David reiterated that its causes were

injustice, hunger, misery, marginalization, terrible exploitation, suffering, the death of our indigenous *pueblos* in Chiapas and throughout Mexico.

As for the genesis of the uprising, Comandante David said:

Indians have never lived like human beings . . . but the moment came when those very same indigenous *pueblos* started to make themselves aware of their reality by means of reflection and analysis, and also by studying the word of God, and thus they began to wake up. (Quoted in *La Jornada,* 21 November 1996)

It is not the purpose of this essay to relate what has happened since. Rather, a consideration of these antecedents will permit us in what follows to scrutinize some of their multiple meanings.

VII

The crisis of the Mexican state community and the crisis of modernization from above could explain the moment at which the *explosion* occurred. But it does not explain its *modes,* which must be sought in history, as I have tried to do. Neither does it explain the singular *reception* of this explosion in Mexican society, whether in the cities or the countryside.

In the first days of 1994, the rebels stirred up a growing movement of support and protection against the federal army offensive. This movement was not headed by any political party; it was initiated by social groups and organizations. The first party to join in was the PRD, with an extensive declaration on 5 January 1994 (*La Jornada,* 6 January 1994). There was a total absence of information in all television news and in the press subordinated to the government. However, some organs of information challenged the blackout and broke through—above all the national daily *La Jornada* (which in the three years following never stopped publishing all the documents and communiqués issued by the EZLN), the national weekly magazine *Proceso,* and the newspapers *El Financiero* (Mexico City) and *El Tiempo* (San Cristóbal). But that is not enough to explain the spirited courage and the movements through which a society, above all urban, managed to create an opening for a peaceful dialogue.

On the other hand, the rebels had risen up with an objective: to unleash a popular war and demolish the federal government. That's what they said, leaving no room for doubt, in their first communiqués. The opposite in fact occurred. Instead of advancing their troops across Mexico, in a short time the government and the EZLN had entered into negotiations, forced to do so because of the mobilizations, because it was an election year, because of the already extant crisis of national power scarred by its internal divisions, and finally because of the impossibility of finishing off the EZLN in a military offensive that would leave hundreds of razed *pueblos* in its wake and an unreachable group of guerrillas that, according to Mexican army estimates, could continue to operate for years from their places of refuge in the *selva.*

The EZLN had hoped that, after them, what were called in their documents the "basements" of society would rise up as well: the marginalized, the poorest of the poor, the excluded, the tens of millions of Mexicans—half the total population, at least—who lived below the official poverty line or were trapped in a life of extreme misery. Without a doubt, many of those people were sympathetic. But the people who mobilized themselves most effectively came from an intermediate sector: not only diverse social movements in Mexico City, but above all the urban youth, especially the students at the UNAM, the UAM, and other universities who later organized a permanent movement of caravans sending support to *zapatista* territory.

As they would declare some time later, this unexpected convergence of what they called "civil society" surprised the *zapatista* leaders and changed the direction of their plans, their objectives, and their strategy. That society did not hear the call to war. Indeed, it responded with its own call— for a truce, peace, and reason. At the same time, though, the rebellion was *adopted* and *protected* by that society, just as Marcos had been adopted by the Indian communities.

My purpose in this chapter is not to explain either the origins or the history of the EZLN; even less, its interior regime or the forms and methods of its relations with the communities, which for now remain opaque to observation from outside. Not even the (variable) numbers of indigenous Chiapan communities that are associated with, neutral toward, or opposed to the *zapatista* movement—though these, I suppose, are observable and quantifiable—are of any pertinence to my objective. I want in this chapter to explain the roots and reasons of the unforeseen and surprising convergence between a movement that declares a civil war and a society that rejects war, yet protects and legitimates that movement under a diverse array of forms and frameworks.

In the search for an explanation of this event, what is called for is to hold fast to the sense of a longer historical duration, rather than fastening onto the political conjuncture or the economic crisis. In my judgment, the historical dimension of Mexican experience, rather than the economy or politics, is the only one wherein one can account for what was unexpected to all of us: first the rebellion, later the convergence, and finally negotiation. To say it with the words of Enrique Florescano:

Reversing the interpretation of the past, which operates from the present, real history models the present from behind, with all the prodigious and multiform force of the historical totality: pouring over the present the multiple load of past sedimentations, transmitting the legacy of the relations and interactions of people with nature, prolonging fragments or complete structures of economic systems and forms of social and political organization from other times, introducing to the present the experiences and knowledges that people's work has been accumulating in the past. (Florescano 1980:105)

A dense and complex conjunction of factors can be taken into account to explain how this effect had operated in the indigenous rebellion of January 1994. What follows does not pretend to be an exhaustive enumeration.

(1) In a culminating *symbolic* gesture, the rebellion began with the entrance of several thousand Indians in military order headed by hundreds of uniformed, armed, and masked women and men into the plaza of San Cristóbal de las Casas, the old Ciudad Real. The image transmitted to the entire country, prior to any proclamation, was that this was an Indian rebellion. It was not a traditional guerrilla movement, it wasn't a *foco,* it wasn't even a mutiny or a disorderly agitation.

The power of this *image* struck with full force upon the historical memory of the country, the memory transmitted in families or studied in school. Indians, those about whom the urban society bore an ancient and unconfessed guilt, had organized themselves and risen up with weapons in their hands. The taking of San Cristóbal by an Indian army touched the historical memory of the occupation of Mexico City by the peasant armies of Villa and Zapata in December 1914. In a single blow the rebellion had *legitimated* itself before Mexicans, this in a country where even the history taught in schools says that the Republic was formed between and as a result of two revolutions of peasants and Indians: 1810 and 1910.

(2) The rebellion explained itself from the very first moment in a word. The very word "zapatismo" invokes national history and addresses the nation not in political cant but in terms accessible to all. The rebellion's right to invoke *zapatismo*—so many other times invoked from other quarters—was based in a fact: entire Indian communities had organized an army. And they affirmed that right through many gestures: for example, since 1993 dictating a body of "revolutionary laws" for their territory,[30] just as the Liberation Army of the South had done in Morelos. In a new way such gestures, tied to a reality and not to a text, address both the present and Mexican memory.

(3) If the rebellion is legitimate, the State ought not squash it, but should *negotiate.* One doesn't negotiate because one has the right to, but because one has the *force* to make that *right* be recognized. These ideas, too, are

---

30. These included the law of war taxes, the law of rights and obligations of the communities in struggle, the law of the rights and obligations of the revolutionary armed forces, the law of urban reform, labor law, industrial and commercial law, security law, the law of justice, and especially the law of women, where among others are established the rights of women "to decide how many children to have and care for," "to select their mate and not be obliged to be forcibly married," and "to occupy leading posts in the organization and to have military rank in the armed revolutionary forces" (EZLN 1994:36–48).

rooted in the common culture within which the Mexican state community has sustained itself, above all since the revolution of 1910 and its aftermath, the *cardenista* reforms. Of course that doesn't guarantee that a rebellion won't be repressed, and ferociously, as occurred many times before and since. But it does permit the State, when events or convenience oblige it, to *negotiate without losing face,* an inescapable requirement for a negotiation to be accepted by both parties. And it knows when public opinion demands truce and negotiation.

Just as the same historical experience teaches both parties, so does negotiation wear down the parties involved in it. If the process of negotiation results in demobilization, it is the party of order that wears down and subordinates the other. But if the opposite occurs, the party in rebellion can hope for a wearing out and crisis for the other. General Alvaro Obregón is the Mexican patriarch of that bit of wisdom.

(4) The demands of the rebellion, its eleven initial points, do not propose to subvert the Mexican state, but rather to replace the existing political regime and its economic policy with another. The rebels declared that their proposition was to *reestablish the Constitution,* not subvert it. They arranged themselves within the law, not outside it. Evidently, given the anomalous linkage of the state and a political regime entrenched in a state party that cannot be removed by elections, the rebel demands were unacceptable. But only by deed, not by right. In any case, in its most general terms the rebellion did not go beyond the margins of a "welfare state," with a democratically elected regime and an independent and reliable system of justice.

The centrality of the Constitution in the discourse of the rebel communities says much about the historical thread of that state community to which the rebels are demanding entrance as Indians with rights. All who had entered before did so by knocking down the doors, in the revolution of 1910 or in the 1930s. Considered together, though, even after a long negotiation the Indian's demands wound up revolving around a constitutional axis: the modification of Articles 4, 27, 41, and 115.

(5) The EZLN rebellion has aroused in Mexico an *Indian movement independent* of the government, concretized in October 1996 during the National Indian Congress. It also set off an unprecedented national debate about the Indian question, especially about culture and autonomy, stimulated by discussion sessions in Chiapas, involving participants from all over

the world, that went on within the framework of the negotiations between the EZLN and the government. This diversification and democratization of Mexican political culture is something new.

In the indigenous composition of its leadership, in the clothing worn by its Indian military chiefs during the negotiations, in its ceremonies, in its texts, in the constant use of symbols and meanings, in its references to time, to nature, and to human beings, the rebels recall and ceaselessly emphasize *Indian identity, history, and culture.*[31]

(6) First *zapatismo* and then the Indian movement that followed put the issue of *national identity* on the table during a period when that notion was (once again) the subject of debate, in light of the globalization of the economy, the entrance into the NAFTA, and the new integration with the U.S. economy and U.S. investment. From the start, it fought with the federal government for the symbols of the nation: the flag, history itself. The First Declaration of the Selva Lacandona, addressed to "the people of Mexico" and written in a style that does not appear to be Marcos', places itself from its first words as facing the national state in that *terreno primigenia:*

We are the product of five hundred years of struggle: first against slavery; then in the insurgent-led war of Independence against Spain; later in the fight to avoid being absorbed by North American expansion; next to proclaim our Constitution and expel the French from our soil; and, finally, after the dictatorship of Porfirio Díaz refused to fairly apply the reform laws, in the rebellion where the people created their own leaders. In that rebellion Villa and Zapata emerged—poor men, like us, to whom are denied the most elementary education so that they can use us as cannon fodder and plunder our country's riches, uncaring that we are dying of hunger and curable diseases, nor caring that we have nothing, absolutely nothing, no decent roof over our heads, no land, no work, no health, no food, no education, we do not have the right to freely and democratically elect our authorities, we have no independence from foreigners, we are without peace or justice for ourselves and our children. *¡Basta!* (EZLN 1994:33–35)

This "challenge from a time before" to the state by those whom the state excludes, this negation of its legitimacy by a prior legitimacy (of which the state cannot be unaware, since it includes Indian ancestry among its own

31. Luis Hernández, "El resplandor," *La Jornada,* 3 December 1996: "The Indian reforms [to the Constitution] suggest a new form of constructing the Mexican nation by recognizing that its constitutive principle is the Indians' *pueblos.*"

myths), and above all the fact of having issued the challenge and consummated the negation by employing the symbolic value of those state attributes which are a territory, a legality, and an organized army, puts the state on the defensive from the very start.

(7) The *communication* of the rebels with society becomes fluid: on the one side, thanks to the prior existence of an independent, democratic press that breaks the state monopoly on televised information; on the other side, thanks to the novelty of the language and symbols used by the rebellion in its communiqués. The rebels' extremely modern management of communication, as much in its substance (text and image) as in its media (press, video, Internet), takes the security organs of the state by surprise and they confess to not having been prepared for this type of assault, so different from a military challenge or the traditional propaganda of the left.

The EZLN has inaugurated a debate about discourse, within discourse and through discourse. In its language of modern images and ancient symbols, the rebellion does not propose a return to a past either distant or near. It suggests instead the possibility of a *nonexcluding modernity,* one that does not destroy history and those who carry it with them but, rather, integrates them into a reality where none are excluded. This idea of a diverse and inclusive modernity is a strong theme that is entwined in the discussions and culture and community shared by intellectuals, writers, and diverse sectors within and without Mexico. To that idea must be assigned a part at least of the international resonance of the movement.

In this singular combination of ancient myths, mobilized communities, clandestine army, *golpes de escena,* literary resources, and political initiatives, the figure of the military chief of the rebellion, Subcomandante Marcos, is immensely important. That much is certain. But that should be the theme of another study, one that ought not to wind up obscuring, as it so frequently has, the *material, human, and historical substance* of this rebellion: the *indigenous communities* and the *Indian leadership* of the movement, without which the combination mentioned above would be impossible. The chief merit of Marcos, if it were necessary to assign one, would thus be that he knew enough, first, to comprehend and assimilate that substance and, then, how to be the mediator or the guide through which its image is transmitted to urban society.

In the early 1980s, a student in the School of Philosophy and Letters at the UNAM, one Rafael Sebastián Guillén Vicente—to whom, according to the government, corresponds the prior identity of Subcomandante Marcos—cited a passage from Michel Foucault's *The Order of Things* [*Les mots et les choses, El orden del discurso*] at the beginning of his *licenciatura* thesis: "Discourse is not simply that which translates struggles or systems of domination, but that for which and by means of which struggle occurs."

The Indian rebels' dispute with the national state started with the oc-cupation of a *physical space*. It wound up growing into a dispute conducted in multiple spaces: *political* spaces, *symbolic* spaces, and *discursive* spaces, inside and outside Mexican territory.

A singular perceptiveness, that of the student.

3. The Obsidian Mirror

I

To explain the encounter between the rebellion of the Indian communities and Mexican society, I have searched for their *common roots* in history and their *shared reasons* in the present. I have tried to specify who speaks through rebellion: the Indian communities. The next questions are: From where do they speak? To whom? And what does their rebellion speak about?

There is a broader dimension to the unexpected repercussions of this movement, what could be called the cultural dimension. The Indian re-bellion has touched the crisis of the Mexican state community, but at the same time it has struck a more universal chord: the crisis of the values and rationality of modernity that the state invokes. In a sense, it has touched the point where the state community in crisis and its historical-cultural construction intersect.

One preliminary clarification. In a general sense, the term "culture" is being used here to indicate the context within which human beings give *meaning* to their actions and experiences and *sense* to their lives (Tomlin-son 1991:7). But the culture concept does not allude only to meaning as subjective experience; it includes as well the practical activities (actions and experiences) in which meaning and sense are constituted and modified. According to this concept, culture may also be seen as a material force present in society (Roseberry 1989:195).

In this expanded sense, the conformation in history of a state commu-nity (Mexican or other) is a cultural construction. Borrowing a phrase from E. P. Thompson, Philip Corrigan and Derek Sayer proposed as an image for this process in England a "great arch" constructed over centuries through the uninterrupted interaction between conflict and consensus. Modern capitalist civilization, they say, is also a cultural revolution, "a revolution as much in the way the world was made sense of as in how goods were produced and exchanged" (Corrigan and Sayer 1985:1–2).

The conformation of the modern state community is the result of that cultural revolution, and this conformation is constituted in a relation of domination/subordination between the superior community (dominators, rulers) and an inferior community (dominated, ruled). The relation is not a dyad, though, as suggested by the two terms, but rather a triad. For both parties, domination and subordination are active relations; between each, molding the one and the other, is interposed and exists a third term, *resistance,* the active part *par excellence,* the most-of-the-time invisible element of the relation in its entirety.

Resistance, it goes without saying, has a place within the ideal and cultural hegemony of dominators over the dominated. Resistance is not an activity that takes place outside a given hegemony but within it, thus influencing the form hegemony assumes (see Roseberry 1994; Sayer 1994). For this very reason, it can and does affect major or minor, visible or subtle displacements of meaning within the hegemonic culture, in which dominators and dominated each have their own discourses and "hidden transcripts" (Scott 1990:intro.).

The common culture shared throughout the historical state community is defined by the form of domination; *to define* is its necessity and its prerogative as domination. But although defining is an attribute of hegemony, it cannot by its own definition ignore counterhegemonic pressures and cultures. As Corrigan and Sayer put it:

The "same" unifying representations from the perspective of "the State" may well be differentially understood from "below." Examples we will encounter include notions of "English" "liberties," or "democracy," or Protestantism, all of which are sites of protracted social struggles as to what they mean and for whom. We should not, in other words, take the state's statements at face value. (1985:6)

Mexican examples of such unifying representations encountered above include Article 27, "land," "zapatista," and, for that matter, "revolution."

The Mexican state community does not ignore counterhegemonic pressures and cultures: it integrates them and, in that very movement, negates and trivializes them. It is the existence and reproduction of hegemony that forms the ideology of the Mexican revolution as response and antidote to a culture of rebellion. Yet, once more, however much this ideology trivializes rebellion, it is unable in principle to delegitimize it. Rebellion is this ideology's force in times of peace, its flaw in times of conflict; it is, finally, what provides ideological sustenance to its art of negotiation.

In this process, oppositional cultures are classified as epiphenomena or curiosities within the ruling idea of a not very well defined "national culture." As Corrigan and Sayer observe, when not marked as dangers to "social health" they are situated as local, archaic, antiquated, vernacular, bad habits or residues that "modernity" (or "progress," in the positivist or Stalinist version) will dissipate: "objects, at best, for a patronizing sentimentalism and nostalgia" (Corrigan and Sayer 1985:7).

Corrigan and Sayer signal how a regulation of relations within the community is inscribed through a definition of meanings by the state:

We call this *moral regulation:* a project of normalizing, rendering natural, taken for granted, in a word "obvious," what are in fact ontological and epistemological premises of a particular and historical form of social order. Moral regulation is coextensive with state formation, and state forms are always animated and legitimated by a particular moral ethos. Centrally, state agencies attempt to give unitary and unifying expression to what are in reality multifaceted and differential historical experiences of groups within society, denying their particularity. The reality is that bourgeois society is systematically unequal, it is structured along lines of class, gender, ethnicity, age, religion, occupation, locality. States act to erase the recognition and expression of these differences. . . .

. . . collective representations . . . are simultaneously descriptive and moral. Typically they present particular moral orders as description. . . . The moral discipline effected by state formation is therefore not, neutrally, about "integrating society." It is about enforcing rule. (1985:4, 6)

The particularity of *zapatista* discourse is that it questions moral discipline and definitions from the standpoint of another ethic and of other definitions based in societies neither "anterior" nor passed over but, instead, alive and living within Mexican territory. From that position, Indian communities cannot accept taking themselves as "the past" of Mexican society's present, nor even that present as the future that awaits them;

rather, they are different, and theirs is another life with its own modes of defining the world and society. This position enters forcibly into conflict with the presentation by the state of its own moral order of domination as though it were a simple description of what is.

In questioning order, discipline, and rule, certain constitutive attributes of a national state community are thrown into question. This questioning occurs when there is a crisis in the relation of command/obedience in the state community, which, without engendering it, legitimates the interrogation. Above all, a wide and theretofore nonexistant space for questioning both to manifest and unburden itself is opened up. Then the Indian questioning comes along to act on that preexisting crisis.

In the negotiations between the government and the EZLN these antagonisms present themselves in forms apparently distant from the subject of debate between the two sides. Discussions about the definition of *dignity* or the concept of *time* (and the insistence on an "Indian time" or a "Southeastern time") have the same root and the same meaning. Far from being trivial, anecdotal, or tactical, they have to do with the question of *who defines* and *for whom are defined* the universal concepts that make up the essence of human beings and their relations to nature.

The ideas expounded by the indigenous leaders are not some creation of the spirit; rather, they are distant but still living fruits of what Guillermo Bonfil called "a negated civilization," a civilization negated but never erased (Bonfil 1991). That is neither to idealize nor to judge this civilization; it is simply to try to detect the persistence of its tracks in the souls of people for generations educated by or subordinated to the ideology and religious representations of the dominant culture, souls wherein these tenacious tracks reappear time and time again. This rebellion introduces something new into Mexican political culture, formed as it was in the *criollo* and *mestizo* dispute between conservatives and liberals from which Indians as such were excluded. In the rebellion, Indians reclaim the right to be *citizens* (which supposes a sort of republican equality in the context of a single collective identity) and at the same time *different* (which supposes a plurality of collective identities within a republican equality).

As has been demonstrated, the Indians' right to plurality is underscored in clothing, symbols, gestures, discourses, and modes of directing themselves to power and to society that do not negate that society (as did the anarchist, socialist, or communist symbols and discourses) but, rather, invoke the rebels' persistence from an earlier time: a time that has arrived until today laid across the time of the society that negates them; a time that is not counterposed to another to substitute for it, but that refuses to be erased and made to disappear into that world (see Dumont 1980:xxix).

The right to name, to order, and to define is the ultimate basis of the dispute. That implies an *ethical* dimension, a *critical* dimension, and a dimension of *modes of knowledge*. It implies verbalizing—and organizing— opposition and resistance to the existing form of domination, not only to its political regime. Further, it implies carrying it out not only theoretically but in terms of a *social practice* that wants to make itself different, even as it formulates itself in the terms of the dominant state hegemony: nation, flag, democracy, Constitution.

Once again, the terms in which that right is formulated obey rules that are shared, albeit in diverse senses, by both sides. A dominant ideology, as the support of a hegemony, consists in precisely this. This common language, setting aside the different baggage of meaning for each side, is at the same time the vehicle for dialogue. In essence, this is not new; what is new is the connection between the novelty of the form and the antiquity of the roots. Corrigan and Sayer write:

State formation is something that has ever been contested by those whom it seeks to regulate and rule. It is, first and foremost, their resistance that makes visible the conditions and limits of bourgeois civilization, the particularity and fragility of its seemingly neutral and timeless social forms. This applies as much to "the State"— the form of forms, *the* distinctive collection (mis)representation of capitalist societies—as elsewhere. *Such practical criticism is a form of knowledge, and like all knowledge, inseparable from its forms of production (whence derived?) and presentation (how said and shown?).* It is also, profoundly, a *moral critique:* what such struggles show again and again is the exact ways in which the regulated social forms of bourgeois civilization effect real, painful, harmful restrictions on human capacities. Such "general knowledge"—disarmed by legitimate disciplines, denied by curricular forms, diluted in its being refused the accolade of scholarship, dissipated as "empirical examples" in a thousand doctoral dissertations—is the "classic ground" for an understanding of bourgeois civilization that does not simply parrot its "encouraged" self-images, as well as for any feasible or desirable social transformation. (Corrigan and Sayer 1985:8–9; emphasis added)

I have thus far tried to elucidate whence the rebellion of the *zapatista* Indians speaks. Now we can consider of what it speaks and who is speaking.

II

Societies based on relations of personal dependence, which is to say all societies prior to modern society, regard themselves as part of the natural order. In their imaginary, their social relations reproduce the principles of the world and of life. The order of the sacred and of the gods are there, whether the Holy Apostles or the Stones that Talk or the Men of the Night. Modernity conceives itself as a radical break from that order. Its defining features are the disenchantment of the world, the quantification of the world, the mechanization of the world, rationalist abstraction, and the dissolution of communitarian social bonds (Löwy and Saury 1992:46–64).

Modern society pretends to be rational or aspires to be so. Reason will be the norm of an autonomous human order different from the natural order. The individual is the measure of humanity, and from the individual the human order is deduced. In this manner of imagining society and the world, the historical past is only a long prelude to the present; in other words, to the modern world of commodity exchange and universal relations between things as the substance of exchange between human beings.

Somewhat differently, Louis Dumont has declared that rather than the counterpositioning of "rationality" to "irrationality" or a succession in which the former slowly and gradually occupies the place of the latter, what is instead entailed is the confrontation or superimposition of two different rationalities, of two diverse modes of making sense of society and the world:

As against societies which believed themselves to be natural, here is the society who wants to find itself to be rational. Whilst the "natural society" was hierarchized, finding its rationality in setting itself as a whole within a vaster whole, and was unaware of the "individual," the "rational" society on the other hand, recognizing only the individual, i.e., seeing universality, or reason, only in the particular man, places itself under the standard of equality and is unaware of itself as a hierarchical whole. (Dumont 1980:261)

Some societies have not arrived at the point of originating the individual; they cannot perceive it in their womb. Modern society, by way of contrast, recognizes only the individual as the subject of reason. This ancient quarrel was inscribed in the language of New Spain: there existed "gentes de razón" and "naturales," it was said, and the same is said today in the province of Chiapas. But modern society is incapable of recognizing the new hierarchies surging from its womb; moreover, it supposes that they are residues of the past without inspecting the modern hierarchical order hidden in money and power. Modern society is capable of seeing the imaginary character that governs social meanings in so-called traditional cultures, in their beliefs or religions; but, assuming for itself a total rationality, it tends to ignore or negate the powerful imaginary nucleus of its own culture (Castoriadis 1987).

In the real life of our day, these two visions of the world are contemporaneous, not successive. "Traditional" societies, crisscrossed and penetrated by the relations of the modern world, remain present in every corner of the planet. In all extant national communities, with the possible exception of the United States, this crossing has given rise to hybrid tones different in each instance: in India it's one thing; in Mexico and Mesoamerica another; in China yet another; in eastern Europe still another, for there the peasant grandfathers are almost silent yet they keep on talking, or so it appears, in the raw material out of which are made the dreams of every solitary individual. Hybrid tones are manifest as well in the diverse flavors of the cheeses from every corner of France and the wines of every village of Italy.

If this is true, we cannot think about the globalization of communications and exchange as a linear and successive process; rather, it presents itself as an arborescent reality in which the unlimited hybridization of both worlds continues unrelentingly. The modern world subverts and disintegrates traditional societies. But in the process of doing so, it interiorizes them as well, unknowingly receiving their practical and silent forms of critique; and this presence alters the modern world's manner of being. Combat, conflict, and suffering preside over this blind, unequal, and (today) universal process. Still, this can hardly be different from the ancient world's absorption of Oriental civilizations and religions, including among others that strange Jewish sect of Jesus Christ which, from out of the Orient, has managed to reach even the province of Chiapas and its diocese of San Cristóbal. What the results of that process will be, for that very reason, are unknown and unforeseeable.

This *compelling totality of the modern dimension,* visible to all in regard to economic relations, appears to be invisible in its cultural and imaginary dimensions, above all to those who consider it from countries where capitalist exchanges and institutions are most dense. Such a gaze tends to see the dimension of modernity country by country or region by region, as though it were a destiny or a goal to which all others ought to aspire, and not a *global reality* which, like the economy, everyone is obliged to take account of and regard as it is: hybrid, changing, confused, and turbulent. What are the great migrations from poor countries to Europe and the United States in search of the utopia that this modernity has postulated if not modernity in culture? (Gilly 1996).

In the same way, once set in motion or awakened by events breaking outside the frame of a "national modernity" (a contradiction in terms), in determined moments the "thirst for community" or the nostalgia for "community" as distinct from "society," without aspiring to replace but rather to contaminate the latter, makes its appearance in unforeseen places with no advance notice. This we could call the invisible presence of the enchanted world from within, from below, and across a globalized modernity.

Since its origin in the Spanish conquest, Mexico has been the fertile ground for a hybrid culture in which at each moment of its history both worlds have been crossed with each other, confused with each other in different combinations. Over this fractured world is constructed a good part of the fecund work of Octavio Paz, and it is perhaps the original source of his poetry. André Breton alluded to it when he called Mexico "the land of choice for surrealism," that movement of ideas about modernity that proposed at once to criticize it, move beyond it, and reenchant the world.

In this strange country, placed on the frontier with and living under the permanent influence of the United States (land of choice for modern instrumental reason materialized in the transparency of commercial exchange), the elaboration of this fractured world and its hybrid result becomes even more complex. Mexico is a modern Western country of 100 million people, most of them urban and educated—in Monterrey, Guadalajara, Mexico City, Tijuana—where still to this day behind every tree, just beyond every hill—right there—in the church in every town or neighborhood, in Saint's Day festivities or on Days of the Dead (whether *El Día de los Muertos Chiquitos* or *El Día de los Muertos*), one still encounters the enchanted world.

The initial theoretical and political baggage of the EZLN left that enchanted world invisible. But by reason and by choice, by recovering its Indian voice it was able to speak from behind, from that world, and at times with the words of that world:

In our heart was so much pain, so much was our death and suffering, that it didn't fit, brothers, in this world that our grandparents gave to us to keep on living and struggling. So great was the pain and suffering that it didn't fit in the hearts of some, and it spilled out, filling the hearts of yet others with pain and suffering, and the hearts of the oldest and wisest in our *pueblos* were filled, and the hearts of young women and men were filled, all of them brave, and the hearts of the children were filled, even the littlest ones, and pain and suffering filled the hearts of the animals and plants, filled the hearts of stones, and all of our world filled with suffering and pain, and the wind and the sun were in suffering and pain, and the earth too. Everything was suffering and pain, everything was silence. (EZLN 1994:118–20)

It would be erroneous to attribute this style of speaking to the literary formation of Marcos. This text, the same as many others, is directed in the first place to Indian communities and would be assessed by them in their own cultural and political terms.

This document is a letter to the Consejo 500 Años de Resistencia Indígena, in the state of Guerrero, and its language alludes to an ancient way of speaking the world:

We speak with each other, we see inside ourselves and we see our history: we see our oldest fathers suffer and struggle, we see our grandparents struggle, we see our parents with fury in their hands, we see that not all of us have been defeated, that we have the most precious thing, what makes us live, what makes our step lift over plants and animals, what makes it so that the stone will be under our feet, and we see, brothers, that it was DIGNITY that we had, and we see that it was a great shame to have forgotten that, and we see that dignity was good so that people could again be people, and dignity came back to live in our heart, and we were still new, and the dead, our dead, saw that we were still new and they called us, once again, to dignity and to struggle.

The voice that writes continues talking between religion and myth, between affront and pride, between supplication and communion ("Don't abandon us brothers, drink our blood as food"):

We leave behind our lands, our houses are far away, we leave everything and everyone, we take off our skin to clothe ourselves in war and death, we die in order to live. Nothing for us, everything for everyone, what is ours and our children's. Everything we leave.

Now they want us to go out alone, brothers, they want our death to be useless, they want our blood to be forgotten between rocks and humus, they want our voice to be shut up, they want our footsteps to go back to being distant.

Don't abandon us brothers, drink our blood as food, fill your hearts, you and all the good people of these lands, Indians and non-Indians, men and women, old folks and children. Don't leave us alone. Don't let this all be in vain.

That the voice of the blood that united us when the land and the skies were not property of the powerful call to us again, that our hearts beat together, that the powerful tremble, that the hearts of the small and miserable be made happy, that the forever dead have life.

Don't abandon us, don't leave us to die alone, don't leave our struggle in the emptiness of the powerful.

Brothers, let our struggle be the same for all of us: freedom, democracy, justice.

I have quoted from this document at length because the evidence is in the very text itself. One could multiply the examples manyfold. This discourse speaks from the *imaginary* and the values of the enchanted world, a world extended and reiterated in gestures and symbols: masked figures, warriors, clothing, fog, forest, stories of the night and nocturnal ceremonies.

III

The discourse of the Indian rebellion has specific audiences: in the first place, the very communities themselves, in which a sense of recognition gives sustenance to the discussion; second, Mexican society, where unexpected resonances are found; third, the government and institutions of State; and, finally, the outside world. The variations and emissaries (the Clandestine Revolutionary Indigenous Committee or Subcomandante Marcos) of the discourse adjust themselves in every instance to each of these various audiences or to all of them.

When Marcos addresses the government, the dividing line is marked by sarcastic and insolent language. Sarcasm directed toward those from above forms part of the *ethic* of rupture involved in a rebellion embodied in its language. In Marcos' letters and stories, by way of contrast, the language is personal, even colloquial. His imagery (night, moon, water, death, storm, fire, obscurity, threat) has a romantic streak. The style could easily be situated within what Michael Löwy calls a "romantic modernism," conceived as a critique from the present not of modernity as such but of a "*social* modernism," of a modernism that dissolves human values and social bonds not quantifiable in monetary terms.

These romantic traits turn out to be even more notable if one recalls that the original political and philosophical formation of Marcos is far from those Marxist currents related to a revolutionary romanticism (E. P. Thompson, William Morris, certain visions of the young Marx and the late Marx) and in fact—a point proved in some of his statements (e.g., Subcomandante Marcos 1995a)—closer to the structuralist school of Louis Althusser. Nevertheless, his thought and its evolution too have become hybrids to which, as Marcos himself says, the forest, the Indians, and "the men of the night" have brought ambiguous and nocturnal images. But neither can one exaggerate the presence of romantic motives, generated in certain ways by some of his followers. At times Marcos' texts ostentatiously wallow in an animated melancholy—which is destroyed in the next paragraph with irony. That game repeats itself; and the only point of demonstrating melancholy is to make fun of it or to convert it into a vehicle against the instrumental reason of impressionable souls.

Very different is the language of the CCRI, whether or not written by the same hand. The Indian leaders are bilingual or multilingual. They speak Spanish and one or another of the indigenous languages. If you correlate their initiatives with their discourse, their words with their silences, one sees that in those discourses, according to the occasion and to whom they're addressed, they effect slight or brusque *displacements* between rationalities, or between the forms reason assumes in the different languages and worlds moved by the discourse. These displacements can be disconcerting for the unprepared listener, who tends to see in them defects of reason—confusion or falsity—rather than the very effect desired by the ordering of the discourse. Those displacements also have a simultaneous place in the various voices that speak from the standpoint of the EZLN: from the communiqué with an address to the story and the personal letter; from the voice of the CCRI to the voice of Marcos to the voice of Old Antonio, a key figure when it comes to getting advice, wild tales, insinuations, and suggestions.

This displacement of discourse between rationalities, languages, and different times produces the effect of a sought ambiguity—once again, romantic—that protects the speaker, disconcerts the hostile listener, and leaves the sympathetic listener open to multiple possible interpretations; which is to say, able to adjust the meaning to their desire. This ambiguity could be seen as a vehicle of manipulation. In any event, it is not the language in which orders may be given. For orders there are other channels and military forms in the army that is also *zapatismo*.

A soldier is a will. A will cannot surrender to conditions or feelings of the soul. Evidence and declarations prove that that will is decisive and that in the will of the leaders is a military discipline, not melancholy or like the beings of the night or the communion of souls—a misleading and dangerous twilight if taken at face value. The EZLN is an army and lives according to its rules; its spokespersons do not tire of repeating so to those who care to listen. In the modern world of its followers, all the same, many don't want the twilight, enchantment, and communion to disappear. At the moment of reason and truth, which in struggle and conflict always arrives, illusion will make them pay the price.

The discursive displacement, further, moves with a temporal displacement. The Chiapan conflict takes place in a "right now"; *zapatismo* legitimates itself in a "back then," a "time before." The communities live these two times as the timelessness of *myth*. Time and again the discourse takes up these timeless myths as the sign of identity of the communities. This mythic thought is not a literary recourse or a nostalgic romance about the past. It exists—it lives—in the Indian community, inextricably woven into the rationality with which that community has to confront the world of the state and the market.[32]

Displacement and ambiguity are the quotidian material reality in which this thought lives, persists, and perdures. Myth, token of common identity and inaccessible territory of refuge in the face of the cruel, tempting, and

32. In his schooled manner of failing to understand a world that evades his experience and mode of thought, Mark Lichbach titled an article "What Makes Rational Peasants Revolutionary? Dilemma, Paradox, and Irony in Peasant Collective Action" (Lichbach 1994). The disconcertion of the title reappears in the conclusion—"In sum, peasant collective action is a dilemma wrapped inside a paradox wrapped inside an irony"—and in the marvelous final sentence: "Peasants, like the rest of us, attempt to balance the public and the private spheres of their lives." And where exactly are "the public" and "the private" in the agrarian community and in the Indian world?

alien presence of the modern, perpetuates itself grounded in the materiality of the social life of the Indians. Confronted by this form of thought, one has two ways to fail to understand it, both of which ignore evidence and reason. The first is to negate it from the outset; the other is to idealize it and imagine it as a model and guide for urban thought. One or the other of these ways is present in the polarizations the rebellion has provoked in Mexico.

The communities, for their part, understand this discourse and feel its tones. For words to be judged "true words" they have to pass the judgment and test of truth of the communities, through their mode of discussing and listening and returning to discuss until a consensus is achieved. When their delegates went in February of 1994 to the dialogue in San Cristóbal, their first communiqué spoke of their coming with "true words," and the terms "truth" and "lie" had a symbolic connotation there:

> For us, the littlest ones of these lands, those without face and without a history, those armed with truth and fire, we who come from the night and the mountain, the true men and women, the dead of yesterday, of today and forever . . . for us, nothing. Everything for everyone.
>
> If the lie returns to the mouth of the powerful, our voice of fire will speak anew, everything for everyone.
>
> Receive our blood, brothers, that so much death not be useless, that the truth return to our lands. Everything for everyone. (EZLN 1994:155–57)

What does not seem reasonable is to suppose that these modes of speaking, discussing, and deciding, born in a different culture, could be a model of democracy for Mexican urban society.

Official thought considers this discourse to be an irritant, a *zapatista* force. But the negotiating wisdom of the Mexican State knows how to cover itself with the mask of tolerance when it cannot, or cannot yet, cut loose with repression or suppression. This State already knows a thing or two about ambiguity and putting on a mask.

What has happened with the urban society? Why the favorable reception to *zapatismo* by a good part of that society (the part that's not irreducibly hostile)? Why has even Octavio Paz proposed dialogue? What chords in this society are struck by the rebellion and its discourse? Several suggestions have been made above. At the most profound level, my hypothesis is that with an unprecedented crisis of *values* and of *security* closing in on

Mexican society in a veritable end of the regime, the words and deeds of the Indian rebellion strike the chord of what I call the enchanted world. Over the course of three years, their words and deeds have restored the *universal and timeless values* in which the left has always located its raison d'être in the face of the bureaucratic rationality of the State, East and West: *dignity*, of which the powerful make so much fun; *ethics*, which is true to everyone's eyes; *myth*, which is community; *justice*, which is fairness in delivery and equality in gift; *freedom*, which in republican law is democracy.

These are words and deeds that come wrapped in the presence, in the literal apparition, of *another world*—New Year's Eve in San Cristóbal—moving itself out of displacement and exclusion, obliged to enter the modern world, the Republic, while clinging to those values and to its own *other-identity*.

This otherworld appears as an enigma and a mystery. In a given moment, the government believed it could unveil the mystery and thereby resolve the enigma. A year into the rebellion, it came to know the prior identity of Marcos and proceeded to publish a history of the arrival of urban guerrillas in the communities of the *cañadas* and highlands of Chiapas. The enigma, in part, was resolved; from that and other sources, the history of Marcos' identity was more or less known. But once known, everyone could also see that it was not relevant. The mystery continues, much like the perennial challenge before which live those who concern themselves with history or histories: enigmas can be resolved, but mysteries can only be pointed to or alluded to.

My hypothesis, to reiterate, is that the rebellion of the otherworld—a world that has always been there—touched Mexican consciousness in the peculiar and hybrid rationality where its culture is nourished, its manner of giving reason to the world and sense to life having been shaped by the persistent presence of the enchanted world below and across the modernity that we all live and want.

The Indian rebellion presents itself as a mirror to that society, the black mirror of obsidian where one sees oneself reflected on the far side of the mirror. The mirror is ambiguous. Each person can see in it their own face and believe that the rebellion speaks to them, to their ideals and hopes, and can draw comfort from the illusion and the consolation thereby offered. Each person can imagine for herself or himself that democracy and equality reign in the communities—ignoring the necessarily and by nature hierarchical and authoritarian character of those communities' internal relations—and invent for himself or herself a new golden age for personal or collective use. Here we are in the ambit of the subjective.

But maybe Mexican society has been gripped by another perception. As a community with a long and complex history, Mexican society itself can perhaps see *through the mirror* on the surface of which we are each reflected but at the base of which can be discerned the still-not-dissolved enchanted world. A *still-not-lost* perception of the past opens the door to a *still-not-reconciled* perception of the future, conforming to the function that Ernst Bloch assigned to utopia: "to cultivate anew all of the past and to deliberate in a new way all of the future" (Bloch [1918] quoted in Löwy and Saury 1992:265). In the obsidian mirror, this world makes itself present as an *otherworld*, instead of absenting itself as a *world-before*. It locates itself in the territory of the *possible*, of the *not-arrived*, and not in the distance of *nostalgia*, of the *come-and-gone*.

Perhaps this mirror reflects the anguished and inflamed conscience of Mexican modernity, a conscience that wants to be modern while preserving its world, that wants to be *society* and at the same time to be *community*. But isn't this (nothing more, and nothing less, than) the tormented conscience of the modern world, where what was to be the end of a lineal and finite history turned out to be the starting point of unending and innumerable arborescent histories?

Epilogue

Several contributors to this volume maintain that a direct link between U.S. intervention and the history of peasant rebellions in Mexico is difficult to discern. By that account, peasants did not rise up in the nineteenth and twentieth centuries to resist the presence of U.S. troops in Mexican territory, nor against U.S. capital's penetration of mining, petroleum, industry, or agriculture. Rather, the identifiable objects of peasant ire were the hacienda, the conversion of land into a commodity, the exactions made against them, and their economic and political oppression; in other words, all that invaded and destroyed their autonomous universe through direct, physical, and palpable intrusions. The persons who figured in these enemy intrusions were the landlord, the boss, the tax collector, the usurer, the policeman, the *jefe político,* the governor, the federal army (*la Federación,* as the peasants name it with strange precision); and all of those persons are Mexican. From this point of view, then, Alan Knight's conclusion that peasants were not concerned with "anti-imperialism," at least in its traditional political meaning, appears well grounded. The United States was not their problem.

All the same, if we recognize the multiform (and not only politico-military) content that John Coatsworth attributes to U.S. intervention, it appears equally evident that U.S. intervention has been a constant factor conditioning—from afar and from up close—the very existence of Mexico as a nation, not excepting its tradition of rural revolts. Further, the indigenous rebellion of Chiapas in 1994 could be understood as a revelatory example of subaltern response to the specific form of presence and conditioning exercised by the United States. From their initial declarations onward, the Indian leaders stated that the reforms to Article 27, the implementation of the NAFTA, and the commercial "opening up" of Mexico snatched the land from rural communities as it deprived the residents of their right to land, expelling them from the market. The reforms and agreements/ treaties in effect announced a death sentence for peasants and Indians.

Neoliberal restructuration of this kind is effected on multiple levels simultaneously, encouraging the unrestricted entry of land into the market throughout Mexico even as it figures as one of the key steps in the homologation of Mexican and U.S. legislation to the end of constituting a unified juridical space for investment, property, and commerce. For peasants, Indians, and small-scale agriculturalists, the essence of the NAFTA is the dual abolition of protective barriers and stimuli for their productive activities; consequently, it demands their surrender to pressure from without, particularly lower prices for basic grains such as maize, wheat, and beans. This pressure, which is more irresistible the more defenseless and small-scale the agricultural direct producer is (Indians being the least protected, conducting agriculture on the smallest scale), also seeks to transform lands that in the past were dedicated to production of basic grains into fields yielding forage for animals or agricultural products destined to be consumed by the more affluent middle and upper classes in the United States and by the urban upper class in Mexico. Here is yet another of the homologations promoted by the mechanisms of the NAFTA.

Recommendations by the International Monetary Fund and the World Bank—tied to their loans and thus, in point of fact, obligations—are the principal support of these transformations, now inscribed in government policy and in the politics of the new and powerful Mexican financial groups. That support conditions and disciplines Mexico with a force more flexible and more irresistible than any traditional-style military or political intervention. In the era of transnational circuits of capital, the punitive expeditions, the landing of U.S. troops on Mexican soil, and the Big Stick are as outdated as the manual typewriter or the steam locomotive.

This disciplining support forms part of a global process that, during the course of the 1980s, restructured the relations among nations, capitals, nation-states, and social classes at a world level. For this very reason, it is invisible and unassailable; it is everywhere and yet seemingly nowhere. It presents itself as the only form of society possible, as an "only way of thinking" to which there is no alternative, neither possible nor even imaginable. Globalization encourages a reorganization of the functions of nation-states, particularly those in a subordinate situation like Mexico, and a new form of global regulation by international finance capital.[33] The crisis of the Mexican state community and its form of state is in part determined by this context. Hence, Mexican government policies cannot be seen as the result of ineptitude, improvisation, or a crisis of the state; rather, they are coherently linked to these global changes, in which they are integrated and from which they secure their logic and force.

Only by recognizing this context does it make sense to speak today of U.S. intervention as the most dynamic pole and center of financial, tech-

---

33. In this regard see Michel and Mihre 1991: "Global regulation supersedes and subordinates prior forms of regulation, and is distinguished on two counts. First, it bypasses the national regulatory structures—a complex built around two principles of the post World War II order: (1) the institutional linking of productivity increases with national-determined wage relations ('Fordism') and (2) the Bretton Woods system of stable exchange rates and international financial institutions that secured national accumulation structures. Second, the emerging form of global regulation depends on the withdrawal of state protection and the reorganisation of the state to secure a 'global wage relation,' anchoring transnational circuits in money, labor and commodities" (p. 85). "There is a growing tendency for the state to act more as a facilitator of the requirements of global capital (which is increasingly independent of metropolitan state control) than as a mediator between global capital and national bourgeoisie and the working class. That is, there is a basic uncoupling of the state from banking capital and control of international monetary relations" (p. 99).

nological and, above all, military force from which the process of globalization of capital and markets is shaped. Located on the other side of an
extensive common border with Mexico, this center or pole of force is
additionally the point from which an epochal transformation of the Mexican state is marked from without (even as that transformation is marked
from within as well, if one considers the NAFTA and the mortgaged loans
to the Mexican government in February 1995). The Mexican state's destruction of its old constitutive pacts with society and its entrance into a
prolonged crisis are the conditions of, and unavoidable prices for, this
change—at once epochal and related to the bourgeois state form and its
insertion in the world.

This process imposes itself on Indians and peasants and their modes of
production, of relating to the land and the market, and of giving sense to
the world and to life. This new great transformation—ruled by the movement of transnational finance capital and by the microelectronic revolution
in communication and in modes of production, exchange, and control—
leaves no place for the peasants, whether in Africa, India, Latin America
generally, or Mexico. It involves an unprecedented spatial-temporal extension and intensification of the quantification, mechanization, and rational-
ization of the world according to a logic of unbridled circulation and
unlimited valorization of capital. It is a process that recognizes neither
Berlin Walls nor national, state, corporate, syndicalist, or juridical barriers.

The first modernity, that of the Enlightenment and the Reformation,
arrived in Mexico wrapped in the feudal dress of the conquest. With that
first modernity in the sixteenth century—and with American precious
metals (which is to say, Indian blood transmuted into gold and silver,
millions of lives sacrificed to the *encomienda* and the mines)—the first
world market was established. The expansion of the United States, the
1847 war against Mexico, the conquest of California, and the division of a
colonial world among European powers by the end of the nineteenth
century constituted the second world market. The unification of markets
under the aegis of transnational finance capital in the present period is
configuring itself as the third great epochal mutation of the world market.

Starting in the middle of the nineteenth century, each successive phase
in the expansion of U.S. influence throughout the world and in the reorganization of production and markets was the most visible (if not the only
and singular) form through which the seemingly accidental and turbulent

conformation with capitalist modernity fell upon Mexico. For better or worse, this modernity has presented itself in Mexico under the visage of the United States.

Hence, this presence of the United States within Mexico's borders is not new. In reality, it is consubstantial with the form of existence of the Mexican Republic, just as the presence and propinquity of Mexico is consubstantial with the form of existence of the United States, even if that reciprocity is more difficult to perceive from north of the border. Since the war of 1847, through Mexico's war against the French intervention, the transformations of the *porfiriato*, the Mexican revolution, the conformation of the postrevolutionary regime, the *cardenista* reforms, and the long period of economic expansion between 1946 and 1976, this presence has been daily and permanent.

There is, however, something novel and distinctive about the present period. The NAFTA, the reform of Article 27, and the new reality of the state and finances in Mexico have dramatically altered the situation. In the rural world particularly, peasants and Indians find themselves weakened and unprotected in the confrontation with globalization—a faceless process against which there is no legal recourse, no constitutional protection, and no acquirable rights. There is not even a concrete subject against which to struggle or before which to reclaim, as there had been in the past with the landlord or the state. Those subjects, it goes without saying, are still around and have by no stretch of the imagination disappeared; but now they speak and act in the name of the unreachable and ungraspable force that is globalization.

The grievances are huge, the aggrieved many, the indignation enormous; but the grievous agent of these multiple affronts has no physical presence. It presents itself instead as a natural act or a divine castigation which threatens to finish off the destruction of the ancient Mesoamerican universe, a destruction begun five centuries earlier with the conquest but never fully accomplished.

Now, though, the Indians of Chiapas, the much abused and rounded-up survivors of that destruction, have risen in revolt against this intervention—if it can be called an intervention. It could very well be that this is the first time that U.S. intervention—once again, if it can be called intervention—encounters the direct and unmediated resistance of rural rebellion.

This resistance is not proposing the conservation of a past world, a past of five centuries of oppression and exclusion. Rather, it demands inclusion in a future world. The hope is that one of the costs of constituting this world is not the extermination of all who resist. The *neozapatistas* claim a place for their universe and their ways of giving sense to life in this world that is re-forming itself in the midst of crisis. They do not rise up against modernity; they demand a place within it with their own identity. They want to enjoy the benefit of it, not become its victim. And in rebelling, they propose in words and deeds another modernity, where there's room for all and none are excluded.

The long series of Mexican rural revolts, which in their vindication of a lost mythical past sought means through which to legitimate their struggle and beliefs, proposed—in each instance of their formulation of plans and proclamations—diverse modes of conceiving the future without surrendering their historical roots or their reasons for living. This culture of rebellion contributed to the establishment and conformation of frameworks and manners of relating to the state, providing structure, solidity, and sense to Mexico's version of the Great Arch alongside determinate channels for the expansion of commercial exchange and the valorization of capital in Mexico, rather than providing obstructions to that process of expansion.

The Indian rebellion of Chiapas, the most recent in this plurisecular series of revolts, has been perhaps the most explicit in its discourse, the most ancient in its roots, and the most modern for the questions it raises.

If we follow these clues, we may find the reasons for their remarkable reception in Mexico, the United States, and even more distant places.

Acknowledgements

This essay was written during a residency at the National Humanities Center in Durham, North Carolina, from September through December 1996, thanks to a grant to the NHC from the Rockefeller Foundation. Research was initiated during the period the author was a visiting professor at the University of Maryland, College Park, from September to December 1995. Final corrections were made at Stanford University, when the author was a Tinker Visiting Professor in the winter and spring quarters of 1997. These sojourns were possible thanks to a leave granted by the Facultad de Ciencias Políticas y Sociales de la UNAM, where the author is a professor. I here express my appreciation to these institutions for valuable support so generously given.

A more detailed and extensive version of this essay was published in Spanish as *Chiapas: La razón ardiente. Ensayo sobre la rebelión del mundo encantado* (Mexico City: Editorial Era, 1997). This translation appears here by permission of the author and the publisher.

On a more personal note, Daniel Nugent's insistence, commentaries, and suggestions for further readings, as well as his trust and friendship, turned out to be indispensable for finishing the essay in its present form. As for the omissions and mistakes, no help was needed; the capacity of the author was quite sufficient.

Bibliography

Archives and Primary Sources

ACD	Archivo de la Catedral de Durango.
ADN	Archivo de la Defensa Nacional, México, D.F.
AE	*Anuario estadístico del estado de Chihuahua.* Vol. 1(1), *año 1905,* was published in 1907. Chihuahua: Imprenta del Gobierno.
AEL	Archivo Ejidal de Lagunitas, Galeana, Chihuahua.
AGE	Archivo General del Estado, Mérida, Yucatán.
AGN	Archivo General de la Nación, México, D.F.
AGN DTN	Archivo General de Notarías, Dirección de Terrenos Nacionales, México, D.F.
AHSRE	Archivo Histórico de la Secretaría de Relaciones Exteriores, México, D.F.
AMCG	Archivo Municipal de Ciudad Guerrero, Cd. Guerrero, Chihuahua.
AMCG CJP	Archivo Municipal de Casas Grandes: Correspondencia del Jefe Político, Casas Grandes, Chihuahua.
AMGVF	Archives de Ministère de la Guerre, Vincennes, France.
AMN	Archivo Municipal de Namiquipa, Namiquipa, Chihuahua.
AMR	Archives of the Martínez del Río Family, México, D.F.
ARO	Archivo de Rubén Osorio, Cd. Chihuahua, Chihuahua.
ATN	Archivo de Terrenos Nacionales. See AGN DTN.
AVC	Archivo de Venustiano Carranza, CONDUMEX, México, D.F.
BLAC	Benson Latin American Collection, University of Texas, Austin.
CHOCH	Colección de Historia Oral de Chihuahua, Cd. Chihuahua, Chihuahua. See ARO.
CPD	Colección Porfirio Díaz, Universidad Iberoamericana, México, D.F.
EZLN	*Ejercito Zapatista de Liberación Nacional: Documentos y comunicados.* Mexico City: Ediciones Era. Volume 1, 1994. Volume 2, 1995.
FO	Foreign Office, London.
HTML	Howard-Tilton Memorial Library, Tulane University, New Orleans, Louisiana.

LC   Library of Congress, Washington, D.C.

MR   Military Reference Branch, National Archives, Washington,
            D.C.

NARA   U.S. National Archives and Records Administration, Washing-
            ton, D.C. Particularly important are the records of the Pershing
            punitive expedition, located in the Military Reference Branch
            and including Record Groups 94, 393, and 395.

NR   Naval Records Collection of the Office of Naval Records and Li-
            brary, National Archives, Washington, D.C.

POch   *Periódico oficial de Chihuahua.*

SACFV   Seis años col el General Francisco Villa, unedited memoirs of
            José María Jaurrieta, 1952. The personal archive of Clinton A.
            Luckett, El Paso, Texas.

SCR   *Crónicas y debates de las sesiones de la Soberana Convención Revolu-
            cionaria.* Two volumes. Mexico City, 1965.

SD   U.S. State Department Archives, Washington, D.C. Various SD
            record groups, including 94, 312, 393, 395, and 812 files, are located
            in the NARA.

STC   Silvestre Terrazas Collection, Bancroft Library, Berkeley, Cal-
            ifornia.

STF   *Shadows of Tender Fury. The Letters and Communiqués of Subco-
            mandante Marcos and the Zapatista Army of National Liberation.*
            Translated by Frank Bardacke, Leslie López, and the Watson-
            ville, California, Human Rights Committee. New York:
            Monthly Review Press, 1995.

USMHI   United States Military History Institute, Carlisle, Pennsylvania.

USS 1919–20 *Investigation of Mexican Affairs: Report of a Hearing before a Sub-
            Committee on Foreign Relations.* 2 vols. Washington, D.C.: U.S.
            Government Printing Office.

USS 1920   *Preliminary Report and Hearings of the Committee on Foreign Re-
            lations, U.S. Senate Pursuant to Senate Resolution . . . Outrages on
            Citizens of the U.S. in Mexico.* 66th Cong. 2 vols. Washington,
            D.C.

WNRC   Washington National Records Center, Suitland, Maryland.

Newspapers

El Agricultor (Mérida, Yuc.)
El Padre Clarencio (Mérida, Yuc.)

El Paso Times/El Paso Morning Times (El Paso, Tex.)
El Popular (Mérida, Yuc.)
El Siglo XIX (Mérida, Yuc.)
La Jornada (Mexico City)
New Era (Marfa, Tex.)
New York Times

Secondary Sources

Abrams, Philip. 1988 [1977]. "Notes on the Difficulty of Studying the State." *Journal of Historical Sociology* 1(1):58–89.

Abrams, Richard M. 1974. "U.S. Intervention Abroad: The First Quarter Century." *American Historical Review* 79:72–102.

Aguilar Camín, Héctor. 1977. *La frontera nómada. Sonora y la revolución mexicana.* Mexico City: Siglo XXI.

Aguirre Beltrán, Gonzalo. 1967. *Regiones de refugio.* Mexico City: Instituto Nacional Indigenista.

Ahmad, Aijaz. 1995. "The Politics of Literary Postcoloniality." *Race & Class* 36(3):1–20.

Alavi, Hamza. 1982. "State and Class under Peripheral Capitalism." In H. Alavi and T. Shanin, eds. *Introduction to the Sociology of "Developing Societies."* New York: Monthly Review Press.

Almada, Francisco. 1938. *La rebelión de Tomóchi.* Chihuahua City: Sociedad Chihuahuense de Estudios Históricos.

———. 1955. *Resumen de historia del estado de Chihuahua.* Mexico City: Libros Mexicanos.

———. 1958. *Juárez y Terrazas.* Mexico City: Libros Mexicanos.

———. 1964. *La revolución en el estado de Chihuahua.* Chihuahua City: Talleres Gráficos de la Nación.

———. 1968. *Diccionario de Historia, Geografía y Biografía Chihuahuense.* 2d ed. Chihuahua City: Ediciones Universidad de Chihuahua.

Alonso, Ana María. 1986. "The Hermeneutics of History: Class Struggle and Revolution in the Chihuahuan Sierra." Paper presented in a History Department seminar, University of Chicago, 21 February.

———. 1988a. "Gender, Power and Historical Memory." *Critique of Anthropology* 8(1):13–33.

——. 1988b. "Gender, Ethnicity and the Constitution of Subjects: Accommodation, Resistance and Revolution on the Chihuahuan Frontier." Ph.D. dissertation, University of Chicago.

Alonso, Jorge, ed. 1982. *El estado mexicano.* Mexico City: CIESAS/Nueva Imagen.

Amerlinck de Bontempo, Marijosé. 1982. *La reforma agraria en la hacienda de San Diego de Río Verde.* In Heriberto Moreno García, ed., *Después de los latifundios: La desintegración de la gran propiedad agraria en México.* Zamora: El Colegio de Michoacán.

Amnesty International. 1986. *Mexico: Human Rights in Rural Areas. Exchange of Documents with the Mexican Government on Human Rights Violations in Oaxaca and Chiapas.* London: Amnesty International.

Anderson, Benedict. 1983. *Imagined Communities: Reflections on the Origin and Spread of Nationalism.* London: Verso/NLB.

Archila, Mauricio. n.d. "Nuevas interpretaciones sobre la formación de la conciencia obrera en algunas regiones de Latinoamérica." Manuscript.

Baitenmann, Helga. 1994a. "Las irregularidades en el programa de certificación ejidal." *La Jornada del Campo,* 6 September, pp. 7–8.

——. 1994b. "La procuraduría agraria: Juez y parte del procede." *La Jornada del Campo,* 31 October, pp. 4–6.

Baldwin, Deborah. 1979. "Variation within the Vanguard: Protestantism and the Mexican Revolution." Ph.D. dissertation, University of Chicago.

Barrón del Avellano, María. 1971. *Habla Elisa, heroína parralense,* Special Issue (September) on the Punitive Expedition, *Boletín de la Sociedad Chihuahuense de Estudios Históricos.*

Bartra, Armando. 1985. *Los herederos de Zapata. Movimientos campesinos posrevolucionarios en México, 1920–1980.* Mexico City: Era.

Beals, Ralph L. 1973. *Cherán: A Sierra Tarascan Village.* New York: Cooper Square.

Becker, Marjorie. 1995. *Setting the Virgin on Fire.* Berkeley: University of California Press.

Beezley, William, Cheryl English Martin, and William E. French. 1994. *Rituals of Rule, Rituals of Resistance: Public Celebrations and Popular Culture in Mexico.* Wilmington: SR Books.

Bendix, Reinhard. 1977. *Max Weber, an Intellectual Portrait.* Berkeley: University of California Press.

Benjamin, Jules Robert. 1977. *The United States and Cuba.* Pittsburgh: University of Pittsburgh Press.

Benjamin, Thomas. 1977. "International Harvester and the Henequen Marketing System in Yucatán, 1898–1915," *Inter-American Economic Affairs* 31 (Winter):3–19.

———. 1981. "Passages to Leviathan: Chiapas and the Mexican State, 1891–1947."
Ph.D. dissertation, Michigan State University.

———. 1989. *A Rich Land, A Poor People: Politics and Society in Modern Chiapas.*
Albuquerque: University of New Mexico Press.

Benjamin, Thomas, and Mark Wasserman, eds. 1990. *Provinces of the Revolution: Essays on Regional Mexican History, 1910–1929.* Albuquerque: University
of New Mexico Press.

Bergquist, Charles. 1986. *Labor in Latin America: Comparative Essays on Chile,
Argentina, Venezuela and Colombia.* Stanford: Stanford University Press.

Bethell, Leslie, ed. 1991. *Mexico since Independence.* Cambridge: Cambridge University Press.

Blasier, Cole. 1976. *The Hovering Giant: U.S. Responses to Revolutionary Change
in Latin America.* Pittsburgh: University of Pittsburgh Press.

Bojórquez Urzaiz, Carlos. 1978. "Estructura agraria y maíz a partir de la 'guerra
de castas.'" *Revista de la Universidad de Yucatán* 20 (November-
December):15–35.

Bommes, Michael, and Patrick Wright. 1982. "'Charms of Residence': The
Public and the Past." In Richard Johnson et al., eds., *Making Histories: Studies
in History-writing and Politics.* Birmingham: Centre for Contemporary Cultural Studies, University of Birmingham.

Bonfil Batalla, Guillermo. 1980. "Historias que no son todavía historia." In
Carlos Pereyra et al., *Historia ¿para que?* Mexico City: Siglo XXI.

———. 1991. *México profundo. Una civilización negada.* Mexico City: Consejo Nacional para la Cultura y las Artes.

Borah, Woodrow. 1983. *Justice by Insurance.* Berkeley: University of California
Press.

Bracamonte y Sosa, Pedro. 1994. *La memoria enclaustrada. Historia indígena de
Yucatán, 1750–1915.* Mexico City: CIESAS.

Brading, David A. 1971. *Miners and Merchants in Bourbon Mexico, 1763–1810.*
Cambridge: Cambridge University Press.

———, ed. 1980. *Caudillo and Peasant in the Mexican Revolution.* Cambridge:
Cambridge University Press.

Brannon, Jeffery, and Eric Baklanoff. 1983. "Corporate Control of a Monocrop
Economy: A Comment." *Latin American Research Review* 18(3):193–96.

Bricker, Victoria Reifler. 1981. *The Indian Christ, the Indian King: The Historical Substrate of Maya Myth and Ritual.* Austin: University of Texas Press.

Brondo Whitt, E. 1940. *La División del Norte 1914–por un testigo presencial.* Mexico City: Editorial Lumen.

Brunhouse, Robert L. 1971. *Sylvanus G. Morley and the World of the Ancient Mayas.* Norman: University of Oklahoma Press.

Burbach, Roger. 1994. "Root of the Postmodern Rebellion in Chiapas." *New Left Review* 205:113–24.

Calagione, John, and D. Nugent. 1992. "Worker's Expressions: Beyond Accommodation and Resistance on the Margins of Capitalism." In J. Calagione et al., eds. *Worker's Expressions: Beyond Accommodation and Resistance.* Albany: State University of New York Press.

Calvert, P. A. R. 1968. *The Mexican Revolution 1910–14: The Diplomatic Anglo-American Conflict.* Cambridge: Cambridge University Press.

Calzadíaz Barrera, Alberto. 1977. *¿Por qué Villa atacó Columbus? Intriga internacional.* Vol. 6 of *Hechos reales de la revolución.* Mexico City: Editorial Patria.

Cardoso, Ciro, ed. 1980. *México en el siglo XIX: Historia económica y de la estructura social.* Mexico City: Nueva Imagen.

Carr, Barry. 1973. "Las peculiaridades del norte mexicano 1880–1927: Ensayo de interpretación," *Historia Mexicana* 22(3):320–46.

———. 1980. "Recent Regional Studies of the Mexican Revolution." *Latin American Research Review* 15(1):3–14.

Cartensen, Fred V., and Diane Roazen-Parrillo. 1983. "International Harvester, Molina y Compañia, and the Henequen Market: A Comment." *Latin American Research Review* 18(3):197–203.

Castañeda, Jorge. 1996. *The Mexican Shock: Its Meaning for the United States.* New York: New Press.

Castoriadis, Cornelius. 1987. *The Imaginary Institution of Society.* Cambridge: MIT Press.

Cervantes, Federico M. 1964. *Felipe Angeles en la revolución: Biografía, 1896–1919.* 3d ed. Mexico City: n.p.

Chakrabarty, Dipesh. 1992. "Postcoloniality and the Artifice of History: Who Speaks for 'Indian' Pasts?" *Representations* 37:1–26.

Chapman, John G. 1967. "Yucatán Secessionism: 1839–1843." Master's thesis, University of Texas, Austin.

Chávez Calderón, Plácido. 1964. *La defensa de Tomochi.* Mexico City: Editorial Jus.

Chevalier, Jacques. 1983. "There Is Nothing Simple about Simple Commodity Production." *Journal of Peasant Studies* 10(4):153–86.

Clendenen, Clarence C. 1961. *The United States and Pancho Villa. A Study in Unconventional Diplomacy.* Ithaca: Cornell University Press, for the American Historical Association.

Cline, Howard F. 1958. *Regionalism and Society in Yucatán, 1825–1847. Related Studies in Early Nineteenth Century Yucatecan Social History.* Part 3. Chicago: University of Chicago Press.

Coatsworth, John H. 1974. "Railroads, Landholding and Agrarian Protest in the Early Porfiriato." *Hispanic American Historical Review* 54(1):48–71.

——. 1975. "Los orígenes del autoritarismo moderno en México." *Foro Internacional* 16(2):205–32.

——. 1985. "El estado y el sector externo en México, 1800–1910." *Secuencia: Revista Americana de Ciencias Sociales* 2.

——. 1988. "Patterns of Rural Rebellion in Latin America: Mexico in Comparative Perspective." In Katz 1988a.

Cockcroft, James D. 1968. *Intellectual Precursors of the Mexican Revolution.* Austin: University of Texas Press, for the Institute of Latin American Studies.

——. 1983. *Mexico: Class Formation, Capital Accumulation and the State.* New York: Monthly Review Press.

Coerver, Don, and Linda Hall. 1984. *Texas and the Mexican Revolution: A Study in State and National Border Policy, 1910–1920.* San Antonio: Trinity University Press.

Cohn, Bernard S. 1987. "History and Anthropology: The State of Play." In *An Anthropologist among the Historians and Other Essays.* Delhi: Oxford University Press. Originally in *Comparative Studies in Society and History* 22 (1980).

——. 1996. *Colonialism and Its Forms of Knowledge: The British in India.* Chicago: University of Chicago Press.

Cohn, Bernard, and Nicholas Dirks. 1988. "Beyond the Fringe: The Nation-State, Colonialism and the Technologies of Power." *Journal of Historical Sociology* 1(2):224–29.

Comaroff, John L. 1982. "Dialectical Systems, History and Anthropology." *Journal of Southern African Studies* 8(2):143–72.

Comaroff, John, and Jean Comaroff. 1987. "The Madman and the Migrant: Work and Labor in the Historical Consciousness of a South African People." *American Ethnologist* 14(2):191–209.

———. 1991. *Of Revelation and Revolution: Christianity, Colonialism, and Consciousness in South Africa.* Volume 1. Chicago: University of Chicago Press.

Cooper, Fred, and Ann Stoler, eds. 1989. Special issue of the *American Ethnologist* 16(4).

———. 1997. *Tensions of Empire: Colonial Cultures in a Bourgeois World.* Berkeley: University of California Press.

Cooper, Fred, et al. 1993. *Confronting Historical Paradigms.* Madison: University of Wisconsin Press.

Córdova, Arnaldo. 1973. *La ideología de la revolución mexicana.* Mexico City: Siglo XXI.

Cornelius, Wayne. 1986. *The Political Economy of Mexico under de la Madrid: The Crisis Deepens.* Research Report Series, no. 43. La Jolla: Center for U.S.-Mexican Studies, University of California, San Diego.

Corrigan, Philip. 1975. "On the Politics of Production: A Comment on 'Peasants and Politics' by Eric Hobsbawm." *Journal of Peasant Studies* 2(3):341–49.

Corrigan, Philip, Harvie Ramsay, and Derek Sayer. 1980. "The State as a Relation of Production." In P. R. D. Corrigan ed., *Capitalism, State Formation and Marxist Theory: Historical Investigations.* London: Quartet Books.

Corrigan, Philip, and Derek Sayer. 1985. *The Great Arch: English State Formation as Cultural Revolution.* Oxford: Blackwell.

Cossío, Lorenzo. 1911. *¿Cómo y por quiénes se ha monopolizado la propiedad rústica de México?* Mexico City: Tipografía Mercantil.

Craig, Ann L. 1983. *The First Agraristas: An Oral History of a Mexican Agrarian Reform Movement.* Berkeley: University of California Press.

Cramer, Stuart W. 1916. "The Punitive Expedition from Boquillas." *U.S. Cavalry Journal* 28:200–227.

Creel, Enrique. 1905. *Informe del gobernador Enrique C. Creel, 1 junio 1905.* Chihuahua: Imprenta del Gobierno del Estado de Chihuahua.

———. 1909. *Informe del gobernador Enrique C. Creel, 1 junio 1909.* Chihuahua: Imprenta del Gobierno del Estado de Chihuahua.

———. 1910. *Informe del gobernador Enrique C. Creel.* Chihuahua: Imprenta del Gobierno del Estado de Chihuahua.

Cruz, Salvador, ed. 1980. *Vida y obra de Pastor Rouaix.* Mexico City: Instituto Nacional de Antropología e Historia.

Cumberland, Charles G. 1954. "Border Raids in the Lower Rio Grande Valley, 1915." *Southwestern Historical Quarterly* 57(3):285–311.

de Janvry, Alain. 1983. *The Agrarian Question and Reformism in Latin America*. Baltimore: Johns Hopkins University Press.

de la Garza, Luis Alberto, et al. 1986. *Evolución del estado mexicano*. Vol. 1. Mexico City: El Caballito.

de la Peña, Guillermo. 1980. *A Legacy of Promises*. Austin: University of Texas Press.

————. 1989. *Local and Regional Power in Mexico*. Texas Papers on Mexico, no. 88-01. Austin: Mexican Center of the Institute of Latin American Studies.

de Szyszlo, Vitold. 1913. *Dix milles kilomètres à travers le Méxique, 1909–1910*. Paris: Plont-Nourrit.

de Vos, Jan. 1980. *La paz de Dios y del rey. La conquista de la selva lacandona*. Mexico City: Fonapas-Chiapas.

————. 1988. *Oro verde. La conquista de la selva lacandona por los madereros tabasqueños, 1822–1949*. Mexico City: Fondo de Cultura Económica.

————. 1992. *Los enredos de Remesal. Ensayo sobre la conquista de Chiapas*. Mexico City: Conaculta.

————. 1995a. "El Lacandón: Una introducción histórica." In Juan Pedro Viqueira and Mario Humberto Ruz, eds., *Chiapas. Los rumbos de otra historia*. Mexico: UNAM.

————. 1995b. "Las rebeliones de los indios de Chiapas en la memoria de sus descendientes." In Jane-Dale Lloyd and Laura Pérez Rosales, eds., *Paisajes rebeldes. Una larga noche de resistencia indígena*. Mexico City: Universidad Iberoamericana.

Delgado, Antonio. 1975. *Romance histórico villista: Diario en verso de un soldado de Villa*. Chihuahua: La Sorbona Librería.

Dennis, Philip A. 1976. *Conflictos por tierras en el valle de Oaxaca*. Mexico City: Instituto Nacional Indigenista.

DeWalt, Billie R., and Pertti J. Pelto. 1985. *Micro and Macro Levels of Analysis in Anthropology: Issues in Theory and Research*. Boulder: Westview Press.

Dirks, Nicholas, ed. 1992. *Colonialism and Culture*. Ann Arbor: University of Michigan Press.

Diskin, Martin. 1986. "La economía de la comunidad étnica en Oaxaca." In A. M. Barabas and M. A. Bartolomé, eds., *Etnicidad y pluralismo cultural, la dinámica étnica en Oaxaca*. Mexico City: Instituto Nacional de Antropología e Historia.

Di Tella, Torcuato S. 1973. "The Dangerous Classes in Early Nineteenth Century Mexico." *Journal of Latin American Studies* 5:79–105.

——. 1996. *National Popular Politics in Early Independent Mexico, 1820–1847.* Albuquerque: University of New Mexico Press.

D'Olwer, Luis Nicolau. 1965. "Las inversiones extranjeras." In Daniel Cosío Villegas, ed., *Historia moderna de México: El porfiriato, la vida económica.* Mexico City: Editorial Hermes.

Duarte Morales, Teodosio. n.d. *Villa y Pershing.* Chihuahua City: n.p.

Dumond, D. E. 1977. "Independent Maya of the Late Nineteenth Century: Chiefdoms and Power Politics." In Grant D. Jones, ed., *Anthropology and History in Yucatán.* Austin: University of Texas Press.

Dumont, Louis. 1980. *Homo Hierarchicus: The Caste System and Its Implications.* Chicago: University of Chicago Press. Originally Paris: Gallimard, 1966.

——. 1985 [1977]. *Homo Aequalis. Génese et épanouissement de l'idéologie économique.* Paris: Gallimard.

Escobar Ohmstede, Antonio. 1993. *Indio, nación y comunidad en el México del siglo XIX.* Mexico City: Ediciones de la Casa Chata.

Estrada, Richard. 1975. "Border Revolution: The Mexican Revolution in the Juarez–El Paso Area, 1906–1915." Master's thesis, University of Texas, El Paso.

Estevez, Dolia. 1994. "Chiapas: An Intelligence Fiasco or Coverup?" *Covert Action Quarterly* 48:44–48.

Evans, Rosalie. 1926. *The Rosalie Evans Letters from Mexico.* Edited by D. C. Pettus. Indianapolis: Bobbs-Merrill.

EZLN (Ejército Zapatista de Liberación Nacional). 1994. *Documentos y comunicados.* Vol. 1. Mexico City: Ediciones Era.

——. 1995. *Documentos y comunicados.* Vol. 2. Mexico City: Ediciones Era.

Florescano, Enrique. 1980. "De la memoria del poder a la historia como explicación." In Carlos Pereyra et al., *Historia ¿Para qué?* Mexico City: Siglo XXI.

——. 1996. "Los indígenas, el estado y la nación." *Proceso* 1049, 8 December, p. 53.

Foster-Carter, Aidan. 1978. "Can We Articulate Articulation?" In John Clammer, ed., *The New Economic Anthropology.* London: Macmillan.

Foucault, Michel. 1978. *Power/Knowledge: Selected Interviews and Other Writings, 1972–1977.* Edited by Colin Gordon. New York: Randon House.

——. 1982. "The Subject and Power." In *Michel Foucault: Beyond Structuralism and Hermeneutics.* Edited by Hubert L. Dreyfus and Paul Rabinow. Brighton: Harvester Press.

Foweraker, Joe, and Ann L. Craig, eds. 1990. *Popular Movements and Popular Change in Mexico.* Boulder: Lynne Rienner Publishers.

French, William. n.d. "Business Attitudes in a Period of Social Change: The Mexico North-Western Railroad Confronts the Mexican Revolution." History Symposium paper, University of Texas, Austin.

Friedman, Jonathan. 1974. "Marxism, Structuralism and Vulgar Materialism." *Man*, n.s., 9(3):444–69.

Friedrich, Paul. 1970. *Agrarian Revolt in a Mexican Village*. Chicago: University of Chicago Press. 2d ed. 1977.

Gall, Olivia. n.d. "Oligarquia, ideología y racismo en el centro de Chiapas: 1876–1994." Research proposal.

Gamio, Manuel. 1971. *Mexican Immigration to the United States*. New York: Dover.

García de León, Antonio. 1985. *Resistencia y utopía. Memorial de agravios y crónica de revueltas y profecías en la provincia de Chiapas durante los últimos 500 años de su historia*. 2 vols. Mexico City: Era.

——. 1994. "Introducción" to EZLN, *Documentos y comunicados*. Vol. 1. Mexico City: Ediciones Era.

——. 1995. "Paradoxes of Development: The New Agrarian Question and the Peasant Movement in Mexico." *Journal of Historical Sociology* 8(4):430–47.

García Díaz, Bernardo. 1981. *Un pueblo fabril del porfiriato: Santa Rosa, Veracruz*. Mexico City: Fondo de Cultura Económica.

Garciadiego Danton, Javier, et al. 1986. *Evolución del estado mexicano*. Vol. 2. Mexico City: El Caballito.

Geertz, Clifford. 1963. "The Integrative Revolution: Primordial Sentiments and Civil Politics in the New State." In Geertz, ed., *Old Societies and New States: The Quest for Modernity in Asia and Africa*. New York: Free Press.

Gilderhus, Mark T. 1977. *Diplomacy and Revolution: U.S.-Mexican Relations under Wilson and Carranza*. Tucson: University of Arizona Press.

Gill, Christopher. 1993. "Wresting Memory from the Violence of the Present: Rape, Martyrdom and Double Narrative in Paul Friedrich's *Agrarian Revolt in a Mexican Village*." *Journal of Historical Sociology* 6(4):430–54.

Gilly, Adolfo. 1971. *La revolución interrumpida*. Mexico City: El Caballito.

——. 1973. *La revolución interrumpida*. 3d ed. Mexico City: El Caballito.

——. 1980. "La historia como crítica o como discurso del poder." In Carlos Pereyra et al., *Historia ¿para que?* Mexico City: Siglo XXI.

——. 1983. "La revolución mexicana." In Enrique Semo, ed., *México: Un pueblo en la historia*. Vol. 2. Mexico City: Nueva Imagen/Universidad Autónoma de Puebla.

———. 1985. *México: La larga travesía.* Mexico City: Nueva Imagen.

———. 1986. *Arriba los de abajo.* Mexico City: Océano.

———. 1988. *Nuestra caída en la modernidad.* Mexico City: Joan Boldó i Climent Editores.

———, ed. 1989. *Cartas a Cuauhtémoc Cárdenas.* Mexico City: Ediciones Era.

———. 1994. *El cardenismo, una utopía mexicana.* Mexico City: Ediciones Cal y Arena.

———. 1996. *México: El poder, el dinero y la sangre.* Mexico City: Editorial Aguilar.

Gilly, Adolfo, Subcomandante Marcos, and Carlos Ginzburg. 1995. *Discusión sobre la historia.* Mexico City: Taurus.

Glantz, Susana, ed. 1987. *La heterodoxia recuperada.* Mexico City: Fondo de Cultura Económica.

Goldfrank, Walter. 1979. "Theories of Revolution and Revolution without Theory: The Case of Mexico." *Theory and Society* 7(1–2):135–65.

González Navarro, Moisés. 1969. "Xenofobia y xenofilia en la revolución mexicana." *Historia Mexicana* 18(4):569–614.

———. 1970. *Raza y tierra: La guerra de castas y el henequén.* Mexico City: El Colegio de México.

———. 1979. Razo y tierra: La guerra de castas y el henequén. 2d ed. Mexico City: El Colegio de México.

González Rodríguez, Blanca. 1984. "Cuatro proyectos de cambio en Yucatán." In Luis Millet et al., eds., *Hacienda y cambio social en Yucatán.* Mérida: Maldonado/INAH.

González y González, Luis. 1981. *Historia de la revolución mexicana. Período 1934–40: Los días del presidente Cárdenas.* Mexico City: El Colegio de México.

Gootenberg, Paul. 1995. "Order[s] and Progress in Developmental Discourse: A Case of Nineteenth Century Peru." *Journal of Historical Sociology* 8(2):111–35.

Gosner, Kevin. 1992. *Soldiers of the Virgin: The Moral Economy of a Colonial Maya Rebellion.* Tucson: University of Arizona Press.

Graham, Richard. 1990. *The Idea of Race in Latin America, 1870–1940.* Austin: University of Texas Press.

Gramsci, Antonio. 1971. *Selections from the Prison Notebooks.* New York: International Publishers.

Grieb, Kenneth J. 1969. *The United States and Huerta.* Lincoln: University of Nebraska Press.

Gruening, Ernest. 1928. *Mexico and Its Heritage.* London: Stanley Paul.

Guerra, Francoise Xavier. 1985. *Le Mexique de l'ancien régime à la révolution.* 2 vols. Paris: L'Harmattam.

Guha, Ranajit. 1982. "On Some Aspects of the Historiography of Colonial India." In *Subaltern Studies I: Writings on South Asian History and Society.* Delhi: Oxford University Press.

———. 1983a. *Elementary Aspects of Peasant Insurgency in Colonial India.* Delhi: Oxford University Press.

———. 1983b. "The Prose of Counterinsurgency." In R. Guha, ed., *Subaltern Studies.* Vol. 2. Delhi: Oxford University Press.

Guha, Ranajit, and Gayatri Chakravorty Spivak, eds. 1988. *Selected Subaltern Studies.* New York: Oxford University Press.

Hackett, Charles W., ed. 1923–37. *Historical Documents Relating to New Mexico, Nueva Viscaya, and Approaches Thereto, to 1773.* Vols. 2 and 3. Washington, D.C.: Carnegie Institution of Washington.

Haley, J. Edward. 1970. *Revolution and Intervention. The Diplomacy of Taft and Wilson with Mexico, 1910–17.* Cambridge: MIT Press.

Hall, Linda B., and Don M. Coerver. 1988. *Revolution on the Border: Mexico and the United States, 1910–1920.* Albuquerque: University of New Mexico Press.

Hamilton, Nora. 1982. *The Limits of State Autonomy.* Berkeley: University of California Press.

Hammond, John Hays. 1935. *Autobiography.* New York: Farrar and Rinehart.

Harper, Henry A. 1910. *A Journey in South-eastern Mexico.* New York: De Vinne Press.

Harris, David. 1992. *From Class Struggle to the Politics of Pleasure.* London: Routledge.

Hart, John. 1978. "The Urban Working Class and the Mexican Revolution: The Case of the Casa del Obrero Mundial." *Hispanic American Historical Review* 58(1):1–20.

———. 1987. *Revolutionary Mexico: The Coming and Process of the Mexican Revolution.* Berkeley: University of California Press.

———. 1988. "Conflicts in a Transitional Society: The 1840's Southwestern Peasants' War." In Katz 1988a.

———. Forthcoming. *Empire and Revolution: The Americans in Mexico since the Civil War.*

Harvey, Neil. 1990. "Peasant Strategies and Corporatism in Chiapas." In Joe Foweraker and Ann L. Craig, eds., *Popular Movements and Political Change in Mexico.* Boulder: Lynne Rienner Publishers.

——. 1994. *Rebellion in Chiapas: Rural Reforms, Campesino Radicalism, and the Limits to Salinismo.* Transformation of Rural Mexico, Number 5. La Jolla: Center for U.S.–Mexican Studies.

——. 1995a. "Rebelión en Chiapas: Reformas rurales, radicalismo campesino y los límites del salinismo." In Juan Pedro Viqueira and Mario Humberto Ruz, eds., *Chiapas: Los rumbos de otra historia.* Mexico City: UNAM.

——. 1995b. "Reformas rurales y rebelión zapatista: Chiapas 1988–1994." In Jane-Dale Lloyd and Laura Pérez Rosales, eds., *Paisajes rebeldes. Una larga noche de resistencia indígena.* Mexico City: Universidad Iberoamericana.

Hawley, C. A. 1964. *Life along the Border.* West Texas Historical and Scientific Society Publications, no. 20.

Hernández Navarro, Luis. 1996a. "Indígenas: Derechos pendientes." *La Jornada,* 26 November.

——. 1996b. "Nuevo tratado para indios insumisos." *La Jornada,* 12 November.

Hewitt de Alcántara, Cynthia. 1985. *La modernización de la agricultura mexicana, 1940–70.* Mexico City: Siglo XXI.

Hill, Larry D. 1974. *Emissaries to a Revolution: Woodrow Wilson's Executive Agents in Mexico.* Baton Rouge: Louisiana State University Press.

Hinkle, Stacy C. 1967. *Wings and Saddles. The Air and Cavalry Punitive Expedition of 1919.* El Paso: Texas Western Press.

Hobsbawm, Eric. 1973. "Peasants and Politics." *Journal of Peasant Studies* 1(1):3–22.

——. 1975. "Reply [to Corrigan 1975]." *Journal of Peasant Studies* 2(3):349–51.

Hobsbawm, Eric, and Terrence Ranger, eds. 1983. *The Invention of Tradition.* Cambridge: Cambridge University Press.

Hoernel, Daniel. 1980. "Las grandes corporaciones y la política del gran garrote en Cuba y en México." *Historia Mexicana* 30(2):209–46.

Holden, Robert H. 1986. "The Mexican State Manages Modernization: The Survey of Public Lands in Six States, 1876–1911." Ph.D. dissertation, University of Chicago.

Hu-DeHart, Evelyn. 1984. *Yaqui Resistance and Survival: The Struggle for Land and Autonomy, 1821–1920.* Madison: University of Wisconsin Press.

——. 1988. "Peasant Rebellion in the Northwest: The Yaqui Indians of Sonora, 1740–1976." In Katz 1988a.

Jackson, Byron. 1976. "The Political and Military Role of General Felipe Angeles in the Mexican Revolution, 1914–1915." Ph.D. dissertation, Georgetown University.

Jones, Grant D. 1971. "La estructura política de los mayas de Chan Santa Cruz: El papel del respaldo inglés." *América Indígena* 31:415–21.

———. 1977. *Anthropology and History in Yucatán*. Austin: University of Texas Press.

Joseph, Gilbert. 1980. "Caciquismo and the Revolution: Carrillo Puerto in Yucatán." In David Brading, ed., *Caudillo and Peasant in the Mexican Revolution*. New York: Cambridge University Press.

———. 1982. *Revolution from Without: Yucatán, Mexico and the United States, 1880–1924*. New York: Cambridge University Press.

———. 1985. "From Caste War to Class War: The Historiography of Modern Yucatán (c. 1750–1940)." *Hispanic American Historical Review* 65(1):111–34.

———. 1986. *Rediscovering the Past at Mexico's Periphery: Essays on the History of Modern Yucatán*. Birmingham: University of Alabama Press.

———. 1988. "Forging the Regional Pastime: Class Dimensions of Baseball in Yucatán." In Joseph L. Arbena, ed., *Sport and Society in Latin America*. Westport, Conn.: Greenwood Press.

Joseph, Gilbert, and D. Nugent, eds. 1994a. *Everyday Forms of State Formation: Revolution and the Negotiation of Rule in Modern Mexico*. Durham: Duke University Press.

———. 1994b. "Popular Culture and State Formation in Revolutionary Mexico." In Joseph and Nugent 1994a.

Joseph, Gilbert, and Allen Wells. 1982. "Corporate Control of a Monocrop Economy: International Harvester and Yucatán's Henequen Industry during the Porfiriato." *Latin American Research Review* 17(1):69–99.

———. 1983. "Corporate Control" and "Collaboration and Informal Empire in Yucatán: The Case for Political Economy." *Latin American Research Review* 18(3):204–18.

———. 1985. "The Crisis of an Oligarchical Regime: Elite Politics, Rural Rebellion, and Patterns of Social Control in Yucatán, 1910–1913." Paper presented at the Latin American Studies Association Conference, Albuquerque, New Mexico.

———. 1986. "Summer of Discontent: Economic Rivalry among Elite Factions during the Late Porfiriato in Yucatán." *Journal of Latin American Studies* 18(2):225–82.

———. 1987. "The Rough and Tumble Career of Pedro Crespo." In William Beezley and Judith Ewell, eds., *The Human Tradition in Latin America*. Wilmington: Scholarly Resources.

———. Forthcoming. *Summer of Discontent, Seasons of Upheaval: Elite Politics and Rural Insurgency in Yucatán, 1890–1915.*

Joseph, Gilbert, Allen Wells, et al. 1986. *Yucatán y la International Harvester.* Mérida: Maldonado.

Kalms, P. G., ed. 1905. *The Directory of Agencies, Mines and Haciendas, 1905–1906.* Mexico City: American Bank and Printing Co.

Kantorowicz, Ernst H. 1951. "*Pro Patria Mori* in Medieval Political Thought." *American Historical Review* 56:472–92.

Katz, Friedrich. 1976. "Peasants in the Mexican Revolution of 1910." In Joseph Spielburg and Scott Whiteford, eds., *Forging Nations: A Comparative View of Rural Ferment and Revolt.* East Lansing: Michigan State University Press.

———. 1978a. "Innen- und aussenpolitische Ursachen des mexikanischen Revolutionsverlaufs." *Jahrbuch für Geschichte von Staat, Wirstschaft und Gesellschaft Lateinamerikas* 15:95–101.

———. 1978b. "Pancho Villa and the Attack on Columbus, New Mexico." *American Historical Review* 83(1):101–30.

———. 1979a. "Villa, Reform Governor of Chihuahua." In George Wolfskill and Douglas Richmond, eds., *Essays on the Mexican Revolution.* Austin: University of Texas Press.

———. 1979b. *Pancho Villa y el ataque a Columbus, Nuevo México.* Translated by Rubén Osorio. Chihuahua City: Regma.

———. 1980a. *La servidumbre agraria en México en la época porfiriana.* Mexico City: Era.

———. 1980b. "Pancho Villa, Peasant Movements and Agrarian Rebellion in Northern Mexico." In David Brading, ed., *Caudillo and Peasant in the Mexican Revolution.* New York: Cambridge University Press.

———. 1981. *The Secret War in Mexico: Europe, the United States and the Mexican Revolution.* Chicago: University of Chicago Press.

———. 1988a. *Riot, Rebellion and Revolution: Rural Social Conflict in Mexico.* Princeton: Princeton University Press.

———. 1988b. "Rural Uprisings in Preconquest and Colonial Mexico" and "Rural Rebellions after 1810." In Katz 1988a.

———. 1988c. "Rural Rebellions after 1810." In Katz 1988a.

Katz, Friedrich, and James Sandos. 1979. Exchange of letters, *American Historical Review* 84(1):304–7.

Katz, Friedrich, et al. 1977. "¿A donde íbamos con Pancho Villa? Un diálogo con

Friedrich Katz" [interview by Segundo Portilla and Héctor Aguilar Camín]. *Siempre* 1229, 12 January.

Kearney, Michael. 1980. "Agribusiness and the Demise or the Rise of the Peasantry." *Latin American Perspectives* 7(4):115–24.

——. 1986. "Integration of the Mixteca and the Western U.S.-Mexico Region via Migratory Wage Labor." In Ina Rosenthal-Urey, ed., *Regional Impacts of U.S.-Mexican Relations.* Monograph Series, no. 16. La Jolla: Center for U.S.-Mexican Studies, University of California, San Diego.

Kearney, Michael, and Carole Nagengast. 1989. *Anthropological Perspectives on Transnational Communities in Rural California.* Working Group on Farm Labor and Rural Poverty, Working Paper no. 3. Davis: California Institute for Rural Studies, University of California.

Kelley, Charles. 1952a. "Factors Involved in the Abandonment of Certain Peripheral Southwestern Settlements." *American Anthropologist* 54(3):356–85.

——. 1952b. "The Historic Indian Pueblos of Junta de los Rios." *New Mexico Historical Review* 27(4):257–95.

Klein, Herbert S. 1966. "Peasant Communities in Revolt: The Tzeltal Republic of 1712." *Pacific Historical Review* 35(3):247–64.

Knight, Alan. 1980. "Peasant and Caudillo in the Mexican Revolution, 1910–1917." In David Brading, ed., *Caudillo and Peasant in the Mexican Revolution.* New York: Cambridge University Press.

——. 1985a. "The Mexican Revolution: Bourgeois? Nationalist? Or Just a 'Great Rebellion'?" *Bulletin of Latin American Research* 4(2):1–38.

——. 1985b. "The Political Economy of Revolutionary Mexico, 1900–1940." In Christopher Abel and Colin M. Lewis, eds., *Latin America, Economic Imperialism and the State: The Political Economy of the External Connection from Independence to the Present.* London: Althone Press.

——. 1986a. *The Mexican Revolution.* 2 vols. Cambridge: Cambridge University Press.

——. 1986b. "Mexican Peonage: What Was It and Why Was It?" *Journal of Latin American Studies* 18(1):41–74.

——. 1987. *U.S.-Mexican Relations, 1910–1940: An Interpretation.* Monograph Series, no. 28. La Jolla: Center for U.S.-Mexican Studies, University of California, San Diego.

——. 1990a. "Revolutionary Project, Recalcitrant People: Mexico, 1910–1940." In Jaime E. Rodríguez, ed., *The Revolutionary Process in Mexico: Essays on*

Political and Social Change, 1880–1940. Los Angeles: UCLA, Latin American Center Publications.

——. 1990b. "Racism, Revolution and Indigenismo: Mexico, 1910–1940." In Graham 1990.

——. 1994. "Weapons and Arches in the Mexican Revolutionary Landscape." In Joseph and Nugent 1994a.

Koreck, María Teresa. n.d. 1. "Social Organization and Land Tenure in a Revolutionary Community in Northern Mexico: Cuchillo Parado, Chihuahua, 1865–1910." Manuscript.

——. n.d. 2. "Why Men Rebel. Villista Villagers in the Mexican Revolution: Chuchillo Parado, Chihuahua." Manuscript.

Krauze, Enrique. 1977. *Historia de la revolución mexicana. Período 1924–1928: La reconstrucción económica*. Mexico City: El Colegio de México.

——. 1987. *Francisco Villa entre el ángel y el fierro*. Mexico City: Fondo de Cultura Económica.

Laite, Julian. 1981. *Industrial Development and Migrant Labor in Latin America*. Austin: University of Texas Press.

Langford, J. O., and Fred Gipson. 1952. *Big Bend: A Homesteader's Story*. Austin: University of Texas Press.

LASSG (Latin American Subaltern Studies Group). 1993. "Founding Statement." In John Beverly and José Oviedo, eds., *The Postmodernism Debate in Latin America*, a special issue of *boundary 2*. 20(3):110–21.

Leal, Juan Felipe. 1985. *México: Estado, burocracia y sindicatos*. Mexico City: El Caballito.

Le Bot, Yvon. 1992. *Le guerre en terre maya. Communauté, violence et modernité au Guatemala (1970–1992)*. Paris: Editions Karthala.

León, María del Carmen, Mario Humberto Ruz, and José Alejos García. 1992. *Del katún al siglo. Tiempos de colonialismo y resistencia entre los mayas*. Mexico City: Conaculta.

Lichbach, Mark I. 1994. "What Makes Rational Peasants Revolutionary? Dilemma, Paradox, and Irony in Peasant Collective Action." *World Politics* 46 (April 1994):383–418.

Lloyd, Jane-Dale. 1983. "La crisis económica de 1905 a 1907 en el noroeste de Chihuahua." *Humanidades Anuario* 7:119–39. Mexico City: Universidad Iberoamericana.

——. 1987. *El proceso de modernización capitalista del noroeste de Chihuahua, 1880–1910*. Mexico City: Universidad Iberoamericana.

Lloyd, Jane-Dale, and Laura Pérez Rosales, eds. 1995. *Paisajes rebeldes: Una larga noche de resistencia indígena.* Mexico City: Universidad Iberoamericana.

Long, Norman. 1984. "Creating Space for Change: A Perspective on the Sociology of Development." Inaugural lecture at the Agricultural University, Wageningen, Netherlands, 15 November.

Löwy, Michael, and Robert Saury. 1992. *Révolte et mélancolie. Le romantisme a contre-courant de la modernité.* Paris: Editions Payot.

Lumholtz, Carl. 1903. *Unknown Mexico.* London: Macmillan.

MacLeod, Murdo J., and Robert Wasserstrom. 1983. *Spaniards and Indians in Southeastern Mesoamerica: Essays on the History of Ethnic Relations.* Lincoln: University of Nebraska Press.

McWilliams, Carey. 1939. *Factories in the Fields: The Story of Migratory Farm Labor in California.* Boston: Little, Brown.

Magagna, Victor V. 1991. *Communities of Grain: Rural Rebellion in Comparative Perspective.* Ithaca: Cornell University Press.

Magaña, Gildardo. 1985. *Emiliano Zapata y el agrarismo en México.* 5 vols. Facsimile edition. Mexico City: Instituto Nacional de Estudios Históricos de la Revolución Mexicana.

Maier, Charles S. 1978. *The Origins of the Cold War and Contemporary Europe.* New York: Watts.

Mallon, Florencia. 1983. "Peasants and the National Questions in Peru and Mexico, 1850–1900." Research proposal.

——. 1988. "Peasants and State Formation in Nineteenth-Century Mexico: Morelos, 1848–1858." *Political Power and Social Theory* 7:1–54.

——. 1994. "The Promise and Dilemmas of Subaltern Studies: Perspectives from Latin American History." *American Historical Review* 99(5):1491–1515.

Manno, Francis Joseph. 1963. "Yucatán en la guerra entre México y Estados Unidos." *Revista de la Universidad de Yucatán* 5(28):51–72.

Margolies, Barbara Luise. 1975. *Princes of the Earth: Subcultural Diversity in a Mexican Municipality.* Special Publication no. 2. Washington, D.C.: American Anthropological Association.

Martínez Alier, Juan. 1977. *Haciendas, Plantations and Collective Farms.* London: Frank Cass.

Marx, Karl. 1906 [1867]. *Capital: A Critique of Political Economy.* Vol. 1. Translated by Samuel Moore and Edward Aveling. New York: Charles Kerr.

——. 1973 [1858]. *Grundrisse.* Translated by Martin Nicolaus. New York: Vintage.

Matute, Alvaro. 1982. "Prólogo." In *Documentos relativos al general Felipe Angeles.* Mexico City: Editorial Domes.

Mena Brito, Bernardino. 1956. *Felipe Angeles, federal.* Mexico City: Publicaciones Herrerías.

Menegus Bornemann, Margarita, and Juan Felipe Leal. 1982. "Los trabajadores en las haciendas de Mazaquiahuac y El Rosario, Tlaxcala." In Heriberto Moreno García, ed., *Después de los latifundios: La desintegración de la gran propiedad agraria en México.* Zamora: El Colegio de Michoacán.

Mexico (Junta Directiva de Colonización). 1848. *Proyectos de colonización presentados por la junta directiva del ramo al Ministerio de Relaciones de la República Mexicana en 5 julio de 1848.* Mexico City: Vicente García Torres.

Meyer, Eugenia. 1978. "Hablan los villistas. Antropología e historia." *Epoca* 3:23.

Meyer, Jean. 1973. *Problemas campesinos y revueltas agrarias (1821–1910).* Mexico City: Sepsetentas.

———. 1977. *Historia de la revolución mexicana. Período 1924–28: Estado y sociedad con Calles.* Mexico City: El Colegio de México.

———. 1979. *El sinarquismo. ¿Un facismo mexicano?* Mexico City: Editorial Joaquín Mortiz.

Meyer, Lorenzo. 1972. *México y los Estados Unidos en el conflicto petrolero (1917–1942).* Mexico City: El Colegio de México. Translated into English as *Mexico and the United States in the Oil Controversy, 1917–1942* (Austin: University of Texas Press, 1977).

———. 1978a. *Historia de la revolución mexicana. Período 1928–34: Los inicios de la institucionalización. La política del maximato.* Mexico City: El Colegio de México.

———. 1978b. *Historia de la revolución mexicana. Período 1928–34: El conflicto social y los gobiernos del maximato.* Mexico City: El Colegio de México.

Meyer, Michael C. 1965. "Albert B. Fall's Mexican Papers: A Preliminary Investigation." *New Mexico Historical Review* 40:165–74.

———. 1967. *Mexican Rebel: Pascual Orozco and the Mexican Revolution.* Lincoln: University of Nebraska Press.

Michel, Philip, and David Mihre. 1991. "Global Regulation vs. the Nation-State: Agro-Food Systems and the New Politics of Capital." *Capital and Class* (London), no. 43.

Moats, Leone. 1932. *Thunder in Their Veins.* London: Century.

Moore, Barrington. 1969 [1966]. *Social Origins of Dictatorship and Democracy:*

Lord and Peasant in the Making of the Modern World. Harmondsworth: Penguin. Originally Boston: Beacon Press.

———. 1978. *Injustice: The Social Basis of Obedience and Revolt.* White Plains, N.Y.: M. E. Sharpe.

NACLA. 1987. Special Issue on Mexico. New York: North American Congress on Latin America.

Nagengast, Carole, and Michael Kearney. 1990. "Mixtec Ethnicity: Social Identity, Political Consciousness, and Political Activism." *Latin American Research Review,* 61–91.

Nash, June. 1979. *We Eat the Mines and the Mines Eat Us.* New York: Columbia University Press.

Nash, June, et al. 1995. *The Explosion of Communities in Chiapas.* Copenhagen: International Work Group for Indigenous Affairs.

Noriega Elío, Cecilia. 1992. *El nacionalismo en México.* Zamora: El Colegio de Michoacán.

Nugent, Daniel. 1985. "Anthropology, Handmaiden of History?" *Critique of Anthropology* 5(2):71–86.

———. 1987. "Mexico's Rural Populations and La Crisis: Economic Crisis or Legitimation Crisis?" *Critique of Anthropology* 7(3):93–112.

———. 1988. "Land, Labor and Politics in a Serrano Society: The Articulation of State and Popular Ideology in Mexico." Ph.D. dissertation, University of Chicago.

———. 1989. *Conflicting Views of State and Revolution in the Chihuahuan Sierra.* Texas Papers on Mexico, no. 88-03. Austin: The Mexican Center.

———. 1991. "Revolutionary Posturing, Bourgeois Land 'Reform': Reflections on the Agrarian Reform in Northern Mexico." *LABOUR, Capital and Society* 24(1):90–108.

———. 1993. *Spent Cartridges of Revolution: An Anthropological History of Namiquipa, Chihuahua.* Chicago: University of Chicago Press.

———. 1994. "The Center at the Periphery: Civilization and Barbarism on the Northern Mexican Frontier." *Identities: Global Studies in Power and Culture* 1(2–3):151–72.

———. 1995a. "Reflexiones sobre la antigüedad de las identidades poscoloniales." *Unicornio. Suplemento Cultural de ¡Por Esto!* 16 April.

———. 1995b. "Northern intellectuals and the EZLN." *Monthly Review* 47(3):124–28.

Nugent, Daniel, and Ana Alonso. 1994. "Multiple Selective Traditions in Agrarian Reform and Agrarian Struggle." In Joseph and Nugent 1994a.

O'Connor, Harvey. 1937. *The Guggenheims.* New York: Covico Friede.

O'Hanlon, Rosalind. 1988. "Recovering the Subject: Subaltern Studies and Histories of Resistance in Colonial South Asia." *Modern Asian Studies* 22(1):189–224.

Olea Arias, Heliodoro. 1961. *Apuntes históricos de la revolución de 1910–1911.* Chihuahua City: Impresora ALFFER.

Oppenheimer, Andres. 1996 *Bordering on Chaos.* Boston: Little, Brown.

Orozco, Victor. 1995. *Tierra de libres: Los pueblos del distrito Guerrero en el siglo XIX.* Vol. 3, pt. 1, of *Historia general de Chihuahua.* Ciudad Juárez: Universidad Autónoma de Ciudad Juárez/Gobierno del Estado de Chihuahua.

Osorio, Rubén, ed. 1986. *La correspondencia de Francisco Villa.* Chihuahua City: Gobierno del Estado de Chihuahua.

———. 1990. *Pancho Villa, ese desconocido: Entrevistas en Chihuahua a favor y en contra.* Chihuahua City: Gobierno del Estado de Chihuahua.

———. n.d. "Tomóchic, la guerra del fin del mundo en la sierra." Manuscript.

Paige, Jeffery M. 1975. *Agrarian Revolution: Social Movements and Export Agriculture in the Underdeveloped World.* New York: Free Press.

Palerm Vich, Angel. 1980. *Antropología y marxismo.* Mexico City: CISINAH/Nueva Imagen.

Paoli, Francisco J., and Enrique Montalvo. 1977. *El socialismo olvidado de Yucatán: Elementos para una reinterpretación de la revolución mexicana.* Mexico City: Siglo XXI.

Patch, Robert. 1976. "La formación de estancias y haciendas durante la colonia." In *Cuatro ensayos antropológicos.* Mérida: Universidad de Yucatán.

Pereyra, Carlos, et al. 1980. *Historia ¿para qué?* Mexico City: Siglo XXI.

Post, Ken. 1978. *Arise, Ye Starvelings.* The Hague: Martinus Nijhoff.

Prakash, Gyan. 1990. "Writing Post-Orientalist Histories of the Third World: Perspectives from Indian Historiography." *Comparative Studies in Society and History* 32(3):383–408.

———. 1994. "Subaltern Studies as Postcolonial Criticism." *American Historical Review* 99(5):1475–90.

———. 1995. "Introduction: After Colonialism." In G. Prakash, ed., *After Colonialism: Imperial Histories and Postcolonial Displacements.* Princeton: Princeton University Press.

Purcell, Anita, ed. 1963. *Frontier Mexico, 1875–1894: Letters of William L. Purcell.* San Antonio: Naylor.

Radical History Review. 1983. Special Issue (no. 27) on Colonialism and Resistance. Edited by Brooke Larson. New York: MARHO.

Ranger, Terrence. 1985. *Peasant Consciousness and Guerilla War in Zimbabwe.* London: James Curry.

Reed, John. 1969. *Insurgent Mexico.* New York: International Publishers.

Reed, Nelson. 1964. *The Caste War of Yucatán.* Stanford: Stanford University Press. Translated into Spanish as *La guerra de castas en Yucatán* [1979] (Mexico City: Ediciones Era).

Reina, Leticia. 1980. *Las rebeliones campesinas en México.* Mexico City: Siglo XXI.

Remmers, Lawrence J. 1981. "Henequen, the Caste War, and the Economy of Yucatán, 1846–1883: The Roots of Dependence in a Mexican Region." Ph.D. dissertation, University of California, Los Angeles.

Reyna Aoyama, Leticia. 1993. "Introducción." In Antonio Escobar Ohmstede, ed., *Indio, nación y comunidad en el México del siglo XIX.* Mexico City: Ediciones de la Casa Chata.

Richmond, Douglas W. 1985. "Provincial Factors during the War of 1847: The Case of Yucatán." Paper presented at the Seventh Conference of Mexican and United States Historians, Oaxaca, October.

Roazen-Parrillo, Diane. 1984. "U.S. Business Interests and the Sisal Industry of Yucatán, Mexico, 1876–1924." Ph.D. dissertation, University of Chicago.

Rocha Islas, Marta. 1979. "Del villismo y las defensas sociales en Chihuahua." Thesis, Universidad Nacional Autónoma de México.

Rodríguez, Jaime E., ed. 1990. *The Revolutionary Process in Mexico: Essays on Political and Social Change, 1880–1940.* Los Angeles: UCLA, Latin American Center Publications.

Ronfeldt, David. 1973. *Atencingo: The Politics of Agrarian Struggle in a Mexican Ejido.* Stanford: Stanford University Press.

Roseberry, William. 1989. *Anthropologies and Histories: Essays in Culture, History, and Political Economy.* New Brunswick: Rutgers University Press.

———. 1994. "Hegemony and the Language of Contention." In Joseph and Nugent 1994a.

Roseberry, William, and Jay O'Brien, eds. 1991. *Golden Ages, Dark Ages: Imagin-*

ing the Past in Anthropology and History. Berkeley: University of California Press.

Ross, Stanley R. 1959. "Dwight Morrow and the Mexican Revolution." *Hispanic American Historical Review* 38:506–28.

Rouse, Roger. 1991. "Mexican Migration and the Social Space of Postmodernism." *Diaspora* 1(1):8–23.

———. 1995. "Questions of Identity: Personhood and Collectivity in Transnational Migration to the United States." *Critique of Anthropology* 15(4):352–80.

Roux, Rhina. 1996. "México: crisis de la forma de estado." In Gilly 1996.

Rus, Jan. 1983. "Whose Caste War? Indians, Ladinos and the Chiapas 'Caste War' of 1869." In MacLeod and Wasserstrom, 1983.

———. 1994. "The 'Comunidad Revolucionaria Institucional': The Subversion of Native Government in Highland Chiapas, 1936–1968." In Joseph and Nugent 1994a. Published in Spanish as "La comunidad revolucionaria institucional: La subversion del gobierno indígena en Los Altos de Chiapas, 1936–1968," in Viqueira and Ruz 1995.

Saul, John. 1979. *The State and Revolution in East Africa*. New York: Monthly Review Press.

Sayer, Derek. 1994. "Everyday Forms of State Formation: Some Dissident Remarks on 'Hegemony.'" In Joseph and Nugent 1994.

Scott, James C. 1976. *The Moral Economy of the Peasant: Rebellion and Subsistence in South East Asia*. New Haven: Yale University Press.

———. 1985. *Weapons of the Weak: Everyday Forms of Peasant Resistance*. New Haven: Yale University Press.

———. 1990. *Domination and the Arts of Resistance: Hidden Transcripts*. New Haven: Yale University Press.

Semo, Enrique, ed. 1983. *México: Un pueblo en la historia*. 3 vols. Mexico City: Nueva Imagen/Universidad Autónoma de Puebla.

Senior, Clarence. 1958. *Land Reform and Democracy*. Gainesville: University Press of Florida.

Sherwell, G. Butler. 1929. *Mexico's Capacity to Pay: A General Analysis of the Present International Economic Position of Mexico*. Washington, D.C.: n.p.

Shields, Karena. 1959. *The Changing Wind*. New York: Thomas Crowell.

Sierra O'Reilly, Justo. 1938 [1848]. *Diario de huestro viaje a los Estados Unidos*. Mexico City: Antigua Librería Robredo.

Simpson, Eyler. 1937. *The Ejido: Mexico's Way Out*. Chapel Hill: University of North Carolina Press.

Sivaramakrishnan, K. 1995. "Situating the Subaltern: History and Anthropology in the *Subaltern Studies* Project." *Journal of Historical Sociology* 8(4):395–429.

Skocpol, Theda. 1979. *States and Social Revolutions.* New York: Cambridge University Press.

———. 1982. "What Makes Peasants Revolutionary?" *Comparative Politics* 14(3): 351–75.

Smith, Carol A. 1984. "Local History in Global Context: Social and Economic Transitions in Western Guatemala." *Comparative Studies in Society and History* 26(2):193–228.

Smith, Gavin. 1985. "Reflections on the Social Relations of Simple Commodity Production." *Journal of Peasant Studies* 13(1):99–108.

———. 1989. *Livelihood and Resistance: Peasants and the Politics of Land in Peru.* Berkeley: University of California Press.

Smith, Robert Freeman. 1972. *The U.S. and Revolutionary Nationalism in Mexico, 1916–32.* Chicago: University of Chicago Press.

Smithers, W. D. 1981. *Circuit Riders of the Big Bend.* El Paso: Texas Western Press.

———. n.d. 1. "The Border Trading Posts." In *Pancho Villa's Last Hangout: On Both Sides of the Rio Grande in the Big Bend Country.* Alpine, Tex.: n.p.

———. n.d. 2. "Bandit Raids in the Big Bend Country." In *Pancho Villa's Last Hangout: On Both Sides of the Rio Grande in the Big Bend Country.* Alpine, Tex.: n.p.

Solís, Gregorio M. 1936. *Acontecimientos chihuahuenses.* Chihuahua City: La Prensa/Bonifacio S. Martínez.

Spicer, Edward. 1980. *The Yaquis: A Cultural History.* Tucson: University of Arizona Press.

Spivak, Gayatri Chakravorty. 1985. "Subaltern Studies: Deconstructing Historiography." In *Subaltern Studies.* Vol. 4. Delhi: Oxford University Press. Also in Guha and Spivak 1988.

———. 1988. "Can the Subaltern Speak?" In Cary Nelson and Lawrence Grossberg, eds., *Marxism and the Interpretation of Culture.* London: Macmillan Education.

Spores, Ronald. 1967. *The Mixtec Kings and Their People.* Norman: University of Oklahoma Press.

———. 1984. *The Mixtecs in Ancient and Colonial Times.* Norman: University of Oklahoma Press.

Stephenson, George M. 1935. *John Lind of Minnesota.* Minneapolis: University of Minnesota Press.

Stern, Steve J. 1987. "New Approaches to the Study of Peasant Rebellion and Consciousness: Implications of the Andean Experience." In Stern, ed., *Resistance, Rebellion and Consciousness in the Andean Peasant World, 18th to 20th Centuries*. Madison: University of Wisconsin Press.

Sterrett, J. E., and J. S. Davis. 1928. *The Fiscal and Economic Condition of Mexico: Report Submitted to the International Committee of Bankers on Mexico*.

Stocking, George W. 1991. *Colonial Situations: Essays on the Contextualization of Ethnographic Knowledge*. Vol. 7 of *History of Anthropology*. Madison: University of Wisconsin Press.

Subcomandante Marcos. 1995a. "Carta a Adolfo Gilly," 22 October 1994. In Gilly, Marcos, and Ginzburg 1995.

———. 1995b. "Historia de Marcos y de los hombres de la noche." Interview with Carmen Castillo and Tessa Brisac, 24 October 1994. In Gilly, Marcos, and Ginzburg 1995.

Taussig, Michael T. 1980. *The Devil and Commodity Fetishism in South America*. Chapel Hill: University of North Carolina Press.

Taylor, William B. 1979. *Drinking, Homicide and Rebellion in Colonial Mexican Villages*. Stanford: Stanford University Press.

Tello Díaz, Carlos. 1995. *La rebelión de las cañadas*. Mexico City: Ediciones Cal y Arena.

Thomas, Keith. 1973. *Religion and the Decline of Magic*. Harmondsworth: Penguin.

Thompson, Edward H. 1932. *People of the Serpent: Life and Adventure among the Mayas*. Boston: Houghton Mifflin.

Thompson, Edward P. 1967. "Time, Work-Discipline, and Industrial Capitalism." *Past and Present* 38.

———. 1971. "The Moral Economy of the English Crowd in the Eighteenth Century." *Past and Present* 50:76–136.

———. 1978. *The Poverty of Theory and Other Essays*. New York: Monthly Review Press.

———. 1991. *Customs in Common*. London: Merlin Press.

Tilly, Charles. 1975. "Revolution and Collective Violence." In *Handbook of Political Science*. Vol. 3. Edited by Fred I. Greenstein and Nelson Polsby. Reading, Mass.: Addison-Wesley.

Tobler, Hans Werner. 1971. "Las paradojas del ejército revolucionario: Su papel en la reforma agraria mexicana, 1920–35." *Historia Mexicana* 21(1)38–79.

Tomlinson, John. 1991. *Cultural Imperialism: A Critical Introduction.* London: Pinter Publishers.

Tompkins, Frank. 1934. *Chasing Villa.* Harrisburg: Military Service Publishing Company.

Traven, B. 1971. *March to Caobaland.* Harmondsworth: Penguin.

Turner, Frederick C. 1968. *The Dynamic of Mexican Nationalism.* Chapel Hill: University of North Carolina Press.

Turner, John Kenneth. 1910. *Barbarous Mexico.* Chicago: C. H. Kerr.

Turner, Terence S. 1986a. "The Politics of Culture: The Movement for Cultural Survival as Political Movement and Anthropological Problem." Manuscript.

———. 1986b. "Production, Exploitation and Social Consciousness in the 'Peripheral Situation.'" *Social Analysis* 19 (August):91–115.

Tutino, John. 1975. "Hacienda Social Relations in Mexico: The Chalco Region in the Era of Independence." *Hispanic American Historical Review* 55(3):496–528.

———. 1976. "Indian Rebellion at the Isthmus of Tehuantepec: A Socio-Historical Perspective." In *Actes des XLIIe Internacional Congress des Americanistes.* Vol. 2. Paris.

———. 1986. *From Insurrection to Revolution in Mexico: Social Bases of Agrarian Violence, 1750–1940.* Princeton: Princeton University Press.

Tyler, Ronnie C. 1975a. "The Little Punitive Expedition in the Big Bend." *Southwestern Historical Quarterly* 78(3):271–91.

———. 1975b. *The Big Bend: A History of the Last Texas Frontier.* Washington, D.C.: National Park Service, Department of the Interior.

Ulloa, Berta. 1971. *La revolución intervenida. Relaciones diplomáticas entre México y Estados Unidos (1910–14).* Mexico City: El Colegio de México.

———. 1979. *Historia de la revolución mexicana: Período 1914–1917.* Mexico City: El Colegio de México.

Van Young, Eric. 1981. *Hacienda and Market in Eighteenth-Century Mexico: The Rural Economy of the Guadalajara Region, 1675–1820.* Berkeley: University of California Press.

———. 1986. "Mexican Regions: Comparative History and Development." Conference proposal.

———. 1990. "To See Someone Not Seeing: Historical Studies of Peasants and Politics in Mexico." *Mexican Studies/Estudios Mexicanos* 6(1):133–59.

———. 1993. "Rebelión agraria sin agrarismo: Defensa de la comunidad, significado y violencia colectiva en la sociedad rural mexicana de fines de la época colonial." In Antonio Escobar Ohmstede, ed., *Indio, nación y comunidad en el México del siglo XIX.* Mexico City: Ediciones de la Casa Chata.

———. 1994. "The State as Vampire: Hegemonic Projects, Public Ritual, and Popular Culture in Mexico, 1600–1990." In William Beezley, Cheryl English Martin, and William E. French, eds., *Rituals of Rule, Rituals of Resistance: Public Celebrations and Popular Culture in Mexico.* Wilmington: SR Books.

———. 1995. "Paisaje de ensueño con figuras y vallados: Disputa y discurso cultural en el campo mexicano de fines de la Colonia." In Jane-Dale Lloyd and Laura Pérez Rosales, eds., *Paisajes rebeldes: Una larga noche de resistencia indígena.* Mexico City: Universidad Iberamericana.

Vázquez, Josefina Zoraida, and Lorenzo Meyer. 1982. *México frente a Estados Unidos. Un ensayo histórico, 1776–1980.* Mexico City: El Colegio de México.

Viqueira, Juan Pedro, and Mario Humberto Ruz, eds. 1995. *Chiapas: Los rumbos de otra historia.* Mexico City: UNAM.

Warman, Arturo. 1976. . . . *Y venimos a contradecir. Los campesinos de Morelos y el estado nacional.* Mexico City: Ediciones de la Casa Chata.

Wasserman, Mark. 1980. "The Social Origins of the 1910 Revolution in Chihuahua." *Latin American Research Review* 15(1):15–40.

———. 1984. *Capitalists, Caciques and Revolution: The Native Elite and Foreign Enterprise in Chihuahua, Mexico, 1854–1911.* Chapel Hill: University of North Carolina Press.

Wasserstrom, Robert. 1983. *Class and Society in Central Chiapas.* Berkeley: University of California Press.

Weber, David J. 1982. *The Mexican Frontier, 1821–1846. The American Southwest under Mexico.* Albuquerque: University of New Mexico Press.

Wells, Allen. 1984. "Yucatán: Violence and Social Control on Henequen Plantations." In Thomas Benjamin and William McNellie, eds., *Other Mexicos: Essays on Regional Mexican History, 1876–1911.* Albuquerque: University of New Mexico Press.

———. 1985. *Yucatán's Gilded Age: Haciendas, Henequen and International Harvester, 1860–1915.* Albuquerque: University of New Mexico Press.

Whetten, Nathan. 1948. *Rural Mexico.* Chicago: University of Chicago Press.

Wilkins, Mira. 1971. *The Emergence of Multinational Enterprise: American Business Abroad from the Colonial Era to 1914.* Cambridge: Harvard University Press.

Williams, Mary W. 1929. "The Secessionist Diplomacy of Yucatán." *Hispanic American Historical Review* 9:132–43.

Wolf, Eric. 1959. *Sons of the Shaking Earth*. Chicago: University of Chicago Press.

——. 1969. *Peasant Wars of the Twentieth Century*. New York: Harper and Row.

——. 1973. *Peasant Wars of the Twentieth Century*. London: Faber and Faber.

——. 1982. *Europe and the People without History*. Berkeley: University of California Press.

——. 1990. "Facing Power: Old Insights, New Questions." *American Anthropologist* 92(3):586–96.

Womack, John. 1969. *Zapata and the Mexican Revolution*. New York: Knopf. Translated into Spanish as *Zapata y la revolución mexicana* (Mexico City: Siglo XXI, 1969).

——. 1986. "The Mexican Revolution, 1910–1920." In *The Cambridge History of Latin America*. Vol. 5. Edited by Leslie Bethell. New York: Cambridge University Press.

Wood, C. D. 1963. *The Glenn Springs Raid*. West Texas Historical and Scientific Society Publications, no. 19.

Worsley, Peter. 1984. *The Three Worlds*. Chicago: University of Chicago Press.

Index

Abrams, Philip, 19

Acculturation, migration-induced, 61–62

Adams Gum, 76

Agrarian reform: American landowners reaction to, 35–36, 38; American losses due to, 37, 37n. 14; Constitution of 1917 legitimization of, 87; and *defensas sociales*, 236; and expropriation (*see* Expropriation); impact of Apache Wars on, 152n. 9; impact on American capital investment, 38–39; Madero on, 79, 82; Obregón role in, 34; and patterns of American investment, 48–50, 74–77; and patterns of Mexican and Spanish investment, 49–50; peasant initiation of, 70; policies of rebel leaders, 255; provisions of Article 27 for, 269–71; reasons for delay in, 66–67; U.S. reaction to, 36–39, 254–55; and *villista* nationalization of haciendas, 86; *villista* versus *carrancista* policy of, 250–55; Woodrow Wilson on, 242; *zapatista*, 86; by *zapatistas*, 86. *See also* Municipal Land Law of 1905; Peasants: dispossession of; Plan de San Luis de Potosí

Agraristas. See Agrarian reform

El Agricultor, 174, 196n. 42

Agriculture: and Caste War, 185–86; coffee monoculture, 286, 290; commercialization of, 68, 72, 132, 139–40, 175, 198, 263, 286, 286n. 20; end of price supports in, 290; henequen monoculture (*see* Henequen monoculture); labor-repressive, 56–57;

maize, 290; subsistence, 139–40; sugar monoculture (*see* Sugar monoculture)

Agroindustrialization. *See* Agriculture: commercialization of

Aguilar, Juan, 117

Aguilar Camín, Héctor, 252

Aguirre, Reidecel, 226

Aldrich-Baruch-Guggenheim, 84

Alonso, Ana María, 6, 13, 224n. 23, 225n. 26, 232, 246

Althusser, Louis, 323

Alvarado, Salvador, 173, 203

Alvarez, Natividad, 164

Amarillas, Ciro, 157

Amaya, Simón, 90, 91

"Americanization in the Americas" (Roseberry), 15

Amnesty International, 289

Anaya, Celso, 90, 91

ANCIEZ (Alianza Nacional Campesina Independiente Emiliano Zapata), 293, 294

Anderson, Benedict, 12, 22, 148, 167n. 48, 210

Anderson Clayton Co., 38

Angeles, Felipe, 89n. 1, 92, 245

Anglo-Canadian Agua Azul, 58

Anti-Americanism: among political parties, 243; due to political interventions, 52; and intellectuals, 47–48, 245; and Mexican nationalism, 70; in Mexican Revolution, 27, 46–47; of middle class, 234n. 51; potential for, 44–45; related to types of American economic interests, 56; revisionist scholarship on, 53; of

Anti-Americanism (*cont.*)
Texans of Mexican descent, 160. *See also* Landowners, American: violence against
Anti-imperialism: in Mexican Revolution, 27, 328; as motivation for revolutionary mobilization, 10, 219–20; of Villa, 219–20, 220n. 18; of *villistas*, 222–23
Apache Wars: and development of imagined community, 213; effect on northern regionalism/localism, 215–16; impact on land distribution, 152n. 9; intragroup social relationships during, 131; oral tradition of, 97n. 17; and settlers, 111
Archila, Mauricio, 138
Arenas brothers, 256
Aron, Raymond, 41
Article 27, of Constitution of 1917: provisions of, 269–71, 273–74; "reforms" to, 11, 17, 276, 287
ASARCO, 53, 56
Ascasillados, 186
ASMIRT (Asociación de los Mixtecos Residentes en Tijuana), 142–43
Atascador colony, 84
Azcarate, Anastasio, 122
Azcarate, Francisco, 122
Azcarate, Santiago, 122

Baca, Cruz, 98n. 19
Baja California, 143, 144
Bancroft, Secretary of the Navy, 183
Bandits, 163–64, 232, 236
Barbachano, Miguel, 182, 183, 189
Barret, Domingo, 184
Barthes, Roland, 20
Bencomo, José, 223
Benjamin, Thomas, 54n. 32
Benton, William, 48, 246
Bergquist, Charles, 45
Bill for the Relief of Yucatán, 188–89
Bill Russell raid, 164
Bloch, Ernst, 327

Bodin, Jean, 28
Bonfil, Guillermo, 264, 277–78, 316
Boquillas raid, 164
Borah, Woodrow, 264n. 5, 273n. 14
Border, Mexican-U.S.: cross-border relationship with Americans, 156–58; impact on Mexican Revolution, 70, 257; Katz on impact of, 69–70, 152, 216; nationalism on, 212–15; and state nonintervention in, 153–54, 213–14
Bourbon boom, 42–43
Braden, Spruille, 34
Breton, André, 320
Brown Brothers, 75
Brownness, 214
Bryan, William Jennings, 244

Cabañas, Lucio, 138
Cabrera, Luis, 241
Caciques, 271, 272, 284–85, 297
Calles, Plutarco Elías, 34, 297–98
Calzadíaz Barrera, Alberto, 207n. 1
Camacho Solís, Manuel, 304
Cámara Agrícola, 196n. 42
Camarilla (divine caste), 193, 195–96, 205
Cambridge History of Latin America, 21–22
Campechano elites, 204
Campeche, 76, 184
Campos, Francisco, 98n. 19
Canada, William, 58
Cananea Copper Company, 76
Canova, Leon, 221, 248, 255
Capital, U.S.: and formation of working class, 61–62; impact of, 8, 216, 262n. 1; increase in, 40, 40n. 18; infusion of, 111; patterns of investment by, 48–50; during *porfiriato,* 39–43; shift of, 38; latent impact of, 27–29; patterns of investment by, 74–77; regional variations in, 43–44, 55n. 33
Capital-intensive enterprises, 55–58, 55n. 33
Cárdenas, Cuauhtémoc, 268, 291

Cárdenas, Lázaro, 36–37, 269, 270
Cárdenas Martínez, León, 207n. 1
Cardenismo, perception of, 302–3
Carothers, George, 48, 240, 244, 255
Carrancistas, 164, 230–31, 250–55. *See also* Constitutionalists
Carranza, Venustiano, 93; agrarian reform policies of, 250–55; defense of *hacendados,* 86; dependency on Obregón Salido, Álvaro, 87; social background of, 250–51; taxation of foreigners by, 243; U.S. influence on, 256–57; U.S. recognition of, 164, 221, 247; U.S. support for, 86–87, 86n. 21, 241, 248; Villa on, 100; versus Villa on expropriation, 254–55
Carrillo Puerto, Felipe, 173, 174, 203
Castellanos, Absalón, 289
Castellanos, Rosario, 278
Caste War (1847), 176, 178–91; consequences of, 190–92; elite perception of, 12, 196–97; elite supporters of, 186n. 23; issue of equality in, 262; Mayan perception of, 12, 185–86; U.S. economic assistance in, 186–87; U.S. military assistance during, 182–84, 187–88
Catholic Church, 288, 291, 297, 297n. 25
CCRI (Clandestine Revolutionary Indigenous Committee), 301, 322, 323
Cedros hacienda, 84
Celaya, battle of, 86n. 21
Ceniceros, Severiano, 253
Central government. *See* State
Certificate of Adhesion, 217
Cervantes, Candelario, 222–24, 223nn. 20, 21, 225n. 27, 226, 227, 227n. 33
Chávez, Cruz, 91
Chávez, Manuel, 91
Chayanov, A. V., 140
Chi, Cecilio, 185
Chiapas: American acquisitions in, 76; colonization in, 285; elites in, 299; Indians in, 283–90; marginalization

of, 278; peasant mobilization in, 288, 293–94; repression in, 288–90, 300–301. *See also* EZLN (Ejército Zapatista de Liberación Nacional)
Chihuahua, 107–33; American acquisitions in, 75; collective identity in, 147–70; common lands in, 111–12; elites in, 108, 235; infusion of capital into, 111; lower-class violence in, 77; Municipal Land Law of 1905 (*see* Municipal Land Law of 1905); peasants and nationalism in, 215–18; peasant-warriors of, 215–17; social classes in, 97–99, 108, 116–17, 129–30, 235; uniqueness of rebel movement in, 97–98. *See also* Identity; Mápula, Donaciano; *Villistas*
CIA (Central Intelligence Agency), 294n. 23
CIOAC (Central Independiente de Obreros Agrícolas y Campesinos), 141, 143
Ciudad Real (Castellanos), 278
Civil society, and revolt, 301, 304, 307
Clements, George, 227n. 33
Clientalism, and U.S. enterprises, 52–53, 56, 212, 232, 236
CNC (Confederación Nacional Campesina), 286
Coatsworth, John, 3, 7; on patterns of rebellion, 265; on U.S. imperialism and Mexican Revolution, 9, 328
Coercion: of labor by American companies, 57–60; of soldiers by *villistas,* 231, 231n. 45
Coffee monoculture, 286, 290
Collaboration: with American invaders, 208, 209, 225, 227–28, 230–31, 231n. 45; with American landed interests, 35, 49–50; and dependent capitalism, 178; and henequen monoculture, 193; reasons for, 13, 51–52
Colonization, 55, 84, 149–50, 219n. 16, 285. *See also* names of individual colonies

Colosio, Luis Donaldo, 4
Columbus raid, 207–8, 221–22, 223, 238, 249
Comaroff, Jean, 168n. 49
Comaroff, John, 6, 15, 168n. 49
Communes, Mixteca, 135–38
"Community in anonymity," 167n. 48
Communities: and collective action, 28n. 18; imagined, 22, 210, 213, 215
Compadrazgo, 130–31, 132
Compañía Constructora Richardson, 75–76, 84
Compañía de Terrenos y Ganados, 76
Compañía Mexicana de Agricultura e Irrigación, 132
Companies, American. *See* Land-owners, American; *names of individual companies*
Conant, Carlos, 98n. 19
Connor, David, 183
Consejo 500 Años de Resistencia Indígena, 321–22
Constitution, Federal (1824), 182
Constitutionalists, 67, 86, 86n. 21, 87–88, 203, 235n. 42. *See also* Carrancistas
Constitution of 1917, 17, 276, 287; codification of agrarian power in, 269–71; EZLN proposition to restore, 310; Indian reforms to, 311n. 31; legitimization of agrarian reform by, 87. *See also* Article 27, of Constitution of 1917
"Contradictory consciousness," 211
Contreras, Calixto, 240, 253
Convenios, of 14 December 1843, 181
Convention of Aguascalientes, 94
Corallitos Land and Cattle Company, 75, 126
Corporatism, 287, 295
Corral, Luz, 229
Corral, Ramón, 229, 230
El Correo de Chihuahua, 98
Corrigan, Philip, 12, 21, 168, 273n. 13, 314, 315, 317
Craig, Ann, 5

Cramer, Lieutenant, 163
Creel, Enrique C., 99n. 20, 119, 276; decrees of, 116; land expropriations of, 252; and Municipal Land Law, 112–13, 261; and privatizations, 10
Crespo, Horacio, 108
Criminal court records, 200, 206
Cristeros, 270, 297
Croix, Teodoro de, 110n. 2
Cruz Sánchez, José de la, 157n. 18, 159, 161
CTM (Confederación de Trabajadores Mexicanos), 141, 141n. 2
Cuba, 28, 38, 39, 41n. 19, 177
Cuchillo Parado, 166–67n. 46, 166–69
Culture, definition of, 313–14
Currency, *villista*, 67n. 2, 243, 255, 257

Daniels, Josephus, 36
David, Commandante, 305
Davis, Lamar, 157
Debt-peonage system, 59, 193
Decree of 24 September 1906, 116n. 16
Defensas sociales: and agrarian reform, 236; establishment of, 227–28, 227nn. 34, 35, 229; mobilization of, 235n. 52; rationale for, 232; social classes in, 231n. 46
Democratic Party (Mexico), 243
Desertions, 231n. 45
Destino, concept of, 151–52, 154
Díaz, Felipe, 92
Díaz, Félix, 251
Díaz, Porfirio, 111n. 1, 73, 81; criticism of, 158; effect of fall of, 202; opponents of, 253; plots to overthrow, 89–90. *See also* Porfiriato
Diéguez, Manuel, 253
Dignity, Indians' demand for, 279–83, 316, 326
División del Norte, 85, 100, 243. *See also* Villa, Francisco
Duarte Morales, Teodosio, 223
Dumont, Louis, 318
Durango, 75, 77, 78, 80

Echeribel, Alejandro, 124
Echeribel, Martín, 124, 125
Education, and formation of working class, 62
Edward Hartman (company), 76
Ejidos, 110–11, 110n. 2, 113, 119–20, 286. *See also* Agrarian reform
Elites, 113n. 8; alienation of, 77–78; alliances of, 202–3, 286–87, 292; anticentrist leanings of, 178–79; apologists for, 201n. 54; Chiapas, 299; Chihuahuan, 108, 235; consolidation of national, 268, 287; dependence on U.S. of, 177, 204; division among, 179, 184n. 20, 202–3, 204, 205; engagement with U.S. influences, 7; and expropriation, 270–71, 273–74; and henequen monoculture, 195–96; historiography of, 18–19; impact of market forces on, 44; Indian supporters of, 186; metropolitan versus provincial, 78, 79; mobilization of, 19, 74, 77–78; modernization of, 285–87; municipal land purchases of, 119–24; pact with peasantry by, 275; power domains of, 20; precautions against rural revolt, 198–99; reaction to U.S. capitalization of land, 74–77; regional, 12; reliance on armed peasants, 267–68; repression by, 73, 197–98, 285–86; revolutionary leadership of, 77–78; speculation by, 195
Ellsworth, Luther T., 159–60
ELN (Ejército de Liberación Nacional), 298
Enchanted world, impact of, 13, 320–21, 327
Enlightenment thought, 279, 280, 330
Enríquez, Ignacio, 227n. 34
Escoffié Zetina, Carlos P., 196n. 42
Estévez, Dolia, 294n. 23
Estrada, Richard, 93–94
Ethnic identity: and active resistance, 11–12, 138–44, 217–18; and passive resistance, 135–38; white versus brown, 214–15
Eusebio Escalante e Hijo, 193–94
Evans, Rosalie, 36
Export-led growth, 42, 68, 97
Expropriation: and land distribution, 10, 34–36, 37n. 14; of oil companies, 271; and peasant land distribution, 73, 252; Villa versus Carranza on, 254–55
External forces, and theories of rural revolt, 14–17
External world, impact of, 263–64, 326–27
Extraction, of value, 137–38
EZLN (Ejército Zapatista de Liberación Nacional), 277; collective reflection of, 302, 303; *la consulta*, 302; decision to rebel, 300–304; demands of, 304–5, 310; discourse on nonexcluding modernity, 312; explanation for revolt of, 309–13, 328; formation of, 292; government denial of, 294, 294n. 23; initiation into communities, 298–99; Marcos on focus of, 298n. 26, 299n. 27; membership of, 292–93, 292n. 21, 295; methodology based on Guha, 294–300; on NAFTA, 300n. 29; negotiations with government, 307–13; news media reports on, 294n. 23, 307, 312; rebellion launched, 304–6; relationship with Catholic Church, 297n. 25. *See also* Marcos, Subcommandante

Fabela, Isidro, 241
Fall, Albert Bacon, 56–57
Fences, 73, 77
El Financiero, 307
First Declaration of the Selva Lacandona, 311
First Indian Congress of Chiapas, 288, 296
Flores, Paulino, 124
Florescano, Enrique, 308
Foucault, Michel, 16n. 2, 20

France, invasion of Mexico, 68, 217
Friedrich, Paul, 5
Frontier regions, 8, border as, 70; colonization of, 149–50; marginalization in, 154–55
Fundos legales, 113, 115, 119

Gamio, Manuel, 60, 60n. 35
García, Mauricio, 110
García, Telésforo, 110
García de León, Antonio, 286n. 20, 289, 299
García Teruel, Luis, 110
Garza, Catarino de la, 89
Garza, Lázaro de la, 161, 245
Gilly, Adolfo, 1, 5, 8, 11, 13
Globalization, 329–30, 329n. 33
Global structures of power, and rural revolt, 14–17, 175
Goldfrank, Walter, 3
Gómez del Campo, Ignacio, 110
Gonzáles Herrera, Carlos, 157n. 16
González, Abrahám, 93, 98, 99, 158, 246, 253
González, Manuel, 126
González, Pablo, 253
González Blanco, Salomón, 291
González Garrido, Patrocino, 291, 292, 299, 304
González Garza, Federico, 245, 249–51
Gramsci, Antonio, 211
Graves, Captain, 226
Greene, Graham, 272
Grienssen, Elisa, 234n. 51
Guccini, Francesco, 280
Guha, Ranajit, 18–19, 266–67, 294–300
Guillén Vicente, Rafael Sebastián, 312–13
Gulf Coast Land and Lumber Company, 84
Gutiérrez Barrios, Fernando, 291–92

Haberman, Robert, 174
Haciendas, 53–55
Hamm, U.S. Consul, 240–41
Hammond, John Hays, 56

Hanna, U.S. Consul, 33n. 8
Harriman, E. H., 76
Hart, John Mason, 7, 8–9, 44
Harvey, Neil, 300n. 29
Hearst, William Randolph, 37, 75, 76, 157
Henequen monoculture, 173; labor recruitment for, 198–99; lack of American landowners in, 201n. 52; and U.S. capital, 177, 191–93, 195–96; worker resistance in, 201–2. *See also* International Harvester Company
Hepburn, John Buchanan, 98
Hernández, Braulio, 32, 158
Herrera, José, 189
Hopkins, Sherburne, 245
Houston, Sam, 188
Huach, 189n. 32
Huerta, Adolfo de la, 93, 94, 202, 203, 256

Identity: active resistance and ethnic, 11–12, 138–44, 217–18; collective, 131, 147–70, 169n. 51, 214, 296, 314–15; and collective reflection, 302, 303; linked with land, 264, 290; loss of, 153–55; and myths, 324–25; national, 12, 148–49, 311, 315–17; and other world, 326; passive resistance and ethnic, 135–38; regional, 153–54, 162; symbols of, 162, 166. *See also Indigenismo;* Localism; Mixteca; Regionalism
Imaginary, the, 271, 321–22
Imagined communities, 22, 210, 213, 215
Imán, Santiago, 179–80
IMF (International Monetary Fund), 4, 329
Imperialism, 9, 70, 328. *See also* Anti-imperialism
India, patterns of rebellion in, 18–19, 266–67, 294–300
Indians: ancient language of, 321–24; demand for dignity by, 279–83, 316; demand for inclusion by, 332; exclusion of, 278, 283, 285, 312; idea of com-

munity of, 280–81; and identity within state, 315–17; mobilization of, 293–94; population of ancient, 265n. 5; public versus private spheres, 324n. 32; right to plurality of, 316–17; subordination to state of, 284–85; and traditional society, 319, 321; vision of mankind, 264. *See also* Peasants

Indigenismo, 142–44, 278, 278n. 17, 295, 310–11, 315–16. *See also* Myths; Symbolism, in revolt

El indio, political significance of, 144, 151 n. 7

Ingenio, 81n. 12

INMECAFE (Institute Mexicano del Café), 286, 290

Insurgent Mexico (Reed), 251

Intellectuals: anti-Americanism of Mexican, 47–48, 245; anti-Villa sentiment of American, 245–46; as supporters of Villa, 249–51, 254

International Harvester Company, 173; and elites, 202, 205; influence of, 193, 199; loans made by, 177; press reports on, 196n. 42; research by, 203n. 57

International Lumber and Development, 75, 76

Investments, U.S. *See* Capital, U.S.; Landowners, American

Jaurrieta, José María, 93, 96n. 15

Jenkins, William, 38, 53

Jennings-Blocker, 75

Joseph, Gilbert, 5, 12, 197n. 44

Juárez, Benito, 167n. 46, 272

Justice, 282, 326

Katz, Friedrich, 7; external/internal historiographies of, 64; on impact of border, 69–70, 152, 216; *Pancho Villa, ese desconocido*, 95–96; on radicalization of revolutions, 65; *The Secret War in Mexico*, 5; on Villa, 95–96; on Villa and U.S., 9, 221

Kearney, Michael, 11–12

Kleinman, I., 161

Knight, Alan, 7; on agrarianism, 270; on agricultural commercialization, 68; Coatsworth on, 64–65; deconstruction of U.S. interventions by, 8; on domestic factors in Madero victory, 256; interpretation of Mexican Revolution by, 205; on nationalism and Mexican Revolution, 220; on nationalism as factor in peasant mobilization, 209n. 4; on northern peasants, 252; studies of macro- and micro-level processes, 5; on U.S. business, 70n. 5; on *villistas* versus *carrancistas*, 250–51; on violence and rural revolt, 201n. 53

Koreck, María Teresa, 6, 12, 21

Labor: coercion of, 57–60; creation of market for, 59, 186; debt-peonage, 59, 193; fixed-price system for, 54n. 31; incentive system for, 54n. 31, 55; migration of, 60–61; recruitment of, 57–58, 76–77, 198–99; relationship with employers, 53n. 29; repressive agricultural, 56–57; supply of, 52–53, 53n. 30; wage, 50, 52–53, 54, 141. *See also* Migration, labor

Labor-repressive agriculture, 56–57

Laguna Corporation, 76, 84

Laite, Julian, 140

Land: and Being, 264, 290; for common use, 110–11; decline in value of, 37, 37n. 13; *denuncias* of municipal, 113n. 8, 116n. 17; effect of capitalization of, 16–17, 73–75, 154; increase in prices of, 74; Municipal Land Law of 1905 (*see* Municipal Land Law of 1905); rental of, 121; rights to, 216, 218; speculation on, 114, 115, 128; titles to, 115, 116, 123. *See also* Agrarian reform; *Ejidos*

Land distribution. *See* Agrarian reform

Landed interests. *See entries beginning with* "landowners"

Land grants, 150, 150n. 6, 167

Landowners, American, 43, 201n. 52;
  acquisitions of, 75–76; and anti-
  American sentiment, 45, 46–47; beneficiaries of, 50; demands on Villa of,
  242; differences from Mexican and
  Spanish, 46; effect of Mexican Revolution on, 66; and henequen industry, 201n. 52; investment patterns of,
  49–50; labor defection from, 52;
  numbers of, 72; *orozquista* threat to,
  82–83; and Porfirian land-tenure system, 73–74; reaction to agrarian reform, 35–36, 38; support for, 49;
  violence against, 80, 81n. 11, 82–86,
  85n. 17, 86n. 20, 87, 157, 162–63. *See
  also* Collaboration
Landowners, Mexican, 48–49, 252. *See
  also* Elites
Landowners, Spanish, 37, 37n. 14, 46–
  47, 47n. 24, 48
Language, traditional, 317, 321–24
Latin American Subaltern Studies
  Group, 20
The Lawless Roads (Greene), 272
Le Bot, Yvon, 296–97, 298n. 26, 302
Liberalism, 218, 218n. 15, 277
Liberal Party, 253
Liberation Army of the South, 309
Lichbach, Mark, 324n. 32
Lind, John, 58, 86, 86n. 21, 239
Livestock industry, 161
Lloyd, Jane-Dale, 5, 10–11, 107–33, 261–
  62
Localism, 236; links to popular mo-
  bilization, 233–34; versus national-
  ism, 224–30, 228–29; and peasant-
  warriors, 149–50, 215–17; as used by
  Villa, 219, 250. *See also* Regionalism
Local leaders, 13, 284, 286, 287, 296–
  97
Long, Norman, 6
López, Alejandro, 124
López, Pablo, 124, 221–22
López Portillo, José, 94
"Los de abajo," 131

Löwy, Michael, 323
Luz Herrera, José de la, 234n. 51

Maderismo: causes of, 92; origins of,
  89–91; schisms in, 162–64; U.S. sup-
  port for (*see* Madero, Francisco: U.S.
  support for)
Madero, Francisco, 78; on agrarian re-
  form, 79, 82; incentives offered by, 79;
  murder of, 99; opponents of, 81–82;
  supporters of, 80, 196–97; U.S. sup-
  port for, 32, 83, 158–61, 256–57; Villa
  loyalty to, 92, 246
Madero, Gustavo, 93
Madrid, Anastasio, 124
Madrid, Cornelio, 124
Madrid, Miguel de la, 287
Magaña, Gildardo, 252
Magón, Enrique, 107
Magón, Ricardo, 107
Maier, Charles, 31, 31n. 5
Maize agriculture, 290
"Manifesto a la Nación" (31 August
  1920) (Villa), 102–3
"Manifesto a la Nación" (October 1916)
  (Villa), 101–2
"Manifesto al pueblo mexicano"
  (Villa), 100
Manuel Dondé y Cia., 194
Mápula, Ascensión, 121
Mápula, Donaciano, 119–21, 122
Mápula, Francisco, 120, 121
Mápula, Jesús, 121
Mápula, Joaquín, 120, 121
Mápula, José María, 120, 121
Marcos, Subcommandante: account of
  EZLN rebellion, 302; background of,
  298–99; on civilians in EZLN, 300–
  301; on displacement of expectations,
  293n. 22; on first EZLN group, 296–
  97; language of, 322–23; on neo-
  zapatismo, 299n. 27; on numbers of
  EZLN members, 292n. 21; role of, 312
Marginalization, of frontier-dwellers,
  154–55, 278

Markets, world, 330

Marx, Karl, 263n. 3, 323

Marxism-Leninism, 174–75, 298

Mateus, Francisco, 116, 125, 130

Mayas, 12, 180, 184–86, 190–91, 283. *See also* Caste War (1847)

Mayos, 48, 49

Maytorena, José María, 251

McWilliams, Carey, 140

Medieros: alliances of, 77, 128–29, 130–31; alternative sources of work for, 111–12; definition of, 108–9; rental of land by, 121; small farmers as, 115, 123–24

Medina colony, 84

Melville, Herman, on dignity, 282

Mena, Ramón, 98n. 19

Méndez, Santiago, 183, 187

Mengel Company, 76, 84

Merchants, 128, 130, 132

Meridano elites, 204

Mexican-American War, 179

Mexican North-Western Railroad, 51, 51n. 26

Mexican Revolution: definition of nation by, 275; financing of, 95n. 14, 243; myths of (*see* Myths, in Mexican Revolution); nationalism in, 211–12, 218–33; PRI view of, 168–69n. 50; revisionist histories of, 26; success of, 66

Middle class: anti-Americanism of, 234n. 51; formation of, 62; support for *maderismo,* 196–97; support for *villismo,* 98–99; *yanquifobia* of, 47–48

Migration, labor, 60–61, 137; radicalizing effect of, 61–62, 140; and search for modernity, 320; and urbanization, 142–44

Mixed Claims Commission, 81n. 11, 84n. 17, 85n. 18

Mixteca, 11–12, 134–46; and active resistance, 138–44; communes of, 135–38; definitions of, 134–35; ethnicity

of, 136, 138–39; as farmworkers, 139–40; identity, 141, 143; influence of U.S. immigration policy on identity of, 144; northern context of ethnicity of, 139; post-conquest, 135–36; resistance to state, 142–44; urbanization of, 142

Mobilization, elite, 19, 74, 77–78

Mobilization, peasant: anti-imperialism as motivation for revolutionary, 10; and commercial agriculture expansion, 175; due to divisions among elites, 179, 184n. 20, 205; effect of hunger on, 200; effects of elite-led, 201; importance of continuities in, 17n. 3; and localism (*see* Localism); and peasant liberalism, 218, 218n. 15; radicalization of, 65–66; relationship to U.S. economic crises, 5–6; relationship to U.S. military intervention, 214, 234–35; role of nationalism in, 12, 209–10, 209n. 4. *See also* Caste War (1847); EZLN (Ejército Zapatista de Liberación Nacional)

Mobilization, working class, 45

Modernity, 312, 318–20, 329–30

Molina, Olegario, 194, 195n. 40, 196n. 41, 199, 203

Molina-Montes *parentesco,* 193

Molinistas, 195n. 40, 196

Montaño, Otilio E., 79n. 9, 82

Montes, Avelino, 196n. 41, 203

Moore, Barrington, 56–57, 281

Morelos, 78–79, 220

Morenistas, 197, 200

Moreno Cantón, Delio, 197

Mormons, 84; impact of, 129; persecution of, 45, 56; resistance to, 132, 220

Morris, William, 323

Morrow, Dwight, as ambassador to Mexico, 34–36

Mortgage foreclosures, 199, 199n. 48

Motines, 198, 199

Motzorongo plantation, 84

Müller family, 222–24, 252

Municipal Land Law of 1905, 10–11, 107–33; background of, 109–12; contradictions in, 127–28; effects on internal power relations, 117–27; effects on large property owners, 119–24; effects on small property owners, 115–17, 123–25, 127–28; and land titles, 115, 116, 123, 127; opposition to, 117–18, 117n. 23, 125–26, 132; provisions of, 112–17; relationship to PLM, 262; terminology of, 108–9. *See also* Chihuahua

Murguía, Francisco, 235n. 52

Myths, in Mexican revolution, 27, 283, 312, 324–25, 326. *See also Indigenismo; Symbolism, in revolt*

NAFTA (North American Free-Trade Agreement): disparity in name of, 300, 300n. 28; EZLN effect on, 294; impact on peasants, 328; and reform of Article 27, 276; and maize monoculture, 290; political implications of, 292

Namiquipa, 208–9n. 3

Nash, June, 138

Nation: consolidation of idea of, 268; definition of, 210; imagined, 213; need to define, 275; versus state, 21–22

Nationalism, 49; and assumptions about state formation, 233; on border, 212–15; celebrations as, 167–68, 167n. 48; as component of *villismo,* 99–103; economic, 9–10; of elites, 268; ideologies of, 148; versus localism, 224–30; in Mexican Revolution, 70, 211–12, 218–33; Osorio on, 9–10; in peasant mobilization, 12, 209–10, 209n. 4; of peasants, 12, 209–11, 209n. 4, 215–18; during *porfiriato,* 212; relationship to anti-Americanism, 70; requirements for development of, 148–49; and state, 210, 233; use of *indigenismo* in, 278,

278n. 17. *See also* Villa, Francisco: nationalism of

Nationalization, of resources, 86, 88, 271

Negotiation: between EZLN and government, 307–13, 316; place in resistance, 272–74; tradition of, 271–77

Neozapatismo, 2, 299n. 27, 332. *See also* EZLN

Neutrality laws, 160

News media: on Baja California issues, 145; on Chiapas Indian issues, 293; and International Harvester Company, 196n. 42; reports on EZLN, 294n. 23, 307, 312; on Villa, 239–40

New York Times, 239–40

Noble and McClellan, 75

Noriega, Iñigo, 78

Obregón Salido, Álvaro, 93, 275, 310; Carranza dependency on, 87; military strategy of, 249; role in agrarian reform, 34

Ochoa, Victor, 89

Oficio de tineblas (Castellanos), 278

Oil, importance of, 36–37

Ojo de Federico hacienda, 126

D' Olwer, Luis Nicolau, 40n. 17

"On Some Aspects of the Historiography of Colonial India" (Guha), 18–19

Oral tradition, 97n. 17, 190

Orozco, Pascual, 78, 79, 82, 91, 99

Orozquismo, 52

Orozquistas, 82–83

Ortega, Toribio, 91, 159, 252, 253

Ortiz Rubio, Pascual, 34

Osorio, Rubén, 9–10

Other, the, reidentification of, 152–55

Pacheco, Anselmo, 124

Pacheco, Florencio, 124

Pacheco, José María, 124

Pacheco, Marco, 124

Pacíficos, 163–64, 230

El Padre Clarencio, 196n. 42

Paige, Jeffery, 55, 56

Palerm, Angel, 14
Pancho Villa, ese desconocido (Katz), 95–96
Pat, Jacinto, 185, 189
Patria chica, 155, 215–16, 232
Patterson, Richard, 34
Paz, Octavio, 320, 325
Peasants: capacity for resistance, 2, 142–44; definition of, 72n. 1; dispossession of, 57, 58, 59–60, 75, 115, 128, 153, 156–57, 300, 300n. 29 (*see also* Agrarian reform; Expropriation); effects of agricultural commercialization on (*see* Agriculture: commercialization of); elite reliance on armed, 267–68; and localism, 215–18; militias of, 227–28; and nationalism, 12, 209–11, 209n. 4, 215–18; organizations of, 286; persistence of, 6, 264, 295–96, 299; proletarization of, 54, 140–41; reaction to U.S. capitalization of land, 74–77; reasons for involvement in Mexican Revolution, 80, 327–28; response to external forces, 16–17; role of religion of, 297; status of, 268; studies of insurgency of, 2–15. *See also* Indians
Peasant-warriors, 77, 149–50, 215–17
Peña, Guillermo de la, 14
Pequeña burgesia, 77, 77n. 6
Pérez, Santana, 91, 91n. 9
Perry, Matthew, 187–88
Pershing, John Joseph, 165, 208, 226, 227n. 33, 231, 234. *See also* Punitive Expedition
Personalismo, 183, 268
Phelps Dodge, 76, 84
Piedra Blanca hacienda, 84
Pinistas, 197, 200
Piñon, Francisco, 96n. 15
Pinos Altos Bullion Company, 98, 98n. 19
Pino Suárez, José María, 197
Plan de Ayala, 79n. 9, 251
Plan de Guadalajara, 182

Plan de San Luis Potosi, 79, 80
Plan Restaurador y Reformista de la Constitución, 90
PLM (Partido Liberal Mexicano), 90, 243; and anti-Americanism, 52; formation of, 117–18; impact on U.S. mining companies, 98; membership in, 131; and Municipal Land Law, 262; opposition to Porfirian regime, 107; opposition to U.S., 246
Politics, definition of, 134
Polk, James, 188
Porfiriato: agricultural commercialization during, 68, 73; and commonalities with plantation and slave societies, 197n. 43; labor coercion during, 59; and modernization, 69; nationalism during, 212; political opposition to, 107; repression during (*see* Repression: during *porfiriato*); U.S. economic influence during, 39–43; U.S. governmental influence during, 30–31, 68–69; wage labor during, 54
Portes Gil, Emilio, 34
Portilla, Enrique, 131
Portilla Chávez, Genevevo, 131
Posadas, Juan Jesús, 4, 294n. 23
Prakash, Gyan, 20
PRD, 307
Precursor revolts, 16–17, 17n. 3
Presidios, 110n. 2, 149
Prieto, Pedro, 126
Primo Tapia, 61
PRI (Partido Revolucionario Institucional), 274, 283–84; definition of, 141n. 2; ideology of, 168–69n. 50; labor opposition to, 141; reaction to "Indian" problem, 143–44
Privatization, 10–11, 276. *See also* Expropriation
Proletarization, 54, 140–41
Protestantism, 70. *See also* Mormons
PSS (Socialist Party of the Southeast), 173

PSUM (Partido Socialista Unificado de México), 141, 143
Public interest, 151, 152–54
Public sphere, 148–49
Pueblos, 78, 130, 150, 311n. 31; northern, 74–75; southern, 79
Punitive Expedition, 33, 165, 207, 225, 226–28, 234, 237. *See also* Pershing, John Joseph
Purcell, Anita, 43n. 21
Purcell, William, 43n. 21

Quintana Roo, 76, 191, 198

Rabel, Sam, 223n. 20
Raids: Bill Russell raid, 164; Boquillas raid, 164; Columbus raid (*see* Columbus raid); Petit raid, 164; Torreón raid, 240–41
Railroads, 97–98
Rancheros: alliances with *medieros,* 77, 130; alternative sources of work for, 111–12; definition of, 77n. 6, 108–9; effect of ejidal land subdivision on, 123; effect of Municipal Land Law on, 115–17; effect of water restriction on, 121; evictions of, 120; peasant-warriors as, 77
Reason, 318–19
Reed, Alma, 173
Reed, John, 219, 246, 251
Reed, Nelson, 182n. 14
Regionalism, 219; definition of, 155–56, 212–13, 213; effect of Apache Wars on, 215–16; and elites, 12; and identity, 153–54, 162; influence of U.S. capital on, 44, 74–77; Mexican concept of, 212–13; and peasant-warriors, 149–50. *See also* Localism
Religion, role of peasant, 288, 297. *See also* Catholic Church
Rentería, Abrahám, 124
Rentería, Amado, 124
Rentería, Ambrosio, 124
Rentería, Angel, 124
Rentería, Jesús, 124

Rentería, Simón, 124
Repression: in Chiapas, 288–90, 300–301; definition of, 134–35; by elites, 73, 197–98, 285–86; during *porfiriato,* 69, 73, 90, 90n. 5, 177
Resistance: active, 11–12, 138–44, 217–18; armed, 268–69; and cultural revolution, 314–15; as culture, 13; definition of, 135; eight elements necessary for, 294–300; ideology of, 202; negotiation in, 272–74; passive, 135–38, 186, 201–2; patterns of, 18–19, 265–67, 294–300, 332; peasants capacity for, 2, 142–44; practices of, 272–73, 273n. 14; as result of Municipal Land Law of 1905, 132; studies of, 2–15
Revolution, definition of, 274, 283–84
Revolutionary laws, 309n. 30
Revolutionary romanticism, 323
Reyes, Bernardo, 243
Rhetoric of contrast, concept of, 168, 168n. 49
Rhodakanaty, Plotino, 79n. 9
Roazen-Parrillo, Diane, 195n. 40
Rockefeller, William, 76
Rockefeller Brothers, 75, 84
Rodríquez, Trinidad, 91
Roosevelt, Franklin, 36
Roseberry, William, 15
Rouaix, Pastor, 240
Roux, Manuel, 165–66
Rueda, Salvador, 108
Ruiz, Samuel, 291, 304, 306
Ruiz Massieu, José Francisco, 4
Rural revolt: areas of generalized, 77; commonalities of, 262–63, 263n. 2; elite precautions against, 198–99; and global structures of power, 14–17, 175; initial American support for, 158–61; molding of political culture by, 274; motives for, 10–11, 156–57, 199–203; patterns of (*see* Resistance: patterns of); process of Chiapan, 309–13; resources for, 158, 161, 163, 225; social classes in, 163–64; studies

of, 2–15, 26–27; violence in (*see* Violence). *See also* Urban revolt

Rus, Jan, 283–84

Said, Edward W., 18n. 5

Salazar, Inés, 157, 157n. 18

Salinas de Gortari, Carlos, 11, 17, 276, 287, 291, 299

Salinastroika, 4

Samuel, Tatic, 297

San Antonio de las Rusias, 84

Santa Anna, Antonio López de, 180–82, 182n. 14

Santa de Cabora (Urrea, Teresa), 90, 297

Sarcasm, 322–23

Sayer, Derek, 12, 21, 168, 273n. 13, 314, 315, 317

Scorza, Manuel, 277

Scott, Hugh, 244–45, 246

Scott, James C., 18, 272n. 13, 273n. 12

Scott, Robert, 211–12

Sheehan, James, 49

Sheffield, James, 34

Shields, Karena, 58

Sierra O'Reilly, Justo, 188, 189

Silliman, Chargé to Mexico, 86n. 21

Silva, Prisciliano, 78

Sivaramakrishnan, K., 20–21

Social classes: Chihuahuan *see* Chihuahua: social classes in); in *defensas sociales,* 231n. 46; engagement with U.S. influences, 7; middle class (*see* Middle class); in rural revolt, 163–64; *villista* versus *carrancista,* 250–51; working class (*see* Working class). *See also* Elites

Solís, Francisco, 225n. 27

Sommerfeld, Felix, 245

Sonora, 35, 62, 75–76, 78

"Southeastern Cartel," 286n. 20, 299

Space, local/regional, 149–50, 264, 290

Speculation: by elites, 195; land, 114, 115, 128

State: definition of, 21–22, 271n. 10;

formation approach of, 19, 21, 148, 210, 212, 216, 233, 273n. 13, 317; and globalization, 329–30, 329n. 33; modernity, 312, 313; and nationalism, 210, 233; and negotiation, 271–77, 307–13, 316; and nonintervention in border issues, 153–54, 213–14; as patrón, 284–85; relationship with new peasant organizations, 288–90; resistance to (*see* Resistance); symbiotic relationship with colonists, 150–51; symbolic gestures against, 277; use of *indigenismo* by, 278, 278n. 17. *See also* Porfiriato; PRI; Repression

Stillman, James, 76

Subaltern politics, definitions of, 18–20

"Subaltern Studies project," 19, 20–21

Sugar monoculture, 78–79, 177, 184–85, 190

Summer of Discontent: Seasons of Upheaval: Elite Politics and Rural Rebellion in Yucatán, 1890–1915 (Wells and Joseph), 197n. 44

Symbolism, in revolt, 162, 166, 277, 277n. 15, 278, 304, 309, 312

Tactical mobility, 185, 185n. 21

Talamantes, Jesús, 125

Talamantes, Porfirio, 117–18, 123, 126, 253

Tannebaum, Frank, 26

Taussig, Michael T., 138

Tejedista "guerrillas," 270

Terrazas, Alberto, 99n. 20

Terrazas, Luis, 98, 99n. 20, 116, 116n. 7

Terrazas, Silvestre, 98, 245, 254

Terrazas-Creel, 75, 98–99

Thompson, E. P., 263n. 2, 314, 323

Titles, land. *See* Municipal Land Law of 1905: and land titles

Tlahualilo Company, 38, 53n. 29, 84

Tompkins, Frank, 207

"To My Compatriots, to the People, and to the Government of the United States" (Villa), 100–101

Torreón raid, 240–41
Tradition, invented, 136–37
Traditional societies, 319–20
Tribute, 136, 137
Turner, Frederick C., 220
Turner, John Kenneth, 58, 201n. 54
Tutino, John, 277n. 15
Typicality, in studies of rural revolt, 26–27

Unionization, 62, 70
United States: and Carranza (*see* Carranza, Venustiano); and Caste War (*see* Caste War [1847]); and cross-border relationships, 156–58; and Díaz regime (*see* Porfiriato); economic crises and peasant rebellion, 5–6; effect on migrants, 61; failure of Mexican Revolution policy of, 32–33; and henequen monoculture (*see* Henequen monoculture); influence of immigration policy, 114, 144; interventions of, 8, 33, 68, 214, 234–35, 249–57; and Madero (*see* Madero, Francisco); opposition to, 246 (*see also* Anti-Americanism); overall impact of, 331; policy debates during Mexican Revolution, 31–32; reaction to agrarian reform, 36–39, 254–55; during reign of Carrillo Puerto, 174–75; role in creation of Mexican Revolution, 68–70; scholarship on interventions by, 2–15; and Villa (*see* Villa, Francisco). *See also* Capital, U.S.; Clientelism; Landowners, American
United Sugar Company, 48, 49
Urban revolt, patterns of, 265, 298, 307, 325–26, 334n. 51. *See also* Rural revolt
Urbina, Erasto, 283
Urbina, Tomás, 240
U.S. Department of State, 85n. 18, 183

Valenzuela, Juan, 98n. 19
Vargas, Silvino, 224–25n. 26

Vasconcelos, José, 62
Venegas, Blas, 98n. 19
Verduzco, Cirilo, 124
Verduzco, Cristóbal, 124
Verduzco, Luis, 124
Verduzco, Ruperto, 118, 124
Verduzco, Tartolo, 124
Vick, R. H., 76
Villa, Francisco: agrarian reform policies of, 250–55; on Americans, 220n. 18; anti-imperialism of, 219–20, 220n. 18; and anti-*villista* campaign, 13; on Carranza, 100; versus Carranza on expropriation, 254–55; erosion of support for, 208, 209n. 5, 224–25, 228–33, 235n. 52, 246–49, 255; finances of, 95n. 14, 243 (*see also* Currency, *villista*); influence of, 93–94; loyalty to Madero, 92, 246; loyalty to U.S., 242–43, 246; manifestos of, 100–103; military career of, 94; nationalism of, 102–3, 207, 218–21, 249–50; national tributes to, 94, 94n. 12; news media on, 239–40; policy toward American interests, 242; proclamations of, 223n. 22; reasons for support of, 209n. 5; relationship with U.S., 9; resources of, 161, 225, 231, 247–48, 255; revolutionary plan of, 101–2; social background of, 250–51; social radicalism of, 243; supporters of, 79–80, 96–98, 97n. 16, 239–41, 244–46, 249–51; taxation of Americans by, 247–48; on U.S. intervention, 100–101, 103, 221; U.S. interventions against, 249–57; U.S. recognition demands on, 248–49; use of diminutive by, 92n. 11; viewed as bandit, 232, 236; Woodrow Wilson on, 78, 239; Zapata alliance with, 251–52
Villismo, 52, 89–103; definition of, 93–94; erosion of support for (*see* Villa, Francisco: erosion of support for); as guerilla movement, 229–30; as pop-

ular movement, 96, 229; resurgence of, 165–66; schisms in, 165

Villistas: versus *carrancistas,* 250–55; defeats of, 87; popular leaders of, 221–24; relationship with U.S., 85, 224, 224n. 24

Violence: against landowners (*See* Landowners, Americans: violence against); lower-class, 77; against *medieros,* 132; and rural revolt, 201n. 53

Vos, Jan de, 272

Wage labor, 50, 52–53, 54, 141

Warman, Arturo, 277n. 16

Water rights, importance of, 80, 120, 121

Waugh, Evelyn, 272

Weber, David, 15n. 7

Welles, Sumner, 34

Wells, Allen, 5, 195, 197n. 44

West, Duval, 220, 248

Wheeler Land Company, 76

Whitt, E. Brondo, 214–15

Wilson, Henry Lane, 34, 240

Wilson, Woodrow, 9, 239, 242, 246, 255

Wolf, Eric, 14, 28, 136

Womack, John, 21–22, 261

Women, in revolutionary period, 49, 143, 175

Working class: formation of, 61–62; mobilization of, 45; regional responses to Mexican Revolution, 74–77, 98, 334n. 51

World Bank, 4, 290

Xenophobia, 46–47. *See also* Anti-Americanism

Xi'Nich, 293

Yanquifobia, 47–48

Yaquis, 184n. 20, 279

Young, Eric Van, 212–13, 263, 279

Yucatán, 173–206; Caste War in, 178–91; description of, 176–77; elites and henequen monoculture, 195–96; fears of reawakening Caste War, 196–97; Marxism in, 174–75; political parties during *maderista* period, 197; reasons for rural revolt in, 199–203; Santa Anna invasion of, 180–81; secession of, 180–82; trade relationship with U.S., 177–78

Zacualapa-Hidalgo Ruber Plantation, 84

Zapata, Emiliano, 251–52, 281

Zapatismo, 82, 309, 311

Zapatistas, 49, 81–82, 83, 86. *See also* EZLN

Zavala, Lorenzo, de, 179

Zozaya, Francisco, 122–23

Zozaya, Guadalupe, 119, 122–23

Contributors

DANIEL NUGENT taught anthropology and Latin American history at the Universities of Arizona, California, and Texas and was a Managing Editor of the *Journal of Historical Sociology* until his death in November 1997. His publications include *Spent Cartridges of Revolution: An Anthropological History of Namiquipa, Chihuahua* (1993); *Worker's Expressions: Beyond Accommodation and Resistance* (co-edited with John Calagione and Doris Francis, 1992); and *Everyday Forms of State Formation: Revolution and the Negotiation of Rule in Modern Mexico* (co-edited with Gilbert Joseph, 1994). Beyond publishing the results of his research on rural Mexico in *Critique of Anthropology*, the *Monthly Review*, and elsewhere, he is co-author, with Joan Holden, Paula Loera, and Eva Tessler, of the play *13 Días/13 Days: How the New Zapatistas Shook the World*, which toured the U.S.A. in 1996–97.

ANA MARÍA ALONSO teaches anthropology at the University of Arizona. In the 1980s she conducted ethnographic and archival research in Mexico and the United States, later holding postdoctoral fellowships at the Pembroke Center for Teaching and Research on Women (Brown University) and the Southwest Institute for Research on Women (University of Arizona). She is the author of *Thread of Blood: Colonialism, Revolution and Gender on Mexico's Northern Frontier* (1995) and of articles on popular resistance, social memory, historical anthropology, gender, and ethnicity.

JOHN COATSWORTH is Monroe Gutman Professor of Latin American Affairs at Harvard University, where he also serves as Director of the David Rockefeller Center for Latin American Studies. He is the author of numerous works on Mexican and Latin American economic, social, and international history. A collection of his articles on Mexican economic history appeared in Mexico under the title *Los orígenes del atraso: Nueve ensayos de historia económica de México, siglos XVIII y XIX* (1990). His most recent book, *The United States and Central America: The Clients and the Colossus* (1994) surveyed U.S.–Central American relations, focusing on the period since World War II.

ADOLFO GILLY is a historian and essayist, and a professor on the Facultad de Ciencias Políticas y Sociales at the UNAM. Over the past decade he has also taught or worked in the United States at the University of Chicago, Columbia and Stanford, and the University of Maryland, and he was a fellow at the National Humanities Center. He is the author of *La revolución interrumpida* (more than thirty editions since 1971; translated into English in 1983). Some of his more recent publications include *El cardenismo, una utopía mexicana* (1994), *Discusión sobre la historia* (with Subcomandante Marcos and Carlo Ginzburg, 1995), and *México: El poder, el dinero y la sangre* (1996). A more detailed version of his contribution to this volume is being published in Mexico as *Chiapas, la razon ardiente: Ensayo sobre la rebelión del mundo encantado* by Editorial Era.

JOHN MASON HART is Professor of History at the University of Houston. His many books include *Anarchism and the Mexican Working Class* (n.d.) and *Revolutionary Mexico* (1987). His forthcoming works include *Meeting the Challenges: Mexican and Mexican American Workers in Transition* and *Empire and Revolution: The Americans in Mexico since the Civil War.* Hart has won several research and writing awards including a postdoctoral grant from the SSRC/ACLS; a Shelby Cullom Davis Fellowship, Princeton University; an NEH University Fellowship; the Conference Prize (CLAH); the Herring Prize (PCCLAS); and the Johnson Prize (SCOLAS).

GILBERT M. JOSEPH is Professor of History at Yale University and Co-editor of the *Hispanic American Historical Review.* He is the author of *Revolution from Without: Yucatán, Mexico and the United States, 1880–1924* (1982); *Rediscovering the Past at Mexico's Periphery* (1986); and, with Allen Wells, *Summer of Discontent, Seasons of Upheaval: Elite Politics and Rural Insurgency in Yucatán, 1876–1915* (forthcoming); as well as many articles on the Mexican revolution and the history of rural crime and protest. With Daniel Nugent he co-edited *Everyday Forms of State Formation: Revolution and the Negotiation of Rule in Modern Mexico* (1994); with Allen Wells, *Yucatán y la International Harvester* (1986); with Jeffery Brannon, *Land, Labor, and Capital in Modern Mexico* (1991); and, with Mark Szuchman, *I Saw a City Invincible: Urban Portraits of Latin America* (1995). Currently he is writing a social and political history of Mexico.

FRIEDRICH KATZ is Morton D. Hull Distinguished Service Professor of Latin American History at the University of Chicago. The author of pathbreaking volumes of historical archaeology (*Die sozialokonomischen Verhaltnisse bei den Azteken im 15. end 16. Jarhundert* [n.d.], *The Ancient American Civilizations* [1972]), diplomatic history (*Deutschland, Diaz, und die mexikanische Revolution* [1964]), and social history (*The Secret War in Mexico* [1981]), he also edited *Riot, Rebellion and Revolution: Rural Social Conflict in Mexico,* published in 1988. His long-awaited study of Francisco Villa and the *villista* movement in the Mexican revolution is being published in English by Stanford University Press and in Spanish by Era.

MICHAEL KEARNEY is Professor of Anthropology at the University of California, Riverside, and an editor of *Latin American Perspectives*. For three decades he has conducted extensive ethnographic fieldwork with Zapotec and Mixtec *indígenas*—in Oaxaca, along the U.S.-Mexican border, and throughout California. He is the author of *Winds of Ixtepeji* (1972), an ethnography of the Zapotecs; *World View* (1984), a study of anthropological theory; many articles on international labor migration which have appeared in the *Annual Review of Anthropology* and elsewhere; and, most recently, *Reconceptualizing the Peasantry: Anthropology in Global Perspective* (1996).

ALAN KNIGHT is currently Professor of Latin American History, Oxford University, and has been Director of the Latin American Center at Oxford and Professor of History at the University of Texas, Austin. The author of *The Mexican Revolution* (2 vols., 1986; translated into Spanish in 1996), of *U.S.-Mexican Relations, 1910–1940* (1987), and of many influential articles on Mexican history and politics, he is currently completing a general history of Mexico and researching a history of Mexico in the 1930s.

MARÍA TERESA KORECK studied anthropology in the United States after leaving her native Argentina in 1976. She has taught anthropology, communications, and women's studies at the University of California, San Francisco, the University of California, San Diego, and the University of Michigan. She conducted ethnographic and archival research in rural Chihuahua for several years while working on her Ph.D. in anthropology from the University of Chicago.

JANE-DALE LLOYD was trained in anthropology and history in Mexico and has taught in the Department of History at the Universidad Iberoamericana for more than a decade. She spent three years investigating *magonismo*, popular mobilization, and related topics while living in the Galeana district of Chihuahua. Results of her investigations have appeared in her book *El proceso de modernización capitalista del noroeste de Chihuahua, 1880–1910* (1987); in many articles; and in her doctoral thesis, which will soon be published as a book in Mexico. With Laura Pérez Rosales, she recently co-edited *Paisajes rebeldes: Una larga noche de resistencia indígena* (1995).

RUBÉN OSORIO, a physician who worked for decades in Ciudad Chihuahua, has interviewed hundreds of Chihuahuan revolutionaries and worked in local archives and private collections never consulted by university-based scholars. Beyond editing the prize-winning collection *La correspondencia de Francisco Villa* (1986), assembling *Pancho Villa, ese desconocido: Entrevistas en Chihuahua a favor y en contra* (1990), and authorizing *Tomóchic, la guerra del fin del mundo en la sierra* (n.d.), Dr. Osorio has skillfully translated important studies by Friedrich Katz which have appeared in popular and accessible Spanish-language versions.